OXFORD ISLAMIC LEGAL STUDIES

Series Editors:
Anver M. Emon, Clark Lombardi, and Lynn Welchman

COERCION AND RESPONSIBILITY IN ISLAM

OXFORD ISLAMIC LEGAL STUDIES

Series Editors:
Anver M. Emon, Clark Lombardi, and Lynn Welchman

Satisfying the growing interest in Islam and Islamic law, the Oxford Islamic Legal Studies series speaks to both specialists and those interested in the study of a legal tradition that shapes lives and societies across the globe. Islamic law operates at several levels. It shapes private decision making, binds communities, and it is also imposed by states as domestic positive law. The series features innovative and interdisciplinary studies that explore Islamic law as it operates at each of these levels. The series also sheds new light on the history and jurisprudence of Islamic law and provides for a richer understanding of the state of Islamic law in the contemporary Muslim world, including parts of the world where Muslims are minorities.

ALSO AVAILABLE IN THE SERIES:

Islamic Legal Revival
Reception of European Law and Transformations in Islamic Legal Thought in Egypt, 1875–1952
Leonard Wood

Sharīʿa and Muslim Minorities
The wasati and salafi approaches to fiqh al-aqalliyyat al-Muslima
Uriya Shavit

Domestic Violence and the Islamic Tradition
Ayesha S. Chaudhry

Sharīʿa and Social Engineering
The Implementation of Islamic Law in Contemporary Aceh, Indonesia
R. Michael Feener

Religious Pluralism and Islamic Law
Dhimmis and Others in the Empire Law
Anver M. Emon

Narratives of Islamic Legal Theory
Rumee Ahmed

Coercion and Responsibility in Islam

A Study in Ethics and Law

MAIRAJ U. SYED
Assistant Professor, University of California, Davis

OXFORD
UNIVERSITY PRESS

OXFORD
UNIVERSITY PRESS

Great Clarendon Street, Oxford, OX2 6DP,
United Kingdom

Oxford University Press is a department of the University of Oxford. It furthers the University's objective of excellence in research, scholarship, and education by publishing worldwide. Oxford is a registered trade mark of Oxford University Press in the UK and in certain other countries

First Edition published in 2017

Published in the United States of America by Oxford University Press
198 Madison Avenue, New York, NY 10016, United States of America

British Library Cataloguing in Publication Data
Data available

Library of Congress Control Number: 2016955719

ISBN 978–0–19–878877–5

To Erum Abbasi Syed, with love.
Without you, I could never have gotten this far.

Series Editors' Preface

With archival depth and theoretical sophistication, *Coercion and Responsibility* provides an innovative, path-breaking study on pre-modern Islamic debates on duress and coercion. The topic is complex, and Mairaj Syed expertly brings into conversation debates that span the fields of law, theology, and ethics. Drawing the reader in with a series of provocative hypotheticals, the study makes the historical tradition come alive for readers who are pressed to think alongside the historical figures examined in this impressive work, thereby giving voice to a historical archive that resonates for scholars today working across relevant fields. A deeply researched study, *Coercion and Responsibility* reveals how a commitment to the archive of Islamic legal studies can, at the same time, address questions that animate contemporary debates about law and ethics beyond the confines of Islamic studies. Indeed, the significance of *Coercion and Responsibility* lies in its ability to draw upon the Islamic literary tradition as a vantage point from which to speak on a wide range of fields, and appeal to a broad readership across the disciplines of political science, philosophy, religious studies, and theological ethics.

Anver M. Emon
Clark B. Lombardi
Lynn Welchman

بسم الله الرحمن الرحيم

Acknowledgements

This work is indebted to numerous individuals and organizations, whom gratitude compels me to acknowledge. My dissertation, "Coercion in Classical Islamic Law and Theology," was the first draft of this book. Michael Cook, Shaun Marmon, Hossein Modarressi, Jeffrey Stout, and Muhammad Qasim Zaman guided me through the process of writing it and provided me regular feedback in making it better. After I left Princeton, Bard College allowed me to teach an undergraduate seminar on coercion and responsibility in the spring semester of 2012. I read much of the Anglo-American philosophical literature that punctuates this book with students who took the risk of taking a seminar on such an arcane and technical topic.

I would like to thank my friend Anver Emon, who not only nurturingly shepherded this manuscript and its author through the publication process, but was the first person outside of Princeton to read the dissertation and provide me with a basic framework for revision. He then read the revised draft a second time and provided me with many helpful comments.

The subsequent drafts of the manuscript would not have been possible without the support of the Fulbright Commission, which awarded me a fellowship to do further research for the book in Istanbul in the spring semester of 2014. The University of California, Davis, gave me time off of teaching and administrative duties to allow me to work on the book while in Istanbul. My colleague Baki Tezcan generously provided me with lodging, a cell phone, and basic introductory knowledge of how to navigate the city. Without his support and encouragement, I doubt I would have been able to so easily and seamlessly integrate into the city's intellectual life. I spent four richly productive months, being hosted by İstanbul Şehir University, where I was able to add to and revise the manuscript.

I benefited immensely from the lively conversations with the theology faculty there, in particular Kasım Kopuz, Mehmet Ali Büyükkara, Mehmet Boynukalın, Özgür Kavak, and Eyyüp Said Kaya. I had the good fortune of becoming friends with a group of talented graduate students in Istanbul: Micah

Hughes, Abdurrahman Mihirig, Niaz Ahmad, and Yakoob Ahmed. I benefited from my conversations with them about this project.

My friends Behnam Sadeghi and Joel Blecher provided me with invaluable feedback and criticism on different portions of the manuscript. My colleagues at the University of California, Davis, Naomi Janowitz, Flagg Miller, Baki Tezcan, Ali Anooshahr, Jocelyn Sharlett, and Wendy Desouza provided me helpful feedback on the introduction. I am in Hanna Siurua's immeasurable debt for editing the manuscript. Much of the conceptual and stylistic clarity it has achieved is because of her always precise and unflagging efforts.

The staff at Oxford University Press has been exceedingly efficient and helpful in making sure the manuscript made it through to publication. I want to especially thank Elinor Shields for her professionalism and responsiveness.

While I was away from my children in Istanbul, my father-in-law, Nishat Abbasi, and mother-in-law, Fatima Abbasi, graciously agreed to move in to our home in Elk Grove and helped my wife juggle the demands of her work and care for our kids. My mother, Zakira Syed, and father, Taj Syed, have gone far beyond the calls of parental duty in supporting my scholarship, particularly in helping us provide a stable and loving home for our children. I thank my children Ibrahim and Maryam for being who they are—just plain awesome. I save acknowledgement of my deepest debt for last, to my wife Erum. Without her encouragement, support, guidance, and at times mere tolerance, this project would simply not have come to fruition.

Table of Contents

Introduction

Consider the following scenarios.

Scenario 1: A man holds a gun to your head. He demands that you divorce your wife, otherwise he shoots. The choice is obvious. You pronounce the formula of divorce. You escape and run to the mosque to find two groups of Islamic legal scholars engaged in debate. You interrupt the session, recount what just happened, and ask: "Am I still married to my wife?" One set of legal scholars, the Shāfiʿites, hold that your pronouncement of divorce is invalid. They say you were clearly coerced, and according to the doctrine of their school, coercion invalidates a pronouncement of divorce. You are relieved. But the other group of scholars, the Ḥanafites, declare that according to the doctrine of their school, coercion, no matter how severe, does not invalidate a pronouncement of divorce. Now you are confused. You ask the scholars to justify their positions.

Scenario 2: A large and imposing man threatens to beat you to a pulp if you do not sell him your camel at well below blue book value. You sell him the camel, then head straight for the mosque, where you find the Ḥanafites and the Shāfiʿites engaged in debate. You recount your story and ask whether the sale is valid. All the Ḥanafites and most of the Shāfiʿites consider the sale invalid. You are confused. In scenario 1, the Ḥanafites refused to invalidate your divorce, despite the fact that you were threatened with death; yet now they are willing to invalidate your sale, although you were threatened only with a beating. Besides, why are the Shāfiʿites now internally divided?

Scenario 3: A man holds a gun to your head. He demands that you kill an innocent bystander, or else he kills you. The choice is not so obvious. You love yourself, but killing another human being is a heinous sin. You kill the innocent bystander. You escape and run to the same mosque, this time with blood on your hands. You find the same two groups of scholars debating some fine point of law. Before you have even finished your story, they intone, united in righteous judgment, "You have sinned!" As you begin contemplating your eternal abode in hell, however, a debate breaks out regarding whom the ruler must execute for the crime of homicide. Though they were united in condemning your sin, the scholars are disunited on this issue. The Shāfiʿites split into two groups: one group says that the ruler must execute you *and* the coercer, whereas the other group holds that *only* the coercer must be punished. The Ḥanafites are even more disunited. They are divided into three groups. One group holds that *only* you must be punished. A second group holds that *neither* you *nor* the coercer must be executed. And a third group holds that the coercer alone ought to be held responsible and that you are off the hook, at least in this world.

Scenario 4: On your way home from the local fermented date drink bar, you meet the Arab poet al-Akhṭal, arguably the composer of the most devastating lampoon in the history of Arabic verse.[1] As fate would have it, he is in a particularly irritable mood. The caliph ʿAbd al-Malik gave him a pittance for his last poem, so he has no money. He threatens to lampoon you in verse if you do not sell him your house for well below market value. You make the sale, fearing the inevitable loss of prestige and social position that would result from being tagged by Akhṭal's verse. You run to the mosque and find only the Shāfiʿites engaged in legal debate. You ask whether you can have the sale invalidated. As usual, the jurists are divided. The Iraqi Shāfiʿites are willing to invalidate it. They regard the threat of a public insult as legally coercive, as long as it is directed against someone who would suffer loss of social rank. A group of particularly cranky Khurasani Shāfiʿites disagree. They hold that only threats against your life are coercive and dismiss the Iraqi Shāfiʿite legal opinion.

[1] The verse in question mocks its targets' stinginess and lack of hospitality on multiple levels by calling them "a people who, when their dog forewarns them of approaching guests, command their mother to piss on the fire."

Scenario 5: A man holds a gun to your head. He does not even get a chance to make a threat before you find yourself, almost instinctually, running away. In the process you run over a child, killing him. After a few moments, you gather yourself and realize what has happened. You head right away for the nearest mosque. Things are a bit different this time. Instead of legal scholars, you find two groups of theologians: the Muʿtazilites and the Ashʿarites. You recount the story. The Muʿtazilites hold that you were compelled by the prospect of suffering great harm and reacted instinctively, and that God, the Most Just, would surely not blame you for an act that was clearly compelled. The Ashʿarites argue that, all things being equal, coercion does not undermine moral agency, and they direct you to the legal scholars for a decision regarding your responsibility for the life of the child.

These scenarios illustrate that coercion poses a number of problems about how responsibility for an action ought to be treated. The problems evoked a variety of responses on the part of Muslim theologians and jurists. By the end of the formative period of Islamic thought in the middle of the second/eighth century, these scholars had started organizing themselves into distinctive theological and legal traditions and had begun to develop and articulate a sophisticated architecture of argument and counterargument on the problems of coercion and responsibility for the range of solutions that their schools favored. This book is a study of how these scholars reasoned about the effect of coercion on moral agency and on legal and moral responsibility. It examines the reasoning underpinning Muslim theological and legal positions on four concrete questions:

1. whether the absence of coercion or compulsion is a condition for moral agency
2. how coercion ought to be defined as a matter of law
3. what effect coercion has on the distribution of responsibility for particular speech acts, most prominently divorce, sale, and legal acknowledgement
4. what effect coercion has on the distribution of responsibility for acts that involve causing harm to innocent bystanders, specifically coerced rape and homicide.

1. TRADITION VS. REASON OR TRADITIONS OF REASON?

This book examines the writings of scholars belonging to two different theological traditions, Muʿtazilism and Ashʿarism, and two different legal traditions, Ḥanafism and Shāfiʿism, from the classical period of Islamic history, defined for the purposes of this study as extending roughly from 150/767 to 505/1111.[2] It adopts a comparativist methodology to identify the characteristic features of reasoning in different disciplines (theology vs. law), traditions (Muʿtazilism vs. Ashʿarism and Ḥanafism vs. Shāfiʿism), and civilizations (classical Islamic vs. modern Western). It seeks to achieve a balance between in-depth analysis of the writings of particular individuals belonging to different traditions and diachronic examination of the development of ideas within a tradition. It also compares the structure of arguments regarding coercion and responsibility within Islamic theological and legal traditions with the arguments proffered by modern Anglo-American philosophers and judges. The result of the book is to suggest, contrary to existing essentialist and largely idealist approaches to analyzing theological, legal, and ethical reasoning in classical Islam, that the most important feature explaining the character of rationality on a given issue is the combination of two primary features which I label constraint and contingency. As I will discuss in further detail later, constraint refers to the features of a given thinker's or tradition's context that are responsive to the logical force of an argument, whereas contingency refers to those features that influence argumentation but are not reducible to an argument's logical force. The book shows that the constraint-and-contingency model better explains the logic and content of argumentation within different traditions and disciplines, accounts for changes in reasoning over time, and allows for cross-cultural ethical analysis.

In this study, the term "tradition" has a specific meaning. By tradition, I do not mean a statement attributed to the Prophet Muḥammad, his companions, or other early religious authorities, although this is a common use of

[2] The classical period for theology falls a little later than that for law. The particular branch of Muʿtazilism examined in this study took decisive shape in the ideas of two members of the Jubbāʾī family, Abū ʿAlī (d. 303/915) and Abū Hāshim (d. 321/933). Ashʿarism is foundationally indebted to Abū al-Ḥasan al-Ashʿarī, who lived from 259/853 to 323/935. I thank Ayman Shihadeh for inspiring this clarification.

the term in the field of Islamic studies. Nor do I mean the cultural practices of a particular people passed on from one generation to the next. I mean something more like the concept of a "school" as it is used in Islamic studies to denote the set of practices, institutions, and social identities associated with a community of scholars organized around the study of either a core set of theological positions, in the case of theology, or a core set of legal opinions, in the case of law.

My understanding of the concept of tradition is influenced by Alasdair MacIntyre's explorations on the issue in some of his major works on ethics.[3] MacIntyre seeks to rescue the concept from the conceptual detritus that originated in the contentious debates between Enlightenment-era philosophers, some of whom saw tradition as the antithesis of rational discourse, and others, most famously Edmund Burke, who advocated adherence to tradition because they saw it as essential to political stability.[4] Against the first party, MacIntyre shows that reasoning cannot take place without some previous tradition of inquiry, to which a community of inquirers is committed. A community of inquirers must share at least some core presumptions about the subject matter they investigate, as well as a set of acceptable methods of reasoning. They must also share a common set of standards by which to evaluate the quality of the answers provided to the problems to which they are devoted. Without these features, rational inquiry could not take place. Moreover, this community of inquirers not only exists at one moment in time but also extends across time, often over many generations.[5] It documents the

[3] One may also refer to Talal Asad's conception of Islam as a discursive tradition. For this see, Talal Asad, *The Idea of an Anthropology of Islam* (Washington, DC: Center for Contemporary Arab Studies, Georgetown University, 1986), especially, 14. I rely on MacIntyre instead of Asad for a few reasons, even though it may be argued that Asad's conceptualization has the benefit of being explicitly articulated to help one think about Islam. MacIntyre provides the fullest argument for how rationality is essentially tradition-based and attempts to identify how and in what contexts such a rationality is capable of conceptual innovation and change. Moreover, MacIntyre works out his theory of tradition-based rationality specifically in the case of schools of thought with a fairly technical shared vocabulary interested in ethics. These are some of precisely the features of classical Islamic thought that make his particular framework insightful.

[4] Alasdair C. MacIntyre, *After Virtue: a Study in Moral Theory* (Notre Dame, IN: University of Notre Dame Press, 1984), 221–22.

[5] For the historical dimensions of the concept of tradition, see MacIntyre's oft-cited definition: "A living tradition then is a historically extended, socially embodied argument precisely in part about the goods which constitute that tradition. Within a tradition the pursuit of goods extends through generations, sometimes through many generations." Ibid., 222.

history of its progress and shortcomings in its common endeavor. In short, it is a tradition, and there can be no rationality without a tradition.[6] Against tradition's Enlightenment-era defenders, MacIntyre holds that traditions are not simply vehicles conducive to stability, impervious to change. Rather, traditions are quite capable of conceptual innovation, and they can accomplish it in a variety of ways. Most straightforwardly, scholars belonging to a tradition often develop it by responding to perceived incoherence in a tradition's received ideas and interpretations of texts. Traditions can also innovate when confronted with a competing tradition, which has its own intellectual and social practices and unique ethical vantage point. In such cases, innovation can arise through the perception of hitherto unforeseen possibilities for solutions to old problems, occasioned by vigorous dialectical exchange with competitors.[7] In MacIntyre's view, traditions are the dynamic carriers of rationality, and it is with this presumption that I approach the Islamic traditions of theology and law. While MacIntyre has done much to prove the dependence of rationality on tradition and in a *general* way sketched an account of what it means to belong to one, his account relies heavily on the historical study of ethical traditions in Western civilization and therefore does not tell us much about what it meant to belong to a tradition in the specific context of classical Islam.

By the fourth/tenth century, Muslim legal and theological scholarship had come to revolve around the legal and theological positions of authoritative masters. Their views formed the basis for the subsequent elaboration and development of theological and legal thought.[8] While there is a basic

[6] MacIntyre, *Whose Justice? Which Rationality?* (London: Duckworth, 1988), 4–11.

[7] Ibid., 355.

[8] In addition to serving as the starting point for intellectual production, the traditions performed a variety of other social and political functions. Not only were they the loci for the massive literary output of numerous disciplines, they also often provided an important element of one's social identity, and they were frequently objects of patronage by rulers and wealthy elites. For a study of the social and political consequences of belonging to legal and theological traditions in medieval Nishapur, see Richard W. Bulliet, *The Patricians of Nishapur: a Study in Medieval Islamic Social History* (Cambridge, MA: Harvard University Press, 1972), 28–46. On the role of state patronage in the establishment of Ḥanafism in the Abbasid empire in the late second/eighth century, see Christopher Melchert, *The Formation of the Sunni Schools of Law, 9th-10th Centuries C.E.* (Leiden: Brill, 1997), 42–43 and 47. References to the role of state patronage in establishing Ḥanafism abound throughout Tsafrir's work. I cite to pages that demonstrate the point in the case of Iraq. See Nurit Tsafrir, *The History of an Islamic School of Law: the Early Spread of Hanafism* (Cambridge, MA: Islamic Legal Studies Program, Harvard Law School, 2004), 18–60. On its role in the establishment of Mālikism in Spain, see Melchert, *Formation*, 156–57. For the

scholarly consensus on the importance of these traditions in Muslim societies, there is a range of views on how belonging to one affected an individual scholar's intellectual production and how ideas developed within traditions over time.

Some premodern Muslims took the establishment of the legal traditions to mean that all the core legal issues facing Muslims' social and individual lives had been addressed decisively by the founders of the legal traditions, and that scholars of law after them were morally bound to follow the laws of their respective traditions. The intellectual work of subsequent tradition-bound scholars consisted of merely clarifying the received law in the face of ambiguity and, if necessary, expanding it to address new cases on the basis of the legal methodology employed by the founders of the traditions.[9]

Modernist Muslim scholars from the nineteenth century onward continued to accept this picture of the history and function of the tradition as wholly true, but they judged it in morally negative terms. They identified the constraints of membership in a tradition as a blight on innovation in legal thought and as the cause of the moral, social, and political decline of Muslim societies, which ultimately culminated in their relative impotence and weakness vis-à-vis the European colonial powers.[10]

Some Western Islamicists in the first half of the twentieth century, most notably Joseph Schacht, also accepted this historical narrative as correct. Schacht limited the dynamic, creative phase of the history of Islamic law to the period before the establishment and ultimate solidification of the legal traditions in the fourth/tenth century. In his view, there were two reasons for the subsequent stagnation of legal thought. After the fourth/tenth century the idea that jurists were obligated to follow the opinions of the founders of the legal traditions became widespread, which effectively prevented Islamic law from participating vigorously in the social and political life of Muslim societies. The intellectual work of the tradition-constrained

role of patronage and other factors in the establishment of Shāfiʿism in Egypt in the second half of the third/ninth century, see Ahmed El Shamsy, *The Canonization of Islamic Law: a Social and Intellectual History* (Cambridge: Cambridge University Press, 2013), 118–44.

9 For a review of the scholarship on this issue, see Sherman A. Jackson, *Islamic Law and the State: the Constitutional Jurisprudence of Shihāb al-Dīn al-Qarāfī* (Leiden: Brill, 1996), 73–79.

10 Indira Falk Gesink, "Chaos on Earth: Subjective Truths versus Communal Unity in Islamic Law and the Rise of Militant Islam," *The American Historical Review* 108, no. 3 (2003): 718, 723–729.

Muslim scholars became limited to expounding a tradition's laws, which had become in practice alienated from the social and political realities of communal life and served merely as a vague and distant moral ideal. Schacht identified a second reason for Islamic law's stagnation—namely, the predominance of a legal theory, articulated in the first instance by the founder of the Shāfiʿite tradition, Muḥammad b. Idrīs al-Shāfiʿī (d. 204/820), that located the source of all legal authority in the scriptural sources, the Qurʾān and the ḥadīth of the Prophet Muḥammad. Shāfiʿī's radical delegitimization of all nonscriptural techniques for justifying laws and his articulation of a religious ideology that constrained legislation to the interpretation of scripture contributed to the growing and ultimately unbridgeable gap between legal practice and legal thought by confining tradition-bound jurists to inherently conservative methods of law-making.[11]

This historical narrative, agreed upon by many premodern Muslims, modernist Muslim intellectuals, and early Orientalists has been challenged by subsequent scholars in many different ways. Wael Hallaq famously contested the factual assertion that after the fourth/tenth century, scholars limited themselves to following the legal opinions of the founders of their respective legal traditions.[12] Sherman Jackson, while not necessarily challenging the idea that legal innovation that departed from the opinions of the founding fathers had become widely viewed as proscribed, criticized the starkly negative portrayal of this development by modernist Muslim scholars and the Western scholars who agreed with them.[13] Jackson noted that any legal system must have a considerable degree of stability and continuity in its laws for it to perform its function, and Islamic law achieved this stability and continuity through the institution of the legal tradition. He also pointed out that, much as Alan Watson had demonstrated in the history of Roman law, legal scholars accomplished legal change not through an explicit renunciation or modification of the existing laws of the tradition, but through a variety of interpretive techniques that modified the existing law's scope of application or through the creation of exceptions to existing rules, a process

[11] Joseph Schacht, *An Introduction to Islamic Law* (Oxford: Clarendon Press, 1964), 69–75.
[12] Wael Hallaq, "Was the Gate of Ijtihad Closed?," *International Journal of Middle East Studies* 16, no. 1 (1984).
[13] Jackson, *Islamic Law and the State*, 77–78.

of legislation that Jackson termed "legal scaffolding." Jackson's aim was to demonstrate both the positive stabilizing function of the institution of the legal tradition in the history of Islamic law and the fact that its emergence did not preclude change in the law.[14]

Wael Hallaq has come to similar conclusions while highlighting the importance of the practice of issuing fatwas in connecting the law to social reality and in continually adjusting the law as elaborated by legal scholars writing works of positive law.[15] Neither of these historians of Islamic law disputes that tradition-bound scholars were overwhelmingly limited to the law of the tradition. They simply dispute the conclusion that this limitation led to legal stasis and argue that tradition-bound legal scholars nonetheless had the conceptual ability to justify change in the law when necessary.

More recently, Eyyüp Said Kaya has argued for a much less restrictive idea of how membership in a legal tradition constrains legal scholars. He notes that in the fourth/tenth century, Ḥanafite scholarship took place in several different geographical regions, and that Ḥanafite scholars of different regions differed in their interpretation of the inherited Ḥanafite legal corpus.[16] Not only did Ḥanafite scholars in various localities take their shared legal heritage in different directions, but, as Kaya also documents, Ḥanafite legal scholars in Central Asia explicitly departed from the version of Ḥanafite laws they had inherited on the issue of compensation for homicide. Based on this evidence, Kaya argues that legal scholars were not, in fact, strictly constrained by their tradition's laws.[17] Rather, what was required of them was merely a general acknowledgment that the inherited laws and attendant legal methodology represent a starting point for legal scholars deliberating

[14] On the idea that legal systems must be sensitive to the values of stability and continuity and that an authority-based discourse best accomplished this in premodern times, see ibid., 79–83. On how jurists achieved change through legal scaffolding, see ibid., 96–102.

[15] Wael Hallaq, *Authority, Continuity, and Change in Islamic Law* (Cambridge: Cambridge University Press, 2001), 166–235.

[16] Eyyüp Said Kaya, "Continuity and Change in Islamic Law: the Concept of Madhhab and the Dimensions of Legal Disagreement in Hanafi Scholarship of the Tenth Century," in *The Islamic School of Law: Evolution, Devolution, and Progress*, ed. P.J. Bearman, Rudolph Peters, and Frank E. Vogel (Cambridge, MA: Islamic Legal Studies Program, Harvard Law School, 2005), 27–30.

[17] Ibid., 31.

on the law.[18] Kaya's discovery of an explicit departure from inherited Ḥanafite law by Central Asian Ḥanafites in the fourth/tenth century is significant, but it constitutes perhaps too small a data set to justify a revision of the majority view of how traditions constrained legal scholars over a much longer period of time, especially in the crucial period after their solidification. Kaya's identification of the importance of region and therefore of differences in customs and social structure in the articulation of Ḥanafite law parallels my own findings regarding the importance of location in explaining similarities in the legal justifications of scholars who may have belonged to different traditions but shared the same locality. Unfortunately, his preliminary findings about the potential significance of geography for explaining the articulation of laws within a tradition have yet to be substantiated by a more detailed and expansive diachronic study.

A second substantial disagreement among historians of Islamic law concerns the question whether tradition-bound scholars were expected to follow not just the laws of their tradition but also the hermeneutical principles used to extract those laws from the Qurʾān and ḥadīth and other conceptual tools, such as analogy or equity reasoning, used to extend them to cases not explicitly covered by scripture. The more common view is that belonging to a tradition required tradition-bound scholars to follow the laws of the tradition as well as the various justificatory techniques used to legitimate them.[19] But the position that tradition-bound jurists were required only to uphold the tradition's laws, as opposed to its laws and legal methodology, also has its adherents, and Behnam Sadeghi provides the fullest

[18] Ibid., 38–40.

[19] Hence Wael Hallaq, in an introductory textbook on Islamic law, writes that "the doctrinal school constituted as much a methodological entity as a substantive, doctrinal one. In other words, what distinguished a particular doctrinal school from another was largely its legal methodology and the substantive principles it adopted in dealing with its own law.... Third, a doctrinal school was defined by its substantive boundaries, namely, by a certain body of law and methodological principles that clearly identified the outer limits of the school as a collective entity.... The fourth characteristic, issuing from the third, was loyalty, for departure from legal doctrine and methodological principles amounted to abandoning the school, a major event in the life of a jurist." Wael Hallaq, *An Introduction to Islamic Law* (Cambridge: Cambridge University Press, 2009), 33–34. For a substantial argument for regarding the legal traditions as schools defined not only by a distinctive set of laws but also by a distinctive and rationally coherent legal methodology, see Umar F. Abd-Allah Wymann-Landgraf, *Mālik and Medina: Islamic Legal Reasoning in the Formative Period* (Leiden: Brill, 2013). For my review of the work, see Mairaj U. Syed, "Review of Mālik and Medina," *Islamic Law and Society* 22 (2015).

substantiation of this position. Through an extensive diachronic analysis of Ḥanafite laws concerning women's public prayer over the course of twelve centuries, Sadeghi demonstrates both the fact of legal change and the remarkable continuity of the laws. Although, as Sadeghi shows, Ḥanafite jurists found it easy to justify changes to the laws, more often than not, once a law was admitted into the corpus of the tradition, it tended to stay the same.[20] However, the cause of the continuity and stability of the law lay neither in scriptural texts (i.e., Qurʾān and ḥadīth), upon which the law of the tradition was putatively based, nor in the hermeneutical principles Ḥanafite jurists deployed to justify the derivation of the law from scripture. In fact, Sadeghi shows that at the basic, logical level, interpretation of scripture, even when constrained by Ḥanafite hermeneutical rules, could easily accommodate a number of conflicting and even opposing interpretations.[21] Neither scripture nor Ḥanafite hermeneutical principles thus completely and strictly determined the laws of the tradition. This does not mean that Ḥanafite jurists were completely unconstrained, or that each generation of Ḥanafite scholars invented the law anew. It simply means that they were not constrained in the ways that they explicitly said they were. Sadeghi notes that despite the considerable leeway that their legal hermeneutics afforded them, Ḥanafite scholars consistently tended to reaffirm the received law of their tradition, even in situations in which holding on to a given law threatened the coherence of the tradition's substantive rationality as exemplified in the body of accumulated scriptural interpretations and legal principles and the laws of the tradition as a whole.[22]

My work confirms Sadeghi's finding that the received laws of each tradition formed the core starting point for legal inquiry within the classical Islamic legal traditions. The justifications given for particular positive rules, whether in the form of scriptural interpretations, citations of legal or moral

[20] Behnam Sadeghi, *The Logic of Law Making in Islam: Women and Prayer in the Legal Tradition* (Cambridge: Cambridge University Press, 2015), 32.

[21] Sadeghi calls this feature of reasoning "hermeneutical flexibility." He classifies the Ḥanafites as having maximal hermeneutical flexibility. Ibid., 26–34.

[22] This is most clearly demonstrated in their invention of the ad hoc adjacency law in order to mitigate the undesirable consequences of continuing to uphold the Ḥanafite law according to which a woman's praying next to a man invalidates his prayer. See Sadeghi, ibid., 50–73, for the case study, and ibid., 74, for the significance of the case to Sadeghi's model of legal change.

principles, casuistry, or competing descriptions of empirical reality, did not determine the rules but rather were generated for them, and there is a much greater variability in the justifications for the laws than in the laws themselves. But can more be said about the character of a tradition's rationality?

This survey shows that, for the past fifty years, the issue of the possibility of legal change in the premodern period and its precise processes and procedures have attracted much attention. Studies on the topic have tended to concentrate on the questions of whether and to what extent Islamic law, as a religious law, is capable of changing over time, how such change takes place, and how that change is justified. Given their focus on change, scholars examining premodern Islamic law have tended to pay only instrumental attention to texts of positive law (*fiqh*), looking only at issues on which legal change and its justifications may be identified. The result was a dearth of knowledge on the structure of reasoning present in the positive law texts, especially on concrete issues of legal and moral thought beyond the narrow question of legal change.[23] Yet, the positive law texts are especially rich sources documenting not only the laws of each tradition but also how the tradition's laws were justified.

Scholars interested in more of a phenomenological approach to Islamic legal thought have largely concentrated their efforts on works of legal theory (*uṣūl al-fiqh*), and this focus has had a deleterious influence on the study of reasoning in positive law. Two particular characteristics of works of legal theory had the effect of generating a set of specific expectations about the type of reasoning actually employed in works of positive law. First, legal theory is a highly systematic and philosophical discipline that devotes substantial attention to the formal logic of different techniques of legal reasoning. Second, it locates the authority for laws predominantly in scripture and therefore is deeply interested in the cogency of the hermeneutical rules used

[23] Exceptions to this trend include Brannon M. Wheeler, *Applying the Canon in Islam: the Authorization and Maintenance of Interpretive Reasoning in Ḥanafī Scholarship* (Albany: State University of New York Press, 1996); Sadeghi, *The Logic of Law Making in Islam*; Kecia Ali, *Marriage and Slavery in Early Islam* (Cambridge, MA: Harvard University Press, 2010); Hina Azam, *Sexual Violation in Islamic Law: Substance, Evidence, and Procedure*, Cambridge Studies in Islamic Civilization (Cambridge: Cambridge University Press, 2015); and Intisar Rabb, *Doubt in Islamic Law: a History of Legal Maxims, Interpretation, and Islamic Criminal Law* (Cambridge, MA: Cambridge University Press, 2015).

to derive law from scripture. Because of these two features, many historians of Islamic legal theory have implicitly adopted the idea that justification and reasoning within all disciplines of Islamic law is largely scripturalist in nature, to the point that one scholar identifies it as one of two main features of Islamic legal thought.[24] But it is incorrect to suppose that an analysis of reasoning within a normative and philosophical field such as legal theory would accurately represent how jurists actually reasoned in the more concrete discipline of positive law. It is as if historians seeking to investigate reasoning in science looked only to the philosophy of science, not its practice. Just as actual scientific reasoning on concrete problems departs significantly from the procedure laid out by philosophers of science, the analysis of positive law texts shows that actual reasoning is neither as formalistic nor as limited to scriptural interpretation as previously assumed.[25]

While the institution of the legal tradition has attracted much attention in Islamic studies scholarship, the same is not true of theological traditions. An examination of how theological traditions influenced individual scholars' intellectual production over a large period of time requires access to texts from that tradition over a period of time. Because Muʿtazilism largely died out by the sixth/twelfth century, this simply is not possible in the case of Muʿtazilism. Hence, most scholarly treatments of Muʿtazilite thought tend to be synchronic studies of various theological issues as represented in just a few texts.

The situation is a bit more promising when it comes to Ashʿarism. Though some of the large encyclopedic works from the early and classical period of Ashʿarism have been lost, the tradition did not die off and in fact flourished in the postclassical premodern period, to the point of becoming recognized as one of three main orientations of theological orthodoxy in Sunnism. Consequently, we have a better idea of how membership in the Ashʿarite

[24] See Bernard G. Weiss, *The Spirit of Islamic Law* (Athens, GA: University of Georgia Press, 2006), 38, who writes: "The universal insistence of Muslim jurists upon the divine authorship of the law and their refusal to accord to human reason any role in the creation of law accounts in large part for the features of Muslim juristic thought . . . textualism and intentionalism. By 'textualism' I mean an approach to the formulation of the law that seeks to ground all law in a closed canon of foundational texts and refuses to accord validity to law that is formulated independently of these texts."

[25] For a similar point, see Sadeghi, *The Logic of Law Making in Islam*, 34–35.

tradition constrained theologians.[26] These studies have revealed a model of constraint that seems remarkably similar to the model found in the legal traditions. Like legal scholars, who were constrained only by their tradition's laws, as opposed to a distinctive legal methodology, Ashᶜarite theologians across the history of their tradition tended to formally endorse a remarkably stable set of theological positions, even if the substantive rationality and methods of reasoning underpinning those positions changed.[27] The most important such change was the gradual integration of Avicennan ontology, cosmology, and philosophical ethics into Ashᶜarite thought, which nonetheless never led to a formal rejection of traditional Ashᶜarite positions, even if the network of inferences that gave substantive meaning to those positions became radically different and thoroughly Avicennan.[28]

In addition to categorizing the ways in which membership in these different traditions influenced scholarly production, historical scholarship has also classified the traditions themselves as more and less rationalist or traditionalist. Historians of Islamic theology routinely identify Muᶜtazilism, specifically, as the theological tradition that epitomizes the primacy of reason in classical Islam.[29] In contrast, Ashᶜarism is depicted as fundamentally committed to a structure of authority that gives primacy to scripture, even if it adopted rationalist methods of defending that structure.[30]

[26] Richard M. Frank, *Al-Ghazālī and the Ashᶜarite School* (Durham, NC: Duke University Press, 1994).

[27] For example, Frank shows that Ghazālī assimilated aspects of Avicennan cosmology and psychology into what he calls Ghazālī's "higher theology." Frank argues that, despite the fact that the integration materially undermined Ashᶜarite occasionalism, Ghazālī continued to formally endorse Ashᶜarite positions that had presupposed an Ashᶜarite occasionalist conception of causality; ibid., 44–45, 71–75. Shihadeh makes similar points regarding Razi's ethics and psychology; see Ayman Shihadeh, *The Teleological Ethics of Fakhr al-Dīn al-Rāzī* (Leiden: Brill, 2006), 13–44. See especially ibid., 44, where he writes that although Ghazālī "maintains a number of central Ashᶜarī doctrines, he often preserves their formulaic, almost creedal, expressions, without much of their theoretical content and details."

[28] On the synthesis of Ashᶜarism with philosophy after Ghazālī, see Ayman Shihadeh, "From al-Ghazālī to al-Rāzī: 6th/12th Century Developments in Muslim Philosophical Theology," *Arabic Sciences and Philosophy* 15 (2005).

[29] Ignaz Goldziher, *Introduction to Islamic Theology and Law*, trans. Andras Hamori and Ruth Hamori (Princeton: Princeton University Press, 1981), 87–89, 92, 103; Richard C. Martin, Mark R. Woodward, and Dwi Surya Atmaja, *Defenders of Reason in Islam: Muᶜtazilism from Medieval School to Modern Symbol* (Oxford: Oneworld Publications, 1997), 10–19; Binyamin Abrahamov, *Islamic Theology: Traditionalism and Rationalism* (Edinburgh: Edinburgh University Press, 1998), x.

[30] On Ashᶜarism mediating between rationalism and either "orthodoxy" or "traditionalism," see Goldziher, *Introduction to Islamic Theology and Law*, 94, 103–4; Duncan Black Macdonald, *Development of Muslim Theology, Jurisprudence, and Constitutional Theory* (New York: Charles

Scholarly descriptions of the legal traditions are more sophisticated, admitting that traditions change over time: the traditions originate in a rationalist ethos in the first/seventh and second/eighth centuries, but became more conservative over the subsequent centuries. Before a thoroughly scripturalist ethos of legal authority came to dominate the legal philosophies of all the Sunnite legal traditions in the third/ninth century, religious scholars drew on a wide variety of law-making methods, including reliance on the authority of communal practice, considerations of public welfare, and the elaboration of laws through casuistry. For example, in contrast to its classical manifestation, Ḥanafism in its infancy is thought to have used rationalist methods inherited from the ancient Iraqi partisans of discretionary reason (*ahl al-raʿy*) for the elaboration of legal rules in response to societal changes.[31] The picture changes after Shāfiʿī. Shāfiʿī articulated his revolutionary and influential legal theory partly as an explicit response to this inchoate, arbitrary method of legislation. He decried the use of reason among his contemporaries as arbitrary and ultimately undisciplined and insisted that scripture, defined as the Qurʾān and the Prophet's statements conveyed through reliable chains of transmission (*isnād*), was the sole legitimate source for law-making.[32] Law must, in this view, be firmly rooted in scripture, whether derived by way of interpretation or through analogy to existing laws. Shāfiʿī's theory proved so influential and irresistible that, over the course of the next two centuries, the rest of the Sunnite legal schools, Ḥanafism included, largely adopted Shāfiʿī's legal philosophy.[33]

Scribner's Sons, 1903), 186–92. In 1962, Makdisi said that the scholarship on Ashʿarism before his time had characterized it as a synthesis between the rationalism of the Muʿtazilites and the traditionalism of "orthodoxy." George Makdisi, "Ashʿarī and the Ashʿarites in Islamic Religious History I," *Studia Islamica* 17 (1962): 38–40; Abrahamov, *Islamic Theology: Traditionalism and Rationalism*, x.

[31] On the Iraqis' use of reason, in the sense of *raʿy*, to formulate laws before the establishment of the classical schools and its relationship to the founders of Ḥanafism, see Joseph Schacht, *The Origins of Muhammedan Jurisprudence* (Oxford: Clarendon Press, 1950), 103–12; Schacht, *An Introduction to Islamic Law*, 60–1.

[32] Schacht, *The Origins of Muhammedan Jurisprudence*, 6–20; El Shamsy, *The Canonization of Islamic Law: a Social and Intellectual History*, 1–13, 69–87.

[33] On the adoption of the main components of Shāfiʿī's theory by the other schools, see Schacht, *An Introduction to Islamic Law*, 55–63. On the "traditionalization" of Ḥanafism, specifically, in the later third/ninth century, see Melchert, *Formation*, 48–53. For the most recent examination of the spread of Shāfiʿī's ideas, see El Shamsy, *The Canonization of Islamic Law: a Social and Intellectual History*, 194–220.

On the basis of this brief survey of the scholarly literature on the influence of tradition membership on the nature of argumentation and the broad characterization of the specific traditions with which we are concerned (namely, Muʿtazilism, Ashʿarism, Ḥanafism, and Shāfiʿism), we might have the following expectations about the type of reasoning that these traditions employ on the issue of coercion and responsibility:

1. Muʿtazilite theologians will rely predominantly on rational arguments, while Ashʿarite theologians base their theological positions largely on interpretations of scripture. Scripture may play a subsidiary, supporting role for Muʿtazilites and reason a similar role for Ashʿarites.
2. Both Ḥanafite and Shāfiʿite argumentation will be largely scriptural, with perhaps a sprinkling of rational arguments in Ḥanafism because of its origins in a pre-Shāfiʿī and therefore a more rationalist age.
3. If it is true that legal authority is vested primarily in scripture, as required by legal theory, the work of defending the legitimacy of a tradition's law, as actually done in works of positive law, ought to consist largely of the interpretation of scripture. Therefore, debates within and between traditions will predominantly take the form of battles over the correct interpretation of scriptural texts.

One of the problems with these expectations is that they originate in the attempt to characterize whole traditions as essentially rationalist or traditionalist/scripturalist. While such characterizations may be useful in describing the broad features of what constituted justification at the theoretical level for these traditions, they are far less helpful when applied to the actual content of norms and argumentation on a concrete issue and the development of that reasoning over time. If proclivity toward rational argumentation or fidelity to textual authority does not accurately characterize the content and structure of argumentation within a tradition over time, what does?[34]

[34] Sherman Jackson has offered a helpful suggestion: to regard the theological schools as traditions of reason, each with different core theological values as the starting point of inquiry. See Sherman A. Jackson, *On the Boundaries of Theological Tolerance in Islam: Abū*

This book shows that the expectations outlined earlier are generally not fulfilled. The Muʿtazilites are no more rationalist than the Ashʿarites. What explains the character of reasoning in both theological traditions is commitment to certain core positions on moral epistemology, the nature of God's justice, and the character of voluntary human action. The two traditions' respective commitments on these three issues explain not only their adherents' specific positions on whether the absence of coercion is a condition for valid moral agency but also the modifications that individual tradition-bound theologians make to the conceptual frameworks they inherit from their predecessors. As for the legal traditions, scriptural interpretation no doubt forms a large component of classical legal thinking, but it is by no means the only component. As we will see, it plays a relatively significant role in scholarly discussions on the impact of coercion on speech acts, but is hardly present in discussions concerning coerced rape or murder or in jurists' attempts to formulate a legal definition of coercion. Casuistry, abstract moral and legal principles, and claims regarding coercion's empirical effects on the coerced are just as important as scriptural interpretation, if not more so, in classical Islamic coercion jurisprudence. Casuistry is the dominant method of analysis in both Ḥanafite and Shāfiʿite discussions of coerced rape and murder, whereas the interplay of empirical observations and moral and legal principles is the defining feature of Shāfiʿite efforts to establish a legal definition of coercion. The very existence of such variations in argumentation indicates that legal traditions are not based on overarching sets of philosophical values that govern a tradition's laws or the types of justifications offered for them. Rather, the actual content of justifications for laws in books of positive law is better explained by constraints such as the strictness of a scholar's commitment to the received laws of a tradition, the extent to which a law is susceptible to criticism by outsiders, and the particular ways of reasoning that emerged and came to be accepted in a given geographical locale.

Ḥāmid al-Ghazālī's Fayṣal al-Tafriqa bayna al-Islam wa al-Zandaqa (Karachi: Oxford University Press, 2002), 17. For the point that argument and the exchange of reasons is an important component to an anthropological conception of Islam, see Asad, *The Idea of an Anthropology of Islam*, 16.

2. THE CONSTRAINT AND CONTINGENCY MODEL OF TRADITION-BASED RATIONALITY

This study reveals that there are two broad features that best explain the rationality exemplified by the traditions of Ashʿarism, Muʿtazilism, Ḥanafism, and Shāfiʿism: constraint and contingency. By constraint, I mean the logical and substantive consequences entailed by commitment to a theological, moral, or legal position, principle, value, or method of reasoning. Avowing any of these constrains the argumentation, either in the writings of a single scholar, or over time in the history of accumulated writings in a tradition.[35] For example, the Ḥanafites held that coercion does not invalidate a pronouncement of divorce, which they identify as a speech act, while simultaneously holding that even the threat of a beating, one of the lowest forms of coercion recognized in the tradition, is sufficient to allow a seller to annul a coerced sale, also a type of speech act. The discrepancy in the effect of coercion on two actions, divorce and sale, that share the feature of being speech acts calls for either a change in one of the laws to restore consistency between them or an explanation that shows why the differential treatment is justified. Despite the fact that the Ḥanafites were the only tradition to hold the position that coercion does not invalidate a pronouncement of divorce, and despite the explicit criticism that this position attracted from other traditions, the Ḥanafites continued to uphold both laws and chose instead to offer increasingly sophisticated defenses of their approach. Their approach to the problem of coercion and speech acts was constrained by an implicit norm that heavily discouraged jettisoning any law of the tradition and by the desire to demonstrate the overall coherence of the tradition's laws.[36]

[35] This way of thinking about how constraint generates and explains the character of reasoning, especially within a tradition, is indebted to Robert Brandom's inferentialist philosophy of rationality. For an assessment of the benefits of Brandom's philosophy for intellectual historians, see David L. Marshall, "The Implications of Robert Brandom's Inferentialism for Intellectual History," *History and Theory* 52, no. 1 (2013).

[36] We may conceptualize the source of this implicit norm that constrained the Ḥanafites to follow the received laws of the tradition in different ways. Perhaps it is a feature of all legal systems, which, all things being equal, tend to encourage following precedent, or deference to authority. The important point for us is not how to conceptualize the source of this constraint, as much as to notice that it exists, and most importantly explains much of the logic and content of justification for Ḥanafite coercion jurisprudence.

To belong to a tradition is to be constrained in some way. There are three types of constraints: internal, external, and domain-specific. Internal constraints are those that are implicitly or explicitly agreed upon by scholars belonging to a tradition. Sometimes these internal constraints are explicitly laid out. For example, the Muʿtazilites identified themselves as the theological school committed to the position that God is just in a way that explains His actions, especially toward human beings, and this position explains the main features of their actual practice of reasoning on various issues involving coercion or compulsion and responsibility. But sometimes scholars within a tradition pay homage to positions, principles, or methods of reasoning that they think constrain them, but in practice actually do not. For example, Shāfiʿite legal theory places a premium on the authority of authentic ḥadīth, but surprisingly, Shāfiʿite reasoning on a number of issues related to coercion and responsibility in works of positive law (*fiqh*) demonstrates little use of ḥadīth. Sometimes the internal constraints are not explicitly acknowledged and remain implicit in the practices of reasoning within a given tradition. For example, Ḥanafite coercion jurisprudence is starkly constrained by the core coercion laws articulated by the founding fathers of the tradition, even though Ḥanafite legal theory largely locates the authority of the tradition in scripture. What is important here is not whether a constraint is acknowledged by the practitioners within a tradition but how powerfully it explains the features of a given scholar's argumentation on an issue or the development of reasoning within a tradition on a problem over time.

External constraints are intellectual positions, principles, value, or methods of reasoning that lie completely outside the tradition or are shared with others beyond it. For example, the fact that the Ḥanafites' position on the validity of coerced divorce conflicted with the position of all other legal traditions on the same issue explains why their justifications consisted largely of interpretations of scripture, a method of argumentation that they shared with the traditions that opposed them. Often, when a position that emerges from within a tradition clashes starkly with broader external values, the scholars of the tradition are motivated to adjust or temper the argumentation for that position. As we will see, this was the case with Ashʿarite argumentation for the position that coercion does not undermine moral agency. And sometimes a conflict between the position of one tradition and that of another is entirely responsible for the form of a scholar's argumentation. Analysis of the coerced speech jurisprudence of the Ḥanafites and the Shāfiʿites provides an example of this phenomenon.

The third class of constraint, consisting of domain-specific constraints, structures the logic of a given domain of inquiry.[37] By a domain of inquiry I mean a specific problem area, such as coerced harm to others, coerced speech, or definitions of coercion. The constraints that structure a given domain transcend individual traditions and in fact seem to guide the thinking of anyone who approaches the problem in question from a shared disciplinary viewpoint, such as law or philosophy. Take the following problems: Is the absence of compulsion a condition for moral agency? How does a legal system define what is coercive? What is coercion's effect on speech acts? What is the proper distribution of moral and legal responsibility for coerced murder? Each of these questions has only a finite set of possible answers. Recall, for example, scenario 3 in the beginning of this introduction, in which a man threatens your life and demands you kill a bystander. The question of who ought to be held responsible and at what level in this scenario can be answered only in a limited number of ways, depending on how many types or levels of responsibility a culture recognizes, since there are only three agents to whom responsibility can be distributed. The fact that Anglo-American philosophers and judges often reasoned about this basic question in ways that are structurally similar to the arguments of their premodern Islamic counterparts is evidence of this particular domain's conceptual structure, a structure that is independent of the internal constraints of a tradition, the external constraints posed by the discursive context of that tradition, and the contingent historical circumstances that influence reasoning on any issue. There is more to domain-specific constraints than just the existence of a finite number of potential solutions. For example, when thinking about whether the coercer or the coerced ought to be held responsible for coerced

[37] This idea is inspired by Arudra Burra's contention that when it comes to moral inquiry, coercion is not a basic moral kind, such that its existence automatically and by itself triggers certain moral judgments. He holds that analysis of particular cases involving coercion reveals that the moral judgments are not triggered by coercion per se, but by the violation of norms that are specific to a given domain, such as the morality of sex (in the case of rape) or property. Arudra Venkata Burra, "Coercion, Deception, Consent: Essays in Moral Explanation" (Ph.D., Princeton University, 2011), 14–15.

homicide, all thinkers, whether Ḥanafites, Shāfiʿites, English or American judges, or Western philosophers, framed the issue as a conflict between the principle that all people have an equal right to security from harm and the idea that life-threatening exigent circumstances normally ought to have some effect on assessment of responsibility.

While internal, external, and domain-specific constraints emerge, in one way or another, from the logical force of avowing a certain legal or theological position, I call the second key determinant of tradition-based rationality contingency. By contingency, I mean those features of a scholar's or a tradition's context that lie outside of the web of logical and substantive commitments entailed by commitment to a particular intellectual position, principle, value, or method of reasoning but that nonetheless shape the character of a scholar's argument at a particular moment or a tradition's argumentation on a given issue over a span of time. These are historical factors, in which accident, luck, and sociopolitical circumstances play a large role. Examples of contingent factors are things like which traditions end up competing with each other in a given geographical locale, or the type of argumentation that becomes the dominant norm in an area, or the extent to which a tradition's position is a minority one vis-à-vis other traditions. These three contingent factors explain significant aspects of the Ḥanafite and Shāfiʿite discussion of various problems in coercion jurisprudence.

Let me use an analogy drawn from chess to explain how I conceive of the relationship between constraint and contingency in explaining the historical trajectory of thought in a given tradition. We might think of constraints as the rules that govern permissible moves that participants in a game of chess are bound to follow. These rules are surely part of the explanation for the moves made in the course of a game. They delimit the logical moves that a player can make in response to the ever-changing arrangement of the board. But there are also factors outside of the rules of the game, the opponent's moves, and the player's own strategy that may explain the latter's moves. It could be that cloudy weather on the day of the game had a depressing effect on the player, encouraging her to adopt a strategy that is more risk-averse than usual. Another factor that may influence the moves made in a game is the personality of the participants, some of whom are more daring and others more deliberate and cautious. These are contingent features that contribute to explaining the moves made in a particular chess match but do not originate in the logical possibilities delineated by the rules of chess or the particular configuration of the board at any given moment in time. Similarly, whether the legal position adopted by a particular tradition conflicts with that of the other major traditions is a contingent historical circumstance that is not rooted in the constraints delimiting the rationality of that tradition. Such historical circumstances represent the main reason that Ḥanafite reasoning on the problem of coercion and speech acts consists largely of scriptural interpretation.

3. COMPARISON: MEDIEVAL ISLAMIC AND MODERN WESTERN TREATMENTS OF COERCION AND RESPONSIBILITY

It goes without saying that freedom is an important value in the history of Western ethical, legal, political, and philosophical thought. Yet it was not until the publication of a seminal article on coercion by the political philosopher Robert Nozick that the examination of coercion was seen as a potentially useful way of thinking about liberty.[38] Juxtaposing this literature with the treatment of coercion and responsibility in classical Islamic thought reveals three fruitful points of comparison between the two discourses.

The first point of comparison reveals a central difference in how the two discourses regard the fundamental character of coercion and why they see an investigation of it as fruitful, and it relates to a core point of disagreement among coercion theorists in the Western philosophical literature: the question whether coercion is a descriptive or a normative concept.[39] Those who hold that it is either entirely or largely a descriptive concept think that the theorist's main task is to develop a satisfactory description of coercion, consisting ideally of necessary and sufficient conditions whose fulfillment

[38] Robert Nozick, "Coercion," in *Philosophy, Science, and Method: Essays in Honor of Ernest Nagel*, ed. Sidney Morgenbesser, Patrick Suppes, and Morton White (New York: St. Martin's Press, 1969).

[39] For a useful survey of the philosophical discourse on coercion, see Scott Anderson, "Coercion," in *The Stanford Encyclopedia of Philosophy (Summer 2015 Edition)*, ed. Edward N. Zalta (2015). See also Alan Wertheimer, *Coercion* (Princeton, NJ: Princeton University Press, 1987), 6–10.

identifies it.[40] Once an instance of coercion has been identified through the application of the criteria developed by the theorist, the normative consequences of the finding flow automatically from the identification and require no recourse to other normative notions. In this view, coercion is a fundamental moral wrong, something that is not reducible to further constituent wrongs and whose existence does not need to be supplemented with the identification of other wrongs in order to have moral effect. In decisions ranging from whether a type of sale ought to be invalidated, whether the responsibility of a criminal perpetrator is diminished, or whether a political system is just, the presence of coercion is by itself sufficient grounds for a judgment. By contrast, those who hold that coercion is a normative concept hold that the mere existence of coercion is often insufficient to generate the relevant normative effects—that a finding of coercion that alters, for instance, responsibility for an action may require the supplementation of other normative judgments.[41] While a threat of imprisonment made by a gangster

[40] The most explicitly and strictly descriptivist approach belongs to David Zimmerman, "Coercive Wage Offers," *Philosophy and Public Affairs* 10, no. 2 (1981). John Lawrence Hill criticizes moralized theories and claims to have developed a strictly nonmoralized approach, but ends up developing a theory of coercion that seems to apply only to responsibility for criminal activity. John Lawrence Hill, "Moralized Theories of Coercion: A Critical Analysis," *Denver University Law Review* 74, no. 4 (1997). I would classify Nozick's theory (in "Coercion") as one that aspires toward a purely descriptive approach but admits that some recourse to other moral standards may be required in some instances. The influence of his theory derives not so much from his attempt to formulate a completely descriptive theory of coercion as from his efforts to identify the necessary and sufficient conditions for the identification of coercion. In the process, he introduced the idea of baselines against which proposals could be judged as coercive threats or noncoercive offers, with lasting effects on the subsequent philosophical discussion. Another semidescriptivist theorist is Scott Anderson, who admits that a purely nonmoralized theory of coercion is untenable but thinks that the philosophical gain in mostly descriptivist theories lies in their significance for political theory. Scott Anderson, "The Enforcement Approach to Coercion," *Journal of Ethics and Social Philosophy* 5, no. 1 (2010).

[41] For a representative set of views criticizing descriptivist approaches and advocating the idea that coercion is a normative concept, see Vinit Haksar, "Coercive Proposals [Rawls and Gandhi]," *Political Theory* 4, no. 1 (1976); Cheyney C. Ryan, "The Normative Concept of Coercion," *Mind* 89, no. 356 (1980). Both Haksar and Ryan frame their responses partly as criticisms of Nozick. For a criticism of the most explicitly descriptivist theorist, Zimmerman, see Lawrence A. Alexander, "Zimmerman on Coercive Wage Offers," *Philosophy & Public Affairs* 12, no. 2 (1983). The most sustained philosophical engagement with coercion is by Alan Wertheimer, who builds his philosophical theory as much on the reasoning found in actual court cases involving coercion as on the writings of previous philosophers. He regards coercion as a normative concept, and his theory of it is explicitly moralized. See Wertheimer, *Coercion*. See also his "Remarks on Coercion and Exploitation," *Denver University Law Review* 74 (1997), for his demonstration that judgments about responsibility for coerced action in concrete cases require recourse to other normative notions such as rationality, fairness, and human dignity. For more recent

might count as legal coercion and thereby cancel the validity of a commercial contract, in most legal systems the threat will not have the same effect when made by a judge. In this case, those who favor a normative analysis of coercion hold that a responsibility-altering finding of coercion relies on a prior normative regime of legal rights and authority. They thus insist that other moral judgments have an intrinsic part to play in deciding whether coercion has normative effects and point to the difficulties that purely descriptivist theories have in dealing with these types of cases.

Closely connected to the debate about whether coercion is a descriptive or a normative notion (though the connection is not always acknowledged) is the question of why a philosophical inquiry into coercion is useful. Does it yield fruitful results for political theory and political philosophy, or are its results limited to law and ethics, in essence to the production of judgments about responsibility for coerced action? Those who hold that coercion is a descriptive concept and a fundamental type of moral wrong do so, for the most part, in order to use the concept to say something relevant to political theory.[42] Those who hold that it is normative regard it as useful only for more practical purposes: to determine its effect on legal and moral responsibility. Some of these latter theorists deny that coercion has any relevance for political theory.[43]

work arguing that coercion is inherently normative and that judgments of responsibility in the presence of coercion require invocation of other normative discourses, see Mitchell Berman, "The Normative Functions of Coercion Claims," *Legal Theory* 8 (2002), and Burra, "Coercion, Deception, Consent: Essays in Moral Explanation".

[42] This is most clearly the case for Nozick, who, in line with liberal and libertarian concerns, conceives of his analysis of coercion "as a preliminary to a longer study of liberty, whose major concerns will be the reasons which justify making someone unfree to perform an action, and the reason why making someone unfree to perform an action needs justifying." Nozick, "Coercion," 440. Zimmerman claims that an analysis of coercion that proves it to be a descriptive concept will allow him to judge capitalist relations of production, and specifically capitalist wage proposals, as unjust *because* they are coercive. Zimmerman, "Coercive Wage Offers," 122. Anderson also favors a largely descriptivist account of coercion, because he thinks that such an approach captures something significant about coercion's social and political importance. Anderson, "The Enforcement Approach to Coercion," 2.

[43] See Berman, "The Normative Functions of Coercion Claims," 47, for this point. Relatedly, although he does not say so explicitly, Burra seems to take aim at liberal and libertarian varieties of political theory by showing how judgments about coercion and exploitation, and by extension freedom, are not basic moral kinds, such that they may serve as an adequate basis for normative political theorizing. Burra, "Coercion, Deception, Consent: Essays in Moral Explanation."

Classical Muslim theologians and jurists did not explicitly identify the conceptual problems associated with coercion in terms of the descriptive/normative distinction, and for the most part their interest in the subject was firmly rooted in the problems it posed for responsibility, as opposed to the discovery of a foundation for political theorizing. Their discussions nonetheless offer three insights on the issue of coercion as descriptive or normative, and the utility of an examination of coercion for political theory. First, even if the Muʿtazilites did not conceive of the matter in this light themselves, they came closest to articulating an entirely descriptivist theory of coercion. This is not accidental and is likely related to the fact that, like the Western philosophers who treated inquiry into coercion as instrumental to the erection of a political theory, the Muʿtazilites treated it as instrumental to their defense of a notion of God's substantive justice, which required, in their system, that humans who are forced to commit an act be subject to neither blame nor praise for it. This indicates that when an inquiry into coercion is instrumental to a larger aim scholars tend to adopt descriptivist approaches—an insight that is made possible only by a comparative study of the two discourses. Second, scholars belonging to Ḥanafism and Shāfiʿīsm do not explicitly identify with contending camps as do Western coercion theorists. If we were to divide them into one of the two categories, they would surely all be normativists, as they all regard the responsibility for at least some acts as impervious to change despite coercion. However, if we conceive of the two categories as anchoring opposite ends of a continuum, we may classify the Ḥanafites as dedicated to a conception of coercion that was more normative, and the Shāfiʿites as favoring a more descriptive view. But more importantly, both traditions struggle with reconciling the formulation of a straightforward and concrete definition of coercion that could effectively guide the legal system in the distribution of responsibility for coerced acts with the appeal of more complex approaches that take a larger number of factors into consideration but by doing so introduce a degree of arbitrariness into the process that some legal scholars found troubling. This struggle mirrors in some ways that of Western philosophers and jurists. Third, although Muslim coercion theorists were not motivated by a concern for elaborating a normative political theory, their inquiry into coercion was by no means entirely divorced from concerns involving political power. At its origin, even before the establishment of the legal traditions, the

Islamic legal discourse on coercion evinced widespread disagreement on the issue of the validity of coerced divorce-contingent oaths, a type of oath whose violation by the oath taker entails automatic divorce from his wife and which rulers used to enforce political loyalty. The founder of the Sunnite legal tradition of Mālikism, Mālik b. Anas (d. 179/795), was even tortured for refusing to countenance the validity of divorce-contingent oaths that were obtained through coercion.[44] In addition, one of the founders of Ḥanafism, Muḥammad b. al-Ḥasan al-Shaybānī (d. 188/804), was reportedly called in for questioning by the caliph when news got around that he had just completed a book on coercion. Whether these reports are true is beside the point. At least in the eyes of those who recorded and disseminated them, coercion jurisprudence was a politicized discourse. Beyond the perception that what the legal scholars had to say about coercion was relevant to politics, the problem of illegal orders from superiors provided the scholars with an opportunity to address the effect of legitimate and illegitimate authority on the distribution of responsibility for coerced harm commanded by others; to debate whether the mere command of a ruler is coercive; and to forcefully insist that the ruler is not above the Sharīʿa (God's law) if he illegally commands his subordinates to harm others.

The second point of comparison between the Western and Muslim discourses involves not Western philosophers but Anglo-American judges and jurists adjudicating cases in which one party claims coercion in order to achieve the cancellation of an adoption, a marriage, or a plea bargain. American judges have historically denied that a claim of coercion can annul the legal consequences of these acts. They have done so despite the fact that in contract law jurisprudence they allow the same types of threats to undermine contracts. This variable approach of making the determination of what is coercive and what is not dependent on the type of legal act being coerced is also found in classical Islamic jurisprudence, where it is the hallmark feature of Ḥanafite coercion jurisprudence. Moreover, both Ḥanafite jurists and American judges tend to articulate their justification for this position in terms that have little to do

[44] Mairaj U. Syed, "Coercion in Classical Islamic Law and Theology" (Dissertation, Princeton University, 2011), 26–34.

with the actual reasons that inspired them to insist that coercion does not cancel a divorce or adoption.

A third point of comparison emerges in Islamic and Western treatments of coerced homicide, and here we find the greatest similarity between the ways in which contemporary philosophers, judges, and lawyers, on the one hand, and classical Islamic scholars, on the other, articulate the moral problem. In contemplating cases in which A coerces B to kill C, the practitioners of both traditions uphold the equality of all life as a starting premise, but they do not apply it to the case uniformly. Nonetheless, the arguments that the various scholars proffer in favor of their preferred ways of distributing moral and legal responsibility between A and B are very similar across the two traditions.

4. OVERVIEW OF CHAPTERS

Chapters 1 and 2 analyze the treatment of compulsion and coercion in two classical theological traditions, Muʿtazilism and Ashʿarism, respectively. The central question for both theological traditions was whether coercion undermines moral agency and whether the lack of coercion or compulsion is a precondition for an agent to be held morally responsible for her acts. The Muʿtazilites answered in the affirmative, the Ashʿarites in the negative. Both traditions were driven to their respective positions by commitments to certain core ideas about God. The Muʿtazilites held that God is just in the sense that He would not hold human beings responsible for acts that they do not freely commit. The Muʿtazilites developed the most extensive psychological theory of the classical period to explain what constitutes a fully volitional act and what constitutes a compelled act.[45] While the Muʿtazilites held God's justice to be a core proposition in their systematic theology, the

[45] By "psychological" I do not mean to imply that the Muʿtazilites put forward a unified naturalistic psychological account similar to that of Muslim philosophers such as Avicenna or of those who appropriated the philosophers' theories of the soul, such as Ghazālī. The Muʿtazilites did not have a theory of the soul as such, but they did have certain systematic ideas about how human beings acquire knowledge and espouse belief and, where relevant, the emotional force such knowledge and belief had to motivate action. My description of their approach as psychological relates only to this aspect of their thought. I thank Ayman Shihadeh for pointing out the potential confusion.

Ashʿarites emphasized God's monopoly on creative agency in the universe. According to the Ashʿarites, God is the creator of all things and events, including volitional human action. For this reason, the Ashʿarites did not consider the absence of compulsion or coercion to be a condition of moral responsibility. However, although all Ashʿarites explicitly noted that coercion does not, prima facie, negate moral responsibility, their justification for this position changed over time. Early Ashʿarites held, contrary to the Muʿtazilites, that there is no rational argument for holding that God would not impose on human beings obligations that they do not have the capacity to perform. Abū Bakr al-Bāqillānī (d. 403/1013) consequently argued that if God may impose impossible obligations on human beings, there is no rational reason to suppose that coercion may cancel moral agency. The later Ashʿarites Imām al-Ḥaramayn al-Juwaynī (d. 478/1085) and Abū Ḥāmid al-Ghazālī (505/1111) explicitly rejected the validity of this line of argumentation, even as they continued to uphold the overall position. Similarly, the Ashʿarites initially argued that since coercion does not compromise an agent's reason, it does not undermine moral agency. Reason was the central capacity that provided the basis for moral agency. But in an effort to bring Ashʿarite thinking further into line with their divine command moral epistemology, some Ashʿarites subsequently changed this criterion to the capacity to understand speech (*fahm*), because it is through this specific intellectual capacity that human beings gain moral knowledge as found only in scripture.

Chapter 3 deals with Ḥanafite attempts to formulate a legal definition of coercion. Classical Ḥanafites articulated a three-tier standard. Threats against life or limb were compellingly coercive such that material responsibility for bodily acts was transferred from the coerced agent to the coercer. Threats of lengthy imprisonment or enchainment were coercive only in commercial transactions, yet did not have the power to transfer responsibility. Threats of a light beating or imprisonment for a short time were not legally coercive. The Ḥanafites were the only group of legal scholars to hold that coercion has no effect on irrevocable speech acts, the paradigmatic instance of which was divorce. I show that the classical Ḥanafite articulation of this three-tiered legal coercion standard was primarily motivated by the desire to account for the coercion laws of the tradition as enunciated by the founding fathers, rather than representing an account of coercion's effects on the psychology of the coerced. Chapter 4 addresses Shāfiᶜite attempts to formulate a legal standard for validating claims of coercion. The standard that they developed was much simpler than that of their Ḥanafite counterparts, largely because all Shāfiᶜites agreed that a coerced speech act is uniformly invalid. But while the Shāfiᶜite standard was in many respects simpler, there was much more internal debate among Shāfiᶜite scholars as to what constitutes that standard. The opinions on this issue broke down along regional lines. With a few exceptions, Iraqi Shāfiᶜites adopted a flexible, contextualist approach to defining coercion that relied mostly on commonsensical empirical judgments. Threats of beating, banishment, imprisonment, and even insult were all potentially coercive, depending on a careful consideration of the coerced's context. In fact, a finding of coercion could vary depending on the social class of the coerced (so, for example, the threat of an insult is coercive when leveled at a member of the upper higher classes but not when made to an individual of low status). By contrast, some Khurasani Shāfiᶜites who held that only threats against life or limb are coercive explicitly opposed this approach. They thought that the flexible standard permitted too much arbitrary discretion in the process of defining legal coercion. They also thought that only threats against life or limb sufficiently undermine the deliberative processes involved in making choices to qualify as coercion.

Chapter 5 focuses on Ḥanafite and Shāfiᶜite jurisprudence on coerced speech. It shows how Ḥanafites sought to defend the coherence of their divergent positions on the effects of coercion on different types of speech actions, and it demonstrates the intimate connection between Shāfiᶜite and Ḥanafite reasoning on coerced speech—remarkable given the two groups' diametrically opposed positions on unilateral coerced speech acts. Out of all the legal issues analyzed in this book, it is coerced speech jurisprudence that best fits the popular description of reasoning in Islamic law as consisting primarily of the interpretation of scripture. I argue that it is precisely because Shāfiᶜism and Ḥanafism were diametrically opposed to each other on this issue that their reasoning on coerced speech was so heavily characterized by scriptural interpretation.

Chapter 6 turns to Ḥanafite and Shāfiᶜite jurisprudence on coerced harm, as exemplified in discussions concerning the distribution of moral and legal responsibility in cases of coerced rape and murder. In both types of cases, the scholars of each tradition confronted a range of conflicting opinions inherited from the founding fathers of the tradition. As a result, much of the jurisprudence of both groups consisted of retrospective reconstruction of the legal and moral reasoning that had led the founders to their divergent opinions. Both the Ḥanafites and the Shāfiʿites held that coercion, even if compelling, cannot ever morally excuse rape or murder. The coerced commits a sin in both cases, because he has preferred his own life to the life of the victim, a preference he cannot legitimately make, because all are equal before God when it comes to protection from unjustified harm. However, the founding fathers of Ḥanafism differed on whether the coerced can escape the legal punishments prescribed for these crimes. What seems to have become the majority position in classical Ḥanafism held that although the perpetrator of coerced rape or murder has committed a sin, he is not to be punished for the crime. This presented the problem of why the legal consequences of the coerced act do not follow its moral evaluation. Much of Ḥanafite jurisprudence on coerced rape and murder is a response to this legal and moral conundrum. Shāfiʿī, too, left his successors with two conflicting opinions on the legal liability of the coerced in cases of coerced homicide. According to one opinion, he held that both the coercer and the coerced are liable for the full punishment; according to another, he limited full liability for the murder to the coercer only. The Shāfiʿites considered the problem of coerced homicide as a species of the problem of orders from a superior, and their discussions often involved consideration of whether it makes a difference that the coercer holds legitimate political authority.

1

Compulsion and Moral Agency in Muʿtazilism

1. INTRODUCTION

In May 2010, a group of activists and academics declared that cetaceans are persons and as such are entitled to the fundamental rights to life, liberty, and wellbeing.[1] Meanwhile, the American Society for the Prevention of Cruelty to Robots is working for the legal affirmation of robotic rights, premised on the idea that at a certain point in the not so distant future, robots will be sentient beings.[2] Both groups raise compelling questions about who deserves legal protection and rights, and why. What is it about cetaceans and robots that might make them merit a moral status that has up to this point been reserved only for human beings? Is it the ability to feel pain? Is it the possession of certain cognitive capacities, such as rationality or language? Is it the capability to form communities?[3]

In the third/ninth century, Muslim theologians and legal theorists started evincing interest in questions that bear a family resemblance to those animating today's debates about the rights of robots and cetaceans. For these theologians, the central issue was the conditions necessary for someone to be subject to God's commandments (*taklīf*)—in short, for moral agency. The lists they proposed of such conditions often combined dispositional features that an agent must have to qualify for moral agency, such

[1] Helsinki Group, http://www.cetaceanrights.org/.

[2] The American Society for the Prevention of Cruelty to Robots, www.aspcr.com/.

[3] Agnieszka Jaworska and Julie Tannenbaum, "The Grounds of Moral Status," *The Stanford Encyclopedia of Philosophy* (Summer 2013 Edition), http://plato.stanford.edu/archives/sum2013/entries/grounds-moral-status/.

as the possession of a certain amount of knowledge (*kamāl al-ʿaql*), physical ability (*qādir*), and the ability to understand language (*fahm*), with temporary features of an agent's context, such as the absence of any impediments to the required act (*manʿ*). One such temporary feature was the absence of coercion (*ikrāh*) or compulsion (*iljāʾ*).[4] According to Muʿtazilite theologians, upholding moral agency on a compelled agent would be morally unjust and thus invalid. Affirming this prerequisite invited consideration of a host of subsidiary issues, including the precise definition of compulsion, its interaction with different types of moral assessment, and the specific conceptual problems that these ideas about compulsion and responsibility posed for the Muʿtazilites' moral epistemology. But why did the Muʿtazilites stipulate the absence of compulsion as a condition for moral agency? This was not the only position that one could have taken in classical Islam, and in fact the Ashʿarites took the opposite stance entirely. The Muʿtazilites' adoption of this position reflects the centrality of Divine justice in Muʿtazilite theology.

In contrast to much existing scholarship on the history of Islamic theology, which characterizes whole traditions as belonging on a spectrum anchored by the pole of reason on one end and tradition on the other, I argue that what drives the argumentation and development of theological thought within the confines of a tradition are commitment to certain core positions, deemed immune from explicit revision and criticism. The different theological traditions were just committed to different core positions. These core positions are the internal constraints of a theological tradition. In the case of Muʿtazilism, they are a commitment to a substantive notion of Divine Justice and an objectivist moral epistemology. These two commitments played three functional roles in Muʿtazilite thought. They ensured that no subsequent

[4] Muʿtazilite discussions of moral agency use the term "compulsion (*iljāʾ*)" as opposed to "coercion (*ikrāh*)". There is a subtle distinction between the two in classical Islamic thought. Both terms denote an agent being forced to do something she does not want to do. When classical Muslim scholars use the term '*ikrāh* (coercion)' they assume that the source of the force is another human being, who usually coerces through threats. The Muʿtazilite use of the term compulsion, as we will see, does not assume that the source of the undesired force must be a human being, though it could be. The source of the external force could be, for example, a predator, who compels one to flee, or a particular circumstance, such as starvation. For the Muʿtazilites, it is not so much the source of the force that is relevant to the analysis, as much as its effect on responsibility for action.

and subsidiary elaboration of Muʿtazilite doctrine could contradict them. Relatedly, they provided Muʿtazilite scholars with the criteria by which to assess, and thereby reject or accept, a subsidiary doctrinal position on an issue which occasioned internal disagreement, and in doing so influenced the historical development of the tradition over time. Finally, the internal constraints helped broadly identify the areas that needed elaboration in order to demonstrate entitlement to the core positions to both insiders and outsiders. In the case of Muʿtazilism, this led to the development of a fairly detailed theory of human psychology: one capable of distinguishing freely-chosen from compelled action.

2. DIVINE JUSTICE AS INTERNAL CONSTRAINT IN MUʿTAZILITE THEOLOGY

The most important sources for Muʿtazilite theology available to scholars today are *Kitāb al-Mughnī fī abwāb al-tawḥīd wa-ʾl-ʿadl* by the celebrated Qāḍī ʿAbd al-Jabbār (d. 415/1025), the chief articulator of the tradition in the fifth/eleventh century, and *al-Kitāb fī ʾl-muḥīṭ bi-ʾl-taklīf* by his student Ibn Mattawayh (d. 435/1044). Both of these theologians belonged to one particular branch of the Muʿtazilite tradition, namely the Basran school. The most important figure of this school was the Basran theologian Abū Hāshim al-Jubbāʾī (d. 321/933), who had studied with his father Abū ʿAlī al-Jubbāʾī (d. 303/915). Unfortunately, the works of these two figures survive only in quotations and paraphrases in later Muʿtazilite and non-Muʿtazilite sources. References to Abū Hāshim's works and doctrines abound in ʿAbd al-Jabbār's and Ibn Mattawayh's works. Often, ʿAbd al-Jabbār begins his discussion of a theological topic or issue by paraphrasing or quoting Abū Hāshim's thoughts on the matter.

Unlike the discipline of law, theology was something of an embattled discipline in classical Islam. The arguments against the legitimacy of the discipline, voiced most vociferously by the traditionalist scholars commonly known as the Ahl al-Ḥadīth, centered on two intertwined suspicions. First, as critics of the entire discipline of theology, they contended that the theologians engaged with topics that were never directly addressed by the Qurʾān, the Prophet, the Companions, or the pious generations after them and should therefore be left alone. And second, they argued that the rationalist methods of speculative inquiry used by the theologians were reprehensible innovations that departed from the methods used by the Prophet, the Companions, and the succeeding pious generations. Yet despite this hostility in early medieval Islamic society, it thrived.[5]

The subjects of theological inquiry were not uniform from one tradition to the next, and what captured the attention of practitioners of the discipline varied historically. Regardless, the core aim of the discipline was to provide a conceptual framework that fleshed out God's relationship to the cosmos, with special attention to the nature of His relationship to human beings. This framework took a largely rationalist form. Formulating such a framework required theorization of the nature of God's essence and attributes and their interrelations, the nature of the cosmos, the nature of physical and moral agency, and the nature of the hereafter and its connection to human action and Divine benevolence. In addition, theologians often ended their works by elaborating on their traditions' doctrines on the legitimacy of the first four historical caliphs and on theories of legitimate governance more broadly.

Theologians typically framed theology as a response to what they considered the first moral obligation of every human being upon reaching maturity: the duty to inquire into the existence of God, His nature, and the bearing of these conclusions on a person's fate in the hereafter. Thus, ideas produced in the course of inquiry into the fundamental nature of the cosmos served as premises for rationalist arguments about God's existence and nature.

The two cardinal features of the Muʿtazilite tradition relevant to compulsion, coercion, and responsibility are its commitment to a conception of God that prioritizes His Justice as His supreme overriding attribute and its commitment to moral objectivism—the position that at least some

[5] For a translation of Ashʿarī's defense of the religious legitimacy of theology (*kalām*), see John Renard, *Islamic Theological Themes: a Primary Source Reader* (Oakland: University of California Press, 2014), 151–60.

judgments on the goodness and evil of acts are ultimately reducible to features of the acts themselves, as opposed to God's will, and discoverable by human reason.

The overwhelming importance of the value of justice for the Muʿtazilites is evident in their works. The Zaydī Muʿtazilite Mānkdīm (d. 425/1034) declares in his supercommentary (*taʿlīq*) on ʿAbd al-Jabbār's commentary (*sharḥ*) on Muʿtazilite theology that God's justice requires commitment to the following substantive propositions: that He "does not commit evil, nor does He neglect duties, nor command evil, nor forbid good, and all of His actions are good."[6] In addition, God's justice allows us to know what "it is permissible for Him to do and what it is not permissible for Him to do."[7] A couple of generations later, the Muʿtazilite al-Ḥākim al-Jishumī (d. 494/1101) adds that a commitment to God as Just entails the following subsidiary positions:

1. The acts of human beings are their own creation.
2. God imposes duties for their (human beings') benefit (*li-nafʿi-him*).
3. God gives human beings the relevant physical capacity (*qudra*), instruments, and act-specific ability (*istiṭāʿa*) before the act.
4. He does not charge one with compliance with a commandment (*lam yukallif*) until eliminating any relevant impediments preventing action.
5. He does not punish unless the person has sinned (*dhanb*), nor does He hold a person responsible for the sins of another.
6. He rewards anyone who obeys Him.
7. It is rationally possible that He punish (*yajūz an yuʿāqib*) one who disobeys Him.
8. He has informed us that He will inevitably (*lā maḥāla*) punish such a disobedient person.[8]

The Muʿtazilites' commitment to God's justice both constrained their theology and generated much of it. The position that God's justice requires that He charge agents only with acts that they are capable of doing and regarding which they have free choice motivated the construction of a rich conceptual picture of what capability and free choice look like. The

[6] Shashdīw Mānkdīm, *Sharḥ al-Uṣūl al-Khamsa*, ed. Samīr Muṣṭafā Rabāb, 1st ed. (Beirut: Dār Iḥyāʾ al-Turāth al-ʿArabī, 2001), 35.17–18.

[7] Ibid., 203.4.

[8] See al-Ḥākim al-Jishumī, *Taḥkīm al-ʿUqūl fī Taṣḥīḥ al-Uṣūl*, ed. ʿAbd al-Salām b. ʿAbbās al-Wajīh, 1st ed. (Sanaa: Muʾassasa al-Imām Zayd b. ʿAlī al-Thaqāfiyya, 2008), 32.17–33.3.

Muʿtazilites produced a perceptive account of the types of motivations that drive human action, its relation to moral goods, and the evaluations (both human and Divine) entailed in the commission of acts of both moral and nonmoral character. Indeed, of the traditions surveyed in this work, it is the Muʿtazilite one that provided the most extensive engagement with the psychology of compulsion. The Muʿtazilites' discussion of the problem of compulsion and responsibility draws on this detailed psychological model, and understanding the former thus requires understanding the latter.

2.1 A Conception of Moral Agency Constrained and Inspired by Divine Justice

Both the Ashʿarite and Muʿtazilite classical traditions hold that basic physical capability (*qudra*) is a condition for moral agency, and both traditions hold that conscious actions are events that occur through this basic physical capacity, which God creates in the human body. In the Muʿtazilite conception, the difference between my shivering when cold (an action that occurs in my body, but not through my physical agency) and my doing "the shiver" on the dance floor is that the former action was created by God in my body, whereas the latter was created by me through my use of the physical capacity created by God in my body. Part of this picture, also important for our later discussion of moral agency in the Ashʿarite tradition, is the Muʿtazilite insistence that God's creation of the physical capacity precedes my autonomous action based on it. Importantly, the presence and temporal precedence of the physical capacity to act mean that I have the power to either perform the action or omit it.[9]

[9] For the picture of physical agency sketched here, see Alnoor Dhanani, *The Physical Theory of Kalām: Atoms, Space, and Void in Basrian Muʿtazilī Cosmology* (Leiden: Brill, 1994), 6; J.R.T.M. Peters, *God's Created Speech: a Study in the Speculative Theology of the Muʿtazilī Qâḍî l-Quḍât Abū l-Ḥasan ʿAbd al-Jabbâr Bn Aḥmad al-Hamadânī* (Leiden: Brill, 1976), 201–3; Richard M. Frank, "The Autonomy of the Human Agent in the Teaching of ʿAbd al-Ǧabbar," *Le Muséon* 95 (1982): 327; Richard M. Frank, *The Metaphysics of Created Being According to Abū l-Hudhayl al-ʿAllāf: a Philosophical Study of the Earliest Kalām* (Istanbul: Nederlands Historisch-Archaeologisch Instituut in het Nabije Oosten, 1966), 29–32; Sophia Vasalou, *Moral Agents and Their Deserts: the Character of Muʿtazilite Ethics* (Princeton, NJ: Princeton University Press, 2008), 142.

However, while the capacity to act is a sufficient condition for *physical* agency,[10] it is a necessary but not sufficient condition for *moral* agency.[11] Other conditions must also be met for moral agency to emerge. ʿAbd al-Jabbār puts forward six general conditions that must be met in order for God's imposition to count as morally good and thus valid:

1. The agent must be provided with the tools (*al-ālāt*) to perform the action that he is charged with, at the time that performance of the action is demanded.[12]
2. The agent must have reached a mature level of knowledge (*kamāl al-ʿaql*).[13]
3. No impediment (*manʿ*) may exist that temporarily prevents the agent from performing or omitting the morally significant act (duty or supererogation) in question.[14]

[10] I use the term "physical" broadly. ʿAbd al-Jabbār lists the following genera of accidents that fall under an agent's fundamental capacity for action: bodily acts (*afʿāl al-jawāriḥ*) and mental acts (*afʿāl al-qulūb*). There are five types of bodily acts: modes of being (*akwān*), pressures (*iʿtimādāt*), compositions (*taʾlīf*), sounds, and pains. And there are five types of mental acts: convictions, will, non-will, assumption, and reflection. For a further explanation of these, see Peters, *God's Created Speech*, 127.

[11] It is important not to lose sight of the explicitly theological sense in which the imposition of morally significant action (*taklīf*) is understood by the Muʿtazilites. God is the one who imposes obligations (*wājib*) and recommends supererogatory acts (*nadb*). For the idea that God is the explicit imposer of morally significant action (obligations and supererogatory acts), see Mānkdīm, *Sharḥ*, 344.18–20.

[12] ʿAbd al-Jabbār, *al-Mughnī fī Abwāb al-Tawḥīd wa al-ʿAdl*, ed. Ṭāhā Ḥusayn and Ibrāhīm Madkūr, 14 vols. (Cairo: Wizārat al-Thaqāfa wa-ʾl-Irshād al-Qawmī, al-Idāra al-ʿĀmma li-ʾl-Thaqāfa, 1960–9), 370–71. See also Maḥmūd b. ʿUmar al-Zamakhsharī, *A Muʿtazilite Creed of Az-Zamaḫšarî (d. 538/1144): (al- Minhâǧ fî uṣûl ad-dîn)*, ed. Sabine Schmidtke, trans. Sabine Schmidtke (Stuttgart: Deutsche Morgenländische Gesellschaft, 1997), 27.

[13] ʿAbd al-Jabbār, *Mughnī*, 11:375.17. For a sustained discussion of this condition along with objections and rebuttals to ʿAbd al-Jabbār's formulation, see ibid., 11:371–87. For a more expansive explanation of the Muʿtazilite concept of *ʿaql*, see Peters, *God's Created Speech*, 92–93. Ibn Mattawayh uses this condition to explicitly exclude from moral responsibility those who are unaware of their actions (*al-sāhī*), asleep (*al-nāʾim*), or insane (*al-majnūn*), as well as animals (*al-bahīma*), and infants (*al-ṭifl*). See al-Ḥasan b. Aḥmad b. Mattawayh, *Kitāb al-Majmūʿ fī al-Muḥīṭ bi-al-Taklīf*, ed. J.J. Houben, Daniel Gimaret, and Jan Peters, 3 vols. (Beirut: Dār al-Mashriq, 1965), 1:243.5–7. Importantly, for the classical Muʿtazilites, the term *ʿaql* refers not to a power, faculty, or tool that the agent uses in the process of reasoning (practical or otherwise), but rather "a specific aggregation of [pieces of] information (lit. knowledges, *jumlatun min ʾl-ʿulūm makhṣūṣa*) such that when they obtain in the [prospective] moral agent (*mukallaf*), [the acts of theological] inquiry, inference, and sustained performance of imposed [duties and supererogations] are possible."

[14] ʿAbd al-Jabbār, *Mughnī*, 11:391–92; Mānkdīm, *Sharḥ*, 264–65. Mānkdīm lists two exemplary ways in which action can be impeded and thus excluded from moral evaluation. The first is by being chained up or physically restricted, so that the act of walking, for example,

4. The agent must not be compelled to perform or omit the act.[15]
5. The agent must perform the action by way of a motivation urging it.[16]
6. The agent must possess natural desires and aversions vis-à-vis the benefits and harms implicit in the pursuit of a prospective course of action.[17]

Of these six conditions, condition 4, the absence of compulsion (*iljāʾ*), is our central concern here. The three Muʿtazilites on whom I focus, ʿAbd al-Jabbār, Mānkdīm, and Ibn Mattawayh,[18] understand most varieties of compulsion as a type of overwhelming motivation. In fact, the concept of motivation is essential to these three thinkers' understanding of human agency in general.

2.2 Constructing a Muʿtazilite Psychology

The Basran Muʿtazilites divide actions into two broad types: those that are directly initiated by an agent (*mubtadiʾāt*) and those that are ultimately but not directly the effect of an act initiated by the agent, yet can still be attributed to her (*mutawallidāt*).[19] Dancing would be an example of the first, while knocking over the punch bowl on the table because of one's bad dancing would be an example of the second. These Muʿtazilites

becomes impossible for the moment. The second is by opposition (*ḍidd*). Here, what ʿAbd al-Jabbār described as an independent condition for the realization for legitimate moral agency, Mānkdīm seems to see as a type of impediment. He gives the situation of a scribe being prevented from writing by the lack of a pen as an example of an impediment caused by opposition. This is very similar to ʿAbd al-Jabbār's instrument condition (no. 1 in his list). See also Ibn Mattawayh, *Majmūʿ*, 1:243.21–22, though in this passage Ibn Mattawayh uses the term *al-aʿdhār*, which I take to be a synonym for impediments (*mawāniʿ*).

[15] ʿAbd al-Jabbār, *Mughnī*, 11:393–400. Discussions about compulsion can be found in multiple volumes of the *Mughnī*. See also Ibn Mattawayh, *Majmūʿ*, 1:243.21.

[16] ʿAbd al-Jabbār, *Mughnī*, 11:400–1.

[17] Ibid., 11:387–90. As we shall see, this is essential to the Muʿtazilite idea that in order to deserve praise or reward for an action, the agent must bear some kind of burden (*mashaqqa*). That an agent be naturally desirous of or averse to certain interactions with the world is a fundamental part of the cost inherent in choosing a course of action, thereby earning praise for the forgone benefit or the encumbrance of harm.

[18] Ibn Mattawayh was a student of ʿAbd al-Jabbār and the author of an important commentary on one of his works. For general biographical information on Ibn Mattawayh, see Martin McDermott, "Ebn Mattawayh, Abū Moḥammad Ḥasan," in *Encyclopædia Iranica*, ed. Ehsan Yarshater (London; Boston; Winona Lake, IN.: Routledge & Kegan Paul, 1982).

[19] Frank, "Autonomy," 326.

further divide immediate actions into two basic categories: acts of the heart and acts of the body.[20] Acts of the heart include things like intending, knowing, believing, and willing. For our purposes, the last is especially important. When an agent has "an object of some event (entity) whose coming to be is actually possible: a concrete act that an agent can do," then an agent can be properly described as willing the prospective act.[21] When an agent initiates an action that is coterminous with his willing that action, then the agent has chosen that action.[22] But what inspires an agent to will a possible prospective action and to undertake it? It is the agent's interaction with the outside world, and these interactions, in Muʿtazilite theology, are mediated by what the Muʿtazilites call motivations (*dawāʿī*).

2.2.1 *Types of Motivations*

The Muʿtazilites' understanding of motivation underpins their account of both compelled and noncompelled action.[23] At the most general level, motivations are an agent's beliefs about prospective courses of action. There are different types of motivations. One important type is beliefs about the benefit or harm that would accrue to an agent in a given course of action.[24] ʿAbd al-Jabbār claims that the fact that human beings act on the basis of such

[20] Ibid.; Margaretha T. Heemskerk, *Suffering in Muʿtazilite Theology: ʿAbd al-Jabbār's Teaching on Pain and Divine Justice* (Leiden; Boston: Brill, 2000), 90.

[21] Frank, "Autonomy," 329. [22] Ibid., 330.

[23] For a brief survey of Islamicist scholarship on the doctrine of motivations, see ibid., 333, footnote 20. I have adopted Frank's translation of *daʿwā/dawāʿī* as "motivation" for the reasons outlined therein and because it fits my own reading of the primary sources. According to Frank, motivations, "in brief, are the concrete bases of the rationality of human actions": ibid., 353–54. Gimaret translates the term as "incentive," but there is little meaningful difference between Gimaret's and Frank's understandings. For Gimaret's elucidation of this concept, see Daniel Gimaret, "La Notion d' 'impulsion irrésistible' (ilǧâʾ) dans l'éthique Muʿtazilite," *Journal Asiatique* 259 (1971): 36–38. For a summary of the theory of motivations in ʿAbd al-Jabbār, see Wilferd Madelung, "The Late Muʿtazila and Determinism: the Philosophers' Trap," in *Yād-Nāma: In Memoria di Alessandro Bausani*, ed. Biancamaria Scarcia Amoretti and Lucia Rostagno, Studi orientali (Rome: Bardi editore, 1991), 245–48.

[24] ʿAbd al-Jabbār argues that beliefs about benefit and harm are further reducible to human beings' natural desire for pleasure and aversion to pain. See Heemskerk, *Suffering*, 114. Frank notes that ʿAbd al-Jabbār further defines pleasure as "the enjoyment of what is desirable (or is actually desired: *ʾidrāku l-muštahá*) and pain as its contrary." Moreover, for ʿAbd al-Jabbār the enjoyment may be physical, psychological, aesthetic, or intellectual. See Frank, "Autonomy," 334.

motivations is undeniable.[25] Motivations can be based on beliefs of differing levels of certitude. In order to result in action, they do not have to have reached the level of certain knowledge (*ʿilm*). They may be motivated by probability (*ẓann*).[26]

Not all motivations to action are based on beliefs about the prospective harm or benefit associated with a given course of action. Some motivations are based on beliefs about the intrinsic goodness or evil of an action. Muʿtazilites held that reason can make judgments independently of revelation about the goodness or evil of some actions. These judgments are based on features of the acts themselves. Examples of such judgments are recognizing the inherent goodness of thanking a generous benefactor or the evil of a gratuitous lie.[27] Acts can be motivated by such judgments.[28] In fact, ʿAbd al-Jabbār stipulates that for an agent to deserve praise and reward for the fulfillment of a duty or a supererogation, it must be motivated by that specific aspect of the act that makes it good or obligatory.[29] In the Muʿtazilite conception, actions are thus motivated by considerations of utility and by their ethical value.

2.2.2 Substantiating a Just Psychology of Free Choice and Action: Conflict of Motivations

Given this picture of human action, Muʿtazilite authors characterize free choice as choosing between conflicting motivations. Making the ethical choice involves choosing to follow the motivation that urges action based on an act's inherent goodness or evil over other motivations that may urge

[25] See Gimaret, "La notion," 37 and the sources cited therein. The idea of deliberating about harms and benefits in pursuing a course of action seems to be old in the Muʿtazilite tradition. See, for instance, Abū ʿUthmān ʿAmr b. Baḥr al-Jāḥiẓ, *al-Ḥayawān*, 2nd ed., 8 vols. (Cairo: Muṣṭafā al-Bābī al-Ḥalabī, 1966), 2:146. However, for al-Jāḥiẓ, motivations do not seem to have the systematic connotations that they acquire with Abū Hāshim. Schwarz identifies Jāḥiẓ as the originator of the idea that action is not possible without a motivation: M. Schwarz, "Some Notes on the Notion of Iljāʾ (constraint) in Muʿtazilite Kalām," *Israel Oriental Studies* 2 (1972): 422.

[26] For an extended presentation of ʿAbd al-Jabbār's and Ibn Mattawayh's views on how human beings perceive pain and pleasure, see Heemskerk, *Suffering*, 81–88.

[27] On this, see, most importantly, George F. Hourani, *Islamic Rationalism: the Ethics of ʿAbd al-Jabbār* (Oxford: Clarendon Press, 1971).

[28] Gimaret, "La notion," 37, and the sources in ʿAbd al-Jabbār's *Mughnī* cited therein.

[29] ʿAbd al-Jabbār, *Mughnī*, 14.177.17–18.

other courses of action on the basis of beliefs about the prospective harm avoided or benefit obtained through them. ʿAbd al-Jabbār writes that "it is necessary that the moral agent (*mukallaf*) is free [to perform] his act (*mukhallan bayna-hu wa-fiʿli-hi*), [characterized by a state of] countervailing motivations between the acts and their opposites."[30] Ibn Mattawayh definitively asserts, "God's imposition of duties (*taklīf*) is completed only with the conflict of motivations."[31]

The conflict between countervailing motivations characterizes the suitability of an agent's act for moral evaluation.[32] In Muʿtazilite thought, this is partly related to the idea that there must be some sort of hardship inherent in the act for an agent to deserve praise or possibly Divine reward for it.[33] ʿAbd al-Jabbār writes that "an agent deserves praise only when he could have done something other than that which [he] was urged to do by a motivation, but he chose not to do it and bore hardship in [performing the chosen act] or [an act] resembling it."[34] A conflict of motivations is rooted in an agent's

[30] See Gimaret, "La notion," 38 and the sources cited therein. As Gimaret notes, in ʿAbd al-Jabbār, *Mughnī*, 6a:186.17–18, ʿAbd al-Jabbār says that it is the equivalence of motivations (*takāfuʾ al-dawāʿī*) that renders the agent free to perform either one of the possible actions in front of him. ʿAbd al-Jabbār uses the idea of conflicting and equivalent motivations to deny the naturalist thesis that acts come to exist in limbs by virtue of some natural constitution inherent in the limbs; see ibid., 9:31.1–2. In addition to the passages cited by Gimaret, see also ibid., 11:393.15–16. For other descriptions of this idea, see Frank, "Autonomy," 336; Madelung, "Late Muʿtazila," 248.

[31] Frank, "Autonomy," 336. The idea that conflicting motivations constitute the context in which an agent chooses one course of action over another seems to have been shared by the Basran Muʿtazilites and their Baghdadi counterparts; see Abū Rashīd Saʿīd b. Muḥammad Naysābūrī, *al-Masāʾil fī al-Khilāf bayna al-Baṣrīyyīn wa al-Baghdādīyyīn*, ed. Maʿn Ziyāda and Riḍwān al-Sayyid (Tripoli, Lebanon: Maʿhad al-Anmāʾ al-ʿArabī, 1989), 293.

[32] On the existence of motivations as a condition for the moral evaluation of actions, see ʿAbd al-Jabbār, *Mughnī*, 11:400–401.

[33] Ibid., 8:175.20–22. The idea appears already in al-Jāḥiẓ, *Ḥayawān*, 4:88.

[34] This passage is found in ʿAbd al-Jabbār, *Mughnī*, 11:393.13–14, cited by Gimaret in Gimaret, "La notion," 58. For an even more explicit connection between forgoing a motivation to act and enduring hardship, see ʿAbd al-Jabbār, *Mughnī*, 16:71.10–12: "Likewise, the obtaining of desire (*shahwa*) and the conflict of motivations (*taraddud al-dawāʿī*) are considered [part of] enabling [an agent to perform an act], because the agent cannot perform the act as charged without them; because hardship and burden are obtained only through them, or through something that takes their place." Ibn Mattawayh explicitly reframes the absence of compulsion condition for moral agency as the positive existence of a conflict of motivations. See Ibn Mattawayh, *Majmūʿ*, 2:265.10. Interestingly, the sixth/twelfth-century Muʿtazilite scholar Ibn al-Malāḥimī completely replaces the negative condition of an absence of compulsion with the positive stipulation that there must simply be a conflict of motivations. See Maḥmūd b. Muḥammad Ibn al-Malāḥimī, *Kitāb al-Fāʾiq fī Uṣūl al-Dīn*, ed. Wilferd Madelung and Martin J. McDermott, 1st ed. (Tehran: Muʾassasa-ʾi Pizhūhishī-i Ḥikmat va Falsafa-ʾi Īrān, 2007), 218.

calculations of comparative utility. Making a choice in the face of a conflict of motivations necessarily implies that some perceived utility will be forgone and that some hardship will therefore be endured.

For the Muʿtazilites, the landscape of moral choice is beset by conflicting motivations that push and pull the agent in opposing directions.[35] Often, utilitarian motivations conflict with motivations rooted in knowledge of the intrinsic evil or good of certain types of acts. The agent deserves praise and sometimes Divine reward when that agent forgoes utility in favor of acting on either an altruistic motivation or an ethical value motivation.

3. WHAT IS COMPULSION?

If a volitional act is one that is made when an agent faces conflicting motivations urging different courses of action, what, then, is a compelled act? A good starting point is provided by the concrete examples of compelled acts in Muʿtazilite literature. ʿAbd al-Jabbār's and Ibn Mattawayh's works yield the following example scenarios:

1. When sick, one is sometimes compelled to groan out loud.[36]
2. When struck by a whip, one is compelled to scream.[37]
3. When one sees an amusing incident, one is compelled to laugh.[38]
4. When healthy, one is compelled to refrain from consuming distasteful medicine.[39]
5. One is compelled to refrain from attempting to kill a king because one thinks the attempt would be futile.[40]
6. In the absence of false belief, people are compelled to not kill themselves.[41]

[35] Frank sees the "conflict of motivations" feature of the Muʿtazilite conception of the moral world as a fundamental principle of their thought. Frank, "Autonomy," 337.

[36] ʿAbd al-Jabbār, *Mughnī*, 8:60.5. [37] Ibid., 8:60.2–3. [38] Ibid., 8:60.6.

[39] Ibid., 11:393.6.

[40] Ibn Mattawayh, *Majmūʿ*, 2:320.13–15; Gimaret, "La notion," 52.

[41] Gimaret, "La notion," 28 and the sources cited therein. The reference to false belief is to the case of "Indians" who commit suicide.

7. A person is compelled to flee when encountering or perceiving a predatory animal, even if this means fleeing into a bed of thorns.[42]
8. One would be compelled to enter heaven if one knew what lies therein.[43]
9. When starving, one is compelled to eat a delicious plate of food placed in front of one.[44]
10. When given knowledge that a treasure is buried under one's feet, one is compelled to dig for it.[45]

Do these examples share a common defining element? While ʿAbd al-Jabbār is skeptical that compulsion may be neatly circumscribed in a formal definition,[46] he does catalog Abū Hāshim's attempts at abstract conceptualization of the phenomenon.

In two such attempts, Abū Hāshim emphasizes the role of the perception of utility in generating the compulsion. In the first instance, ʿAbd al-Jabbār quotes Abū Hāshim as writing that "the compelled is one who, [when] impelled to two harms (*man yudfaʿ ilā ḍararayn*), prefers the lesser over the greater (*fa-yuʾthiru ʾl-adwana min-humā ʿalā ʾl-aʿẓam*)."[47] This characterization emphasizes the difference in prospective harm between alternative courses of action. In a second utility-focused attempt, Abū Hāshim argues that a perception of benefits may also compel and adds that the perception, whether of harm or benefit, need not be limited to oneself.[48]

[42] This example was cited most often and may have been the paradigmatic case. See ibid., 28–29 and the sources cited therein. In addition, see ʿAbd al-Jabbār, *Mughnī*, 6a:16, 11:394, and 13:489–99; Mānkdīm, *Sharḥ*, 16.2–11; Ibn Mattawayh, *Majmūʿ*, 2:321.3–4.

[43] See Gimaret, "La notion," 28 and the sources cited therein.

[44] See ibid., 30 and the sources cited therein.

[45] Mānkdīm, *Sharḥ*, 143.7–8.

[46] For his skepticism on the possibility of a formal definition similar to those given for "body" (*jism*) and "physical mover" (*mutaḥarrik*), see ʿAbd al-Jabbār, *Mughnī*, 11:395.17–396.1 and 8:166.9–10. Even Abū Hāshim concedes that the most a conceptualization of compulsion can achieve is an approximation (*taqrīb*), not a formal definition. For this, see ibid., 11:395.12–13.

[47] Ibid., 8:165.3–4 and 11:394.9–10. ʿAbd al-Jabbār notes that this definition is found in Abū Hāshim's work *Naqḍ al-Ṭabāʾiʿ*. For an analysis of citations of this text in later Muʿtazilite sources, see Daniel Gimaret, "Matériaux pour une bibliographie des Ǧubbāʾī," *Journal Asiatique* 264, no. 3 (1976): 327–28.

[48] He also shows how the concept of compulsion is related to the concept of prudential obligation. He quotes from Abū Hāshim's work *al-Aṣlaḥ*: "In certain states, the human agent is compelled to [procure] benefit for or repel harm from himself or those in his care (*ʿamman yamassa-hu amru-hu*). It is true for every agent compelled to a thing that had he not been compelled, it would have been prudentially necessary for him [to do it]." See ʿAbd al-Jabbār, *Mughnī*, 11:395.6–7. For an analysis of references to this text in later Muʿtazilite texts, see Gimaret, "Matériaux," 307.

In another attempt by Abū Hāshim to conceptualize compulsion, it is not the perception of utility but rather that of futility that compels. According to ʿAbd al-Jabbār, Abū Hāshim holds that

> compulsion occurs sometimes with respect to omitting an action regarding which the agent knows that should he try to perform it, he would be prevented, even if the omission was something one could have chosen (*wa-in kāna ʾl-tark mimmā yaṣiḥḥu ʾl-takhyīr fī-hi*).[49]

In a different attempt, Abū Hāshim does not try to identify the positive features that characterize compulsion but rather describes it as a category delimiting those acts that an agent is in some sense forced to do. Compulsion is something that prevents the agent from pursuing alternative courses of action even if he is physically capable of doing so and free from external impediments.[50] In other words, there are cases in which moral evaluation fails that are not covered by the absence of basic capacity or the presence of an impediment, and this category of cases is labeled compulsion.

Abū Hāshim's final attempt, which ʿAbd al-Jabbār prefers over the others, identifies compulsion not by the psychological features of the compelled (perceptions of utility or futility) but rather as generated by the judgment that an agent does not deserve praise for the act under consideration.[51] ʿAbd al-Jabbār may prefer this conceptualization because it is consistent with a fundamental principle of his ethics, namely his view that our knowledge that it is good to praise or blame an agent for a given action is epistemically

[49] ʿAbd al-Jabbār, *Mughnī*, 8:165.20–1. ʿAbd al-Jabbār does not provide a reference for this position.

[50] ʿAbd al-Jabbār quotes Abu Hāshim as defining compulsion as something that "makes it impossible for the agent to perform any act except that which he is compelled to perform, given that he has the basic physical capacity [to do it] and no impediments [obstructing it] exist." Ibid., 11:394.11–12.

[51] ʿAbd al-Jabbār quotes Abū Hāshim as follows: "Compulsion is not a type of act (*laysa ʾl-iljāʾa bi-jinsi ʾl-fiʿl*). It is merely something done to a capable agent that has the effect of excluding him from deserving praise for an action or an omission." Ibid., 8:165.8–10 and 11:396.2–397.7. For an analysis of references to these texts in later Muʿtazilite texts, see Gimaret, "Matériaux," 306. The reason that only praise and not blame is mentioned in this passage is that the entire discussion of Abū Hāshim's attempts to conceptualize compulsion occurs in the context of his discussion of moral agency, which consists first and foremost of commandments that God imposes upon human beings to give them opportunities to merit Divine reward. In Muʿtazilite thought, meriting Divine reward plays a role parallel to that of meriting human praise. As we will see later on, compulsion not only makes one undeserving of praise, but also undeserving of blame when the compelled act is evil.

the most immediate type of moral knowledge.[52] According to ʿAbd al-Jabbār, we reason from this gut reaction to the discovery of rational moral truths. Similarly, in the case of compulsion, we reason from the immediate knowledge that a person does not deserve praise or blame for committing a particular act to the conclusion that he must have been compelled.

Whereas ʿAbd al-Jabbār relegates the variety of phenomena denoted as compulsion to a single essential element—the failure of valid moral appraisal—his successors Ibn Mattawayh and Mānkdīm are not as singularly reductive. Instead of defining compulsion by its normative effects, Ibn Mattawayh and Mānkdīm prefer those of Abū Hāshim's conceptualizations that emphasize the roles of utility and futility in explaining compelled action.[53]

Utilitarian motivations can compel action in one of two ways.[54] If the agent knows or believes that a pure benefit, either completely untainted or only trivially tainted by harm, will be the result of a given action, the agent is compelled to undertake the action. For example, if food is placed before a really hungry person, and if no other factor diverts her from eating it, and if she believes that no present or future harm will result from partaking of the food, she is compelled to eat it.[55] Compulsion in this case is an overwhelming motivation to action produced by a probable belief in or certain knowledge of a predominant benefit to be gained through the action. Conversely, compulsion can result from overwhelming motivations produced by beliefs in or knowledge of a predominant harm. Suppose the agent is faced with a decision between the harm that would ensue from omitting an action and the harm involved in performing it. If the difference between

[52] For a discussion of what ʿAbd al-Jabbār considers the most immediate of ethical judgments, see Vasalou, *Moral Agents*, 102–15. There are places in the works of both Ibn Mattawayh and ʿAbd al-Jabbār where the most immediate moral truth is not that it is good to praise or blame an agent for a given act, but that an agent deserves praise or blame for it. For these passages, see ibid., 222, footnote 91. Vasalou thinks that the equivocation between the two conceptions is reflective of larger tensions within the system of Muʿtazilite ethics.

[53] Ibn Mattawayh, *Majmūʿ*, 2:320.11–321.4; Mānkdīm, *Sharḥ*, 143.1–8.

[54] ʿAbd al-Jabbār, *Mughnī*, 12:425.16–18. ʿAbd al-Jabbār sums up the idea as follows: "When a rational agent knows or believes that a great benefit will ensue, he becomes compelled to perform the act, and when the ensuing harm is great, he becomes compelled to omit it; he thereby becomes exempt from being a moral agent (*mukallaf*) because of the strength of these motivations."

[55] Ibn Mattawayh, *Majmūʿ*, 2:321.1–2.

the two harms is great, the agent is compelled to choose the act associated with the lesser harm in order to ward off the greater harm. The textbook example of this scenario for the Muʿtazilites is the case of an agent's perception of or encounter with a predator.[56] The agent's belief in or knowledge of the overwhelming harm associated with staying in place when faced with a predatory animal produces an overwhelming motivation—that is, compulsion—to flee.

These examples explain compulsion as the result of the magnitude of the quantitative difference in the harm or benefit involved in alternative courses of action. The strength of utilitarian motivations is affected not only by the quantity of the benefit or harm contemplated but also by its temporal proximity to the agent. For example, in the process of arguing against the idea that an agent can practically be compelled to engage in the theological inquiry necessary to establish the existence of God and His attributes, ʿAbd al-Jabbār writes:

> If [the harms] are far off, time-wise, or if one of them is far off, then the compulsion no doubt does not exist. We know that the omission of inquiry in the domain of religious matters is characterized by a far-off harm. The act in question is [undertaking] contemplation to eliminate this harm. It is not possible to identify [it as] a case of compulsion.[57]

Utilitarian motivations are, at a basic level, rooted in perceptions of harm and benefit, and for this reason they underlie Muʿtazilite analysis of the psychology and ethics of action even beyond their role in explaining compulsion. A perception of harm that is great and imminent compels action. But what about a perception of harm that is not great? For the Muʿtazilites, such perceptions result in prudential obligations.[58] And what about a perception of harm that is balanced by a perception of equal benefit? This situation results in free choice. Compulsion is merely one end of a spectrum

[56] Ibid., 2:265.14–15.

[57] ʿAbd al-Jabbār, *Mughnī*, 12:353.6–8. Likewise ibid., 14:25.4–7.

[58] This is connected to the utility-based definition of compulsion listed above. When Abū Hāshim identifies utilitarian motivations as a possible basis for compulsion, he also notes that compulsion is related to obligation. See ibid., 11:395.6–10, where ʿAbd al-Jabbār attributes the idea to Abū Hāshim's *Kitāb al-Aṣlaḥ*. Abū Hāshim asserts that the presence of a slight harm in a given benefit excludes the case from being considered as one of compulsion.

charting the effects of motivations on the psychology of action in Muʿtazilite thinking.[59]

That compulsion is merely on one end of a spectrum of types of actions linked to motivations is most clearly articulated in ʿAbd al-Jabbār's explanation for the basis of the obligation to inquire into God's existence. Ultimately the obligation to inquire is a species of the more general rational obligation to avoid harm to oneself, which also happens to be a basic fact about human nature—human beings are naturally inclined to avoid harm. The inclination to avoid harm is an endemic feature of how human agents make decisions about their affairs in this life. It also serves as part of the explanation for why agents are obliged to engage in theological inquiry to substantiate God's existence and nature. The Muʿtazilites imagine that after reaching maturity, all agents are motivated, by a variety of factors, not excluding God's gracious intervention, to consider the question of their salvation. The fear of possible harm in the hereafter motivates them to undertake inquiry to quiet their souls. Here ʿAbd al-Jabbār observes:

> As for a case in which the two harms are equal and the agent knows that this is the case, the inquirer is fully free to choose. It is not obligatory for the agent to undertake the action, and the obligation fails to hold (*sāqiṭ*). When the difference in harm is tremendous, [choice] is extinguished and the basis of compulsion has been realized (*la-ḥaqqa thabātu ʾl-iljāʾ*). When there is a [mere] difference, the basis of obligation has been realized (*la-ḥaqqa thabātu ʾl-wujūb*), especially when the harm is far off (*muʾajjal*) and not immediate (*muʿajjal*).[60]

The explanation of compulsion as rooted in motivations brings it into line with other features of Muʿtazilite psychology, because motivations are what lie behind freely chosen actions as well as prudential obligations.

[59] Gimaret, "La notion," 38–44 and the sources cited therein. For Abū Hāshim and ʿAbd al-Jabbār, obligation and compulsion are related. Indeed, as noted by Gimaret, Abū Hāshim coined the dictum, affirmed and used by ʿAbd al-Jabbār elsewhere, that "compulsion is a more intense form of obligation" (*inna ʾl-iljāʾa ākadu mina ʾl-ījāb*).

[60] See ʿAbd al-Jabbār, *Mughnī*, 12:358.12–18.

The understanding of motivations as beliefs explains other interesting facts about compulsion. First, an agent can very easily slip into and out of a state of being compelled through changes in beliefs alone, or a counter-motivation may arise that effectively dilutes the overwhelming effect of a hitherto compelling motivation. Muʿtazilite authors adduce a number of examples demonstrating this point.[61] ʿAbd al-Jabbār has us consider the case of an agent suffering from severe hunger,

> who is fully able to eat (*al-mutamakkin min ʾl-akl*) and will eat, no doubt, if there is nothing to divert him (*idhā lam yakun hunāka ṣārif*). But should someone inform him while he is severely hungry that the delicious food is poisoned, he will be diverted from eating it.[62]

Or consider this variation on the textbook Muʿtazilite example of compulsion:

> One who witnesses a predator approaching him is compelled to flee. But what if he is told: "The predator is a reminder [from God]. If you persevere by staying in place, you will be [rewarded] with heaven"? The agent stops being compelled to flee.[63]

In yet another example, ʿAbd al-Jabbār highlights the role of beliefs, even false ones, in shifting an agent into and out of a state of being compelled, thus changing the moral evaluation of him. For ʿAbd al-Jabbār, we are compelled to not kill ourselves. Even though suicide is a major sin, we do not

[61] As an example of an agent escaping compulsion through a change in beliefs about a situation, which cancels the compulsion, ʿAbd al-Jabbār says that one would normally be compelled to laugh at an amusing incident, but this compulsion evaporates if the amusing incident takes place in the presence of an awe-inspiring personality. See ibid., 8:59.12–60.7.

[62] Ibid., 12:253.17–20. This example is cited and translated in Gimaret, "La notion," 47. The present translation is my own.

[63] ʿAbd al-Jabbār, *Mughnī*, 12:352.19–353.2. ʿAbd al-Jabbār is trying to show how easily an agent can go from being compelled to not being compelled. The function of the argument is to show that the obligation to inquire into the existence and nature of God does not in practice turn into a compulsion. If the act of initially seeking knowledge of God were compelled, the compulsion would undermine the free-will position of the Muʿtazilites and their view of seeking knowledge of God as a meritorious action. The ease through which, by God's agency an agent can sometimes stop being compelled, as demonstrated by this example, is equally applicable to the case of seeking knowledge of God. It is the fact that a change in beliefs alone can motivate seeking knowledge of God that practically prevents it from ever being compelled. Another example demonstrating how the state of compulsion can be altered by beliefs is the case of a man who resists crying out when lashed with a whip because he has been promised a large sum of money if he stays silent. For these, see Gimaret, "La notion," 32 and the sources cited therein.

deserve praise for not killing ourselves, because we are usually constantly in a state of being compelled not to kill ourselves. The fact of being compelled excludes us from deserving praise or blame for acts. But it is possible that this de facto state of being compelled not to kill ourselves can be changed by way of false beliefs. ʿAbd al-Jabbār explains:

> Despite the fact that the Indians (*al-hind*) believe that there is a benefit in killing themselves, insofar as it entails releasing light from darkness, if they refrain from doing it, they deserve praise for their refusal. But if the false beliefs [about the benefits of suicide] cease to exist, they no longer deserve this praise because compulsion (*iljāʾ*) has entered into force. For this reason, the false beliefs occupy the same position as natural aversion, in the sense that the action of the one holding the false belief falls into the category of a burdensome act and thus garners praise and reward.[64]

All of these examples fall into the general category of compulsion through the predominance of a utilitarian motivation, which is a belief about the relative harms or benefits in a given course of action. Ibn Mattawayh identified one other major type of compulsion—that produced by belief in the ultimate futility of a course of action in achieving an agent's objective. Compulsion by futility is likewise ultimately based on an agent's beliefs about prospective courses of action. But instead of being compelled by a great and immediate harm or benefit, in cases of futility the agent is compelled by the belief that a given act would be futile. The most illustrative example used by ʿAbd al-Jabbār and Ibn Mattawayh is the case of a person compelled to not kill the king of the Byzantines because he knows or believes that the attempt would be futile. This belief in the act's futility, ʿAbd al-Jabbār and Ibn Mattawayh argue, is the reason for the agent's being compelled not to attempt it.[65]

[64] ʿAbd al-Jabbār, *Mughnī*, 11:394.1–5. In addition, ʿAbd al-Jabbār also quotes this example from Abū Hāshim: "The human being is compelled to not kill himself. The latter example also contains the elements of prudential obligation (*fa-inna dhālika yataḍammanu maʿnā ʾl-ījāb*). [Consider:] if an agent had doubts [about whether it would be moral for him to kill himself, he would stop from being compelled to not kill himself], and it would then be obligatory for him to leave the act of killing himself (*la-wajaba ʿalay-hi tarku qatli nafsi-hi*). This is what we say about the Indians who have doubts about whether it is moral for them to kill themselves. [When this happens] they deserve praise if they do not kill themselves and blame if they do." Ibid., 14:20.2–5.

[65] See Gimaret, "La notion," 29 and the sources cited therein.

4. WHAT DOES COMPULSION DO TO RESPONSIBILITY?

4.1 Compulsion Does Not Negate Basic Capability (*Qudra*) or Choice

Thus far we have seen what the Muʿtazilites considered compulsion to be at the empirical level. This leaves the question of what they thought the normative consequences of a finding of compulsion to be in their theological system. The Muʿtazilites held that the presence of compulsion is morally incompatible with God's impositions of obligations: for God to hold a human being responsible for an act he was compelled to perform would be unjust, and in the Muʿtazilites' view God can never act unjustly. Compulsion also impedes an agent's deserving of praise, blame, reward, or punishment. What it does not do is negate choice (*ikhtiyār*) or the physical capacity (*qudra*) to perform an action. ʿAbd al-Jabbār writes:

> Compulsion (*iljāʾ*) does not make the compelled incapable of the action, nor is it connected to choosing it. Someone who perceives a predatory animal and fears for his life is compelled to flee. His [act of fleeing] takes place by choice, because when he flees, there are [multiple] paths [he could take] and he chooses to take one of them. This act is also in accordance with his capacity, because he runs fast or slow, according to his capacity, and takes a path according to his knowledge of the shortness or length of a path. Compulsion (*iljāʾ*) does not mean he cannot be a capable agent of the act he performs, even though compulsion diverts him from one action to another through the force of knowledge of harm and intense fear.[66]

The fact that the compelled agent chooses the path and speed of escape shows that compulsion has not categorically eliminated choice or capability. In addition, ʿAbd al-Jabbār gives another reason why compulsion does not negate capacity: it is ultimately caused by a motivation, which is essentially a belief (*iʿtiqād, ẓann*)—and beliefs cannot negate capacity.[67]

[66] ʿAbd al-Jabbār, *Mughnī*, 12:317.6–12. See also ibid., 6b:56.17–57.7, where ʿAbd al-Jabbār asserts that compulsion does not eliminate choice and uses the same example of someone compelled to flee but exercising choice as to how and where to flee. See further ibid., 8:59.114–16, where ʿAbd al-Jabbār describes the one compelled to flee as being still in possession of basic capacity and as capable of making a choice. On this issue generally, see Gimaret, "La notion," 46–52.

[67] ʿAbd al-Jabbār, *Mughnī*, 12:316.17–18. Elsewhere (ibid., 6a:188.18), ʿAbd al-Jabbār notes that while a motivation may "require an act, it does not causally necessitate it (*wa-ʾl-dāʿīyu*

4.2 Compulsion Negates Praise and Blame

While the Muʿtazilite scholars assert that compulsion impedes all varieties of moral evaluation,[68] it does not do so in a uniform way. Specifically, in order to understand its differential impact on assessments of praise and blame, we need to understand what the Muʿtazilites meant by good and evil acts.

In Muʿtazilite thought, there are three categories of acts that are good: simply permitted acts, supererogations, and obligations. Agents who perform actions that are simply permitted do not deserve praise for their performance. Most often, such actions are understood as motivated by the perceived benefit procured or harm avoided through the act. But, praise is deserved for the performance of obligations and supererogations.[69] The difference between obligations and supererogations hinges on the evaluation of their respective omission. An agent deserves blame for failing to satisfy an obligation but does not deserve blame for not satisfying a supererogation.[70]

In a volume of the *Mughnī* devoted to debates on how an agent comes to deserve moral evaluations (*istiḥqāq*), ʿAbd al-Jabbār lists the following summary conditions that must be satisfied in order for an agent to deserve praise and reward for satisfying an obligation or a supererogation:[71]

1. The agent must be aware of the obligatory nature of the act or any necessary preconditions to the act.[72]

wa-in iqtaḍā ikhtiyāra ʾl-fiʿli fa-laysa bi-mūjibin li-dhālika)." For greater elaboration of ʿAbd al-Jabbār's assumed distinction between "requiring" or, in Gimaret's terms, "determining" and "causing" an act, see Gimaret, "La notion," 46–52. Gimaret considers ʿAbd al-Jabbār's distinction contrived and philosophically inconsistent: ibid., 49. Frank disagrees and provides an explanation of ʿAbd al-Jabbār's distinction between "requiring" (*iqtiḍāʾ*) and "causing" (*ījāb*) in Frank, "Autonomy," 340–43. Madelung similarly criticizes Gimaret's characterization of ʿAbd al-Jabbār; see Madelung, "Late Muʿtazila," 247–48.

[68] For an example, see ʿAbd al-Jabbār, *Mughnī*, 12:425.16–18. For a translation of the passage, see footnote 54 above.

[69] For a fuller treatment of the moral varieties of acts in ʿAbd al-Jabbār's thought, see Hourani, *Islamic Rationalism*, 39–44.

[70] Ibid., 39.

[71] The section of the volume in which this discussion occurs is entitled "How praise and reward are deserved for an obligation or a supererogation" (*faṣlun fī kayfiyyati istiḥqāqi ʾl-madḥi wa-ʾl-thawābi bi-ʾl-wājibi wa-ʾl-nadb*). ʿAbd al-Jabbār, *Mughnī*, 14:177.14–15.

[72] Ibid., 14:177.16–17.

2. He must perform the act because of the aspect of the act that makes it good or obligatory.[73]
3. He must be free to perform the act (*an yakūna mukhallan bayna-hu wa-bayna-hu*).[74]

ʿAbd al-Jabbār notes that compulsion is a violation of the third condition[75] and gives two reasons why compulsion impedes the agent's deserving of praise for an action or an omission. Both reasons are ultimately grounded in broader Muʿtazilite values about why agents deserve praise in the first place. One reason agents deserve praise for certain actions is that they involve bearing some type of hardship; hardship is a necessary feature of free choice, which is in turn defined as a conflict of motivations (*taraddud al-dawāʿī*).[76]

In one passage, the connection between conflicting motivations, the hardship at stake in performing an imposed obligation, and compulsion is made explicitly:

> The stipulation that compulsion must be absent is subsumed under the [more general] condition of enabling [the agent to perform the given act], as we have already explained. Likewise, that desire (*shahwa*) and conflicting motivations (*al-dawāʿī al-mutaraddida*) must obtain is connected to enablement, because the agent cannot do the act in the way it was imposed without one or both of them [i.e., desire and conflicting motivations]. This is because hardship (*mashaqqa*) and burden (*kulfa*) obtain only through them, or through something that takes their place.[77]

The conflicting motivations to act stem from the conflicting goods at stake in a choice. The source of the hardship in this situation is the value forgone, as represented by the motivations ignored in the choice that is made.[78] Compulsion occurs when either only a single motivation is present or when one motivation has overwhelming strength. In a case of compulsion, the forgone good, as represented to the agent in the form of a motivation, is

[73] Ibid., 14:177.17. [74] Ibid., 14:177.17–18. [75] Ibid., 14:178.14–17.
[76] Ibid., 11:393.13–14. [77] Ibid., 16:71.9–12.
[78] In another part of the *Mughnī*, ʿAbd al-Jabbār asserts that "the agent deserves praise for not doing evil if there is a motivation to do it" (*wa-qad yastaḥiqqu ʾl-madḥa bi-an lā yafʿalu ʾl-qabīḥa idhā kāna la-hu ilā fiʿli-hi dāʿan*). Ibid., 8:176.13–14.

nonexistent or negligible in comparison with the overwhelming motivation. The agent bears no hardship in committing the compelled act because the utility forgone is nonexistent or negligible. Thus, the agent deserves no praise for the compelled performance or omission.

The second reason that agents of compelled acts do not deserve praise relates to the type of motivation driving the act. As we saw, ʿAbd al-Jabbār stipulates that only duties or supererogations performed for the right reasons deserve praise: an agent merits praise for telling the truth only if she did it because she knows that it is morally good to tell the truth, not because she gained some benefit for doing it. Compelled agents do not perform acts for the sake of their ethical value. Most compelled acts are compelled by utilitarian motivations—beliefs about a prospective benefit or harm that is enormous and immediate. ʿAbd al-Jabbār notes that

> an agent deserves praise for an act only when he does it for what he knows of its intrinsic goodness (*li-ḥusni-hi fī ʿaqli-hi*). If, however, he does the act in order to repel an immediate harm or to procure an immediate benefit (*li-dafʿi ʾl-maḍarrati aw li-ijtilābi ʾl-manfaʿati ʾl-ḥāḍiratayn*), he does not thereby deserve praise. What he is compelled to do he does only for its benefits or harms and therefore does not deserve either praise or reward.[79]

In contrast to his discussion of the two reasons why compulsion impedes the attachment of praise, ʿAbd al-Jabbār does not provide reasons why an agent does not deserve blame for being compelled to perform an evil act beyond stating that "what an agent cannot escape or guard against he does not deserve blame for."[80] ʿAbd al-Jabbār notes, however, that there is a structural difference between deserving praise and deserving blame. An agent deserves praise for doing a good act only when he does it for its intrinsic goodness. But he deserves blame if he commits an evil act as long as it would be possible for him to avoid it (*idhā amkana ʾl-taḥarruzu min-hu*).[81] What compulsion does is

[79] Ibid., 11:393.10–12. For a repetition of the same idea, see ibid., 16:71.6–9. See also ibid., 6a:16.16–17.2, where ʿAbd al-Jabbār describes the compelled agent as performing the compelled act "for its benefits and in order to repel harm from himself, not for its intrinsic goodness. What is not done for the latter reason does not deserve praise."

[80] Ibid., 14:16.6. See also ibid., 6a:17.1–3.

[81] Ibid. See also ibid., 6a:26.9–11. This definition of an evil act is also cited by Hourani. See Hourani, *Islamic Rationalism*, 50. For another example of how guarding against or avoiding evil (*taḥarruz*) is connected to deserving blame, see ʿAbd al-Jabbār, *Mughnī*, 11:399.10–16.

negate the possibility of avoidance and thus impede the agent's deserving of blame for the commission of the evil act.

One question addressed by the Muʿtazilites is whether compulsion or coercion changes the value of an act from evil to good. The answer depends on the type of evil act under consideration. Broadly speaking, Muʿtazilite thought recognizes two different types of evil acts: acts of injustice that involve harm to others and evil acts that involve no such harm, such as disbelieving in God or lying.[82] The former type attracts the bulk of the Muʿtazilites' attention. Other than the presence or absence of harm to others, one other feature distinguishes these two broad types of evil acts: the specific intention of the agent in performing the act.[83] For lying, for example, to count as evil for ʿAbd al-Jabbār, the liar must do it for the purpose of conveying information,[84] but this intention requirement does not hold for acts of injustice, such as illegitimately attacking someone. In order for the latter type of act to count as evil, there is no stipulation that the perpetrator of the act must act with a specific purpose.

The question of whether compulsion may change the moral quality of a prima facie evil act has a more conflicted history in Muʿtazilism than the unanimously endorsed idea that it impedes blame. The later Muʿtazilite scholars—ʿAbd al-Jabbār, his immediate teachers, and Ibn Mattawayh—firmly held that though compulsion impedes the deserving of blame, it does not change the value of the act itself. This position was in potential conflict with the position of the founders of the Basran school, Abū ʿAlī al-Jubbāʾī and Abū Hāshim al-Jubbāʾī, on a different issue, namely the moral valuation of acts committed by individuals who are asleep or unaware of what they are doing. The two Jubbāʾīs held that the actions of the sleeping and the unaware cannot be described as either good or evil.[85] The potential analogy to the case of acts committed under compulsion is evident, and in fact, ʿAbd al-Jabbār frames his discussion of the issue as a response to an anonymous interlocutor who asks why the

[82] Vasalou, *Moral Agents*, 84. [83] Hourani, *Islamic Rationalism*, 89–92.
[84] Lies told for the purpose of entertainment would thus presumably be excluded.
[85] ʿAbd al-Jabbār, *Mughnī*, 6b:338.8–9 and ibid., 6a:11.15–17.

Jubbāʾīs' contention that the asleep and the unaware do not commit evil acts cannot be extended to the case of the compelled.[86] ʿAbd al-Jabbār considers the objection in relation to both types of acts, using the examples of coerced lying and coerced commission of an act of injustice. In both cases, he argues, coercion does nothing to the value of the evil act, but for different reasons. In the first case, ʿAbd al-Jabbār points to a dissimilarity between the sleeping or unaware, on the one hand, and the coerced, on the other: a coerced liar intends the act of lying in exactly the same way as a willing liar, whereas no intention can be ascribed to people who lie while asleep or without awareness.[87] Thus, coercion has no effect on the evilness of the lie; a coerced lie is still evil. In the case of coerced injustice, ʿAbd al-Jabbār disagrees with the Jubbāʾīs' view that the sleeping and the unaware cannot commit evil acts. Because the evilness of acts of injustice in no way depends on the perpetrator's intention, individuals who are compelled, coerced, asleep, and unaware alike do evil when they commit an injustice, even if they deserve no blame for it.[88] In addition, according to ʿAbd al-Jabbār, the act of injustice is perpetrated in exactly the same way by the aware and the willing as by the compelled, the sleeping, and the unaware.[89] Ibn Mattawayh adds an additional argument for why compulsion, sleep, and inattentiveness do not change the core ethical value of an unjust act. He argues that if the commission of unjust acts by agents characterized by these and other qualities is not considered evil,[90] it would not be considered good to prevent nonmoral agents such as animals and the insane from committing injustice, which is clearly not the case.[91]

[86] Ibid., 6b.338.12–13. [87] Ibid., 6b:338.10–11.

[88] For ʿAbd al-Jabbār's position that the compelled does not deserve blame for committing an act of injustice, see Gimaret, "La notion," 55 and the sources cited therein.

[89] ʿAbd al-Jabbār, *Mughnī*, 6b:338.16–17. Later on ʿAbd al-Jabbār asserts categorically that "for an act of injustice to be deemed evil, it is sufficient that it be an act of injustice, and its being such is not connected to intention." Ibid., 6b:339.3–4.

[90] Examples of nonmoral agents (*ghayr mukallaf*) are individuals who are unaware (*sāhī*), asleep (*nāʾim*), and insane (*majnūn*), as well as infants (*ṭifl*) and animals (*bahīma*). See Ibn Mattawayh, *Majmūʿ*, 2:243.5–6.

[91] Ibid., 2:243.11–12. See also ibid., 2:243.20–22 for Ibn Mattawayh's statement of the position that compulsion impedes an agent's deserving of blame for the commission of an evil act, but it does not change the value of the act itself.

4.3 Compelled Harm Merits Restitution

We know that compulsion impedes an agent's deserving of praise, blame, reward, and punishment. But what consequences, if any, do the actions of a compelled agent have if they cause harm to the agent or to others? Muʿtazilite scholars stipulated that the occurrence of unjustified harm creates an entitlement to restitution for the sufferer from the agent who caused or, as in the case of God, allowed the harm.

The Muʿtazilite theologians' discussions on the character and conditions of entitlements to restitution are formally similar to those found in the legal literature. But the restitution assumed in Muʿtazilite theology is not financial compensation for bodily harm suffered or for property damaged or destroyed; rather, it applies to the hereafter.[92] All unsettled claims for compensation will be administered on the Day of Judgment, and God is the Divine administrator of these claims.[93] The restitution for harm suffered is to be paid in the currency of benefit (*nafʿ*), the opposite of harm.

4.3.1 Compelled Harm to the Agent or to Someone Else

Regardless of who the compeller is, ʿAbd al-Jabbār and Ibn Mattawayh hold that compulsion creates an entitlement to restitution for harm suffered by the compelled agent in the process of either repelling harm or enduring it. The material consequences of the compelled act are attributed to the compeller, and if they include harm, the compeller bears the duty to compensate the harmed party, on the condition that the harm in question was unavoidable.[94] Ibn Mattawayh grants an entitlement to restitution even if the object of the compelled harm is not the compelled himself but someone

[92] For the Muʿtazilites, God can be the subject of a duty to provide restitution for harm suffered by agents. Thus, Heemskerk notes that ʿAbd al-Jabbār held that God could restitute sufferers in this world. See Heemskerk, *Suffering*, 180.

[93] For further examination of this idea, see ibid., 176–79.

[94] ʿAbd al-Jabbār, *Mughnī*, 8:172.12–14. The compelled act has "become like the act of the compeller, insofar as [the compelled agent] did what was required because of him [i.e., the compeller]." In the next passage, in which he uses the predator example to illustrate his larger argument for why the compeller is responsible for the harm caused, ʿAbd al-Jabbār again asserts that the compelled act is judged "as if it were the act of the predator" (*ka-anna-hu fiʿlu ʾl-subuʿ*). See ibid., 8:172.20–1.

under that person's care, such as a son.[95] When the compelled agent is the one who suffered the harm caused by the compulsion, the value of the restitution is determined by the amount of harm suffered in the act of repelling the greater harm represented by the threat causing the compulsion. If the course of action that the compelled agent was forced to take and through which he suffered harm was the only option available to him, then the compelled agent is entitled to restitution from the compeller for the harm he suffered. But if the agent had other options, he is judged to have initiated the harm to himself and no entitlement to restitution exists.[96]

As we have seen, the Muʿtazilites held that the level of certainty of the belief upon which a motivation is based is irrelevant to the effectiveness of the motivation in compelling an action and thereby canceling its moral evaluation. One may either surmise or know that a treasure is buried under one's feet. Either way, one is compelled to dig for it. Knowing something compelling to be the case and surmising it to be probable both suffice to establish compulsion. But this is not the case in creating entitlements to restitution for compelled harm. If the agent is compelled not by knowledge but by surmise, the surmise must be vindicated for an entitlement to restitution to arise.[97]

4.3.2 Harm Caused by God's Command or Compulsion

Claims to restitution for compelled harm apply also when the compeller is God. If God compels a human being to inflict harm, God is obliged to restitute for that harm. As an example, Ibn Mattawayh cites the case of a person compelled to slaughter an animal in order to stave off death by starvation; in this case, God is responsible for the harm done to the animal by the person and

[95] Ibn Mattawayh, *Majmūʿ*, 3:110.8.

[96] ʿAbd al-Jabbār, *Mughnī*, 13:490.11–491.1. One of ʿAbd al-Jabbār's examples of compulsion producing harm is the case of an agent who is compelled to act by someone brandishing a sword and who harms himself when fleeing. In this case, the duty of restitution is on the person wielding the sword. See ibid., 13:490.13–14. Animals can also compel the production of harm and are likewise obliged to compensate for it on the Day of Judgment. See ibid., 13:490.11–13.

[97] Ibn Mattawayh writes: "Sometimes one is compelled by a belief based on probability (*ghalaba fī ẓanni-hi*). In this instance, the compulsion is due to the belief (*li-ajli ʾl-ẓann*), not the object of the belief (*lā lil-maẓnūn*), because sometimes the agent gets the belief right and sometimes wrong (*lammā kāna qad yukhṭiʾu ʾl-ẓanna wa-yuṣīb*). If one is compelled by a belief, it is necessary that the situation not remain doubtful in order to establish [the duty of] restitution upon another." Ibn Mattawayh, *Majmūʿ*, 3:110.13–111.2.

owes the animal restitution for the harm it has suffered, presumably because God both created the circumstances that compelled the agent to harm the animal and permitted its slaughter.[98] The same principle applies to a situation in which God obliges or recommends an action that results in harm to a bystander.

But what if the human agent was acting in response to God's command? Does a duty of restitution arise in such a situation? The following exchange in Ibn Mattawayh's *Majmūʿ* demonstrates his answer to this question:

> [Anonymous interlocutor:] Are you saying that God, not human agents, is responsible for restitution for any harm that He has required?
>
> [Ibn Mattawayh:] This is the case if He is alone [in causing the harm]. If He is joined by someone else, the situation is different. Consider the following explanation (*wa-bayānu dhālika*): God requires the judge to hand over property to Zayd based on the legitimate testimony of two persons, even if the recipient of the property does not know that he does not deserve it or is a minor, insane, or something similar. The recompense for this act is on God, because He required it. This is not the case if the one who takes the property knows [that it does not rightfully belong to him] and thus takes it unjustly. [In this latter case] he has the duty to provide recompense, and his way out is to return the property to its prior owner.[99]

In this passage Ibn Mattawayh imagines an entirely plausible scenario in which the formal application of the Islamic law of testimony leads to a substantively unjust outcome, the responsibility for which cannot be traced to any freely chosen human action.[100] Because God is the source of the law of testimony, and because He requires judges to abide by it, He must, in order for His actions to be considered good, compensate the wronged party for any

[98] Ibid., 3:96.3–17. In this passage it is not quite clear how God is compelling, as opposed to simply permitting, the slaughter of the animal and thus creating the basis for a claim to restitution; God permits the slaughter of most animals for the purpose of consumption. Since the Muʿtazilites categorically deny that God directly compels human action, it is probable that Ibn Mattawayh is imagining a situation in which God permits the slaughter for food of an animal that is normally prohibited, such as a pig, when compelled by exigent circumstances.

[99] Ibid., 3:97.5–11.

[100] This is the function of Ibn Mattawayh's stipulation that the recipient of the property not know (or be unable to know) that the transfer of the property is unjust, in order to relieve the recipient of the positive duty to rectify the wrongful transaction.

material injustice that results from the application of the law that He has authorized.

In another case involving political power, Ibn Mattawayh denies that responsibility for restitution is transferred because he denies that compulsion has occurred. He considers whether a duty of restitution applies to a person who slanders another to an unjust ruler by insinuating that the slandered person has been unjust to the ruler. Ibn Mattawayh asserts that the slanderer indeed owes restitution to the slandered for any anxiety (*ghamm*) that the latter suffers in anticipation of possible retribution by the ruler. But the slanderer is not responsible for any actual harm initiated by the unjust ruler. Ibn Mattawayh reasons that the ruler is not *compelled* or *forced* by the slanderer. The slanderer merely incites the ruler to injustice. Moreover, God has made known the evil of the act in the mind of the ruler, and this knowledge conflicts with the motivation to do evil triggered by the slanderer's incitement to harm. Where there is a conflict of motivations, there is free choice, and where there is free choice, there is responsibility. Thus, the ruler bears the obligation for restitution if he decides to harm the slandered individual.[101]

5. INTERNAL CONSTRAINTS VS. EXTERNAL CONSTRAINTS: THE CURIOUS CASE OF LYING AND ʿABD AL-JABBĀR'S INGENIOUS SOLUTION

The issue of apostasy brought the Muʿtazilites' thinking on compulsion's effect on responsibility into conflict with their moral objectivism, a prominent value in their theology. Coerced apostasy usually involves a Muslim being coerced to apostatize by uttering words that explicitly repudiate or contradict core Islamic theological ideas. When performed willingly, the act of apostasy has a host of theological and legal effects. Among other things, it renders the apostate a non-Muslim and potentially liable for the death penalty. Few issues in coercion jurisprudence united all Muslim scholars, and coerced apostasy was one of them.[102] Based on an interpretation of Qurʾān

[101] Ibn Mattawayh, *Majmūʿ*, 3:112.21–113.4.

[102] Ibn Ḥazm cites two points of consensus on issues related to coercion: that God does not hold a person responsible for the coerced utterance of disbelief, and that fear for one's life is

16:106 ("except one coerced [to utter disbelief], while his heart is at peace with faith"), Muslim scholars agreed that coercion made it permissible to utter words of disbelief.[103] But this position posed two potential problems for the Muʿtazilites. First, they regarded the utterance of words of disbelief as an objective and intrinsic evil, and they held that God never wills evil. However, if God permits people to utter words of disbelief when coerced, then God has indeed willed evil. Second, the Muʿtazilites construed God's permission for the (insincere) utterance of disbelief when coerced as permission to likewise lie about one's true theological convictions. But just as expressions of disbelief constitute an objective and intrinsic evil, so does lying, so by permitting either, God effectively wills evil. It is for these reasons that ʿAbd al-Jabbār cites the scenario of coerced apostasy in the form of an objection to his broad defense of the Muʿtazilite position that God does not will evil.[104]

ʿAbd al-Jabbār documents two Muʿtazilite responses to the objection in the history of the tradition. The solution of the very early Muʿtazilite master Abū ʾl-Hudhayl al-ʿAllāf (d. 227/841) was to admit that the presence of fear and coercion *does* make it at a minimum permissible to utter words of disbelief.[105] The reason the coerced individual does not deserve blame for the act of apostasy is because, according to Abū ʾl-Hudhayl, the act is in some way the act of another agent. Abū ʾl-Hudhayl assimilates the case of coerced apostasy to compulsion in general: just as someone who is compelled does not deserve blame for the compelled act, neither does someone who is coerced to apostatize.[106]

coercive. Abū Muḥammad ʿAlī b. Aḥmad b. Ḥazm, *Marātib al-Ijmāʿ fī al-ʿIbādāt wa al-Muʿāmalāt wa al-Muʿtaqadāt*, 1st ed. (Beirut: Dār al-Āfāq al-Jadīda, 1978), 70.

[103] The translations of the Qurʿānic verses in this work are my own, though I did consult the following translations: *The Qurʾan: a New Translation*, trans. Thomas Cleary (United States: Starlatch, 2004); *The Message of the Qurʾān*, trans. Muhammad Asad (Lahore, Pakistan: Maktaba Jawahar ul Uloom, 1979); *The Glorious Qurʾan: Text and Explanatory Translation*, trans. Marmaduke William Pickthall (New York: Alavi Foundation, 2001).

[104] For the objection, see ʿAbd al-Jabbār, *Mughnī*, 6b:336.7–11.

[105] On Abū ʾl-Hudhayl, see Josef van Ess, "Abu ʾl-Hḏahyl al-ʿAllāf," in *Encyclopædia Iranica*, ed. Ehsan Yar-Shater (London: Routledge & Kegan Paul, 1982); H.S. Nyberg, "Abu ʾl- Huḏhayl al-ʿAllāf," in *Encyclopedia of Islam, Second Edition*, ed. P. Bearman, et al. (Leiden: Brill, 1980–2004) for an examination of Abū ʾl-Hudhayl's theology, see Josef van Ess, *Theologie und Gesellschaft im 2. und 3. Jahrhundert Hidschra: eine Geschichte des Religiösen Denkens im Frühen Islam*, 6 vols. (Berlin: Walter de Gruyter, 1992), 3:209–296.

[106] For ʿAbd al-Jabbār's citation of Abū ʾl-Hudhayl's position and his reasoning, see ʿAbd al-Jabbār, *Mughnī*, 6b.337.7–11.

While agreeing with Abū ʾl-Hudhayl on the general idea that compulsion impedes the deserving of blame for the commission of an evil act, ʿAbd al-Jabbār rejects Abū ʾl-Hudhayl's overall response to the problem of coerced apostasy, arguing that it undermines moral objectivism:

> We hold that his position is false, because what accounts for the evil of a lie told in a situation of security is its being a lie. Fear does not preclude its being [a lie], and therefore it does not preclude its being evil; and if it is evil, then permitting it is evil as well.[107]

The Muʿtazilite position was that lying is evil because of the specific features that make it what it is, and that neither coercion nor fear changes the evil-making features of the act of lying.[108] ʿAbd al-Jabbār cautions that in addition to threatening Muʿtazilite moral objectivism, Abū ʾl-Hudhayl's position approaches the slippery slope of seeing it as potentially good that God can do evil if the needs of human beings require it:

> If it is possible that fear requires deeming an action that has an element of evil as good, then we have made it possible that it require deeming every evil act good. And if it is possible to deem this good, then what is to stop one from deeming good God's doing of an evil action in order to meet the needs of human beings? Because what is deemed good for them to do in order to [fulfill] a need is also deemed good for God to do in order to [fulfill] their need. [Accepting] this leads to accepting [that] God may command evil and utter lies in His declarative speech (*ikhbāri-hi*). This [absurdity] has proved that what we have said regarding this issue is correct.[109]

Rejecting Abū ʾl-Hudhayl's position, ʿAbd al-Jabbār relates and endorses a second solution to the dilemma, which seems to have become the dominant opinion of the Muʿtazilites and which he regards as responding to the

[107] Ibid., 6b:337.16–18.

[108] For an examination of the Muʿtazilite position on lying, see Sophia Vasalou, "Equal before the Law: the Evilness of Human and Divine Lies ʿAbd al-Ǧabbār's Rational Ethics," *Arabic Sciences and Philosophy* 13, no. 2 (2003). Vasalou argues that the Muʿtazilites' insistence on the intrinsic evil of lying as something that is independent of calculations of benefit and harm stems from their desire to preclude the possibility that God could lie, a premise they thought needed to be excluded in order to safeguard the integrity of revelation and properly ground moral motivation. See also Hourani, *Islamic Rationalism*, 76–81.

[109] ʿAbd al-Jabbār, *Mughnī*, 6b:338.3–7.

anonymous interlocutor's objection more effectively.[110] This position relies on a different interpretation of what God requires of an individual who is coerced to apostatize. Instead of permitting the uttering of disbelief, Qurʾān 16:106 merely permits the insinuation (*taʿrīḍ*) of disbelief. ʿAbd al-Jabbār explains the position in the following way:

> That which we have judged to be good is similar to the utterance of disbelief, but without being a factual statement. Rather, it is an insinuation or merely an act of repelling harm, without one intending it as a factual statement. Or one may say it as a factual statement, but as a quotation from another person, so that it is true. All of this would be evil to do in the absence of [the need for] dissimulation (*taqiyya*).[111]

By interpreting Qurʾān 16:106 as requiring something like insinuation, the Muʿtazilites are able to escape the charge that God wills evil by permitting either the utterance of disbelief or lying about one's true theological commitments.[112]

6. CONCLUSION: A REPRISAL OF DIVINE JUSTICE AND MORAL OBJECTIVISM AS INTERNAL CONSTRAINTS AND COMPARISON WITH ANGLO-AMERICAN PHILOSOPHY

Muʿtazilite thinking on compulsion's effects on moral agency was driven primarily by an internal constraint: the Muʿtazilites' commitment to a substantive notion of Divine justice. Muʿtazilites interpreted this commitment as requiring that only free, uncompelled human acts are blameable, praiseable, rewardable, and punishable, because a just God would not hold human beings responsible for acts they were compelled to do. In addition, this position inspired the development of the most detailed psychological description of compulsion and free choice in classical Islam. Much of

[110] ʿAbd al-Jabbār identifies the position as that held by Abū ʿAlī al-Jubbāʾī and Abū Hāshim al-Jubbāʾī as well as by his teachers, Abū Isḥāq b. ʿAyyāsh (n.d.) and Abū ʿAbdullāh al-Baṣrī (d. 369/979). See ibid., 6b:336.12–13 and 6b:338.14–16.

[111] Ibid., 6b:337.1–5.

[112] This solution to the problem, while ingenious, is not unique to the Muʿtazilites. The Ashʿarite Shāfiʿite Juwaynī identifies a similar approach in the proposition that a man who is coerced to divorce his wife ought to do so with a mental reservation in order to have the divorce subsequently deemed invalid.

the psychology on which the Muʿtazilites relied to paint this picture was derived from general ideas about how assessments of benefit and harm motivate action.

The Muʿtazilite analysis of the psychology of compulsion and free choice is very similar to some contemporary Western philosophers' analysis of coercion and responsibility. This is especially true of philosophers who think that the proper analysis of coercion is largely a descriptive endeavor involving the correct triangulation of the empirical conditions that characterize the presence of coercion. Some of the philosophers are similiar to Muʿtazilite authors who held that what often causes compulsion is merely the difference in the utility between alternative courses of action. As proof, Muʿtazilite authors cited the example of one compelled by prospects of great benefit. A modern bioethicist has made the same type of claim:

> Dangling thousands of dollars in front of a poor person ... is simply coercive—just short of putting a gun to someone's head and telling them to do something.[113]

Robert Nozick, the author of a highly influential article on coercion, relies on the difference in utility between courses of action as an important component of identifying an instance of coercion. He constructs the following philosophical view of how to differentiate between threats and offers in the case of an agent, *Q*, facing possible courses of action belonging to a set *A*:

> According to this view, any action of *P*'s which results in A_1's being significantly greater or A_2's being significantly less in utility than the other actions in *A* may coerce *Q*. It makes no difference, according to this view, how the difference in utility is brought about. ... It is only the resulting *relative* positions, however arrived at, which count.[114]

These convergences indicate that regardless of the philosophical or theological traditions to which one belongs, whether medieval or modern, Western or Islamic, theorists that adopt largely descriptivist approaches to analyzing

[113] Cited in Wertheimer, *Coercion*, 68.

[114] Nozick, "Coercion," 459. For a couple of theorists who rely on differences in utility to determine coercion, see Michael J. Murray and David F. Dudrick, "Are Coerced Acts Free?," *American Philosophical Quarterly* 32, no. 2 (1995): 113.

compulsion or coercion also adopt a psychology that relies on a type of utilitarian calculus to explain the psychology of compulsion and free choice.

There is another point of similarity between these descriptivist traditions. The Western philosophers such as Nozick and Zimmerman who have argued extensively for a descriptivist approach to the issue of coercion and responsibility have tended to do so in order to substantiate foundationalist political philosophies. For the libertarian Nozick, the foundational political value is liberty, and the job of the political philosopher is to work out the arrangement of political institutions that maximizes it. The analysis of coercion is one way to define liberty or a variety of forms of "unfreedom," which are instrumental to the construction of Nozick's larger political project. In the case of Zimmerman, a descriptivist analysis of coercion serves as an element in arguments against the legitimacy of market-based wage offers.[115] In some sense, then, the descriptivist analyses of both Nozick and Zimmerman are instrumental to a larger philosophical aim, whether that be substantiating a philosophical vision of institutions that maximize freedom or providing arguments against market-based wage offers.

Can something similar be said about the Muʿtazilites? Was their analysis of compulsion instrumental to a larger theological vision? Of the theological and legal traditions surveyed in this book, the Muʿtazilites were by far the most descriptivist in their analysis of compulsion and responsibility. Why is this the case? Compared to the field of law, tradition-based theological thought was much more systematically based on just a few core positions. This commitment to a small set of core positions prioritized internal coherence. Part of the theologian's job was to elaborate theological ideas in such a way as to ensure that the derived theological doctrine did not contradict a core systemic position. For the Muʿtazilites, their specific conception of Divine justice and their moral objectivism were the core conceptual pillars upon which they erected their theological system. On the basic issue of whether the absence of compulsion is a necessary condition for moral agency (*taklīf*), the Muʿtazilites were motivated by their Divine justice commitments. Given their commitment to the free will position in classical Islam, they could not but hold that compulsion impedes the attachment of

115 Zimmerman, "Coercive Wage Offers".

blame for the commission of evil acts. To say otherwise would have been to acquiesce to the determinist position: that God, as the author of human acts, could nonetheless blame and punish human beings for committing evil acts that He had created. That they saw these two issues as intimately related is quite clear in ʿAbd al-Jabbār's work. Given the nature of theology as a discipline and the Muʿtazilite construal of Divine justice as requiring a pro-choice position in the free-will/predestination debate, it is not surprising to find them fairly uniformly committed to the idea that compulsion impedes moral assessment. In this sense, their descriptivist analysis of compulsion and responsibility can also be explained as instrumental to their larger theological vision.

Before concluding this chapter, I want to make one further observation. Thus far, I have largely treated the Muʿtazilites as a tradition that spoke in a unified voice. Part of the reason for this treatment is that the available substantial sources on the Muʿtazilites' views on the issue of compulsion are essentially limited to three works, all from roughly the same time period. However, there are two cases that allow us to see disagreement, contestation, and change within the tradition, and these speak directly to my contention about the nature of change and reasoning in theological traditions, a point taken up again in the next chapter on the Ashʿarites. Recall that Abū ʾl-Hudhayl, a very early Muʿtazilite, had held that the reason why God permits an individual being forced to apostatize to lie is that coercion changes the moral quality of the otherwise evil act. ʿAbd al-Jabbār rejected this position, insisting that coercion does not change the quality of the act. His argument on this issue is a good example of how external constraints influence the solutions that can be proposed for theological problems. ʿAbd al-Jabbār could not simply have asserted that coercion cannot legitimize anything resembling apostasy, because non-Muʿtazilite scholars agreed unanimously that the Qurʾānic verse 16:106 granted the coerced some sort of dispensation to do something that would normally be prohibited. ʿAbd al-Jabbār was also internally constrained from arguing that 16:106 allowed lying because of his construal of what the Muʿtazilite commitment to moral objectivism entailed. His ingenious solution was to reinterpret exactly what 16:106 permitted in the case of coercion. It allowed not lying per se, but giving one's persecutors an impression or insinuation of having apostatized.

On the issue of how the moral quality of a compelled agent's acts compares with the quality of acts committed by sleeping or unaware agents, both ʿAbd al-Jabbār and Ibn Mattawayh rejected Abū ʿAlī's and Abū Hāshim's contention that the reason the latter do not deserve blame if they commit ostensibly evil acts is that their acts cannot really be labeled evil. ʿAbd al-Jabbār and Ibn Mattawayh both held that while such agents do not deserve blame, their acts are still evil.

What the two discussions on the evilness of acts committed by those asleep and unaware and the issue of coerced apostasy have in common is that in both cases, the later Muʿtazilite scholars rejected their forebears' positions out of deference to one of the two core principles of the tradition, namely moral objectivism: the positions of Abū ʾl-Hudhayl and the two Jubbāʾīs implied a weakening of the reach of moral objectivism into these subsidiary issues, and were therefore criticized and rejected in favor of solutions that did not endanger it. We shall see an even clearer example of exactly this type of doctrinal modification in the Ashʿarites' argumentation for their position on coercion and moral agency.

2

Coercion and Moral Agency in Ashʿarism

1. INTRODUCTION

As described in the previous chapter, the Muʿtazilites held that the absence of compulsion is a necessary condition for moral agency. They also held that compulsion renders an agent immune to praise, blame, reward, and punishment. The driving force behind the Muʿtazilites' articulation of these two positions was their desire to extend and protect two core positions of their tradition: the primacy of Divine justice (which requires that God hold human beings accountable only for freely chosen acts) and moral objectivism (which holds that reason can know at least some moral truths). Both of these positions were roundly rejected by scholars belonging to the Ashʿarite theological tradition, which represented one of the Muʿtazilites' principal rivals from the fourth/tenth century onward. Drawing on the core positions articulated by the founder of the tradition, Abū al-Ḥasan al-Ashʿarī (d. 323/935), particularly his theory of physical human agency, later Ashʿarites considering the problem of coercion (*ikrāh*) and moral agency arrived at the conclusion that there is nothing inherent in coercion itself that would make its absence a necessary condition for moral agency. The Ashʿarites approached the issue with internal constraints that were very different from those of the Muʿtazilites. The Ashʿarites construed the Muʿtazilite insistence on moral objectivism as a limitation on God's freedom and as implying the existence of a morality external to God. By contrast, they held that the legal and moral value of acts is solely the result of God's command, which can only be discerned in scripture. Contrary to the Muʿtazilites, who held that human beings are the creators of their volitional acts, the Ashʿarites insisted that God is truly the creator of all events in the universe, including human volitional acts. The Ashʿarites thus considered the Muʿtazilite position a restriction of God's creative power and omnipotence.

Given these two core theological ideas—affirmation of God's monopoly on creation and a Divine command epistemology—Ashʿarite thinking about the conditions for moral agency took on a different flavor than in Muʿtazilite thought. Unlike their Muʿtazilite counterparts, Ashʿarite scholars could not rely on substantive notions of what would be just or unjust for God to do in defining the type of agent that can properly be the object of God's moral impositions. The history of Ashʿarite thinking on the effect of coercion on moral agency is, in part, a history of attempts to find a basis for moral agency that preserves the Ashʿarites' fundamental theological commitment to God's monopoly on creative agency and was simultaneously compatible with a moral epistemology centered on Divine command.

Unlike the Muʿtazilites, who explained compulsion largely in terms they had developed to explain the possibility and psychology of human action in general, the Ashʿarites did not rely on an account of human psychology. They did not need to. Having adopted a version of the determinist position in the free will/predestination debate in classical Islam, the Ashʿarites had no need for an account of free choice or an account of how compulsion interacts with free choice; hence the disinterest in and absence of such accounts in Ashʿarite thought.

The Ashʿarites deployed a number of different types of arguments to defend their position on coercion, and this chapter highlights an explicit change in the arguments used in the course of the history of the tradition. The change was inaugurated by Abū ʾl-Maʿālī al-Juwaynī (d. 478/1085), a towering scholar of Shāfiʿite law and an Ashʿarite theologian, and consolidated by his student Abū Ḥāmid al-Ghazālī (d. 505/1111). This shift in the tradition gives us a unique glimpse into the values that must have been at stake for Juwaynī to initiate a modification of key components of Ashʿarī's ideas about agency. It also provides an illuminative example of the mechanics of change internal to a theological tradition.

In order to understand how authors after Ashʿarī, beginning with Abū Bakr al-Bāqillānī (d. 403/1013), argued for the Ashʿarite position on coercion's effect on moral agency, we need to take into account how Ashʿarites thought about physical agency more broadly.

2. PHYSICAL AGENCY IN ASHʿARISM: THE DOCTRINES OF ACQUISITION (*KASB*) AND SIMULTANEOUS CAPACITY (*ISTIṬĀʿA*) AS INTERNAL CONSTRAINTS

2.1 Ashʿarī

Abū ʾl-Ḥasan al-Ashʿarī, the founder of the Ashʿarite theological tradition, began his scholarly career as a Muʿtazilite, the favored pupil of Abū ʿAlī Muḥammad al-Jubbāʾī.[1] In middle age, he abandoned some Muʿtazilite teachings in favor of theological beliefs espoused by Sunnī traditionalists, but he retained the methods of investigation characteristic of theology at the time.[2]

Though hundreds of works have been attributed to Ashʿarī in Islamic biographical and bibliographical literature, only six are extant. Of these six, three works—namely, *al-Lumaʿ*, *al-Ibāna ʿan Uṣūl al-Diyāna*, and *Risāla ilā Ahl al-Thaghr bi-Bāb al-Abwāb*—provide a snapshot of Ashʿarī's theological system.[3] This picture is complemented by the work of a fourth/tenth-century Ashʿarite scholar, Ibn Fūrak (d. 406/1015),[4] titled *Maqālāt al-Shaykh*

[1] C.E. Bosworth, "Ašʿarī," in *Encyclopaedia Iranica*, ed. Ehsan Yar-Shater (London; Boston, Winona Lake, IN: Routledge & Kegan Paul, 1982). A major point of disagreement among Islamicists concerns the nature and extent of Ashʿarī's departure from the teaching of Abū ʿAlī al-Jubbāʾī, the founder of Basran Muʿtazilism. Makdisi views Ashʿarī's conversion from Muʿtazilism as the *in toto* embrace of a Ḥanbalite Ahl al-Ḥadīth traditionalist position. See George Makdisi, "Ashʿarī and the Ashʿarites in Islamic Religious History II," *Studia Islamica* 18 (1963): 41–42. Frank interprets it as a radical modification of key tenets of Muʿtazilite theology that does not amount to a repudiation of the methods of argument and key elements of physical theory shared among those engaging in speculative theology (*kalām*). See Richard M. Frank, "Elements in the Development of the Teaching of al-Ashʿarī," in *Early Islamic Theology: the Muʿtazilites and al-Ashʿarī, Texts and Studies on the Development and History of Kalām*, ed. Dimitri Gutas (Aldershot: Ashgate, 2007).

[2] For Ashʿarī's defense of theology as a discipline against the criticisms of the Ahl al-Ḥadīth, see Renard, *Islamic Theological Themes: a Primary Source Reader*, 151–60.

[3] For a brief description of Ashʿarī's oeuvre, see Richard M. Frank, "al-Ashʿarī" in *Encyclopedia of Religion, Second Edition*, ed. Lindsay Jones (Detroit: Macmillan Reference USA, 2005).

[4] On Ibn Fūrak, see W. Montgomery Watt, "Ibn Fūrak, Abū Bakr Muḥammad b. al-Ḥasan," in *Encyclopedia of Islam, Second Edition*, ed. P. Bearman, et al. (Leiden: Brill, 1980–2004).

Abī ʾl-Ḥasan al-Ashʿarī, Imām Ahl al-Sunna. Just two generations after Ashʿarī, it seems that many contradictory opinions on theological issues had come to be attributed to him. Ibn Fūrak, therefore, took it upon himself to properly identify and clarify Ashʿarī's theological positions.[5]

Ashʿarī's theology shares two features with Muʿtazilite thinking on the issue of human agency. First, he conceptualizes basic human physical agency (*qudra*) in atomistic terms. And second, despite his disagreement with the Muʿtazilites on the nature of God's omnipotence and moral independence, he does think that certain conditions need to obtain before God's imposed commandments on human beings can become operative.

Ashʿarī notes that in order for an agent to be eligible for moral agency, the agent must possess the basic capacity for bodily action (*qudra*) and knowledge (*ʿilm*). Like the Muʿtazilites before him, Ashʿarī notes that this basic capacity for bodily action results from the distribution of an adequate number of quanta of capacity (*qudar*) to the body parts necessary to undertake or, in Ashʿarī's own terms, *acquire* the action in question. The same principle applies to knowledge. Both knowledge and capacity are discrete, divisible components that agents can possess in greater or lesser quantity. If the level of *qudar* in the body parts through which a divinely imposed action should be performed is inadequate, God's imposition of the act is not operative, because the agent simply does not possess the fundamental physical ability to perform the act.[6]

Ashʿarī elaborates the knowledge condition for moral agency specifically with reference to the pre-revelational duty to know God through reason.[7] The agent must possess a sufficient amount of knowledge (*ʿulūm*) in order to perform the duty to reason (*istidlāl*) his way to God's existence and nature. If the agent does not possess the requisite amount of knowledge, the duty to reason about God's existence and nature fails to arise. Ashʿarī sums up his discussion by asserting that

[5] Abū Bakr Muḥammad b. al-Ḥasan b. Fūrak, *Maqālāt al-Shaykh Abī al-Ḥasan al-Ashʿarī, Imām Ahl al-Sunna*, ed. Aḥmad ʿAbd al-Raḥīm Sāyiḥ (Cairo: Maktabat al-Thaqāfa al-Dīniyya, 2005), 3.5–17.

[6] Abū al-Ḥasan ʿAlī b. Ismāʿīl al-Ashʿarī, "Risāla al-Ashʿarī," *Darülfünun İlâhiyat Fakültesi Mecmuası* (1928): 102.15–18.

[7] See, for instance, ibid., 102.4–13, where Ashʿarī discusses the knowledge and capacity conditions necessary for God to validly impose the duty to believe in Him.

> the imposition of duties on [potential moral agents] is valid only given the proper functioning of their intelligences and body parts (*ṣiḥḥat ʿuqūli-him wa-abdāni-him*) necessary for the performance of the imposed actions.[8]

The use of atomistic vocabulary to understand human action at a basic level and the idea that agents must possess at least some features before God can impose commandments on them are continuous with Muʿtazilite ideas on moral agency.

Ashʿarī's departure from Muʿtazilism was motivated by a desire to remedy what he saw as Muʿtazilism's insufficient emphasis on and deference to a conception of God as the *sole* creative power in the cosmos. Ashʿarī achieves this deference himself at the level of subsidiary theological doctrine by articulating two ideas related to human physical agency: the doctrine of acquisition[9] and the doctrine of God's creation of the capacity to act *simultaneously* with the act itself.

The Muʿtazilites subscribed to the idea that human beings are truly the creators of their volitional actions in order to preserve human accountability. If a person is truly the creator of his volitional acts, it follows that the person can be held morally and legally responsible for those acts. From the Muʿtazilite perspective, however, Ashʿarī's insistence on God's sole creative agency destroyed the distinction between volitional and nonvolitional acts and thereby undermined the possibility of both Divine and human

[8] Ibid., 102.17–18.

[9] Watt, based mostly on a reading of Ashʿarī's heresiological work, *al-Maqālāt al-Islāmiyyīn*, determines the second/eighth-century Kufan theologian Ḍirār b. ʿAmr to have been the originator of the doctrine of acquisition. Watt notes that the doctrine was developed further by a group of early Muʿtazilites and thus already had a substantial, though conflicted, history before Ashʿarī's own deployment of it. See W. Montgomery Watt, "The Origin of the Islamic Doctrine of Acquisition," *Journal of the Royal Asiatic Society of Great Britain and Ireland*, no. 2 (1943). Harry Wolfson identifies al-Najjār's (d. circa beginning of third/ninth century) doctrinal version of acquisition in the formative period as the closest to Ashʿarī's interpretation; see Harry Austryn Wolfson, *The Philosophy of the Kalam* (Cambridge, MA: Harvard University Press, 1976), 686–88. Gimaret identifies both Ḍirār b. ʿAmr and Najjār as the originators of the doctrine of acquisition and asserts that the doctrine was elaborated in opposition to Jahm b. Safwān's (d. 128/746) thorough determinism in order to explain how human beings are the agents of their acts. See Daniel Gimaret, *Théories de l'Acte Humain en Théologie Musulmane* (Paris: J. Vrin, 1980), 68–67. For the most comprehensive account of the development of the doctrine of acquisition in the formative period, see M. Schwarz, "'Acquisition' (*kasb*) in Early Kalām," in *Islamic Philosophy and the Classical Tradition: Essays Presented by his Friends and Pupils to Richard Walzer on his Seventieth Birthday*, ed. S.M. Stern, Albert Hourani, and Vivian Brown (Columbia, SC: University of South Carolina Press, 1973), 355–73.

accountabilities for action. If God creates all events in the cosmos, including human action, is there any way of distinguishing between different types of human acts? Is there a difference, for example, between my writing this chapter and my shivering when cold? Ashʿarī's doctrine of acquisition was meant to respond to just such a question.

At a basic level, the doctrine of acquisition is a theological description of human action in relation to God's all-encompassing creative agency. For Ashʿarī, "acquisition" denotes all volitional human acts, which are created by God like all other acts but are acquired by human beings.[10] He defends the distinction between volitional and nonvolitional action by arguing that we know by an immediate, introspective knowledge that there is a difference between movement that occurs by way of "shaking from palsy or shivering from fever"[11] and the movement of "a man who goes and comes, and approaches and recedes."[12] We recognize this difference through introspection into our own internal states when experiencing these different types of acts and by observing others. Moreover, this knowledge is immediate (*ʿilm iḍṭirār*) and does not admit doubt (*lā yajūz maʿa-hu shakk*).[13]

[10] Modern scholars have identified three arguments for Ashʿarī's doctrine of acquisition:

1. All created things need a creator who has full knowledge of the object created. The human being can be mistaken about the acts he undertakes; thus he cannot be their true creator. It is not possible that acts exist without a creator; therefore God is the Creator of volitional human action. See Hammouda Ghoraba, "Al-Ashʿarī's Theory of Acquisition (*al-Kasb*)," *Islamic Quarterly* 2 (1955): 3; Gimaret, *Théories*, 80–81; Mohammed Yusoff Hussain, "Al-Ashʿarī's Doctrine of Human Actions," *Islamic Quarterly* 36, no. 2 (1992): 78–79.
2. All the arguments that apply to God as the creator of necessary, nonvolitional human action (e.g., shivering from a fever) apply equally to volitional human action. Thus God is the creator of volitional human action. See Hussain, "Al-Ashʿarī's Doctrine of Human Actions," 81–82.
3. If creators other than God are admitted, then the proof for God as the creator of the cosmos is weakened, as one could never be sure that the power to create was not delegated to some other creature. For this argument, see Schwarz, "'Acquisition' (*kasb*) in Early Kalām," 374.

[11] For McCarthy's translation, see Abū al-Ḥasan ʿAlī b. Ismāʿīl al-Ashʿarī, *The Theology of al-Ashʿarī: the Arabic Texts of al-Ashʿarī's Kitāb al-Lumaʿ and Risālat Istiḥsān al-Khawḍ fī ʿIlm al-Kalām: with Briefly Annotated Translations, and Appendices Containing Material Pertinent to the Study of al-Ashʿarī*, trans. Richard Joseph McCarthy (Beirut: Imprimerie Catholique, 1953), 59, §92. For the Arabic, see ibid., 41, §92.

[12] For McCarthy's translation, see ibid., 59, §92. For the Arabic, see ibid., 41, §92.

[13] For the Arabic, see Ashʿarī, *Theology*, 41, §92. For a substantially similar discussion of Ashʿarī's epistemological justification for the distinction between volitional and nonvolitional action, see Schwarz, "'Acquisition' (*kasb*) in Early Kalām," 374; Wolfson, *Philosophy*, 685; Gimaret, *Théories*, 82; Abrahamov, "Re-examination," 211. Wolfson notes that the Muʿtazilites, starting

But at the ontological level, what separates volitional from nonvolitional acts is not the agent's experience or observation of the two types as categorically different, but rather the fact that volitional acts occur by way of a simultaneous, yet mediate capacity for the act God creates in the human agent.[14] An act that occurs in this way is described as acquired by the human agent. Such acts contrast with acts that occur by necessity, such as shivering when cold. God creates the latter acts directly in the body of the agent without a mediating capability created in the agent.

In Ashʿarī's theology, then, the volitional act accepts two ontological descriptions: it is a creation and an acquisition. It is, on the one hand, created by God, as it is impossible to apply the term creator nonmetaphorically to anything besides God.[15] The human being who performs the act is not its creator, she is its acquirer.[16] God cannot be described as the act's acquirer, and the human being cannot be described as its creator. In Ashʿarī's theology, the terms "creator" and "acquirer" are mutually exclusive when applied to a single agent. The volitional act itself, though, is capable of receiving two descriptions. It is God's creation and the human agent's acquisition.[17]

If all things, including volitional human acts, are God's creations, what is the purpose and function of describing these acts as a human agent's

with Wāṣil b. ʿAṭāʾ (d. 131/748–9), as quoted in Shahrastānī's heresiographical work, *al-Milal*, used this same argument to establish the reality of free choice. Wolfson, *Philosophy*, 617–18.

[14] Ashʿarī defines an acquired act as one that "proceeds from its acquirer through a created power (*al-shayʾ waqaʿa mina ʾl-muktasibi la-hu bi-quwwatin muḥdathatin*)." See Ashʿarī, *Theology*, 42, §92; for McCarthy's translation, see ibid., 60, §92. Gimaret also cites a definition proffered by Ashʿarī in his *Maqālāt*; see Gimaret, *Théories*, 83. Ibn Fūrak attributes essentially the same definition of acquisition (*kasb*) to Ashʿarī: "what occurs *through* a created power (*mā waqaʿa bi-qudratin muḥdathatin*)." See Ibn Fūrak, *Maqālāt*, 93.15. He also notes that Ashʿarī frequently sought to distinguish acquisitions from nonacquisitions, indicating that it was a primary conceptual concern of Ashʿarī's. See ibid., 101.18–19.

[15] Ibn Fūrak notes that Ashʿarī held that the term "agent" (*fāʿil*) applies nonmetaphorically only to God, and additionally that the variety of verbal nouns denoting creation apply nonmetaphorically only to God. See *Maqālāt*, 93.3–8.

[16] Ibid., 93.7–8. Ibn Fūrak describes Ashʿarī as "consistently describing the temporally originated being (*muḥdath*) as being truly the acquirer (*wa-kāna yaṣifu ʾl-muḥdatha alā ʾl-ḥaqīqati anna-hu muktasibun*)."

[17] Ibid., 95.19. Ibn Fūrak observes that Ashʿarī expressed the same idea using the following formulation: the act occurs by way of a created capacity as an acquisition, and by way of an eternal capacity as a creation (*inna-hu yaqaʿa bi-ʾl-qudrati ʾl-muḥdathati kasban, wa-yaqaʿa bi-ʾl-qudrati ʾl-qadīmati khalqan*). Ashʿarī's doctrine is in this sense the inverse of the Muʿtazilite conception of human agency. In Muʿtazilite doctrine, the term "creator" can be applied nonmetaphorically to either God or the human agent. The occurrence that is the act is merely someone's creation, and there is no need for a perspectival description of it.

acquisitions? As we shall see, Ashʿarī's need to describe volitional acts as acquisitions points to the importance of defining the scope of human action that can properly be the object of God's command. God's monopoly on creative agency pulled Ashʿarī in one direction, but the fact that God imposes moral, legal, and religious duties pulled him in the opposite direction. The doctrine of acquisition was Ashʿarī's response to this tension. Epistemologically, it was born of the drive to account for the indubitable distinction between voluntary and involuntary action. Ethically and legally, it provided an answer to the need to differentiate the actions that fall under the purview of God's command. Without acquisition, how could Sharīʿa get off the ground? It is this same tension between the need to conceptually preserve God's monopoly on creation and, simultaneously, an intelligible account of the moral agent that led the later Ashʿarites Juwaynī and Ghazālī to either modify or reject central components of the Ashʿarism they inherited.

Some modern commentators have expressed reservations about the conceptual cogency of Ashʿarī's doctrine of acquisition. Like the Muʿtazilite ʿAbd al-Jabbār, they see the doctrine as nothing more than a rhetorical attempt to frustrate the application of the pejorative "determinist" (*jabrī*) label without, in reality, offering a view of human agency that substantially differs from that of the derided determinists of early Islam. However, the doctrine of acquisition does more than simply serve as an attempt to soften the thrust of the determinist implications of God's creative monopoly. From an ethical and legal perspective, the doctrine of acquisitions allows Ashʿarī to think about the conditions necessary for God to institute moral, legal, and religious duties. God can only command an act that is acquirable.[18] It is for this reason that we find Ashʿarī stipulating, similarly to the Muʿtazilites, basic physical capacity (*qudra*) and the lack of incapacity (*ʿajz*) as conditions for the imposition of duties (*taklīf*).

Two further features of Ashʿarī's thought help to explain later Ashʿarite authors' attempts to grapple with the impact of coercion on moral agency from within the framework of Ashʿarism:

1. The simultaneity of God's creation of the human capacity (*istiṭāʿa*) to perform a specific act with His creation of the acquirer's act

[18] Ibid., 94.12–13.

2. The possibility that God could impose impossible or unbearable obligations (labeled the *taklīf mā lā yuṭāq* issue in later theological and legal-theory literature).

Both positions contrast with those taken by the Muʿtazilites.

The Muʿtazilites conceived of capacity as a type of accident that endures through time. More specifically, they asserted that it precedes the act for which it is a capacity and, as mentioned earlier, that it covers the capacity to both perform an action and refrain from it. To what extent this formulation of capacity was merely an outcome of the commitments that made up the Muʿtazilites' physical theory and to what extent its specific construction was motivated by the desire to substantively protect the human agent's free choice is not clear. The same is true of the position taken by Ashʿarī, who disagreed with the Muʿtazilites on this issue. For Ashʿarī, God creates the specific capacity to perform an act simultaneously with the act itself. The capacity neither precedes the act nor endures after it.[19] Moreover, the capacity is limited to the performance of the act in question;[20] it does not, in contrast to the Muʿtazilite conception, extend to the option of refraining from it.

The debate on impossible obligations centers on the question whether God can impose duties that are impossible to perform. Ashʿarī does not address the idea of impossible obligations directly,[21] but Bāqillānī and Juwaynī, inferring his position from his collateral commitments on other issues, argue that Ashʿarī's specific conception of agency effectively

[19] On this point, see Ashʿarī, *Theology*, 76–78, §123–25, for the English translation and ibid., 54–55, §123–25, for the original Arabic. Ashʿarī's arguments for his position derive entirely from his physical theory. His argument against the existence of the capacity before the act stems from the fact that he does not think that an accident can endure over time. To have the capacity precede the act would be to posit that it has endurance from the time of its beginning before the act till the time of the performance of the act. Things cannot endure without the accident of endurance (*baqāʾ*) that comes to inhere in the substrate. Accidents cannot inhere in other accidents, and since capacity (*qudra*) is already an accident, it cannot serve as the substrate for the accident of endurance. Therefore, it is impossible that a capacity can precede the act and endure till the performance of the act itself.

[20] Ibid., 78–79, §126–28 (English translation) and ibid., 55–56, §126–28 (original Arabic).

[21] Where Ashʿarī does address the issue of impossible obligations in his *Kitāb al-Ibāna*, his treatment amounts to no more than the citation of Qurʾānic verses that he interprets as validating the idea that God could impose obligations that are incapable of being fulfilled. See Ashʿarī, *al-Ibāna ʿan Uṣūl al-Diyāna*, 1st ed. (Beirut: Dār Ibn Zaydūn, n.d.), 55.

commits him to the idea that God does indeed impose impossible obligations. Bāqillānī endorses this position and then uses it as a premise in an a fortiori argument for why coercion does not impede moral agency. Juwaynī rejects the idea that God imposes impossible obligations but nonetheless remains committed to the claim that coercion does not compromise moral agency.

3. MORAL AGENCY AND COERCION

3.1 Bāqillānī: Extension of Ashʿarī's Ideas to Coercion and Moral Agency

The earliest extant treatment of the issue of coercion's impact on moral agency within the Ashʿarite tradition is found in the work of the famous Mālikite chief judge of Baghdad, Abū Bakr al-Bāqillānī (d. 403/1013).[22] Bāqillānī discusses the issue in his book on legal theory (*uṣūl al-fiqh*), *al-Taqrīb wa-ʾl-Irshād "al-Ṣaghīr."*[23] This is noteworthy because in the formative and classical periods, the problem of coerced acts generally received the most attention in works devoted to articulating positive law (*fiqh*). To a large extent, Bāqillānī's treatment of the issue of moral agency (*taklīf*) in his work on legal theory consisted of showing how a theological description of agency cohered with widely accepted legal positions.[24] At times this

[22] See ʿAbbās Ziryāb, "Bāqillānī," in *Dānishnāmah-ʾi Jahān-i Islām*, ed. Aḥmad Ṭāhirī ʿIrāqī, Muṣṭafā Mīr Salīm, and Naṣr Allāh Pūrjavādī (Tehran: Bunyād-i Dāʾirat al-Maʿārif-i Islāmī, 1996–).

[23] The tradition of addressing the issue in works of legal theory, ostensibly inaugurated by Bāqillānī, is continued by Juwaynī and Ghazālī.

[24] For summary remarks on the relationship between the disciplines of legal theory and theology, see Wael Hallaq, *A History of Islamic Legal Theories: an Introduction to Sunnī Uṣūl al-Fiqh* (Cambridge; New York: Cambridge University Press, 1997), 134–36. Hallaq highlights the assimilation of theological epistemology and certain Sunni metaphysical commitments about the nature of causality into the discipline of legal theory as an important component of its historical emergence. For the integration of Ashʿarite ideas about God's creation of human acts in the work of a later Ashʿarite-Shāfiʿite legal theorist, al-Āmidī (d. 631/1233), see Bernard G. Weiss, *The Search for God's Law: Islamic Jurisprudence in the Writings of Sayf al-Dīn al-Āmidī* (Salt Lake City: University of Utah Press, 1992), 61–64. Makdisi makes the case that the formation of the discipline of legal theory is intimately tied to the bid for legitimacy made by what he calls "moderate rationalism" in an increasingly traditionalist Sunnī society by way of latching on to the more "orthodox" and socially accepted discipline of positive law (*fiqh*). Thus, he argues, the

involved merely the integration of a theological doctrine into a legal discussion. For instance, Bāqillānī starts his discussion of the conditions necessary for moral agency (*taklīf*) by asserting that it is a necessary but not sufficient condition that the act that is the object of the Divine command be an acquisition (*kasb*).[25] As in Ashʿarī's teaching, part of the conceptual function of the doctrine of acquisition is to denote volitional action. By stipulating that only acts that count as acquisitions are subject to moral assessment, Bāqillānī excludes nonvolitional actions by definition and requires that the agent have the requisite knowledge and physical capacity.[26] In addition, Bāqillānī states that the agent must be rational (*ʿāqil*). Examples of agents who are capable of performing acquirable acts but do not qualify as moral agents include animals (*bahāʾim*), minors (*aṭfāl*), and the insane (*majānīn*). Bāqillānī asserts that the existence of agreement (*ittifāq*) on not regarding the actions of these types of agents as valid performances of a Divine command is because they lack intellect (*ʿaql*), the capacity for discernment (*tamyīz*), and the ability to engage with full knowledge and intent in the specific acts meant to satisfy the Divine commands.[27]

For Bāqillānī, the possession of the capacity for rationality is also a necessary but not sufficient condition for subjection to God's commands. An agent might possess the capacity to reason, but temporary states might impede the

generation of moderate rationalists in the early fifth/eleventh century pursued the surreptitious acceptance of moderately rationalist methods of theological inquiry and substantive theological ideas by inventing a new discipline that was intimately connected to positive law—namely, legal theory. Makdisi claims that it is around this time that we see the "infiltration" of the Sunnī Shāfiʿite and Ḥanafite legal traditions by Muʿtazilite and Ashʿarite theologians. See George Makdisi, "The Juridical Theology of Shâfiʿî: Origins and Significance of Uṣûl al-Fiqh," *Studia Islamica* 59 (1984): 24–46. Hallaq sees the formation of the discipline of legal theory as an indication of the emerging rationalist-traditionalist synthesis being worked out from the third/ninth century onward. See Hallaq, *A History*, 33.

[25] Abū Bakr Muḥammad b. al-Ṭayyib al-Bāqillānī, *al-Taqrīb wa al-Irshād "al-Ṣaghīr"*, ed. ʿAbd al-Ḥamīd b. ʿAlī Abū Zunayd, 1st ed., 3 vols. (Beirut: Muʾassasa al-Risāla, 1993–1998), 1:236. Note that Bāqillānī is not so much making an argument that acquisitions are the object of moral imposition as merely introducing the vocabulary of acquisition as relevant to defining the features of moral agency.

[26] Bāqillānī specifies that this is what he means when he talks about factors that either prevent or eliminate the emergence of moral agency in ibid., 1:236.8–10: "The only thing we mean by the cessation of moral agency is the omission of accountability (*muṭālaba*) for either eschewing or performing [an act] and thereby obtaining the promise [of heaven] (*waʿd*), the threat [of hell] (*waʿīd*), reward (*thawāb*), punishment (*ʿiqāb*), praise (*madḥ*), or blame (*dhamm*) for it."

[27] Ibid., 236.8–10.

agent's use of that rational capacity. The agent could perform or omit an act out of forgetfulness, or heedlessly, or while asleep, or in a state of intoxication. Each one of these states negates moral agency because, for Bāqillānī, it cuts the agent off from "the foundation of the intellect and discernment."[28]

What about coercion? Is its absence a condition of moral agency akin to the presence of physical ability and rationality? Bāqillānī claims that a person can be coerced to do only actions that are acquirable and within the scope of that person's basic physical capacity.[29] An act that is coerced is nonetheless acquired by the agent and takes place through the agent's knowledge and intention. For these reasons, coercion does not undermine moral agency.[30] Bāqillānī then offers five different arguments to rebut the opposing position. His defense of the Ashʿarite position consists of theological arguments, inference from laws addressing the problem of coercion, and empirical observations, and his quoted opponents include both Muʿtazilite theologians (to whom he refers as the Qadariyya) and legal scholars.

He directs two arguments against the Muʿtazilite position. According to Bāqillānī, the Muʿtazilites hold that coercion invalidates moral agency because the agent cannot do anything other than the coerced act.[31] Bāqillānī's first argument against this position asserts that the agent possesses the basic physical capacity (*qudra*) to perform or omit the coerced act, or even perform an act that contradicts it. Bāqillānī notes that the Muʿtazilites, too, describe the coerced agent as nonetheless capable (*qādir*). Therefore, the fact that the agent could refuse to perform the act demanded through the use of coercion and bear the harm associated with the refusal undermines the Muʿtazilite contention that it is not possible for the coerced agent to do any other act.[32]

While this argument is based on the shared premise that coercion has no effect on basic physical capacity, Bāqillānī's second argument is based on a premise that only Ashʿarite scholars hold: that God can validly impose obligations that are in some sense impossible. This argument is rooted in Ashʿarī's conception of God's creative monopoly as encompassing even human beings'

[28] Ibid., 241.6–7.

[29] Ibid., 250.1–3. The section is entitled "the doctrine regarding the validity of subsuming the act of the coerced under moral agency and the disagreement regarding it" (*Bāb al-qawl fī ṣiḥḥat dukhūl fiʿl al-mukrah taḥta al-taklīf wa-al-ikhtilāf fī-hi*).

[30] Ibid., 1:250.4–7. [31] Ibid., 1:251.1–2. [32] Ibid., 1:251.4–6.

volitional actions. Bāqillānī bases the argument on the cardinal Ashʿarite position that God creates the capacity for a specific act simultaneously with the agent's performance of the act. He then construes commitment to this doctrine as necessarily committing one to the position that it is impossible for the agent to omit the act at the moment of God's simultaneous creation of the capacity and the act itself. Yet despite the metaphysical impossibility of the agent's refraining from the act at that moment, he is still, according to Ashʿarite theology, held morally responsible for it. Bāqillānī implies that since moral agency survives this metaphysical description of human action, a fortiori there is no reason to regard coercion as fundamentally compromising it.[33] As we will see, the later Ashʿarites Juwaynī and Ghazālī reject this argument, despite their overall commitment to the Ashʿarite position on coercion and moral agency.

Bāqillānī's third argument consists of merely asserting that the majority of orthodox theologians (*akthar ahl al-ḥaqq*)[34] hold that it is rationally possible for God to impose obligations on living rational agents (*al-aḥyāʾ al-ʿuqalāʾ*) for whom such actions or omissions would be impossible to perform, even if revelation limits the realization of this rational presumption.[35] Like the previous argument, this is an a fortiori argument that effectively takes God's determination of human volitional action for granted. Bāqillānī does not explain the reasoning behind this position.[36]

[33] The entire argument is found in ibid., 1:251.7–12.

[34] The referent of the label *ahl al-ḥaqq* (lit. people of truth) is at first sight ambiguous—does it refer to jurists, ḥadīth scholars, or theologians? That it most likely denotes specifically theologians can be gleaned from Bāqillānī's use of the phrase "the theologians among the *ahl al-ḥaqq*" in another location in the *Taqrīb*, ibid., 1:186. Moreover, the subject of the *ahl al-ḥaqq*'s putative agreement is a topic likely to be debated by theologians, not jurists or ḥadīth scholars. In another place in the *Taqrīb*, Bāqillānī describes the position of the *ahl al-ḥaqq* as contradicting that of the Muʿtazilites: ibid., 3:384.14. In yet another passage, Bāqillānī not only asserts that the *ahl al-ḥaqq* oppose the Muʿtazilites on an issue but also says that those "*fuqahāʾ* (jurists) who disagreed with the Qadariyya" were committed to the same position as the *ahl al-ḥaqq*. This last phrase distinguishes the *ahl al-ḥaqq* from the jurists, which strengthens my contention that it is the theologians to whom Bāqillānī is referring here.

[35] See ibid., 1:251.13–14.

[36] It is probable that Bāqillānī's treatment of the issue in his now lost larger works on the same subject presents the argument more fully. As it stands, this argument seems to be based on the authority and competence of orthodox theologians. It may be related to a broader concern for Bāqillānī: boosting the social legitimacy of theologians in society. This concern is evidenced by his unusual positions on whose opinions count toward a consensus and what qualifications are required of a scholar to merit the rank of a *mujtahid*. On the former question, Bāqillānī held that the opinions of the scholars specializing in legal theory (*uṣūl al-fiqh*), even those who do not qualify as *mujtahids*, must be included in order for a legislating consensus to be reached. See

As one might expect in a work of legal theory, Bāqillānī's fourth and fifth arguments involve legal doctrine. Bāqillānī begins the fourth argument by acknowledging that

> many jurists assert that the basis for excluding (*al-maʿnā ʾl-muzīl*) the act of the coerced from moral significance (*taḥta ʾl-taklīf*) is that it issues from the agent without will or intent (*bi-ghayri irādatin wa-qaṣd*), such that it occupies the same position as the act of someone who is asleep or overcome [with insanity] (*al-maghlūb*), neither of whom has intent.[37]

Bāqillānī rejects this view, noting that the rejection accords with the consensus of the theologians (*ittifāq al-mutakallimīn*), as opposed to the jurists.[38] He points out that someone who is coerced to divorce his wife or to kill another person knows what he is doing and intends to do that specific action as opposed to some other one.[39]

Éric Chaumont, "Bâqillânî, Théologien Ash'arite et Usûliste Mâlikite, contre les Légistes à Propos de 'l'Ijtihâd' et de l'Accord Unanime de la Communauté," *Studia Islamica*, no. 79 (1994): 94–96. On the latter, he claimed that in order to qualify as a *mujtahid*, a scholar must have expertise in theology. See ibid., 85–86. Both of these positions are out of the ordinary and indicate a concern with strengthening the relevance and legitimacy of the practitioners of theology.

[37] Bāqillānī, *Taqrīb*, 1:251.15–252.2.

[38] The argumentative function of the reference to the theologians' agreement is not clear. It could be that the agreement of the theologians is motivated by the empirical fact that a coerced agent does not lose the capacity to form intentions or to have a will in the process of performing the coerced act. Bāqillānī could also be asserting that given the theological nature of the question, it is the opinion of the theologians that carries weight; and they happen to agree, contra many jurists who do not have the right competence to judge the issue, that the jurists' argument is false.

[39] It is important to note that as a Mālikite, Bāqillānī was most probably committed to the Mālikite *legal* position that coercion does in fact invalidate a pronouncement of divorce. As a matter of legal doctrine, all legal schools recognize that coercion has the effect of either mitigating or canceling altogether the moral and legal responsibility for some if not most types of coerced acts. Yet here, Bāqillānī asserts that coercion by itself does not necessarily impugn moral agency. Unfortunately, Bāqillānī's legal writings, if he had any, do not seem to have survived. But we do have an encyclopedic collection of Mālikite legal thought compiled by a scholar contemporaneous with Bāqillānī, the famous Ibn Abī Zayd al-Qayrawānī (d. 386/996), who records Mālik's (d. 179/796) opinion that coercion invalidates pronouncements of divorce. Moreover, the eighth/fourteenth-century Mālikite Ibn Farḥūn notes in his biographical entry on Bāqillānī that he apparently sought permission from Ibn Abī Zayd to transmit two of his works on Mālikite positive law (*fiqh*), *Mukhtaṣar* and *al-Nawādir wa-ʾl-Ziyādāt*. We know therefore that Bāqillānī must have been familiar with Mālikite positive laws on coercion. On the connection between Ibn Abī Zayd and Bāqillānī, see the notice devoted to Bāqillānī in Ibrāhīm b. ʿAlī Ibn Farḥūn, *al-Dībāj al-Mudhahhab fī Maʿrifat ʿUlamāʾ al-Madhhab*, ed. Maʾmūn b. Muḥyī al-Dīn al-Jannān, 1st ed. (Beirut: Dār al-Kutub al-ʿIlmiyya, 1996), 354.7. For Ibn Abī Zayd's discussion of the debates surrounding the legal positions on the validity of coerced pronouncements of divorce, see Ibn Abī Zayd al-Qayrawānī, *al-Nawādir wa al-Ziyādāt ʿalā mā fī al-Mudawwanah min Ghayri-hā min al-Ummahāt*, ed. ʿAbd al-Fattāḥ Muḥammad al-Ḥulw,

Bāqillānī's final argument relies on a position commonly held not just by Ashʿarites but also by Ḥanafites and Shāfiʿites. It is based on the fact that

> God has imposed on us the duty (*taklīf Allāh*) to refrain from killing an innocent person (*al-barīʾ*) even in the presence of compulsion and has commanded us to desist from that.

From this statement, Bāqillānī infers that it is likewise "possible for God to impose on us the duty to refrain from every action we are coerced to perform."[40]

Indeed, despite the lack of a clear text explicitly prohibiting murder even when coerced, all jurists and theologians regardless of theological affiliation or legal tradition held that under no circumstances is a coerced agent permitted to commit murder. Bāqillānī uses this unanimously shared core position to argue against the idea that coercion can, prima facie, invalidate moral agency. If, as all agree, the moral imposition to refrain from unjust killing survives coercive threats against one's own life, then there is nothing inherent in coercion itself that would undermine God's imposition of duties.

Bāqillānī ends his discussion of the relationship of coercion to moral agency by considering the question of whether there is any standard definition of coercion that can invalidate a standing legal prohibition. In other words, can coercion permit a previously forbidden action? To the extent that coercion (*ikrāh*) is conceptually related to necessity (*iḍṭirār*), this question has a long history in Islamic intellectual discourses owing to the fact that the Qurʾān itself permits, on several occasions, the consumption of forbidden food under circumstances of necessity. Bāqillānī's treatment of the problem centers on whose authority illicit acts could be deemed licit in situations of coercion. Is it revelation or reason?[41] Bāqillānī's response evinces commitment to Ashʿarite moral epistemology:

> The [knowledge of] acts as evil is conveyed only through revelation. If revelation did not make them evil, they would not be evil. Thus, it is [rationally]

1st ed., 15 vols. (Beirut: Dār al-Gharb al-Islāmī, 1999), 10.253–57. That Ibn Abī Zayd considers the Mālikite position to be that coercion invalidates a pronouncement of divorce is made obvious by his citation of Saḥnūn's (d. 240/855) arguments against the pro-validity Ḥanafite position. See ibid., 10:255.14–257.15.

[40] Bāqillānī, *Taqrīb*, 1:253.11–13.

[41] Ibid., 1:254.9–255.1. Bāqillānī cites the Muʿtazilite position that coercion cannot render evil acts (*qabāʾiḥ*) permitted. Muʿtazilite moral epistemology stipulates that certain fundamental judgments about the evil or goodness of actions are caused by characteristics intrinsic

> possible that *everything* can be permitted, meaning that the rational agent is not prohibited from doing anything, nor is he threatened with punishment for doing it.[42]

Given that reason cannot establish the goodness or evil of actions, it is scripture (*samʿ*) and the extension of scriptural proofs to unprecedented cases (*ijtihād*) that determine when coercion can and cannot render forbidden acts permitted. Though only scripture can change the normative status of acts occasioned by coercion, the description of what is coercive, for Bāqillānī, does not seem to necessarily depend on scripture. In response to a query about the possibility of defining the type of coercion that invalidates a standing prohibition, he cites a formulation of legal coercion that is found throughout the legal literature: in the presence of fear of a harm that would result in loss of life or other consequences that may be less severe than death but greater than a "slight harm," Bāqillānī notes that the law (*al-sharʿ*) invalidates a standing prohibition and renders its object permitted.[43]

3.2 Tradition in Motion: Imām al-Ḥaramayn al-Juwaynī's New Arguments for Old Positions

In many ways the famous Imām al-Ḥaramayn al-Juwaynī's (d. 478/1085) work, in both theology and legal theory, represents an extended engagement with Bāqillānī's oeuvre.[44] Juwaynī's work *al-Shāmil fī Uṣūl al-Dīn*, now mostly lost, is a detailed exposition of Bāqillānī's commentary on Ashʿarī's *Lumaʿ*.[45] And Chaumont notes that in Juwaynī's work on legal theory, *Burhān fī Uṣūl al-Fiqh*, Bāqillānī is the scholar cited most frequently after Shāfiʿī, the

to the action itself. For this reason, nothing extrinsic to the action (such as coercion) can change its moral character. Thus you have the Muʿtazilite position that coercion cannot make an evil action permissible.

[42] Ibid., 1:255.2–4. [43] Ibid., 1:254.3–5.

[44] For basic biographical information, see C. Brockelmann and L. Gardet, "al-D̲juwaynī, Abu ʾl-Maʿālī ʿAbd al-Malik," in *Encyclopedia of Islam, Second Edition*, ed. P. Bearman, et al. (Leiden: Brill, 1980–2004); Ḥusayn Hūshangī, "Juwaynī," in *Dānishnāmah-ʾi Jahān-i Islām*, ed. Aḥmad Ṭāhirī ʿIrāqī, Muṣṭafā Mīr Salīm, and Naṣr Allāh Pūrjavādī (Tehran: Bunyād-i Dāʾirat al-Maʿārif-i Islāmī, 1996–).

[45] Richard M. Frank, "Ashʿarīyah," in *Encyclopedia of Religion, Second Edition*, ed. Lindsay Jones (Detroit: Macmillan Reference USA, 2005).

eponymous founder of the legal tradition to which Juwaynī belonged—an indication of the deep intellectual debt Juwaynī owed to Bāqillānī.[46]

On the basic question of whether coercion by itself undermines moral agency (*taklīf*), Juwaynī, as a good Ashᶜarite, holds the same position as Bāqillānī—namely, that it does not. However, he changes two major components of Bāqillānī's argumentation. The most fundamental change is Juwaynī's move from identifying the possession of a general capacity for rationality (*ᶜaql*) as the basis of moral agency to insistence on the more specific capacity for linguistic understanding (*fahm*) as the key criterion. The second change is his rejection of the proposition that God could impose impossible obligations on His human subjects. As a consequence, he also rejects the use of this idea as an argument for why coercion does not undermine moral agency. As we saw, Ashᶜarī himself did not directly address the issue of impossible obligations, and Juwaynī notes disagreement regarding what exactly Ashᶜarī's position was on the issue and what his system effectively commits him to. Some scholars thought that Ashᶜarī held the view that God *could* impose impossible obligations (*kāna yujjawizu taklīfa mā lā yuṭāq*); some of these same scholars thought that Ashᶜarī held that God in fact *does* impose impossible obligations (*wuqūᶜ mā jawwazu-hu min dhālika*).[47] Juwaynī himself thinks that Ashᶜarī's conception of physical agency effectively committed him to both the rational possibility and the actuality of God's imposition of impossible duties, for two reasons. First, Juwaynī notes that Ashᶜarī claimed that the capacity to perform a specific act does not precede the performance itself, whereas God's command to perform the act is directed at the agent before the act's occurrence, when he is not actually yet able to perform it.[48] For Juwaynī, this qualifies as God's imposition of impossible duties: the command to perform an act exists at a time when the agent is simply not able to fulfill it. Second, in Ashᶜarī's account of human agency, a human being's act occurs by way of God's power (*fiᶜlu ʾl-ᶜabdi wāqiᶜun bi-qudrati ʾllāh*).[49] Juwaynī adds that this means,

[46] Chaumont, "Bâqillânî, Théologien Ash'arite et Usûliste Mâlikite, contre les Légistes à Propos de 'l'Ijtihâd' et de l'Accord Unanime de la Communauté," 80.

[47] Abū al-Maᶜālī ᶜAbd al-Malik b. ᶜAbdillāh al-Juwaynī, *al-Burhān fī Uṣūl al-Fiqh: Makhṭūṭ Yunsharu li-Awwal Marra*, ed. ᶜAbd al-ᶜAẓīm al-Dīb, 1st ed. (Qatar: Jāmiᶜa Qatar, 1399[/1979]), 1:102.10–103.1.

[48] Ibid., 1:103.4–5. [49] Ibid., 1:103.12.

in effect, that the human being is held accountable for an act that is actually that of his Lord (*al-ʿabdu muṭālabun bi-mā huwa min fiʿli rabbi-hi*)![50] In response to an anonymous interlocutor who asks, "So what, then, is the correct position in your view regarding the imposition of impossible obligations?" Juwaynī summarizes his position thus:

> If what is meant by the imposition (*taklīf*) is the demand for acts (*ṭalab al-fiʿl*) that are unbearable, by [a demander] who knows that the occurrence of the demanded act is impossible (*min ʾl-ʿālimi bi-istiḥālati wuqūʿi ʾl-maṭlūb*)—that is absurd (*muḥāl*).[51]

Juwaynī seems to be saying that God would not impose an obligation that He knew was impossible for the human agent to satisfy, not because it would be unjust, as the Muʿtazilites held, but because it would be incoherent.[52] This position comes close to limiting what God could and could not do. At the very least, Juwaynī's arguments against the impossible obligations position imply a rejection of Ashʿarī's conception of agency. This rejection is confirmed by the fact that Juwaynī twice asserts, in the course of his discussion of impossible

[50] Ibid., 1:103.12–13. He adds specifically that the doctrine of acquistion does *not* remedy the situation.

[51] Ibid., 1:104.2–3. See also his short exposition on the orthodox creed, in which he asserts that "it is a fundamental creedal principle (*qāʿidatu ʾl-aqīda*) that [God's] slave is held accountable (*muṭālab*) according to what is possible (*jāʾiz*), not [what is] impossible (*mustaḥīl*)." Juwaynī, *al-ʿAqīda al-Niẓāmiyya fī al-Arkān al-Islāmiyya*, ed. Muḥammad Zāhid b. al-Ḥasan Kawtharī (Cairo: al-Maktaba al-Azhariyya li-ʾl-Turāth, 1992), 55.18–19. In fact, consistent with his statements in the *Burhān*, he rejects the idea that God could impose an obligation that requires simultaneous, mutually exclusive actions. See ibid., 55.14.

[52] The specific nature of the impossibility is hard to discern in this text. There are three possible ways to construe its nature: moral, metaphysical, and linguistically incoherent. A moral construal would amount to accepting the Muʿtazilite conception: it is morally impossible for a Just God to hold human beings responsible for the acts that He creates for them. Juwaynī rejects this construal. See *Burhān*, 1:105.12–13. As for the metaphysical construal: Juwaynī does think that some things are metaphysically impossible for God to do, such as creating two atoms in the same place at the same time, or creating the action of motion and rest in the same substrate at the same time. For this see Ayman Shihadeh, "The Argument from Ignorance and Its Critics in Medieval Arabic Thought," *Arabic Sciences and Philosophy* 23, no. 2 (2013): 197. It certainly does not seem that Juwaynī would think it metaphysically impossible for God to command a person to do a thing without giving him the capacity to do it at the moment of the command, nor that it is metaphysically impossible for God to hold human beings responsible for acts that occur through His capacity. The remaining possible explanation, then, is that he thinks impossible obligations are simply incoherent, a view that fits well with his emphasis on the specific capacity of linguistic comprehension as the basis of moral agency. I thank Ayman Shihadeh for helping me clarify these points.

obligations, that he has his own specific doctrine on the creation of human acts (*khalq al-afʿāl*).[53] But this alternative doctrine is not consistently upheld in all his works. In his book on the general principles of Ashʿarite theology, the *Irshād*, he in fact affirms the very conception of agency that he criticizes in the *Burhān*.[54] But in a work devoted to explaining what he took to be the orthodox creed, *al-ʿAqīda al-Niẓāmiyya fī ʾl-Arkān al-Islāmiyya*, he provides the alternative conception of agency that he hints at in the *Burhān*.[55] Both medieval and modern commentators have tried to make sense of the discrepancies between the views found in the *Irshād* and those found in the *ʿAqīda al-Niẓāmiyya*.[56] The question of what caused Juwaynī to change his mind has prompted much speculation, and I will engage in some speculation myself in a moment.

[53] Specifically, Juwaynī alludes to his own theory by writing: "We would mention the essence (*sirr*) of what we believe regarding the creation of acts, but this is not the place for it." Juwaynī, *Burhān*, 1:103.14–15. On the next page he notes, again, that "as for the essence (*sirr*) of what we believe regarding the creation of acts, this is not the place for it." Ibid., 1:104.6–7.

[54] See Juwaynī, *Irshād ilā Qawāṭiʿ al-Adilla fī Uṣūl al-Iʿtiqād*, ed. Muḥammad Yūsuf Mūsā and ʿAlī ʿAbd al-Munʿim ʿAbd al-Hamīd (Cairo: Maktabat al-Khānjī, 1950), 187–226, where Juwaynī's theological ideas on human agency seem much closer to Ashʿarī's. For his thoughts on the prospect that God could impose impossible obligations on human agents, see ibid., 226–28, where he does not seem to reject the doctrine outright. He notes that the doctrine could refer to a number of different types of scenarios, from asking an agent to perform two mutually exclusive actions at the same time (*jamʿu ʾl-ḍiddayn*) to asking him to perform an action that he is only physically unable to perform (*īqāʿu mā yukhraju ʿan qabīli ʾl-maqdūrāt*). Juwaynī affirms it as rationally possible that God could impose both of these types of obligations. See, specifically, ibid., 226.5–7. When pressed on whether he thinks the scenarios are valid from the perspective of revelation, he answers in the affirmative, citing the example of God's imposing the obligation to believe in the Prophet on Abū Jahl while asserting that Abū Jahl will in fact never believe as an instance of the imposition of an impossible obligation of the mutually exclusive actions type. See ibid., 228.1–3. Yet in the *Burhān* he cites the case of Abū Jahl as one that does *not* imply the imposition of an impossible obligation, and specifically rejects the case as an instance of God imposing an obligation to perform two simultaneous, yet mutually exclusive actions. For this, see *Burhān*, 1:104.8–13.

[55] What we have of the *ʿAqīda al-Niẓāmiyya* is actually only part of a larger work. See the comments of the editor Muḥammad Zāhid al-Kawtharī, who notes that what survives is merely a creedal introduction to a Shāfiʿite text on the fundamental religious institutions of the Sharīʿa, namely prayer, fasting, *zakat* (religious tax on wealth), and the *ḥajj* pilgrimage. *al-ʿAqīda al-Niẓāmiyya*, 3. Juwaynī's discussion of physical agency takes place in the course of his discussion of moral agency (*taklīf*); see ibid., 42–59. For a presentation and analysis of Juwaynī's conception of physical agency as found in the *ʿAqīda al-Niẓāmiyya*, see Gimaret, *Théories*, 122–24.

[56] See Schwarz, "'Acquisition' (*kasb*) in Early Kalām," 379–80. See also Gimaret, *Théories*, 120–28, who cites a number of medieval commentators trying to determine Juwaynī's position. Frank asserts that Juwaynī's own student, Abū ʾl-Qāṣim al-Anṣārī, accuses him of inconsistency regarding the creation of human acts because of the differences between the *ʿAqīda al-Niẓāmiyya* and his other works. See Frank, *Al-Ghazālī and the Ashʿarite School*, 115, footnote 2. No one, to my knowledge, has considered the material found in the *Burhān*, however.

The second substantial change from Bāqillānī to Juwaynī is a shift in the conception of the basis of moral agency from the possession of a *general* capacity for rationality to the *specific* ability to understand speech. Bāqillānī argued that it is the absence of the capacity for rationality that undermines the imposition of duties on the intoxicated, the sleeping, and the heedless. For this reason, the actions of agents in these states are not morally significant, in contrast to the actions of the coerced. Bāqillānī thought that since coercion does not compromise rationality, it does not invalidate moral agency. The form of Juwaynī's argument is exactly the same, but for him the basis for moral agency is possession of the specific capacity to understand speech (*fahm*). Thus, the moral agency of the intoxicated is undermined by the latter's inability to understand the Divine address (*istiḥālatu fahmi ʾl-khiṭāb*),[57] which precludes the imposition of obligations (*al-sukrānu, yamtaniʿu taklīfu-hu*).[58] Compliance with a command (*al-imtithāl*) and intending a performance to be an act of such compliance (*qaṣdan ilay-hi*) are not possible without the capacity to understand the Divine address.[59] But these impediments do not apply to a coerced agent. Juwaynī writes:

> Imposing obligations on the coerced is not impossible because of the possibility of linguistic understanding (*fahm*) and compliance [with a command] (*imtithāl*) even when [one is] coerced.[60]

The basis for moral agency is the capacity to understand God's command. Since coercion does nothing to the ability to understand this command, it does not undermine moral agency. In sum, although Juwaynī, like Bāqillānī, denies that coercion, prima facie, prevents the imposition of moral duties,

[57] Juwaynī, *Burhān*, 1:106.1.

[58] Ibid., 1:105.15. In the following paragraph Juwaynī affirms that it is likewise impossible to impose duties on someone who acts forgetfully even if the forgetfulness persists over time, for exactly the same reasons as those offered in justification in the case of the intoxicated. Ibid., 1:106.6–7.

[59] Ibid., 1:106.1–2.

[60] Ibid., 1:106.9–10. Juwaynī then notes that the Muʿtazilite position that someone coerced to engage in acts of worship cannot be regarded as a proper moral agent is based on the principle that God has a duty to recompense the moral agent for the willing performance of a moral duty, and someone forced to commit a duty is thus not rewarded for it. Juwaynī argues that the claim that God is *obliged* to reward the performance of duties is false, and there is no reason that a moral duty cannot be imposed even without a corresponding reward.

he departs from Bāqillānī's justification for this position in two ways: by eschewing the argument that God can impose impossible obligations on human beings, and by replacing rationality as the criterion of valid moral agency with the more specific capacity to understand speech. Are these two developments in any way connected?

If we interpret Ashʿarism, writ large, as a reaction against Muʿtazilism, then Juwaynī's interventions in the history of the tradition point in conflicting directions. On the one hand, he rejected the idea that God can or does impose impossible obligations, contradicting the standard Muʿtazilite interpretation of what Ashʿarī's conception of agency effectively entailed. Bāqillānī had no problem biting the bullet: he explicitly affirmed the doctrine and went on to use it unashamedly as a premise in his argument that coercion does not invalidate moral agency. Juwaynī rejected the doctrine outright in two of his works and effectively ended up tacking *closer* to the Muʿtazilite position on this signature issue. Yet on the issue of the basis for moral agency, Juwaynī moved the tradition further *away* from Muʿtazilism. On this issue, Bāqillānī had been closer to the Muʿtazilites.

Gimaret interpreted Juwaynī's attempts at reformulating Ashʿarite ideas on physical agency as a result of the growing influence and penetration of philosophical ideas about causality as they relate to volitional human action. This may be partly true. But Gimaret did not take into consideration Juwaynī's work of legal theory, the *Burhān*. Moreover, he did not track the change in Juwaynī's own positions on the doctrine of impossible obligations. Is there an explanation that can account for all three developments—the shift in Juwaynī's position on the doctrine of impossible obligations, his attempt at reformulating ideas on agency, and the change he proposed in the basis for agency? If we look once more at the *ʿAqīda al-Niẓāmiyya*, we find that Juwaynī himself correlated two of the three changes. He notes that the imposition of impossible obligations is logically unfeasible because it is *un intelligible*. He writes that

> it is a stipulation that duties be imposed on the human being (*tawjīh al-taklīf ʿalā ʾl-ʿabd*) when he has presence of mind (*ḥuḍūr al-ʿaql*), such that he is able to understand the [Divine] address (*fahm al-khiṭāb*). If the agent is not in such a state, it is inconceivable that he could intend to comply with the command before understanding it and knowing [it is from] the [Divine] Commander, the

> Exalted. If this condition does not obtain, the command would be an impossible obligation (*taklīf mā lā yuṭāq*), and that is logically impossible (*mustaḥīl*).[61]

Juwaynī goes on to explicitly link his rejection of a specific type of impossible obligation—namely, a command to perform two mutually exclusive actions at one and the same time—to the fundamental principle of the orthodox creed (*qāʾidat al-ʿaqīda*), from which all other principles relating to moral agency are derived: "that the human subject is held accountable according to what is possible, not impossible" (*anna ʾl-ʿabda muṭālabun bi-jāʾizin dūna ʾl-mustaḥīl*).[62] It thus seems that the fundamental concern that motivated Juwaynī's changes was the doctrinal threat that he perceived in the legacy of Ashʿarite thought to the concept of God's command—a conceptual cornerstone of the Sharīʿa. It was perhaps as a committed adherent of Divine command theology and a textually conservative Shāfiʿite that Juwaynī was reacting to what he saw as an overly determinist Ashʿarite doctrine. It is tempting to see Juwaynī as attempting to save Shāfiʿism from what he took to be the pernicious features of Ashʿarism. Yet in a sense, Juwaynī was merely reenacting a tension that was already inherent in the thought of Ashʿarī himself and represents an enduring conflict in Islamic moral, theological, and legal thought: the tension of viewing God simultaneously as the Supreme Creator and as the Supreme Commander.

Did Juwaynī's modifications to Ashʿarism stick? To answer this question, we turn to the work of his illustrious student, Abū Ḥāmid al-Ghazālī.

3.3 Ghazālī: Continuing and Consolidating Juwaynī's Teachings

On the issue of coercion and moral agency, Ghazālī was not an innovator. In fact, in his writings, he hews closely to Juwaynī's teaching. He rejects the doctrine of impossible obligations and identifies the capacity to understand speech as the fundamental basis of moral agency. Since coercion does not undermine the latter, it does not, prima facie, undermine moral agency. We have seen all of these arguments in Juwaynī's work, and we see them repeated, though more clearly and in a more organized way, in Ghazālī's writings.

61 *al-ʿAqīda al-Niẓāmiyya*, 55.3–6. 62 Ibid., 55.19.

Like the Ashʿarite writers before him, Ghazālī addresses the issue of the effect of coercion on moral agency in his works of legal theory (*uṣūl al-fiqh*). Two such works are extant, the *Mankhūl* and the *Mustaṣfā*. The former has been dated to Ghazālī's early scholarly career, whereas the latter is considered one of his last works.[63] The *Mankhūl* tends to follow Juwaynī's *Burhān* in terms of order and content alike. Compared to the *Mankhūl*, the *Mustaṣfā* is a much more substantial work, as Ghazālī himself acknowledges in the introduction to the *Mustaṣfā*.[64] Whereas the *Mankhūl*, like Juwaynī's *Burhān*, has the quality of an oral lecture,[65] the *Mustaṣfā* reads like a well-polished and analytically organized monograph.[66]

Since there are some differences between Ghazālī's respective justifications of the standard Ashʿarite position in the *Mankhūl* and in the *Mustaṣfā*, for the sake of simplicity, the following analysis is based on Ghazālī's treatment of coercion and moral agency as found in the *Mustaṣfā*. I have confined my comments on the *Mankhūl* to the footnotes.

Ghazālī begins his discussion by identifying the possession of the faculty of linguistic comprehension (*fahm*) as the basis for moral agency:

> The object of moral and/or legal evaluation is the moral agent (*mukallaf*). One condition is that he must be a rational agent (*ʿāqil*) who can understand

[63] For a chronology of Ghazālī's writings, including the early composition of the *Mankhūl* compared with the late composition of the *Mustaṣfā*, see George F. Hourani, "A Revised Chronology of Ghazālī's writings," *Journal of the American Oriental Society* 104 (1984): 290–91 and 301–2.

[64] See Abū Ḥāmid Muḥammad b. Muḥammad al-Ghazālī, *al-Mustaṣfā min ʿIlm al-Uṣūl*, ed. Muḥammad Sulaymān Ashqar, 1st ed., 2 vols. (Beirut: Muʾassasat al-Risāla, 1997), 1:33.20, where Ghazālī notes that one of his major aims in writing the book was combining good organization with a forceful vindication of the correct position (*aṣrifu ʾl-ʿināyati fī-hi ilā ʾl-talqīni bayna ʾl-tartībi wa-ʾl-taḥqīq*). See also ibid., 1:33.21–34.1, where Ghazālī places the *Mustaṣfā* as a work of median length between the now lost larger work entitled *Tahdhīb al-Uṣūl* and the briefer *Mankhūl*. For a review of the debates within the Shāfiʿite biographical tradition about whether the *Mankhūl* was written either during Juwaynī's life or shortly after his death, see the editor's introduction to Ghazālī, *al-Mankhūl min Taʿlīqāt al-Uṣūl*, ed. Muḥammad Ḥasan Hītū, 2nd ed. (Damascus: Dār al-Fikr, 1970), 34–36.

[65] The *Mankhūl* is essentially based on Juwaynī's teachings in the field of legal theory. In the closing statement, Ghazālī explicitly notes that he restricted himself to his notes from Juwaynī's lectures (*taʿlīqāt*) in composing the work. Ghazālī, *Mankhūl*, 503.18–19.

[66] Already in the medieval period, Ghazālī enjoyed a reputation for composing extremely well-organized works. See Michael Cook, *Commanding Right and Forbidding Wrong in Islamic Thought* (Cambridge: Cambridge University Press, 2000), 250, where Cook reports that Ibn Ṭumlūs (d. 620/1223f.), the Spanish doctor and philosopher, lauded the "unprecedentedly well-ordered and well-arranged character" of Ghazālī's writings.

> the Divine address (*yafhamu ʾl-khiṭāb*). It is not possible to address inanimate bodies or animals or even insane people or children who do not have the capacity for discernment (*al-ṣabiyu alladhī lā yumiyyiz*). This is because the imposition of a moral duty requires an act of obedience (*al-ṭāʿa*) and compliance (*al-imtithāl*). These are possible only when there is an intent to comply (*qaṣd al-imtithāl*), and a condition for intending [an act] is knowledge of the object intended (*al-maqṣūd*) and comprehension (*fahm*) of the imposed duty (*al-taklīf*). Inherent (*mutaḍammin*) in every Divine address (*khiṭāb*) is the command, "Understand!" How can it be said to one who does not understand, "Understand"? Or how can someone who does not hear the voice (*al-ṣawt*), such as an inanimate object, be spoken to? And if a person sometimes linguistically comprehends (*yafhamu*) something but does not possess rationality or circumspection (*wa-lā yatathabbatu*), such as a person who is insane or lacks discrimination—addressing him is possible, but requiring compliance from him is not possible because it is not possible that he have a valid intention.[67]

If, as Ashʿarites hold, God's command is the only valid source for the imposition of duties, then it follows that the specific capacity relevant to the validity of any moral imposition should be the capacity to understand speech. Juwaynī's departure from Bāqillānī, confirmed and more explicitly articulated by Ghazālī, can be seen as an attempt to integrate this fundamental Ashʿarite theological commitment more closely with the relevant issues debated in legal theory. In a sense, the integration represents a further consolidation of legal theory along lines dictated by Ashʿarite moral epistemology—a moral epistemology that was defined against the reason-centric Muʿtazilite version.

Ghazālī takes the integration a step further along the argumentative lines Juwaynī set out in his creedal text, the *ʿAqīda al-Niẓāmiyya*, in which he rejected the Ashʿarite teaching that God could impose impossible obligations.[68] In the *Burhān*, his work on legal theory, Juwaynī based his rejection partly on a conception of agency different from that of Ashʿarī and partly on dismissal of the interpretation of certain Qurʾānic proof texts used by Ashʿarī and

[67] Ghazālī, *Mustaṣfā*, 1:158.6–14.

[68] Ghazālī's presentation of the Ashʿarī position on the possibility of God's imposing impossible obligations is essentially identical to Juwaynī's. Ibid., 1:163.10–15. For essentially the same argument in the *Mankhūl*, see Ghazālī, *Mankhūl*, 22.4–24.2.

those of his followers who agreed with him on the issue of impossible obligations. Ghazālī similarly rejects the idea that God could impose impossible obligations. But it is not clear from the *Mustaṣfā* alone whether his rejection draws on a different conception of agency.[69] At the very least, Ghazālī seems to think that neither commitment to the idea of God's simultaneous creation of capacity and act nor commitment to the lack of a capacity's effectiveness (*taʾthīr*) over the act commits one to the doctrine of impossible obligations.[70] His arguments against the proof texts adduced by Ashʿarī and his followers mirror, for the most part, those of Juwaynī.[71] Ghazālī argues that God's imposition of impossible duties is itself impossible not "because of its intrinsic evil,[72] or because of the corruption that originates from it,[73] or because of [the impossibility of the] grammatical form [which institutes it]."[74] Rather, the impossible obligation

[69] In the *Mankhūl*, Ghazālī notes that the temporally created power has a "connection" to the act over which it is a power, even if they are simultaneous (*lil-qudrati ʾl-ḥādithati taʿalluqun bi-ʾl-maqdūr*). The editor of the *Mankhūl*, Muḥammad Ḥasan Hītū, glosses "connection" (*taʿalluq*) as meaning that the power effectuates the act (*lil-qudrati ʾl-ḥādithati taʾthīrun fī ʾl-maqdūr*) and observes that the same position is ascribed to Bāqillānī. He notes that the effectiveness position is attributed to Ashʿarī by others but that Ashʿarī explicitly endorses the anti-effectiveness position in two of his works. See Ghazālī, *Mankhūl*, 26.1 and footnote 1. On Ghazālī's conception of physical agency, see Gimaret, *Théories*, 128–32; Frank, *Al-Ghazālī and the Ashʿarite School*, 42–47.

[70] See Ghazālī, *Mustaṣfā*, 1:167.1–2, where he says that "our objective regarding this issue [i.e., impossible obligations] does not depend on inquiry into either the way in which power (*qudra*) is effective [over the act] or its time."

[71] For the Abū Jahl argument, see ibid., 1:164.2–13. For the argument based on Qurʾān 2:286 (the prayer "Do not burden us with what we cannot bear!"), see ibid., 1:163.17–164.1. For the arguments based on verses 7:166 and 2:65 ("Become apes, despised!"), 17:50 ("Become stones or iron!"), 2:117 ("Be! And it is"), see ibid., 1:164.3–10. Ghazālī cites more examples of verses demonstrating this phenomenon, but his argument is essentially the same as Juwaynī's, namely that while these verses employ the grammatical imperative form, God is not expressing a demand in them, and therefore they do not constitute imposition of a duty. Rather, the command form, usually construed as indicating an imposition, is in these verses used to express either the impossibility of human endeavor (*taʿjīz*) or God's greatness. For this argument, see ibid., 1:165.3–7. For arguments of the same type in the *Mankhūl* against the construction given to proof texts by those on the other side of the issue, see Ghazālī, *Mankhūl*, 24.4–8 and 27.5–28.3.

[72] The idea that the imposition of impossible obligations is invalid because it would be intrinsically evil or unjust is a Muʿtazilite argument, hence Ghazālī's explicit denial of it as the motivating reason behind his rejection.

[73] What this corruption (*mafsada*) refers to is not clear to me.

[74] Ghazālī mentions this possibility because in a previous paragraph he quotes an interlocutor who asserts that the potential reasons for rejecting the doctrine of impossible obligations can be enumerated as the impossibility of the grammatical form that conveys the imposition, the impossibility of the content of the imposition, a corruption connected to the putative imposition, and the argument that it contradicts wisdom. See Ghazālī, *Mustaṣfā*, 1:164.14–15.

> is logically impossible because of its unintelligibility (*yumtanaʿ li-maʿnā-hu*). The meaning of the imposition of an obligation (*taklīf*) is a demand (*ṭalab*) [to do] something that involves hardship (*kulfa*), and a demand requires (*yastadʿī*) an object that is demanded (*maṭlūb*). It is agreed (*bi-ʾl-ittifāq*) that this must be something understandable (*mafhūm*) to the moral agent (*mukallaf*). It is valid to say, "Move!" (*taḥarruk*), if movement is understandable. If the agent is told, "Shlove!" (*tamarruk*—a nonsensical word), it does not impose a duty, because its meaning is neither intelligible (*maʿqūl*) nor understandable (*mafhūm*). It has no meaning in and of itself. It is a vacuous utterance (*lafẓ muhmal*).[75]

As argued earlier, Juwaynī's and Ghazālī's identification of the specific capacity to understand speech as the basis of moral agency can be interpreted as a move to bring aspects of legal theory into tighter integration with a fundamental theological commitment to a Divine command moral epistemology, and thus as a move *away from* Muʿtazilism. By contrast, the use of arguments based on the same capacity to reject the doctrine that God can impose impossible obligations can be seen, at the very least, as a mitigation of the determinist implications of a core Ashʿarite doctrine and thus as a contradictory move *toward* Muʿtazilism. These contradictory conceptual movements can be explained by the overall motivation to preserve the integrity of the Sharīʿa as well as by a Shāfiʿite ideology of textual conservatism. Both Ashʿarī's conception of agency as consisting in a simultaneous and noncausal relation between the power to act and the act itself and the possibility of impossible obligations posed acute threats to a believer's commonsensical connection to the moral duties enshrined in the Sharīʿa. Juwaynī's and Ghazālī's ingenuity lies in using the logic inherent in an Ashʿarite-inspired Divine command morality to alleviate the pernicious effects of a similarly Ashʿarite-inspired conception of agency—the doctrine that God could impose impossible obligations.

Like Juwaynī, Ghazālī uses the idea that the capacity for linguistic comprehension is the basis of moral agency to argue that coercion does not

[75] Ibid., 1:165.8–11. In the *Mankhūl*, Ghazālī provides essentially the same argument, noting that a command is a demand, which requires that there be an object that is demanded. If the object demanded is inherently unintelligible, the act of demanding is logically impossible. Ghazālī, *Mankhūl*, 24.9–11.

undermine moral agency in the way that intoxication, heedlessness, and forgetful acts do.[76] Ghazālī writes:

> The condition for the imposition of moral duties (*taklīf*) on the moral agent (*mukallaf*) is the [capacity for] listening (*samāʿ*) and linguistic understanding (*fahm*), and this is missing from insane individuals and animals. A coerced person understands, and his actions lie within the ambit of possibility (*wa-fiʿlu-hu fī ḥayyizi ʾl-imkān*), because he is capable of realizing the act or of omitting it.[77]

The rest of Ghazālī's engagement with the issue of coercion and moral agency revolves around a law-inspired argument, specifically relating to cases in which a person is coerced to perform a duty.[78]

In form, the law-inspired argument is similar to that advocated by Bāqillānī and also those found in Ḥanafite sources. It amounts to the following inductive argument: if the law does not allow coercion to cancel out responsibility in at least some cases, then there is nothing intrinsic to it that impedes moral agency. Ghazālī identifies three such cases in which coercion does not affect the agent's obligation to carry out a duty:

1. An agent can be coerced to, for example, kill a snake that is on the verge of killing another Muslim.[79]
2. A non-Muslim who does not belong to a contractually protected group can be coerced to convert to Islam.[80]

[76] Ghazālī, *Mustasfā*, 1:159.22.

[77] Ibid., 1:170.5–7. In the *Mankhūl*, Ghazālī identifies the ability to comply with the command as a condition for valid moral agency (*sharṭu ʾl-taklīfu ʾl-tamakkunu mina ʾl-imtithāl*). He also notes that even when an agent is coerced, his choosing an action remains (*īthāra-hu bāqun*) and she is capable of performing it (*mutamakkinun mina ʾl-iqdām*). Notably, Ghazālī does not explicitly make reference to the capacity for linguistic comprehension (*fahm*) here, but he does make reference to the act of compliance, which he relates specifically to linguistic comprehension in the *Mustaṣfā*. See Ghazālī, *Mankhūl*, 32.7–8.

[78] Ghazālī, *Mustaṣfā*, 1:170.12–13. [79] Ibid., 1:170.9–10.

[80] Ibid., 1:170.10. Ghazālī also addresses the issue of forced conversion in one of his books on Shāfiʿite positive law, arguing that the coerced conversion to Islam of a non-Muslim combatant (*ḥarbī*) is valid, whereas that of a non-Muslim member of a contractually protected group (*dhimmī*) is not. Ghazālī, *al-Wasīṭ fī al-Madhhab*, ed. Abū ʿAmr al-Ḥusaynī b. ʿUmar b. ʿAbd al-Raḥīm, 1st ed., 4 vols. (Beirut: Manshūrāt Muḥammad ʿAlī Bayḍūn; Dār al-Kutub al-ʿIlmiyya, 2001), 3:273.9–10. The fact of coercion does not undermine the unprotected non-Muslim's successful performance of the universal duty to convert to Islam (*qad addā mā kullifa*), Ghazālī, *Mustaṣfā*, 1:170.11. For a general survey of some Sunnī ḥadīth and exegetical and legal materials on debates surrounding the categories of persons whom it is legitimate to coerce to convert, see Yohanan Friedmann, *Tolerance and Coercion in Islam: Interfaith Relations in the Muslim Tradition* (Cambridge: Cambridge University Press, 2003), 106–20.

3. A person can be coerced to pour out wine, since drinking it is prohibited (*īrāqat al-khamr*).[81]

Since coercion is legitimate in these cases, Ghazālī concludes that there is nothing in coercion per se that undermines moral agency.

Ghazālī ends the section on coercion and moral agency by addressing a possible conceptual difficulty. He notes that complicity with a command counts as an act of obedience only when the agent is motivated by and responding to the call of duty. Yet when a coerced agent performs the same act in order to escape from someone's sword, he is not responding to the call of duty. He could only be considered to respond to the call of duty if he would have performed the act even if uncoerced.[82] Ghazālī does not attempt to solve the dilemma but simply ends the section by encouraging his readers to be aware of this subtle point—*fal-yantabihu li-hādhi-hi ʾl-daqīqa*.[83]

4. CONCLUSION: EXTERNALLY MOTIVATED AND INTERNALLY JUSTIFIED CHANGE IN ASHᶜARISM

All three of the Ashᶜarites surveyed in this chapter were committed to the position that coercion does not undermine moral agency, but why they thought so varied. The explicit change over time in the arguments used to defend a constant position is the most interesting feature of classical Ashᶜarite thinking on coercion and moral agency. Ashᶜarite work on this issue brought out a tension between commitment to God's monopoly over creation, including volitional human acts, and commitment to the idea that human beings are responsible for their acts, a position taken for granted in Islamic law. This tension surfaced most clearly and forcefully in Bāqillānī's use of the impossible obligations argument as a justification for his position that coercion cannot undermine moral agency. Juwaynī rejected this argument's validity, even as he acknowledged that the founder of his theological tradition, Ashᶜarī, had

[81] Ghazālī, *Mustaṣfā*, 1:170.16. Coercing someone to pour out wine is probably related to the general duty to command right and forbid wrong, and specifically to the legitimacy of destroying forbidden objects. For Ghazālī's take on this duty, see Cook, *Commanding Right and Forbidding Wrong in Islamic Thought*, 440.

[82] Ghazālī, *Mustaṣfā*, 170.17–21.

[83] Ibid., 170.20.

accepted the rational possibility that God could impose impossible obligations. Juwaynī's rejection of the possibility of impossible obligations was grounded not in a substantive ethical commitment (i.e., that it would be unjust for God to impose such obligations, as the Muʿtazilites argued), but in the view that the conveyance of an impossible obligation is linguistically unintelligible. This argument drew on another core value of Ashʿarism—its Divine command epistemology of morality, which relates to the second modification Juwaynī made to his Ashʿarite inheritance. For Bāqillānī, the basis for moral agency had been the possession of reason. Juwaynī changed this basis to the specific capacity to understand language (*fahm*). This modification added to the force of his rejection of the possibility of impossible obligations. Together, the two modifications amount to an ingenious solution that allowed Ashʿarite theology to jettison a concept that challenged widespread ideas, external to Ashʿarism, about moral responsibility without falling into Muʿtazilite objectivism, and further enabled the integration of the Ashʿarite position on coercion and moral agency with Ashʿarism's other core position, Divine voluntarism.

The modification of Ashʿarite arguments over time illustrates two points, which also apply to the Muʿtazilite tradition. It seems that, in contrast to jurists, classical theologians put a premium on systematic coherence, with a few core positions taking pride of place in the center of their theoretical frameworks. These core positions controlled the elaboration of subsidiary positions within a given domain (the domain for both the Muʿtazilites and the Ashʿarites being moral agency) by imposing a rule of noncontradiction. The example of change in argumentation also demonstrates the mechanics of change within theology, which has not garnered as much scholarly attention as that within law. In many respects, the way in which change unfolded in these theological traditions bears a strong resemblance to the processes of change and elaboration that Kuhn identified as taking place in the "normal science" phase of scientific traditions.[84] In the normal science phase, scientists work to fill in gaps suggested by the paradigms to which they are committed, or they strive to refine the paradigm's internal coherence. This

[84] Thomas S. Kuhn, *The Structure of Scientific Revolutions* (Chicago: University of Chicago Press, 2012), 23–34, especially 33–34.

is similar to what we witnessed in Ashʿarism. Neither Juwaynī nor Ghazālī suggested abandoning the inherited position that coercion does not impede moral agency. Instead, they rejected some of the arguments put forward by previous Ashʿarite theologians because these placed the tradition in too overt a conflict with external constraints. However, their rejection of these arguments was not justified on grounds external to the tradition, but rather on grounds valued internally.

Similarly, within the Muʿtazilite tradition, ʿAbd al-Jabbār and Ibn Mattawayh rejected Abū ʾl-Hudhayl's position that coercion renders apostasy (construed as lying about one's true beliefs) permitted. They also rejected the position of the Jubbāʾīs that acts committed by agents who are asleep or negligent cannot be evil. In both cases, the adjustment to inherited doctrine was motivated by a desire to sustain a morally objectivist epistemology, an internal constraint within Muʿtazilism.

3

Defining Coercion in Ḥanafism

1. INTRODUCTION

The following four hypothetical cases illustrate the issues at stake in this chapter.

Scenario 1: You are a pious Muslim and consequently avoid the consumption of foods that God has forbidden, such as pork. One day you find yourself confronted by a well-known gangster who loves humiliating people for no reason other than that it gives him pleasure. He says to you: "If you don't eat this pork-based pepperoni pizza, I'll kill you." You eat the pizza, then run to the local Ḥanafite mufti and explain what happened. You ask: "Was it permissible for me to eat the pizza?"

Scenario 2: On another day, the gangster accosts you again. He's eating a club sandwich. Stupidly, you ask whether the bacon is pork-based. He replies, "Why yes it is and if you don't eat this sandwich, I will slap you." You were an only child with overprotective parents and hence turned out kind of a wimp. You give in and eat the club sandwich, then run to the local Ḥanafite mufti and ask him: "Was it permissible for me to eat the club sandwich?"

Scenario 3: You are a happily married Muslim man and you love your wife. She's the apple of your eye. Unfortunately, the gangster fancies your wife and he intends to get you out of the picture. According to Ḥanafite law, a man may irrevocably divorce his wife merely by uttering the words "I divorce you" three times. The gangster says to you: "If you don't irrevocably divorce your wife, I'll kill you." You comply and run to the local Ḥanafite mufti and ask him: "Have I really irrevocably divorced my wife?"

Scenario 4: You are walking along the road. The gangster accosts you. He says: "If you don't kill Zayd, I'll kill you." You kill Zayd. You run to the mufti to tell him what happened. You ask him: "Have I sinned? And can I be prosecuted?"

The question posed by Muʿtazilites in Chapter 1 and by Ashʿarites in Chapter 2 was simple and direct: does the presence of compulsion or coercion negate moral agency? The questions of coercion that classical legal scholars grappled with were much more intricate. As can be seen in these hypothetical cases, a much larger number of factors are at play. Does it matter whether the gangster's threat is of death or a single slap? Does the presence of a threat against one's life undermine the validity of a divorce? Does such a threat have any effect on the moral quality of the act of homicide? What about legal responsibility for homicide? Who is held legally responsible for the death?

The issues that arise in concrete cases involving coercion are often as varied as the types of norms that govern the wide variety of acts addressed by Islamic law. The jurists not only made laws that prohibited, permitted, and punished, but also identified the features that made a given performance legally valid. For example, in cases related to ritual observance, legal scholars devoted considerable efforts to the precise description of the acts that satisfy a given ritual duty: only a person in a state of ritual purity may perform a religiously valid prayer (*ṣalāt*). In cases of contract, the issues discussed in the legal literature have to do with the conditions necessary for the validity of particular kinds of transactions: a legally insane person cannot engage in valid commercial transactions. In criminal law, they spilled much ink about the conditions necessary to establish liability for punishment: the presence of doubt in the case of a crime has the potential to impede the application of a defendant's punishment. For torts, the central issues often revolve around duties of financial compensation. Each domain of the law is governed by concerns specific to that domain, and thus the effects of coercion within the domain differ from one field of law to the next. Yet underlying all coercion cases is one vexatious question: how does one determine that an instance of coercion that affects responsibility in some way has occurred? The answer to this question, as discussed in the Introduction, has divided coercion theorists in the contemporary Anglo-American philosophical tradition into two broad camps, the descriptivists and the normativists.

Although the classical Islamic legal scholars who grappled with formulating a legal standard for coercion do not themselves explicitly articulate similar concerns about the role of moral judgments as their Anglo-American counterparts, it is possible to divide the Ḥanafite and Shāfiʿite approaches broadly into less and more descriptive camps. The distinction is only relative because both legal traditions acknowledge at least some cases in which they admit that coercion has absolutely no effect on the normative consequences of an act. While the Shāfiʿites explicitly recognize a very small number of such cases, the Ḥanafites, in contradistinction to all other Sunnite and Shīʿite legal traditions, exclude a rather large number of practices from the potential purview of coercion's consequence-altering effects. Put this way, the Shāfiʿites tend to adopt a *more* descriptivist approach than the Ḥanafites.

What sets the Ḥanafites apart is their unique position on coercion's ineffectiveness in undermining the validity of unilateral speech acts. The paradigmatic instance of a unilateral speech act is the pronouncement of divorce, but other speech acts such as emancipations, marriages, vows, and oaths are similarly regarded as valid even if coerced. Ḥanafites also regarded the validity of certain ritual acts such as fasting, the performance of the formal prayer (*ṣalāt*), and the state of consecration for pilgrimage (*iḥrām*) as unaffected by the presence of coercion. This stance meant, for example, that no matter how severe the threat issued by a credible coercer, and no matter what the resultant effect on the psychology of the coerced, a pronouncement of divorce is still valid.[1] These coercion-resistant laws greatly constrained the Ḥanafite formulation of a definition of coercion, and thus form the main internal constraint on the elaboration of Ḥanafite coercion jurisprudence.

Ḥanafite attempts at a legal definition of coercion started with attention to its specific potential effects on different classes of legal acts, and these consequently form the starting point of our investigation, too. We begin by examining the writings of one of the founders of the tradition,

[1] However, coercion does have an effect on some of the normal financial consequences of a divorce. The Ḥanafites hold that a man who is coerced to divorce a wife with whom he has not consummated the marriage has the right to recover the market value of the marriage gift (*mahr*) from the coercer, even though the coercion has no effect on the validity of the divorce. Similarly, a man coerced to emancipate his slave has the right to recover the market price of the slave from the coercer, even though the coercion has no effect on the validity of the emancipation.

Muḥammad b. al-Ḥasan al-Shaybānī, who wrote an incredible amount on the topic. After that, we survey the rules that made up the bedrock of classical Ḥanafite coercion jurisprudence as presented in the most popular handbooks of the tradition from the fourth/tenth and fifth/eleventh centuries. Against this background, we then look very closely at three specific questions: How did the Ḥanafites justify their position that coercion can, at times, render previously prohibited acts permissible or excused? How did they justify the related claim that coercion can, in some situations, transfer the legal consequences of a coerced act from the coerced to the coercer? And how did the Ḥanafites square the fact that coercion's ability to alter the consequences of an act depend on the type of act coerced with their remarks on its uniform effects on the psychology of the coerced?

The answers that the Ḥanafites developed for these questions constitute an important component of Ḥanafite coercion jurisprudence, and as was the case with the theological traditions, Ḥanafism's internal constraints go a long way in explaining the character and development of its rationality over time. While in the theological traditions, the internal constraint consisted of the tradition's commitment to a couple of core positions, Ḥanafite scholars were constrained by commitment to a corpus of inherited laws defining the effects of coercion on responsibility for a set of paradigmatic acts. Throughout the history of classical Ḥanafism, no Ḥanafite ever attempted to revise these laws. Even as Ḥanafites developed an ever-refined legal formulation of coercion, these core Ḥanafite laws formed the boundary which no attempted conceptualization transgressed or diluted. However, this did not mean that commitment to the corpus of coercion laws precluded development in Ḥanafite coercion jurisprudence. In fact, the inherited corpus of laws encouraged scholarly inquiry in particular directions. As was the case with Muʿtazlism, the Ḥanafites ended up developing an empirical account of coercion's impact on human psychology consistent with and supportive of their coercion laws. Over time, there was a discernible development towards an ever more coherent legal formulation of coercion culminating in a classical theory that synthesized scriptural interpretation with empirical ideas about the psychology of coercion and was fully consistent with Ḥanafite coercion laws.

2. THE SOURCES FOR ḤANAFITE COERCION JURISPRUDENCE

My discussion of Ḥanafite legal thought relies on the legal works of six Ḥanafite jurists: Muḥammad b. al-Ḥasan al-Shaybānī (d. 188/804), Abū Jaʿfar al-Ṭaḥāwī (d. 321/933), Abū Bakr al-Jaṣṣāṣ (d. 370/981), Abū Zayd al-Dabūsī (d. 430/1039), Abū Bakr al-Sarakhsī (d. 483/1090), and ʿAlī b. Muḥammad Bazdawī (d. 482/1089).

Muḥammad b. al-Ḥasan al-Shaybānī is regarded as one of three most important figures in the Ḥanafite tradition, along with Abū Ḥanīfa (d. 150/767), the eponymous founder of the school, and Abū Yūsuf (d. 182/798), Abū Ḥanīfa's student.[2] Shaybānī, too, was a student of Abū Ḥanīfa, but only for a couple of years. He studied with Abū Yūsuf for a much longer time, collecting his legal opinions and those of Abu Ḥanīfa. His legal writings form the basis of what later Ḥanafites would come to identify as the most authoritative expression of the opinions of the tradition's founders (*ẓāhir al-riwāya*). He also studied with Mālik b. Anas (d. 179/795), hearing one recension of the latter's famous legal work, *Muwaṭṭaʾ*, from him and transmitting it accompanied by his own comments.

Among his many works, Shaybānī wrote extensively on the problem of coercion, devoting an independent "book," or major chapter, to it.[3] The chapter is divided into twenty-seven sections, each section devoted to a particular aspect of the problem.[4] In terms of length, this chapter far

[2] For basic biographical information on Shaybānī, his context, and his place in Ḥanafism, see Eric Chaumont, "al-Shaybānī," in *Encyclopedia of Islam, Second Edition*, ed. P. Bearman, et al. (Leiden: Brill, 1980–2004); Mehmet Boynukalın, *al-Aṣl: al-Muqaddima* (Beirut: Dār Ibn Ḥazm li-ʾl-Ṭibāʿah wa-al-Nashr wa-al-Tawzīʿ, 2012); Aḥmad b. Muḥammad Naṣīr al-Dīn Naqīb, *al-Madhhab al-Ḥanafī: Marāḥilu-hu wa Ṭabaqātu-hu, Ḍawābiṭu-hu wa Muṣṭalaḥātu-hu, Khaṣāʾiṣu-hu wa Muʾallafātu-hu*, 1st ed., 2 vols. (Riyadh: Maktabat al-Rushd, 2001), 1:65–67 and 1:112–14.

[3] Coercion is not typically addressed as an independent chapter in the writings of other legal traditions. For example, in Shāfiʿite works, discussion of the definition of legal coercion occurs in the chapter on divorce in the context of coercion's impact on divorce, and discussion of the problems of superior orders, rape, and coerced homicide occurs in the chapters devoted to criminal law.

[4] Norman Calder doubts that the published texts attributed to some of the earliest Muslim jurists can really be taken to represent their own work, as opposed to the cumulative legal thought of scholars belonging to succeeding generations. See Norman Calder, *Studies in Early Muslim Jurisprudence* (Oxford: Clarendon Press, 1993), 39–66. Behnam Sadeghi has persuasively criticized this view and shown that the features of the works that Calder took to be indicative of collective authorship were actually the result of the lecture/audition method of composing

surpasses anything written on the topic by his predecessors, his contemporaries, or his successors in any Islamic legal tradition,[5] and it served as the basis of coercion jurisprudence in the Ḥanafite tradition.

This naturally raises the question of why Shaybānī decided to devote such attention to the issue of coercion. It is possible that Shaybānī merely found the topic interesting and useful, and one that is especially conducive to the type of analysis for which he was (in)famous—elaboration and testing of the cogency of laws through casuistry and the positing of hypothetical scenarios. But there may be another motivation. The late fifth/eleventh-century Ḥanafite Sarakhsī records a report from one of Shaybānī's students, Muḥammad b. Samāʿa (d. 833/847), on the circumstances surrounding Shaybānī's completion of his book on coercion. Ibn Samāʿa recounts that when word got out that Shaybānī had finished a work on coercion, one of Shaybānī's colleagues reported him to the caliph, claiming that Shaybānī had called the caliph a criminal in the book. The caliph sent his police force to investigate. Apparently Ibn Samāʿa got wind of the impending arrival of the police force and was able to hide the volume by throwing it into a well on Shaybānī's property. As a result, the police could not find the incriminating book, and the caliph ended up apologizing to Shaybānī and sending him away with some money for his trouble. The book, though lost for a while, was eventually rediscovered, still intact, lying on a brick near the bottom of the well![6]

What is most interesting about the report is the suspicion and concern of the political authorities evinced in the legal discourse on coercion. Evidence of this phenomenon is not limited to Ibn Samāʿa's report: the founder of the Mālikite tradition, Mālik b. Anas, was reportedly beaten for transmitting a report that implied that coercion invalidates a pronouncement of

legal works. See Behnam Sadeghi, "The Authenticity of Two 2nd/8th Century Ḥanafī Legal Texts: the Kitāb al-Āthār and al-Muwaṭṭaʾ of Muḥammad b. al-Ḥasan al-Shaybānī," *Islamic Law and Society* 17 (2010).

[5] Shāfiʿī addresses the problem of coercion in several different places in his magnum opus, the *Umm*, but taken together, these discussions amount to fewer than ten pages. Shaybānī's discussion, by contrast, runs to 120 pages.

[6] For the report, see Abū Bakr Muḥammad b. Aḥmad al-Sarakhsī, *Kitāb al-Mabṣūṭ*, ed. Abū ʿAbd Allāh Muḥammad Ḥasan Muḥammad Ḥasan Ismāʿīl al-Shāfiʿī, 1st ed., 30 vols. (Beirut: Dār al-Kutub al-ʿIlmiyya, 2001), 24:49.1–15.

divorce—the legal position he himself held.[7] In light of these reports, might Shaybānī's composition of a work of substantial length on the topic of coercion be at least in part politically motivated? I cannot undertake a thorough investigation of this issue here, but it is interesting to note that Shaybānī pays specific attention to the question of the possible effect of the political legitimacy of a power holder's coercion on responsibility for coerced acts by considering, in separate sections, the scenarios of coercion by a criminal,[8] by the agent of a legitimate ruler,[9] by a rebel, and even by a non-Muslim combatant.[10] The general thrust of his discussion is that coercion's effect on responsibility does not depend on the legitimacy of the political authority issuing the coercive threat. Shaybānī's jealous enemy who reported him to the caliph was thus largely right. If holding legitimate political authority is immaterial to coercion's effects on the cases considered in Shaybānī's book, then the caliph is indeed equal to the common criminal!

The intellectual activity of the generation of Ḥanafites after Shaybānī consisted of transmitting Ḥanafite doctrines, largely as recorded in the works of Shaybānī himself. The first Ḥanafite to compose a legal handbook summarizing the main positions of the tradition across all legal issues was the Egyptian scholar Abū Jaʿfar al-Ṭaḥāwī (d. 321/933).[11] Legal handbooks such

[7] For this report, see Yūsuf b. ʿAbd Allāh b. ʿAbd al-Barr, *al-Intiqāʾ fī Faḍāʾil al-Umma al-Thalātha al-Fuqahāʾ: Mālik b. Anas al-Aṣbaḥī al-Madanī, Muḥammad b. Idrīs al-Shāfiʿī al-Muṭṭalibī, wa Abī Ḥanīfa al-Nuʿmān b. Thābit al-Kūfī*, ed. ʿAbd al-Fattāḥ Abū Ghudda (Aleppo, Syria: Maktab al-Maṭbūʿāt al-Islāmiyya, 1997), 87–88. For a discussion of the politics surrounding the attitudes of early legal authorities toward coercion, see Syed, "Coercion in Classical Islamic Law and Theology," 55–58.

[8] For this, see the second section in Shaybānī's book on coercion in Muḥammad b. al-Ḥasan Shaybānī, *al-Aṣl*, ed. Mehmet Boynukalın, 13 vols. (Beirut: Dār Ibn Ḥazm lil-Ṭibāʿah wa-al-Nashr wa-al-Tawzīʿ, 2012), 7:305–13. The title of the section is "Chapter on that which is coerced by criminals who do not rely on interpretation" (*Bāb mā yukrihu ʿalay-hi ʾl-luṣūṣ ghayr al-mutaʾawwilīn*).

[9] See the third section in ibid., 7:322–27, entitled "Chapter on coercion in which a ruler's agent transgresses the limits of his delegated authority" (*Bāb min al-ikrāh alladhī yataʿaddā fī-hi al-ʿāmil mā umira bi-hi*).

[10] See the fifth section in ibid., 7:359–61, entitled "Chapter on the coercion by rebels who rely on a legitimating interpretation" (*Bāb ikrāh al-khawārij al-mutaʾawwilīn*). In this section, Shaybānī explicitly asserts that the political identity of the coercer, whether a criminal, a rebel, or a non-Muslim enemy combatant, is immaterial in the cases in which coercion renders normally prohibited things permitted. See ibid., 7:359.4–14.

[11] For information on Ṭaḥāwī, see Norman Calder, "al-Ṭaḥāwī, Aḥmad b. Muḥammad b. Salāma b. ʿAbd al-Malik al-Azdī al-Ḥad̲j̲rī Abū D̲j̲afar," in *Encyclopedia of Islam, Second Edition*, ed. P. Bearman, et al. (Leiden: Brill, 1980–2004). See also Muḥammad Zāhid al-Kawtharī, *al-Ḥāwī fī Sīrat al-Imām Abī Jaʿfar al-Ṭaḥāwī* (Cairo: Maṭbaʿat al-Anwār, 1368 [/1949]). According to Aḥmad al-Naqīb, a historian of Ḥanafism, Ṭaḥāwī was the first to collect the opinions of the three

as Ṭaḥāwī's contain little if any analysis or justification of the rules they present. Therefore, for a better sense of Ṭaḥāwī's legal thought, we must rely instead on his law-oriented ḥadīth commentary, *Sharḥ Maʿānī ʾl-Āthār*. The purpose of this work is to defend Ḥanafite laws against opponents who claim that the laws contradict established Prophetic ḥadīth.

The Baghdad-based Abū Bakr al-Jaṣṣāṣ (d. 391/982) was the leading Ḥanafite scholar in his day and age.[12] A number of his works have survived. Of particular relevance to the topic of coercion are his work on Qurʾānic exegesis and his recently published commentary on Ṭaḥāwī's legal handbook. Jaṣṣāṣ's works represent the first extensive sources for Ḥanafite coercion jurisprudence after the work of Shaybānī.

The Central Asian jurist Abū Zayd al-Dabūsī (d. 430/1039) is a prominent figure in the next generation of Ḥanafites.[13] Of his works, my analysis draws mostly on his recently edited book on comparative legal argumentation, the *Asrār*. The chapter organization of the book resembles that of books of positive law, though it is not a commentary on a legal handbook. It presents the basic Ḥanafite legal rules on each issue along with legal and scriptural justifications for those rules. Dabūsī's discussion unfolds largely in the form of a dialogue with Shāfiʿite legal rules and justifications. I also use, to a lesser extent, Dabūsī's work of legal theory (*Taqwīm Uṣūl al-Fiqh wa-Taḥdīd Adillat al-Sharʿ*). This work has recently been recognized as inaugurating a specifically Ḥanafite approach to legal theory (*uṣūl al-fiqh*).[14] It is the first Ḥanafite work of legal theory to devote a section to the topic of coercion.

founding jurists of Ḥanafism—Abū Ḥanīfa, Abū Yūsuf, and Shaybānī—and arrange them under chapter headings inspired by the organizational scheme found in the famous *Mukhtaṣar* of the Shāfiʿite scholar al-Muzanī. Muzanī was Ṭaḥāwī's uncle. Naqīb, *al-Madhhab al-Ḥanafī*, 2:462.

[12] On Jaṣṣāṣ, see O. Spies, "al-Djaṣṣāṣ, Aḥmad b. ʿAlī Abū Bakr al-Rāzī," in *Encyclopedia of Islam, Second Edition*, ed. P. Bearman, et al. (Leiden: Brill, 1980–2004). See also Murteza Bedir, "The Early Development of Ḥanafī *Uṣūl al-Fiqh*" (PhD, University of Manchester, 1999), 21–26.

[13] For information on Dabūsī, see Bedir, "Early Development," 26–30.

[14] Murteza Bedir identifies Jaṣṣāṣ as the originator of this tradition and Dabūsī as the introducer of important modifications to Jaṣṣāṣ's legacy in the field. Bedir isolates two features of a particularly Ḥanafite way of doing legal theory. He writes: "In the dominant Ḥanafī *uṣūl* tradition, every principle of *uṣūl* is put to the test of practical law of the school. This works in two ways, i.e. they, on the one hand, test practical law (*furūʿ*) with the theoretical law (*uṣūl*) (test of justification); on the other hand, more interestingly, they test the theoretical principles of *uṣūl* with the cases drawn from the practical jurisprudence (*furūʿ*)." Bedir, "Is there a Ḥanafī Uṣūl al-Fiqh?," *Sakarya Üniversitesi Ilahiyat Fakültesi Dergisi (Journal of Sakarya University Faculty of Theology)* 4, no. 2 (2001): 165–66 and 169.

Abū ʾl-Ḥusayn al-Qudūrī (d. 428/1037) is most famous within the Ḥanafite tradition for his legal handbook, which served as the object of a vast commentarial tradition.[15] His much larger, multivolume work of comparative law (*al-Tajrīd*) has also recently been edited and published. Much like the work of his contemporary Dabūsī's *Asrār*, this work is devoted to defending the legitimacy and coherence of Ḥanafite coercion jurisprudence, framed mostly as a response to Shāfiʿite positions and arguments.

The most important Ḥanafite of the succeeding generation is undoubtedly the Transoxanian jurist Abū Bakr al-Sarakhsī (d. 483/1090).[16] Sarakhsī's chapter on coercion in his monumental work of positive law, the *Mabsūṭ*, is the most voluminous source for coercion jurisprudence in the postformative period. The *Mabsūṭ* is a commentary on the legal handbook of an earlier Ḥanafite scholar, Marwazī.[17]

Our final source is the Transoxanian ʿAlī b. Muḥammad al-Bazdawī's (d. 482/1089) work of legal theory, *Kanz al-Wuṣūl ilā Maʿrifat al-Uṣūl*.[18] Bazdawī transforms Dabūsī's few remarks on coercion in his work of legal theory into an independent chapter. Unlike the previously mentioned works, Bazdawī's aim is not primarily to justify Ḥanafite positive legal rules. In fact, he cites scripture only once, and unlike other jurists, he does not indicate which legal rules were subject to disagreement among the founding fathers of the tradition. Rather, Bazdawī provides a legal principle-based discussion of how Ḥanafite coercion jurisprudence works in general.

[15] Naqīb claims that it is the most widely studied and commented-upon text in Ḥanafite history. See Naqīb, *al-Madhhab al-Ḥanafī*, 2:465. For a description of Quduri's handbook, including its influence within Ḥanafism through the ages, see ibid., 2:464–67. For basic biographical information, see the editors' introduction to a recently published work of his in Aḥmad b. Muḥammad al-Qudūrī, *al-Mawsūʿa al-Fiqhīyya al-Muqārana: al-Tajrīd*, ed. Muḥammad Aḥmad Sirāj and ʿAlī Jumʿa Muḥammad, 1st ed., 12 vols. (Cairo: Dār al-Salām li-ʾl-Ṭibāʿa wa al-Nashr wa al-Tawzīʿ wa al-Tarjama, 2004), 1:6–23.

[16] For biographical information, see Norman Calder, "al-Sarakhsī, Muḥammad b. Aḥmad b. Abī Sahl Abū Bakr, Shams al- Aʾimma," in *Encyclopedia of Islam, Second Edition*, ed. P. Bearman, et al. (Leiden: Brill, 1980–2004) and Bedir, "Early Development," 30–35.

[17] For information on Marwazī's work, see Naqīb, *al-Madhhab al-Ḥanafī*, 1:145. For basic biographical information, see ʿAbd al-Qādir b. Muḥammad al-Qurashī, *al-Jawāhir al-Muḍiyya fī Ṭabaqāt al-Ḥanafiyya*, ed. ʿAbd al-Fattāḥ Muḥammad al-Ḥulw, 2nd ed., 5 vols. (n.p.: Hajar li-ʾl-Ṭibāʿa wa al-Nashr wa al-Tawzīʿ, 1993), 3:313–15.

[18] For basic biographical information, see Bedir, "Early Development," 35–38, and Sayyid Riḍā Hāshimī, "Bazdawī," in *Dānishnāmah-ʾi jahān-i Islām*, ed. Aḥmad Ṭāhirī ʿIrāqī, Muṣṭafā Mīr Salīm, and Naṣr Allāh Pūrjavādī (Tehran: Bunyād-i Dāʾirat al-Maʿārif-i Islāmī, 1996–).

3. SHAYBĀNĪ'S LEGAL FORMULATION OF COERCION

Shaybānī's most focused attempt to formulate a legal definition of coercion is found in his discussion of the circumstances in which necessity renders certain prohibited acts either completely permitted or excused.

It is clear that the basis for Shaybānī's thinking about coercion's effect on moral responsibility is the Qurʾānic verses that permit believers to consume typically forbidden foods in circumstances of necessity. The specific verse cited by Shaybānī in his discussion of the issue (Qurʾān 2:173) reads as follows:

> God has only forbidden you carrion, and blood, and the flesh of the swine, and that over which other than God has been invoked. But there is no sin on one who is driven by necessity, without wanting to or going too far. For God is most forgiving, most merciful.[19]

Shaybānī regards this verse as the paradigm case legitimating the possibility that circumstances may transform something absolutely prohibited by God into something excused or even completely permissible. The two paradigmatic prohibitions Shaybānī deals with explicitly in his discussion of necessity are related to diet and apostasy. The reason why the necessity verses of the Qurʾān are applicable to coercion is because Shaybānī considers coercion a species of necessity.[20] The conceptual difficulty inherent in the invocation of necessity is establishing its precise boundaries. In the case of coercion, the central question is the following: threats of what kinds of harm, precisely, are coercive to the point of making previously prohibited acts as something wholly permissible or excused? After considering a number of concrete cases, Shaybānī asserts that the degree of coercion that may render a prohibited act as something permissible or excused arises only from threats against one's life or limb, or from threats of any act that may result in the loss of either life or limb.[21] He also stipulates that the coerced need not be certain

[19] For Shaybānī's citation of the verse, see Shaybānī, *al-Aṣl*, 7:414.3–5.

[20] See ibid., 7:306.11–12, where he states explicitly that "coercion is merely an analogical extension of necessity in the specific cases under discussion" (*wa-inna-mā yuqāsu ʾl-ikrāhu fī dhālika bi-ʾl-ḍārūra fī hādhihi ʾl-ashyāʾ*).

[21] See ibid., 7:305.14–16. The concrete cases that Shaybānī considers are demands that the victim consume carrion, pork, or wine, first on pain of death; then on pain of having a hand cut off, an eye poked out, or an ear, limb, or finger severed; and finally on pain of one hundred lashes of the whip. In all these cases, according to Shaybānī, the coercion is severe enough that

that the proposed threat would result in such loss; a probable expectation is sufficient to change the moral quality of the act demanded by the coercer.[22]

That only threats against life or limb are compellingly coercive was not the only position available to Shaybānī in his time. Shaybānī notes one position which held that the threshold is forty lashes, equivalent to the least severe divinely mandated punishment (*ḥadd*).[23] But he disagrees. For Shaybānī, what is dispositive is not the type of the act threatened by the coercer, but the fear experienced by the coerced. In response to the forty-lash proposal, he writes:

> Sometimes a man fears the loss of his life or limbs through fewer than forty lashes. Sometimes he does not fear it. What he ought to do, in our view, is [act according to] what he thinks in his heart will happen (*fa-huwa ʿinda-nā ʿalā mā waqaʿa fī ʾl-qalb min dhālika*).[24]

Shaybānī also applies the life-limb standard to the threat of imprisonment. If the threat is imprisonment, it is not automatically permitted for the victim to partake of the forbidden foods, because there is no immediate threat to life or limb, and Shaybānī's core criterion of necessity is thus not met. Only if the imprisoned victim is denied water and food to the point that he fears the loss of life or limb through starvation is he allowed to consume the forbidden substances.[25]

What if the coerced does not comply with the demand, perseveres against the threat, and ends up dying? Shaybānī's answer depends on the act demanded. If the demand is the consumption of prohibited foods, the refusal to the point of dying constitutes a sin. This is not the case when the coercer demands that the coerced apostatize, utter words of disbelief, or blaspheme against the Prophet. If the coerced refuses to give in to these demands and is killed as a consequence, he is Divinely rewarded. What

the consumption of the prohibited substances is permitted. But Shaybānī draws the line at the threat of a single lash of the whip, deeming it not legally coercive. See ibid., 7:305.1–11. But if the coerced thinks that the coercer will not in fact follow through with the threat, he is not permitted to consume the forbidden substances. *Wa-yakūnu ʿalay-hi akbar al-raʾy*; ibid., 7:305.16.

22 *Wa-yakūnu ʿalay-hi akbar al-raʾy*; ibid., 7:305.16.
23 For Shaybānī's presentation of this view, see ibid., 7:305.17–18.
24 Ibid., 7:305.20–21.
25 Ibid., 7:306.4–11.

accounts for the difference? Shaybānī points out that the only reason for the prohibition of foods such as carrion, pork, and wine is a Divine command. This being the case, Qurʾānic verses such as 2:173 render these specific prohibited foods wholly permitted in the presence of necessity, with the result that they become wholly similar to foods that are not prohibited in any way. By contrast, uttering words of disbelief or committing acts of injustice, such as sexual slander (*qadhf*), against other human beings are acts that God has never made permissible in any situation. In the case of apostasy, the presence of necessity merely creates a temporary dispensation to utter the words.[26] Refraining from these types of actions to the point of dying is meritorious because the intent of the coerced in defying the threat and refusing to comply with the demand is to glorify the religion (*arāda bi-tarki-hi an yaʿizza ʾl-dīn*), an intent that Shaybānī considers missing in the refusal to consume forbidden foods.[27]

While the standard for rendering certain prohibited actions either permitted or excused is fear of the loss of life or limb, a different standard applies to legal acknowledgments. Acknowledgments are statements that confirm a normatively significant past legal action, the legal significance of which is to confirm the legal effects of that past legal action. The paradigmatic example of an acknowledgment is a person's affirmation of an existing debt to another person. But there are other types of acts that also fall under the Ḥanafite category of acknowledgments, such as confessions to crimes or torts and admissions of paternity. The legal question for Shaybānī is whether coercion invalidates an acknowledgment. Does the fact that a person was coerced into making an acknowledgment render its legal consequences null and void? Shaybānī responds in the affirmative.[28] What, then, is coercive in the case of acknowledgments? Shaybānī claims that any threat whose actualization would result in severe pain is coercive in this context, in addition to threats against life or limb. As for imprisonment, Shaybānī refuses to identify a specific time limit, but he concludes that any threat of imprisonment or enchainment that causes severe anxiety (*ightimām*) is legally coercive. While he does not think that the threat of a single day's

[26] Ibid., 7:326.1–9 and 7:416.22–418.3.
[27] Ibid., 7:417.3.
[28] Ibid., 7:307.11–14.

imprisonment or enchainment meets that criterion, he ultimately favors delegating the empirical inquiry into what is and what is not coercive in such cases to a judge.[29]

Shaybānī's approach to coercion and responsibility was highly differentiated and domain-specific. For him, what is coercive to the point of affecting legal responsibility, either that of the coerced or that of the coercer, depended on what the coercer is demanding of the coerced. The impact of Shaybānī's approach on the subsequent development of Ḥanafite tradition was threefold. Most importantly, he enunciated the core legal rules that came to form the bedrock of Ḥanafite coercion jurisprudence—that is, the specific responsibility outcomes of coerced actions, such as coercion's lack of effect on the validity of divorce, its excusing of utterances of disbelief, and its invalidation of legal acknowledgments. None of the Ḥanafite jurists discussed in this book departed from the laws articulated by Shaybānī, even regarding those cases in which Shaybānī recorded disagreements among the founding members of the tradition. Shaybānī also bequeathed to his successors a substantial justificatory framework for many aspects of Ḥanafite coercion jurisprudence. He provided a list of earlier esteemed authorities who had held the same positions and cited Prophetic ḥadīth and reports from the Prophet's companions that supported the Ḥanafite positions. His interpretation of coercion as a type of necessity and therefore rooted in the Qurʾānic text and his identification of the fear of loss of life or limb as the empirical standard that triggers the normative transformation of some types of prohibited acts are the foundations for later Ḥanafite jurisprudence on the issue of coercion, even as later Ḥanafites continued to add to and refine this aspect of his legacy.

4. INTERNAL CONSTRAINT: ḤANAFITE COERCION LAWS

Shaybānī's work on coercion is large and unwieldy, two features that did not make it a very useful introductory text to the core laws of the tradition. About a hundred years after Shaybānī, Ḥanafite scholars sought to rectify these deficiencies by producing slim, single-volume summations of the entire corpus

[29] Ibid., 7:307.16–308.2: "What the judge (*ḥākim*) sees as coercive is coercive, and what he does not see as coercive leads him to uphold the validity of the acknowledgment."

of Ḥanafite laws as found in Shaybānī's and Abū Yūsuf's legal works.[30] I rely on these volumes for much the same reason that they are taught to this day by Ḥanafite scholars and memorized by students: they provide a succinct overview of the core laws that make up Ḥanafite coercion jurisprudence. These laws are presented over the next few pages and subsequently summarized in Table 3.1. Because Ḥanafite coercion jurisprudence is highly differentiated, an overview of the entire corpus of coercion laws is necessary before delving deeper into the conceptual structure of Ḥanafite legal thinking on coercion and responsibility.

The following discussion focuses on attempts to formulate standards for defining legally admissible coercion and laws concerning the impact of coercion on different types of speech acts, on prohibitions related to the consumption of illicit foods and beverages, and on prohibitions related to causing physical or financial harm to others.

Like Shaybānī, the authors of the legal handbooks define the type of threat that justifies the consumption of normally forbidden items such as carrion, pork, or wine as a threat that is directed against one's life or limb or entails some other form of physical harm that one fears will lead to the likely loss of life or limb.[31] Confronted with such a threat, the coerced is permitted to consume substances that are ordinarily illicit. If the coerced refuses and perishes

[30] The emergence of such summations in the early part of the third/ninth century seems to have been a trans-tradition phenomenon originating in Egypt. See, for instance, the handbook of the Mālikite Ibn ʿAbd al-Ḥakam (d. 229/814), the Shāfiʿite handbooks of Buwayṭī (d. 231/846) and Muzanī (d. 264/877), and the Ḥanafite handbooks of Ṭaḥāwī (d. 321/933) and Marwazī (d. 334/975). For basic information on the Ḥanafite handbooks, see Kaya, "Continuity and Change in Islamic Law: the Concept of Madhhab and the Dimensions of Legal Disagreement in Hanafi Scholarship of the Tenth Century," 212, footnote 5. For an analysis of Buwayṭī's legal handbook, see Ahmed El Shamsy, "The First Shāfiʿī: the Traditionalist Legal Thought of Abū Yaʿqūb al-Buwayṭī (d. 231/846)," *Islamic Law and Society* 14, no. 3 (2007). For a comparison of Buwayṭī's and Muzanī's legal handbooks, see ibid., 334–336. For an analysis of Ibn ʿAbd al-Ḥakam's handbook, see Jonathan E. Brockopp, "The Minor Compendium of Ibn ʿAbd al-Ḥakam (d. 214/829) and Its Reception in the Early Mālikī School," *Islamic Law and Society* 12, no. 2 (2005). Fadel argues that the legal handbooks of the seventh/thirteenth century sought to simplify and pare down the legal doctrines accumulated over the previous centuries. He thus interprets the emergence and popularization of the legal handbooks in this period among the Mālikites specifically as a type of codification of Islamic law. See Mohammad Fadel, "The Social Logic of Taqlīd and the Rise of the Mukhtaṣar," *Islamic Law and Society* 3 (1996): especially 219–33. It is not clear, however, that the same argument can be made for the handbooks of the third/ninth and fourth/tenth centuries.

[31] See, for instance, Aḥmad b. Muḥammad al-Ṭaḥāwī, *Mukhtaṣar al-Ṭaḥāwī*, ed. Abū al-Wafā al-Afghānī (Hyderabad: Lajnat Iḥyāʾ al-Kutub al-Nuʿmānīyya, 1370[/1950]), 405.13–407.9. Ṭaḥāwī lists the following examples: a threat against one's life, the threat to chop a hand or

as a result, he has sinned.[32] Lesser threats, such as the threat of imprisonment, do not transform the prohibition into permission.

The authors add that the threat must be credible. As Qudūrī puts it, the threat must be made by someone who can follow through with its execution.[33] This qualification for the coercer is stated explicitly only in the law on consuming illicit foods, but it is safe to assume that it applies also to all other rules that deal with coercion.

Life- or limb-threatening coercion *excuses* but does not fully permit apostasy. The coerced individual is not held legally or morally responsible for blasphemous utterances. However, in contrast to the coerced consumption of prohibited foods and beverages, in the case of apostasy the Ḥanafites considered refusal to comply with the coercer's demands to the point of being killed or harmed meritorious.[34]

The prohibitions against the consumption of illicit foods and apostasy do not involve the interests of other people, but the prohibitions against murder and rape do. These prohibitions involve protecting innocents from harm. How coercion interacts with these moral valuations elicited disagreement within the tradition. In fact, these issues tended to be the ones that garnered the lowest degree of consensus amongst Muslim scholars. On the issue of coerced homicide, for example, the discussion centered on a hypothetical case in which a coercer threatens the life of the coerced if the latter does not kill a particular person. What is the legal penalty if the coerced actually commits the act in these circumstances? According to Ṭaḥāwī, the founding fathers disagreed on whether the coerced, the coercer, or both are held legally responsible for the homicide. Abū Ḥanīfa held that the coercer is liable for retaliation (*qiṣāṣ*), the most severe punishment, which in this case would be execution,

other limb off, and the threat of a hundred or so lashes of the whip. Marwazī similarly says that the threat of death renders the consumption of prohibited substances permitted. He adds that some scholars defined coercion in such cases as the threat of a minimum of forty lashes, the least severe *ḥadd* penalty. See Sarakhsī, *al-Mabsūṭ*, 24:59.1–2. See also Aḥmad b. Muḥammad al-Qudūrī, *Mukhtaṣar al-Qudūrī fī al-Fiqh al-Ḥanafī*, ed. Kāmil Muḥammad Muḥammad ʿUwayḍa, 1st ed. (Beirut: Dār al-Kutub al-ʿIlmiyya, 1997), 229.1–230.6.

[32] For this position, see Sarakhsī, *al-Mabsūṭ*, 24:172.1–2 and Qudūrī, *Mukhtaṣar*, 229.7–10. Ṭaḥāwī does not address the issue of whether refraining from committing the demanded act in an instance of coercion is sinful.

[33] Ṭaḥāwī speaks of a threat made by a thief or someone else; for Marwazī, such a coercer is the leader of a Muslim or *dhimmī* gang.

[34] Ṭaḥāwī does not discuss the issue of apostasy. See Qudūrī, *Mukhtaṣar*, 229.10–230.1.

while the coerced is not. Abū Yūsuf held that the coercer is liable for paying the appropriate amount of blood money to the victim's heirs, while the coerced is entirely absolved of legal responsibility for the act. Finally, Zufar, another early Ḥanafite authority, held that the coerced is to be executed, arguing that coercion does not legitimize murder. Ṭaḥāwī explicitly endorses the latter position as being better than the other two.[35] Qudūrī does not mention the difference of opinion among the founding jurists and simply states that even life-threatening coercion does not excuse murder. If the coerced individual succumbs to the coercion and carries out the murder, she has committed a sin (*ithm*) and becomes subject to retaliation.[36] Marwazī presents only Abū Ḥanīfa's and Shaybānī's position: when the life of the coerced is threatened and he kills another person as a result, the coercer is held liable for the maximum possible penalty (retaliation), and the coerced is not legally liable.[37]

The case of coerced rape is similar to that of coerced murder. All three handbook authors record disagreement among the founding jurists on the appropriate legal penalty in a case in which a coercer threatens a man's life if he does not rape a particular person. Ṭaḥāwī records two different opinions for Abū Ḥanīfa. According to one, the coerced is to be punished (*yuḥadd*) for the crime of fornication (*zinā*). According to the other, apparently shared by Abū Yūsuf, if the coercer is the ruler, the coerced is not to be punished, but if the coercer is someone other than the ruler, the coerced is liable for punishment. Shaybānī opined that if the coercer is not the ruler but his method of coercion resembles that of the ruler, the coerced is not to be punished for the crime. Ṭaḥāwī derives Zufar's position on the issue via analogy from his stance on coerced murder—the coerced ought to be punished—and proclaims that this is the correct position. Both Marwazī and Qudūrī reproduce the same opinions, with slight differences, but unlike Ṭaḥāwī, neither endorses a specific view.[38]

In all of these cases, the coercer demands that the coerced commit a forbidden act, whether the consumption of illicit foods or the unwarranted harming of others. But how does coercion interact with acts that are in the vast majority of circumstances morally not prohibited, such as contracting a sale or marriage,

[35] Ṭaḥāwī, *Mukhtaṣar*, 409.14–410.19. [36] Qudūrī, *Mukhtaṣar*, 230.3–4.

[37] Marwazī enunciates the rule in the context of the case of a government agent sent to a rural district by the caliph, who commands someone, on pain of death, to kill someone else illegally. Sarakhsī, *al-Mabsūṭ*, 24:84.1–3.

[38] See ibid., 24:103.1–104.1 and Qudūrī, *Mukhtaṣar*, 230.6–8.

or performing a divorce? Here the Ḥanafites make a curious distinction. On the one hand, in contrast to the cases where the coercer demands the consumption of illicit substances, in which only threats against life or limb count as coercive, in cases where the coercer demands one to engage in a commercial transaction, such as selling or buying property or to acknowledge a debt, threats of beatings, amputations, and imprisonment are also deemed legally coercive. Such threats, just like threats against life or limb, permit the coerced to cancel commercial exchanges after the coercion has passed and immediately invalidate legal acknowledgments.[39] On the other hand, in accordance with ancient Kufan legal doctrine,[40] not even threats against one's life can invalidate the legal consequences of acts such as divorce and emancipation. The same law applies to contracting a marriage, revoking a pronouncement of divorce, and vows.[41] A coerced pronouncement of divorce has the same legal consequences as one that is made freely. Coercion has no effect on the validity of the divorce, no matter how severe the threat. However, if the coerced has not yet consummated the marriage, he has a claim to half of the value of the marriage gift from the coercer, an amount that he would have owed his divorced wife had he not been coerced.[42] Likewise, a person who has been coerced to emancipate a slave has recourse to the value of the slave against the coercer, and the former owner also retains the patronage relationship (*walāʾ*) with the emancipated slave that customarily follows emancipation. Ṭaḥāwī provides a cursory justification for the distinction between acts such as divorce, on the one hand, and commercial transactions such as sales, on the other. He points out that in the case of sales, the law recognizes the possibility of ex post facto invalidation due to either a defect (*ʿayb*) in the product exchanged or a stipulation in the sales contract of the option to return the product after review (*khiyār al-ruʾya*).[43] Because these acts accept other types of cancellations, they also accept

[39] See Ṭaḥāwī, *Mukhtaṣar*, 407.4–7. See also Qudūrī, *Mukhtaṣar*, 229.2–4.
[40] See Syed, "Coercion in Classical Islamic Law and Theology," 47–58.
[41] See Ṭaḥāwī, *Mukhtaṣar*, 408.8; Sarakhsī, *al-Mabsūṭ*, 24:67.1–3; Qudūrī, *Mukhtaṣar*, 230.4–5. Qudūrī does not mention marriages and vows.
[42] All of the Islamic legal traditions require the husband to pay a marriage gift to the wife as an essential condition for the validity of a marriage. When the husband divorces his wife before the marriage is consummated, the jurists, relying on the Qurʾānic verse 2:237, hold that the husband must pay a sum equivalent to half of the marriage gift to the wife as compensation. See Ṭaḥāwī, *Mukhtaṣar*, 407.9–14.
[43] See ibid., 408.7–10.

cancellation because of coercion. But this is not the case for acts such as marriage, divorce, or emancipation. The law does not recognize any means of ex post facto invalidation for these types of acts, and therefore there is no basis for allowing coercion to invalidate them.

Table 3.1. Summary of Coercion Laws in Ḥanafism

Coercer's Minimum Effective Threat	Coercer's Demand	Normative Consequence on Demanded Act	Normative Consequence of Defying Coercer's Demand
Loss of life or limb	Consumption of a prohibited substance	Substances become temporarily permitted	Sin
Loss of life or limb	Apostasy	Utterance of disbelief is excused	Reward
Loss of life or limb	Murder	Abū Ḥanīfa and Shaybānī: Only coercer is liable for full legal punishment Abū Yūsuf: Only coercer is liable for payment of blood money Zufar: Coerced is liable for full punishment	Reward
Loss of life or limb	Rape	Abū Ḥanīfa (opinion 1): Coerced liable for full punishment Abū Ḥanīfa (opinion 2) and Abū Yūsuf: Only if coercer is ruler, coerced not punished Shaybānī: If method of coercion resembles that of ruler, coerced not punished	Reward
Beating or imprisonment	Commercial transaction	Coerced has option to cancel transaction after coercion ceases	
Beating or imprisonment	Acknowledgment (e.g., of existing debt)	Acknowledgment is invalid	
Loss of life or limb	Divorce	Divorce remains valid, but if marriage not consummated, coerced can claim half of marriage gift from coercer	
Loss of life or limb	Emancipation of a slave	Emancipation remains valid, but coerced can claim restitution of slave's market value from coercer	

Unfortunately, there are few sources that document the arguments behind these coercion laws in the second/eighth and third/ninth centuries. But for subsequent generations of scholars, they served as objects of written and oral commentary, often composed through the process of teaching, from which many of the arguments that make up coercion jurisprudence in subsequent centuries originated.

5. DEFINING COERCION EMPIRICALLY AND SCRIPTURALLY SUBSTANTIATING ITS LEGAL EFFECTS IN LIGHT OF ḤANAFITE INTERNAL CONSTRAINTS

The earliest evidence of the development of Ḥanafite jurisprudence on coercion beyond Shaybānī's initial analysis is found in two works by the Baghdadi Ḥanafite Abū Bakr al-Jaṣṣāṣ. In his Qurʾān commentary on the verses relevant to coercion, Jaṣṣāṣ further develops Shaybānī's basic position on coercion's effects on dietary prohibitions by employing a more technically systematic conceptual vocabulary, explicitly developed in his work of legal theory. Jaṣṣāṣ's ideas unfold most substantially in his commentary on the Qurʾānic verse 2:173, quoted earlier, which permits the eating of otherwise forbidden food in cases of necessity.[44] He interprets the verse as indicating not only permission to consume illicit foods in the presence of necessity but also, more generally, a connection between necessity and permission, regardless of the type of act under consideration. He accomplishes this by reading verse 2:173 in conjunction with verse 6:119, which reads, "God has clarified for you what is forbidden, exempting that to which you are driven by necessity." Jaṣṣāṣ argues that

> in these verses God has mentioned necessity, and in some of them he has indicated permissibility when necessity exists without qualification, such as in 6:119. The latter [verse] requires the inference (*fa-aqtaḍā*) that permissibility exists when necessity does in every case in which necessity exists.[45]

[44] Other, similar verses are 5:3, 6:115, 6:119, 6:145, and 16:119.
[45] Abū Bakr Aḥmad b. ʿAlī al-Jaṣṣāṣ, *Aḥkām al-Qurʾān*, ed. ʿAbd al-Salām Muḥammad ʿAlī Shāhīn, 3 vols. (Beirut: Dār al-Kutub al-ʿIlmiyya, n.d.), 1:154.13–16.

Jaṣṣāṣ interprets 6:119 as expressing a universal principle that necessity lifts prohibition because it does not explicitly link the lifted prohibition to the specific case of illicit foods, as other verses do. This is a key step in extending the possible dispensatory effect of coercion to acts beyond the consumption of forbidden foods.

Like other similar passages, 2:173 qualifies the necessity exemption by stressing that the eater should consume the food without "coveting it or exceeding his immediate need." Jaṣṣāṣ reports a dispute about the meaning of this phrase, mentioning two opposing camps. "Without coveting" (*ghayra bāghin*) can also be translated as "without rebelling" and for this reason one camp held that the permission to eat the illicit foods in circumstances of necessity applies only to those who have not rebelled against legitimate political authority nor engaged in a journey in the pursuit of a sinful goal.[46] The other camp, by contrast, interprets the phrase as setting limits on the amount that can be consumed in a situation of necessity.[47] Jaṣṣāṣ holds this to be the right opinion.[48]

He then turns his attention to defining the nature of the limits implied by the phrase "neither coveting it nor exceeding his immediate need." He classifies this verse as inherently indeterminate (*ijmāl al-lafẓ*)[49] and in need of clarification (*iftiqāri-hi ilā bayān*), to the point that it cannot, in isolation, be taken to indicate a law. The indeterminacy must first be remedied through

[46] Jaṣṣāṣ attributes this view to the second/eighth-century Meccan scholars Mujāhid and Saʿīd b. Jubayr, as well as to Shāfiʿī. See ibid., 1:154.20–22.

[47] Jaṣṣāṣ attributes this view to Ibn ʿAbbās, al-Ḥasan, Masrūq, Mālik b. Anas, and the Ḥanafites generally. See ibid., 1:154.17–19.

[48] See ibid., 1:154.19–155.15 for his criticism of the alternative and his substantiation of the opinion held by the Ḥanafites.

[49] For his classification of the verse as inherently indeterminate and thus in need of clarification, see Jaṣṣāṣ, ibid., 1:155.16. The conceptual pair of *bayān* (clear) vs. *mujmal* (indeterminate) is very important in Jaṣṣāṣ's legal hermeneutic. On the meaning of *mujmal*, see *Uṣūl al-Jaṣṣāṣ al-Musammā al-Fuṣūl fī al-Uṣūl*, ed. Muḥammad Muḥammad Tāmir, 1st ed., 2 vols. (Beirut: Manshūrāt Muḥammad ʿAlī Bayḍūn, Dār al-Kutub al-ʿIlmiyya, 2000), 1:19–29; on the conceptual consequences for legal rules of classifying a text as indeterminate, see ibid., 1:182–88; on the mechanics of clarification (*bayān*), see ibid., 1:238–79. For a short explanation in English of the term "indeterminate," see Mohammad Hashim Kamali, *Principles of Islamic Jurisprudence*, Revised ed. (Cambridge, UK: Islamic Texts Society, 1997; repr., 1997), 101–2, as well as Aron Zysow, *The Economy of Certainty: an Introduction to the Typology of Islamic Legal Theory* (Atlanta, GA: Lockwood Press, 2013), 55–56. On the role of *mujmal* in the postclassical hermeneutic of the Shāfiʿite legal theorist al-Āmidi, see Weiss, *Search*, 447–67.

clarification from other sources before it can serve as a basis for a law. Jaṣṣāṣ writes:

> When we are able to use the law given by the verse, it is incumbent on us to use it. The way that it becomes possible [for us] to use it is by affirming the construction of the phrase "coveting and exceeding" as referring to consuming only the amount of food necessary to stave off death and to extinguish the fear of loss of one's life. Does not God say: "Do not kill yourselves" [Qur'ān 4:29]? Whoever refuses to eat what is permitted to the point of dying kills himself, according to all of the scholars.[50]

He thus implies that the circumstance of necessity that renders forbidden foods permitted is a situation in which one fears for one's life. He argues that in such a situation, not consuming the amount of food necessary to stave off death is akin to suicide, which is prohibited. Later on he makes the point explicit and connects the concept of necessity to that of coercion:

> The meaning of necessity (*ḍarūra*) here is fear of harm to oneself or one's limbs by not eating. The verse covers (*qad inṭawā*) two meanings. One meaning refers to a situation in which only carrion is available. The other meaning [refers to] situations in which foods other than carrion are available, but a person is coerced to eat carrion by a threat against his life or limb. We hold that both meanings are intended by the verse, because it bears both [meanings] (*li-iḥtimāli-himā*). It is narrated that Mujāhid used to interpret the verse as referring to the necessity present in coercion (*wa-qad ruwiya ʿan Mujāhid anna-hu taʾawwala-hā ʿalā ḍarūrati ʾl-ikrāh*). If it is the case that the necessity of the case of carrion is the harm that one fears for one's life from not consuming it, then this is present also in the necessity of coercion.[51]

The basis of the Ḥanafite law permitting the eating of forbidden food when confronted with a threat against life or limb are the Qurʾānic verses that address situations of necessity. The Qurʾān does not define what the necessity consists in, nor does it define the limits of the permissibility of consuming the previously forbidden foods. The law indicated by these verses thus cannot be operationalized unless this indeterminacy is resolved. Jaṣṣāṣ clarifies the indeterminacy by defining necessity as fear of the loss

[50] Jaṣṣāṣ, *Aḥkām*, 1:155.17–21.
[51] Ibid., 1:157.14–20.

of life or limb and notes that such fear can arise not only from finding oneself in exigent circumstances but also from being coerced by another person, who threatens one's life or limb unless one complies. He bolsters his argument by citing an early Meccan authority (Mujāhid) as also interpreting the verse in this way. His argument for why one sins if one refuses to eat the otherwise prohibited food and consequently dies relies on the rule against suicide.

Though this argument relates only to the law about coercion and forbidden foods, Jaṣṣāṣ also makes the seemingly general claim that necessity and permission go together. But there are many types of forbidden acts, including murder and rape. Can the necessity engendered by threats against one's life or limb also permit rape and murder? Can it do more than change the moral valuation of an act? Can it transfer responsibility from the coerced to the coercer? If so, how is this justified?

These questions are addressed in Jaṣṣāṣ's work of positive law, *Sharḥ ʿalā Mukhtaṣar al-Ṭaḥāwī fī ʾl-Fiqh al-Ḥanafī*. In terms of structure, the work departs both from Shaybānī's extensive but unwieldy discussion of coercion and from the legal handbooks, which had simply followed Shaybānī's topical order. Jaṣṣāṣ organizes his chapter on coercion according to the types of potentially coercive threats and the different moral and legal effects they have on different types of acts. Unlike the authors of the handbooks, who used concrete examples of coercers such as thieves, leaders of criminal gangs, and agents of rulers, Jaṣṣāṣ simply says that a coercer is anyone who holds power (*al-musalliṭ*) and who commands obedience (*al-nāfidh al-amr*).[52]

He begins by dividing potentially coercive threats into three types:[53]

1. Threats against life or limb
2. Threats of imprisonment or enchainment that result in severe anxiety and great harm but do not reach the point of endangering life or limb
3. Threats of a beating, or a lash or two, or imprisonment for a day or so.

[52] Jaṣṣāṣ, *Sharḥ Mukhtaṣar al-Ṭaḥāwī fī al-Fiqh al-Ḥanafī*, ed. ʿIṣmat Allāh ʿInāyat Allāh Muḥammad and Saʿīd Bakdāsh, 1st ed., 8 vols. (Beirut: Dār al-Bashāʾir al-Islāmiyya lil-Ṭibāʿa wa al-Nashr wa al-Tawzīʿ, 2010), 8:437.3.

[53] Ibid., 8:437.4–8.

Let us begin with the first category. We have already seen that in both the legal handbooks and Jaṣṣāṣ's Qurʾān commentary on the necessity verses, these types of threats permit previously prohibited foods and excuse apostasy. This type of coercion also has the potential to transfer the legal consequences of the coerced act from the coerced to the coercer, especially when the act involves material liability for harm of some sort or the law of retaliation (*qiṣāṣ*). The positive laws reviewed earlier in the chapter provide examples of such transference. Coercion based on a threat to life or limb, at least according to Abū Ḥanīfa's opinion, results in the transference of the legal punishment for murder from the coerced to the coercer. While coercion cannot invalidate pronouncements of divorce or emancipation, coercion of this type allows the coerced to seek subsequent compensation from the coercer for the value of the emancipated slave or for half the value of the marriage gift in case he had not consummated the marriage with the divorced wife. It is precisely these types of acts that Jaṣṣāṣ points to as examples of the transferring effect of this kind of coercion.[54]

Unlike Shaybānī, Jaṣṣāṣ does not specifically identify the preponderant subjective belief of the coerced as dispositive in cases that admit compelling coercion. About a hundred years after Jaṣṣāṣ, the Central Asian Ḥanafite Sarakhsī reintroduces Shaybānī's view on the matter and his arguments against a forty-lash objective standard. Sarakhsī adds the following empirical argument: given that individuals differ in the severity of the beatings that their bodies can bear, there is no alternative to admitting that what is coercive depends on what the coerced thinks is the probable result if the coercer fulfills the threat. If the coerced feels confident that he will neither perish nor lose a limb if the coercer executes the threat, he is not compelled. But if he thinks that his life or limbs are indeed in peril, he is compelled, even if the threat is only of ten lashes.[55]

In addition, Sarakhsī argues that certainty is not required of the coerced victim's subjective beliefs about the result of the threatened act: probability suffices. Sarakhsī points to the case of a person who kills an intruder in her home without giving a warning. Killing the intruder without warning is permissible because of the likelihood that issuing a warning would lead to the

[54] Ibid., 8:443.8–14. [55] Sarakhsī, *al-Mabsūṭ*, 24:59.14–18.

intruder killing the owner of the home. If probability has the effect of protecting a person from legal and moral liability in this case, then it is also legally effective in coercion jurisprudence.[56]

While threats of a lesser severity, such as a beating or imprisonment cannot transfer the legal consequences of bodily acts, such as murder, from the coerced to the coercer,[57] they can result in the cancellation of speech acts that stipulate contentment (*riḍā*) as a condition for their validity. The paradigmatic example of such acts for the Ḥanafites is sales.

Much as Shaybānī did, Jaṣṣāṣ justifies the coercive nature of the threats of imprisonment or beating by citing reports from the Prophet's companions and other early authorities, as well as unanimously accepted legal practice. He cites texts attributed to ʿUmar (d. 23/644) ("No man who is beaten, fettered, or deprived of food is safe from himself") and to an early religious authority, Shurayḥ (d. 78/698) ("Imprisonment is coercive; being fettered is coercive"), to justify the claim that imprisonment and enchainment can be coercive in certain cases. In addition to referring to these precedential texts, also documented by Shaybānī, he makes an empirical argument based on an accepted legal practice. He notes that all jurists agree on the validity of the practice of imprisoning a debtor who refuses to pay his debt. In this case, the use of force is legitimate because the debtor has refused to honor a rightful claim,[58] but Jaṣṣāṣ uses the case as evidence for the fact that imprisonment does indeed successfully change the debtor's mind. The coercion is effective.

The last of Jaṣṣāṣ's categories is threats of a slight beating or a brief imprisonment or enchainment. Such relatively mild threats, he says, are not to be considered legally coercive. They have no effect on the legal consequences of the action demanded by the person making the threat.[59]

Thus far, my discussion has focused on sources that attempt to formulate a legal definition of coercion. In Jaṣṣāṣ's three-tier framework, threats against life or limb belong to the highest tier. These types of threats are compellingly coercive. They have the potential to transform the moral categorization of forbidden acts and to transfer the attribution of legal responsibility for the

[56] Ibid., 24:61.7–10.
[57] Bodily acts contrast with speech acts. Homicide, murder, rape, and the destruction of property are examples of bodily acts.
[58] Jaṣṣāṣ, *Sharḥ*, 8:440.8–13. [59] Ibid., 8:438.15–18.

coerced act from the coerced to the coercer in cases in which the coerced act is a bodily one. Jaṣṣāṣ provides a scriptural argument for why compelling coercion can transform the moral categorization of some prohibitions, but he does not explain why it can transfer legal responsibility or why the moral transformation applies only to certain types of acts. The first Ḥanafite to provide arguments for these aspects of compelling coercion is Dabūsī. It is in Dabūsī's writings that we first see a justification of Ḥanafite coercion rules that makes reference to its effects on the coerced's psychological capacities. Subsequently, at the end of the fifth/eleventh century, Bazdawī developed a theory of coercion that fully integrated Ḥanafite coercion laws with the effects of different types of threats on the psychological capacities of the coerced.

6. THE PSYCHOLOGY OF COERCION, MORAL AGENCY, AND CHOICE: THE CULMINATION OF A CLASSICAL SYNTHESIS

In his work of comparative law, *al-Asrār fī ʾl-Uṣūl wa-ʾl-Furūʿ*, Dabūsī provides a psychological account to explain why threats against life, specifically, are compelling and why they therefore result in transference. Dabūsī writes:

> When an agent fears the loss of a limb or something greater, his ability to reason becomes degraded (*fasada raʾyu-hu*) and his discernment vanishes (*dhahaba tamyīzu-hu*). The human being [in this scenario] uses his reason only to save his own life and admits no other consideration. The ability to [actively] distinguish between saving oneself and [some other good] does not remain. His sole intention is to save himself, and this intention is equivalent to the intention of an animal that has no reason at all.[60]

Compelling coercion has an effect on the coerced's choice:

> No valid choice (*ikhtiyār ṣaḥīḥ*) for anything else remains when a person fears being killed. By a natural cause (*bi-ḥukmi ʾl-ṭabīʿa*), he becomes compelled (*muljaʾan*) to the act that will repel being killed. He becomes as if he had no choice.[61]

[60] Abū Zayd ʿAbd Allāh b. ʿUmar al-Dabūsī, *al-Asrār fī al-Usūl wa al-Furūʿ*, ed. Salim Özer (Keyseri, Turkey: Erciyes University, Turkey, 1997), PhD Dissertation, 1000.27–29.

[61] Ibid., 1006.25–26.

Threats against life or limb, according to Dabūsī, have the unique ability to degrade the psychological faculties involved in the balancing of this-worldly goods when making choices about courses of action.

One would assume that Dabūsī's remarks on the debilitative effects of threats against life or limb in fact eliminate the coerced's moral agency entirely or her choice. This is not the case. Dabūsī argues for two ideas that would become staples of Ḥanafite coercion jurisprudence in subsequent generations: coercion does not eliminate moral agency and it does not eliminate choice. Despite the coercion, the coerced agent continues to be an addressee of the Divine law:

> We say that the coerced is [still] the addressee (*mukhāṭab*) of the Divine law. We agree on the fact that if the coerced is coerced to commit fornication and performs that act, he sins, and that if he perseveres and is killed, he is rewarded. If he is coerced to eat carrion and eats it, he does not sin, and if he perseveres to the point of being killed, he sins.[62]

In his work on legal theory, he explicitly describes the coerced as choosing to do what he does, intending to do it. The coerced is confronted with two bad choices, and he chooses the lesser of two evils based on his knowledge and intent.

Sarakhsī refines Dabūsī's ideas about coercion's effect on choice. He defines coercion in the following terms:

> Coercion denotes an action that one directs toward another, through which [the coercer] negates [the coerced's] contentment and degrades his choice (*yufsidu bi-hi ikhtiyāra-hu*), without thereby eliminating the coerced's suitability (*ahliyya*) [for moral and legal accountability] or excluding [him from address by] the Divine law (*khiṭāb*).[63]

Dabūsī said simply that coercion does not eliminate the coerced's choice: a coerced agent still chooses what she does. Sarakhsī modifies this formulation by arguing that while coercion does not eliminate choice, it renders it defective. He goes on to make the same argument as Dabūsī, though in more generic terms. The coerced is tried by the ordeal of being coerced, and the fact that she is tried confirms that she is subject to the address of the

[62] Ibid., 998.26–27. [63] Sarakhsī, *al-Mabsūṭ*, 24:47.25–27.

Divine law: under coercion, she is sometimes obliged to do what the coercer demands, sometimes permitted to do it, sometimes excused for doing it, and sometimes forbidden to do it. The fact that some type of command is present even when the agent is coerced is evidence that she is still under moral charge.

There seems to be a tension, most acute in Dabūsī's writings, between the idea that coercion does not undermine moral agency and the idea that compelling coercion degrades choice to the point that it transfers legal responsibility from the coerced to the coercer. On the one hand, in his work of legal theory, Dabūsī affirms that agents exercise choice even in situations of coercion, although it may be an unnaturally burdened choice; the coerced is faced with two bad options and redirects his intention to saving himself from impending harm, but his actions are still governed by Divine command. Yet in his work of comparative law, Dabūsī describes the deleterious effects of coercion on various psychological processes and capacities in order to justify why certain types of threats can result in the transference of the act's legal consequences. So coercion does not undermine moral agency, because it does not actually eliminate choice, but Dabūsī must rationalize why compelling coercion can nonetheless change the moral valuation of prohibited acts and make the coercer rather than the coerced liable for crimes against the body or against property. To do that, Dabūsī offers a picture of the psychological impact of a threat against life or limb—a picture that acknowledges, at a minimum, a severe impairment of choice.

The tension is mitigated by Sarakhsī, and especially Bazdawī. The late fifth/eleventh-century Transoxanian legal theorist Bazdawī classifies types of coercion according to its psychological effects, using the distinct analytical terms used by Dabūsī and Sarakhsī before him. His three categories of potentially coercive threats match Jaṣṣāṣ's tripartite framework, but instead of differentiating the categories with reference to concrete threats (life or limb vs. imprisonment vs. slight beating), Bazdawī differentiates them by the effect that the coercion has on the psychology of the coerced, specifically his degree of contentment and his capacity to choose. The first category, which he calls compelling coercion (*al-mulji*ʾ), eliminates contentment and degrades choice.[64] The second category eliminates contentment but does not degrade choice, and the last category has no effect on either.[65] Like Dabūsī and Sarakhsī, he affirms that, regardless of its effects on choice and contentment, coercion does not undermine moral agency, and he repeats Sarakhsī's generic version of Dabūsī's argument.[66] He adds that it makes no sense to say that coercion can obliterate choice, for if the coerced "is forced to choose [the coerced act], he has effectively agreed with the coercer, so how, then, could he be someone who does not choose?"[67] For this reason, the coerced must be regarded as the subject of the Divine command (*mukhāṭab*) despite the coercion.

7. REACHING FOR COHERENCE: THE HISTORY OF THE INSTRUMENT TEST

From the very beginning of the tradition, Ḥanafite doctrine held that threats against life and limb are compellingly coercive and have the potential to drastically alter the normative effects of coerced acts. Jaṣṣāṣ developed Shaybānī's justification for how coercion could change the moral valuation of the act demanded of the coerced. In the next generation, Dabūsī added a psychological argument to explain why such threats are compellingly coercive to the point of transfering, in certain circumstances, the legal consequences of the coerced act from the coerced to the coercer and was the first scholar to develop the instrument test to justify transference in a wide variety of cases. It is probably the case, however, that the instrument metaphor emerged before Dabūsī as a way of understanding Abū Ḥanīfa's and Shaybānī's opinion specifically on coerced murder. Both had held that it is the coercer and not the coerced who is held fully liable for the legal sanctions for the crime. The instrument metaphor makes its earliest appearance in Jaṣṣāṣ's work of positive law. Jaṣṣāṣ argues that given a compelling threat,

[64] ʿAlī b. Muḥammad al-Bazdawī and al-Ḥusayn b. ʿAlī al-Saghnāqī, *al-Kāfī: Sharḥ al-Bazdawī*, ed. Fakhr al-Dīn Sayyid Muḥammad Qānit, 1st ed., 5 vols. (Riyadh: Maktabat al-Rushd, 2001), 5:2429.1.

[65] Ibid., 5:2429.2.

[66] Ibid., 5:2429.3–5.

[67] Ibid., 5:2430.2–3.

> the coerced . . . becomes like an instrument in the coercer's act of killing, as if he had fastened a sword to the hand of the coerced and then struck the victim with it. In this case, the retaliation (*qiṣāṣ*) is on the coercer and not on the coerced.[68]

Dabūsī extends the instrument metaphor to all coerced acts that Jaṣṣāṣ had categorized as capable of transferring the legal consequences from the coerced to the coercer—that is, all bodily acts caused by compelling coercion. Dabūsī formulates the principle that compelling coercion has the effect of transferring the legal consequences of an action from the coerced to the coercer in all cases in which it is empirically conceivable that the coerced serves as the coercer's instrument. For Dabūsī, the instrument test not only justifies transference but also serves as a test of its applicability. If it is empirically conceivable in a given situation that the coerced serves as the instrument of the coercer, then the transference is successful. If it is not empirically conceivable, then the legal consequences of the coerced act remain restricted to the coerced. Paradigmatic cases of the successful application of the instrument test are bodily acts that cause harm to the body or property of others. In such cases, the coercer is liable for the harm caused, because it is empirically possible that the coercer could have used the body of the coerced to cause the harm. According to Dabūsī, compelling coercion renders the action of the coerced akin to that of "a rock that has no choice, which the coercer uses to destroy, thus turning the physical agent (*al-mubāshir*) into an instrument of the coercer."[69] But coerced legal speech acts, rape, and certain ritual acts such as breaking one's fast, one's prayer, or one's state of consecration on pilgrimage (*iḥrām*) are examples of acts whose legal consequences cannot be transferred from the coerced to the coercer. Given Dabūsī's psychological account of how compelling coercion turns the coerced into an instrument of the coercer, "like a rock that has no choice," how can he justify the apparently contradictory claim that legal speech acts, for example, cannot be invalidated by compelling coercion?

[68] Jaṣṣāṣ, *Sharḥ*, 8:452.9–11. Before introducing the instrument metaphor, Jaṣṣāṣ argues that everyone agrees that the coerced and the intended victim have every right to attempt to defend themselves, using lethal force if necessary, against the coercer, as if he were attacking them physically. The fact that the coercer's blood can legitimately be spilled in such a situation, Jaṣṣāṣ argues, indicates that the legal consequence of his action attaches solely to him.

[69] Dabūsī, *Asrār*, 1000.30–1001.1. See also ibid., 999.18–19, for a similar idea.

Dabūsī offers the following argument. He emphasizes that the instrument test must be construed in a strictly empirical fashion: "At the empirical level it is not possible for a human being to speak with the tongue of another, so that no choice remains for the speaker."[70] For this reason, the case of coerced speech fails the instrument test, and the consequences remain attached to the coerced. The same goes for being coerced to break one's fast and being coerced to rape someone.[71]

After Dabūsī, the instrument test played a key role in the Ḥanafite understanding of the legal effects and limits of threats against life or limb. Both Sarakhsī and Bazdawī used it systematically to both justify transference and limit its scope.[72] Sarakhsī added, and Bazdawī reproduced, an additional argument for why compelling coercion can transfer consequences in those cases in which the instrument test succeeds. Sarakhsī writes:

> The most correct opinion is that the effect of [compelling] coercion is to make the coerced an instrument of the coercer. The action then becomes attributed to the coercer, and the coerced is rendered an instrument. This does not amount to considering coercion to fundamentally eliminate his choice. But coercion does degrade his choice when it reaches the level of compulsion. This is because man is naturally disposed to love his life, and this forces him to do what the coercer demands. In this way his choice is degraded. The degraded [choice], when compared with a [fully] valid one, should be considered as if completely absent. Therefore, the action is attributed to the coercer, because he has a completely valid choice, whereas the coerced has become an instrument of the coercer.[73]

According to Sarakhsī, in any compelling coercion case there are in fact two choices being made, by two different agents. There is the free choice the coercer makes to use coercion to accomplish his aim, and there is the degraded choice of the coerced. A judge deliberating on a coerced crime is thus faced with the decision of giving effect to one of these two choices. The judge ought to give effect to the free choice, and this involves transferring the attribution of the legal consequences of the coerced act from the coerced

[70] Ibid., 1001.4–5.
[71] For the case of fasting, see ibid., 1001.2–3, and for rape, see ibid., 1001.2.
[72] See these two examples: Sarakhsī, *al-Mabsūṭ*, 24:48.10–18; Bazdawī, *al-Kāfī*, 5:2438.4–8.
[73] Sarakhsī, *al-Mabsūṭ*, 24:48.10–14.

to the coercer.[74] Bazdawī reproduces this two-choice analysis of compelling coercion in his own work.[75]

8. CONCLUSION: THE EXPLANATORY POWER OF INTERNAL CONSTRAINTS AND ORGANIC DEVELOPMENT OVER TIME

This chapter has outlined two important features of Ḥanafite coercion jurisprudence:

1. The relative stability over time of the laws that govern different types of coerced acts within the tradition
2. The organic growth and systematic adjustment of the justifications given for these laws.

Classical Ḥanafite jurists did not attempt to modify the laws first articulated by the authors of the legal handbooks. In fact, Jaṣṣāṣ took the laws describing the legal and moral effects of coercion on different types of acts as the starting point of his legal definition of coercion. Subsequent Ḥanafite scholars pursued the same approach.[76]

What does change over time in the Ḥanafite jurisprudence is the justifications offered for the tradition's definition of coercion. Jaṣṣāṣ justified the compelling effect of threats against life or limb by an interpretation of the necessity verses in the Qur'ān. Dabūsī added an empirical argument about the effects of compelling coercion on the decision-making process of the coerced agent. He argued that a threat against life or limb compromises the deliberative capacity of the coerced agent to such an extent that the agent metaphorically becomes an instrument of the coercer, which justifies why compelling coercion can result in the transference of legal responsibility for the coerced act from the coerced to the coercer. However, Dabūsī's analysis of the psychology of the coerced created a problem. It implied that compelling

[74] Sarakhsī enunciates the same principle later on in connection with cases involving the destruction of property: when it is possible to regard the coerced as a tool of the coercer, preference is given to the valid choice over the degraded choice. Ibid., 24:73.12–13.

[75] Bazdawī, *al-Kāfī*, 5:2437.1–2438.4.

[76] As we will see, the Ḥanafites, in contrast to the Shāfiʿites, did not disagree about what is and what is not coercive.

coercion eliminates choice entirely. If this were true and moral agency could not coexist with compelling coercion, then coercion ought to eliminate also the legal consequences of unilateral speech acts. But the instrument metaphor could not be taken as a global coercion principle, because it would contradict Ḥanafite laws on coerced speech acts. For this reason, Dabūsī limited the impact of the instrument test by stipulating that it can successfully transfer legal responsibility only in cases in which it is physically conceivable for the coercer to use the coerced to perform a given act. According to Dabūsī, it is impossible for the coercer to use the coerced to perform a speech act; therefore, compelling coercion does not result in the transference of the legal consequences of speech acts. Ḥanafite coercion laws constrain the impact of the empirical psychological picture of the effects of compelling coercion and the use of the instrument metaphor.

The instrument metaphor and test became staple features of Ḥanafite jurisprudence in the legal thought of Sarakhsī and Bazdawī, who incorporated and systematized Dabūsī's arguments. According to them, compelling coercion eliminates contentment and degrades, but does not eliminate, choice. These are not simply psychological categories. The reason the Ḥanafites would want coercion to wholly eliminate contentment is that contentment is an essential feature of valid commercial transactions, as opposed to unilateral speech acts. The reason the Ḥanafites would not want compelling coercion to eliminate choice is that they want to preserve the idea that coercion does not eliminate moral agency, and choice is the fundamental basis for moral agency. Yet compelling coercion does degrade choice, because Sarakhsī and Bazdawī compare the degraded choice of the coerced agent to the valid choice of the coercer for an additional argument for transference. For this same reason, the second category of threats (of imprisonment, for example) also eliminates contentment but does not degrade or eliminate choice. This second category of threats, not coincidentally, has a legal effect only on commercial exchanges. The Ḥanafites thus calibrated their empirical observations about the impact of different forms of coercion on the psychology of the coerced with a view toward preserving the inherited Ḥanafite laws.

4

Defining Coercion in Shāfiʿism

1. INTRODUCTION

In many respects, Shāfiʿite coercion jurisprudence is less complicated than its Ḥanafite counterpart. This is in large measure because the Shāfiʿites took a much more straightforward approach to coerced speech acts. For the Shāfiʿites, coercion canceled the legal consequences of all speech acts. A coerced pronouncement of divorce was as invalid as a coerced sale. The Shāfiʿites did not, therefore, face the challenge of explaining how coercion could have different effects on different types of speech acts.

The history of Shāfiʿite attempts at formulating a legal standard for coercion upends current scholarly understandings of the justificatory tendencies of classical Ḥanafism and Shāfiʿism. Unlike the Ḥanafites, classical Shāfiʿites show little concern for substantiating their legal formulation of coercion with scriptural arguments, either by reference to the Qurʾān or ḥadīth. In addition, unlike the Ḥanafites, who dutifully followed and built upon Shaybānī's arguments for Ḥanafite coercion laws, including his empirical observations, the classical Shāfiʿites did not follow Shāfiʿī as closely.

By the late fifth/eleventh century, a disagreement regarding the legal definition of coercion had emerged within Shāfiʿism. One approach favored a flexible, contextualist definition. According to this approach, what is coercive depends on a variety factors, such as the ability of the coerced agent to withstand the coercer's threat, the coerced agent's social status, and the relationship between the demand and the threat made by the coercer. This approach seems to have dominated among the Iraqi Shāfiʿite jurists of the fifth/eleventh century. The second approach eschewed contextualist considerations and favored what I call a "red line" standard for defining coercion. According this standard, only credible threats against one's life or limb are legally coercive. Factors such as the subjective ability of the coerced individual to bear the threat, his social status, and the correlation between the coercer's demand and the threat are immaterial to identifying legally valid claims of coercion. This approach was favored by some Khurasani Shāfiʿite jurists of the time.

2. SHĀFIʿĪ: DEFINING COERCION AND ITS EFFECTS

Muḥammad b. Idrīs al-Shāfiʿī (d. 204/820) has garnered much attention in Western scholarship.[1] He has been seen as a pivotal figure in the emergence of legal traditions oriented toward the laws and methodology of a founding figure, as opposed to a region.[2] Unlike Mālikism and Ḥanafism, Shāfiʿism did not emerge in a direct way out of the legal culture and teaching of a particular area. Shāfiʿī traveled quite a bit in the pursuit of knowledge: he studied with Mālik in Medina, engaged in vigorous debate with Shaybānī in Iraq, and ultimately settled, taught, and died in Egypt. The main source for his legal thought is his work of positive law, the *Umm*.[3] This work preserves not only Shāfiʿī's legal positions but also his justifications for them as well as his criticisms of competing positions.

Unlike Shaybānī, who consolidated questions about coercion into a single chapter, Shāfiʿī distributes his remarks on the topic in a host of different places the *Umm*. Naturally, most of his opinions deal with the normative consequences of coercion. For Shāfiʿī, it invalidates the legal consequences of all speech acts. He uses the coerced apostasy verse (16:106) to justify this position. He argues that if God cancels the legal effects

[1] For basic biographical information, see Éric Chaumont, "al-Shāfiʿī," in *Encyclopedia of Islam, Second Edition*, ed. P. Bearman, et al. (Leiden: Brill, 1980–2004).

[2] See Schacht, *The Origins of Muhammedan Jurisprudence*, 1–39. For a criticism of this view, see Wael Hallaq, "From Regional Schools to Personal Schools of Law? A Reevaluation," *Islamic Law and Society* 8, no. 1 (2001).

[3] For an analysis of the contents and authenticity of Shāfiʿī's texts, including the *Umm*, see El Shamsy, *The Canonization of Islamic law: a Social and Intellectual History*, 149–166.

of an act as serious as apostasy if the act is coerced, then a fortiori[4] the legal consequences of other types of coerced speech acts should be considered invalidated as well.[5] Elsewhere, Shāfiʿī uses the same reasoning, based on the apostasy verse, to justify the position that coercion renders consuming pork or entering a church permitted. He states generally that coercion can make prohibited acts permitted as long as they do not involve harm to others; he notes specifically that even coercion cannot render homicide licit.[6] While these laws clarify coercion's normative effect in certain cases, they do not by themselves identify the empirical features that characterize it. In the process of articulating the position that coercion invalidates speech acts, Shāfiʿī makes the following remarks indicating the threats he thinks are legitimately coercive:

> the agent finds himself in the hands of someone whom he cannot refuse, whether a ruler (*sulṭān*), a thief (*liṣṣ*) or an usurper of authority, such that the coerced (*mukrah*) fears that if he refuses to say what he is commanded to say, the coercer will inflict on him either a painful beating or something more severe still, up to the loss of his life.[7]

Later, Shāfiʿī adds that threats of imprisonment and enchainment have a similar effect. But, if the coerced thinks that her imprisonment or enchainment will not last long (e.g. an hour), and the coercer's demand consists of committing a sin, and she complies, then she has sinned.[8] Shāfiʿī further adds that if the coerced person confesses that she believed the coercer would not have been able to follow through on the threat, she is bound by the consequences of her speech act.[9]

Surprisingly, even as later Shāfiʿites uphold Shāfiʿī's opinions on the normative consequences of coercion, his sparse remarks on the types of threats that constitute it attract little attention. After Shāfiʿī, extant Shāfiʿite writings on coercion before the early fifth/eleventh century are limited. The most influential Shāfiʿite text in the generation immediately after Shāfiʿī was

[4] For an analysis of the legitimacy of a fortiori reasoning among the Shāfiʿites, see Zysow, *The Economy of Certainty: an Introduction to the Typology of Islamic Legal Theory*, 96–100.

[5] Muḥammad b. Idrīs al-Shāfiʿī, *al-Umm*, ed. Rifʿat Fawzī ʿAbd al-Muṭṭalib, 1st ed., 11 vols. (al-Manṣūra: Dār al-Wafāʾ li-ʾl-Ṭibāʿa wa al-Nashr wa al-Tawzīʿ, 2001), 4:496.13–15. Specifically, Shāfiʿī refers to legally relevant speech acts (*aḥkām al-ikrāh ʿalā ʾl-qawli kulli-hi*).

[6] Ibid., 5:701.14–702.3.

[7] Ibid., 4:496.16–19.

[8] Ibid., 4:497.4–12.

[9] Ibid., 4:496.8–9.

undoubtedly the legal handbook written by one of his students, Abū Ibrāhīm Ismāʿīl al-Muzanī (d. 264/877).

Muzānī reduces Shāfiʿī's discussion of coercion to two sentences. In his handbook, he reproduces Shāfiʿī's opinion on the effect of coercion on a pronouncement of divorce in the chapter devoted to divorce, not, as Shāfiʿī himself did, in that on legal acknowledgments. He states succinctly that Shāfiʿī held that pronouncements of divorce made by the coerced and the insane are not effective (*wa-law mukrahu wa-maghlūbu ʿalā ʿaqli-hi fa-lā yalḥaqu-hu ʾl-ṭalāq*).[10] In his second reference to the issue of coercion, Muzānī adds that the reason Shāfiʿī held that a coerced pronouncement of divorce is invalid is that the coerced agent lacks the positive will to perform the action in question. For the same reason, pronouncements of divorce by individuals who are intoxicated and incapable of understanding or who are asleep are likewise invalid.[11] All subsequent Shāfiʿites follow Muzanī's lead by discussing the legal definition of coercion in the context of divorce rather than legal acknowledgments. They typically use Muzanī's remarks as the starting point for offering empirical standards for what is legally coercive and discuss competing theories circulating among classical Shāfiʿite scholars, without making direct reference to Shāfiʿī's ideas.

3. MĀWARDĪ AND SHĪRĀZĪ: THE FLEXIBLE CONTEXTUALIST APPROACH OF IRAQI SHĀFIʿISM

By the beginning of the fifth/eleventh century, Shāfiʿism had split into two competing orientations: the Khurasani school and the Iraqi school. Little research has been done on the cause of this bifurcation of the Shāfiʿite tradition. ʿAbd al-Aẓīm Maḥmūd al-Dīb, the editor of Juwaynī's work of positive law, *Nihāyat al-Maṭlab*, hypothesizes that as Baghdad in Iraq and Nishapur in Khurasan emerged as the two intellectual centers of Shāfiʿite teaching in the

[10] Ismāʿīl b. Yaḥyā al-Muzanī, *Mukhtaṣar al-Muzanī fī Furūʿ al-Shāfiʿīyya*, ed. Muḥammad ʿAbd al-Qādir Shāhīn, 2nd ed. (Beirut: Dār al-Kutub al-ʿIlmiyya, 1998), 258.30.

[11] Ibid., 268.12–13.

third/ninth century, the jurists associated with the two locations gradually diverged on certain issues of positive law over the course of the next century and a half.[12] According to Dīb, this initial divergence solidified into recognizably distinct approaches to Shāfiʿite law in the fifth/eleventh century, with each represented by a central scholar. For Iraq, this scholar was Abū Ḥāmid al-Isfarāʾīnī (d. 406/1015), and for Khurasan, it was Abū Bakr al-Qaffāl al-Ṣaghīr (d. 417/1026).[13] The scholarly production of these two scholars provided the base of opinions, principles, justifications, and legal arguments for subsequent scholars of Shāfiʿite law in the two intellectual centers, respectively.[14]

The primary sources on classical Iraqi Shāfiʿism are the encyclopedic *al-Ḥāwī* of Abū al-Ḥasan al-Māwardī (d. 450/1058), and the much smaller but highly influential *al-Muhadhdhab* of Abū Isḥāq al-Shīrāzī (d. 475/1083). Māwardī was Isfarāʾīnī's direct student, and his work of positive law is based on Isfarāʾīnī's scholarship.[15] Shīrāzī also belonged to the Iraqi school, and his work is representative of the Iraqi approach.[16] Shīrāzī's treatment of coercion is substantially similar to Māwardī's in its analytical approach and substantive content. The nature of the relationship between Shīrāzī's and Māwardī's texts is unclear. It could be that both simply express the Iraqi Shāfiʿite consensus on coercion. Because of their similarity, I use Māwardī's text as my primary source and cite the corresponding passages in Shīrāzī's work in the notes.

Māwardī's discussion of the legal definition of coercion is located in his chapter on divorce, following his treatment of the issue of coerced divorce.[17] He begins by noting that legal acts relating to coercion can be divided into

[12] Abū al-Maʿālī ʿAbd al-Malik b. ʿAbdillāh al-Juwaynī, *Nihāyat al-Maṭlab fī Dirāyat al-Madhhab*, ed. ʿAbd al-ʿAẓīm Maḥmūd al-Dīb, 1st ed., 21 vols. (Jeddah: Dār al-Minhāj li-ʾl-Nashr wa-al-Tawzīʿ, 2007), 1:148–49. Chaumont asserts that the Khurasani Shāfiʿites were "more speculative" than the Iraqis. See Chaumont, "al-Shāfiʿī."

[13] Juwaynī, *Nihāyat*, 1:134. [14] Ibid., 1:141. [15] Ibid. [16] Ibid., 1:142.

[17] His treatment of the issue of coerced divorce consists of a criticism of the Ḥanafite position and a justification of the contrasting Shāfiʿite position. See Māwardī, *al-Ḥāwī al-Kabīr fī Fiqh Madhhab al-Imām al-Shāfiʿī Raḍiya Allāh ʿanh: wa Huwa Sharḥ Mukhtaṣar al-Muzanī*, ed. ʿAlī Muḥammad Muʿawwaḍ and ʿĀdil Aḥmad ʿAbd al-Mawjūd, 1st ed., 19 vols. (Beirut: Dār al-Kutub al-ʿIlmiyya), 10:227–31. None of the other classical Shāfiʿite authors treated in this chapter defend the Shāfiʿite position against Ḥanafite arguments or criticize the Ḥanafite position on coerced divorce. For Shīrāzī's discussion, see Shīrāzī, *al-Muhadhdhab fī fiqh al-Imām al-Shāfiʿī*, ed. Zakarīyā ʿUmayrāt, 3 vols. (Beirut: Dār al-Kutub al-ʿIlmiyya), 3:4–5 and *al-Tanbīh fī al-Fiqh ʿalā Madhhab al-Imām al-Shāfiʿī*, 2nd ed. (Cairo: Muṣṭafā al-Bābī al-Ḥalabī), 112.

three generic types: those that are invalidated by coercion and are not treated as equivalent to freely chosen acts, those that are valid despite the presence of coercion and are treated the same as freely chosen acts, and those about which conflicting legal opinions are attributed to Shāfiʿī.[18]

In the second category, Māwardī lists the following as examples of acts unaffected by coercion:

1. An enemy combatant's conversion to Islam (*islām ahl al-ḥarb*)[19]
2. The generation of kinship ties caused by the ingestion of breast milk (*riḍāʿ*)[20]
3. The loss of a state of ritual purity,[21] specifically the loss of a state of ritual purity by someone who qualifies for the dispensation to wipe the feet instead of washing them when performing the ablution but whose foot covering is forcibly made to come into contact with a ritual pollutant (*ṭarḥu al-najāsa ʿalā ʾl-muṣallī ʿalā khuffi-hi idhā kāna māsiḥan*).[22]

For two of these cases—the coerced conversion of an enemy combatant and the coerced ingestion of breast milk—he offers a justification for why coercion does not invalidate the consequences of the act in question. On the former case he simply notes that forcing enemy combatants to accept Islam is a religious duty laid down by the sources of the law, in contrast to the prohibition on the coerced conversion of protected non-Muslims (*dhimmīs*) who have paid the poll tax (*jizya*).[23] In the breast milk case, Māwardī argues that drinking breast milk is a bodily act that does not admit legal consideration of intent (*fiʿlu lā yurāʿā fī-hi ʾl-qaṣd*), as opposed to legal speech acts such as pronouncements of divorce and legal acknowledgments.[24]

[18] Māwardī, *al-Ḥāwī*, 10:231.20. The cases of coercion regarding which two opinions are attributed to Shāfiʿī are coerced homicide, coerced rape, coerced breaking of the fast at the proper time, and coerced speaking during the ritual prayer. See also ibid., 10:231.22–25.

[19] Ibid., 10:231.20. Shīrāzī also lists it as an act of legitimate coercion, *al-Muhadhdhab*, 3:4.11.

[20] Māwardī, *al-Ḥāwī*, 10:231.20. [21] Ibid., 10:231.20–21. [22] Ibid.

[23] Ibid., 10:229.27–30. Māwardī notes that coercing the protected non-Muslim to convert would be an act of injustice and that coercion in that instance would invalidate the legal consequences of the conversion.

[24] Ibid., 10:229.12.

For the Shāfiʿites, coercion invalidates the legal consequences of most types of acts. Specifically, Māwardī lists the following: apostasy or cursing the Prophet; divorce; emancipation; contracts, such as marriages, sales, leases, delegations of authority, and contracts of emancipation; and oaths of divorce. Given their relatively expansive conception of coercion's potential, most Shāfiʿite coercion jurisprudence is oriented toward formulating a legal standard for validating claims of coercion. Māwardī divides his coercion standard into three distinct analytical components: conditions related to the coerced agent, those associated with the coercer, and those that must characterize the act of coercion itself.[25] The bulk of Māwardī's discussion focuses on the last set of conditions. The structure of his argument is simple: once these three sets of conditions are met, a legally relevant instance of coercion has occurred—one that alters the normative consequences of the coerced act.

Māwardī begins with the coercer. In order for a claim of coercion to succeed, the coercer must possess overwhelming power (*qāhir*). Māwardī divides coercers into two types. One type is rulers, whom he characterizes as holding a generalized type of power (*ʿāmm al-qudra*). The other type, which encompasses criminals and slave masters, has a more specific type of power (*khāṣṣ al-qudra*). Regardless of type, the important point for Māwardī is that the power that the coercer exerts over the coerced must be effective (*nāfidha*).[26]

Not only must the coercer possess power; his threat must be credible. The coercer must be able to fulfill the threat made against the coerced. However, Māwardī does not say that the credibility of the threat must be an objective feature of the coercer. Rather, as Shaybānī and the later Ḥanafites insisted, the credibility of the threat is evaluated according to the subjective beliefs of the coerced, with the caveat that the latter must be convinced through empirical signs (*bi-ʾl-imārāt al-ẓāhira*) that the coercer will indeed realize the threat if the demand is refused. In other words, the threat must be credible, and the coerced ought to be able to point to concrete signs that justify his belief that it is so. If the coerced believes that the coercer is probably not able to

[25] Ibid., 10:231.28–10:232.1.

[26] Ibid., 10:232.2–5. Shīrāzī simply stipulates that the coercer must possess power. See *al-Muhadhdhab*, 3:4.14.

fulfill the threat (*lam yaghlib ʿalā ʾl-nafs*), the threat's realization is considered merely possible, and the claim of coercion fails.[27]

The second set of conditions applies to the situation of the coerced agent. Māwardī stipulates that the coerced must not be able to defend himself against the threat. First, he must not be able to flee from the coercer. If he is able to flee, the claim of coercion fails. Second, if the coerced knows that appeals that the coercer fear God and desist from the coercion would be effective, no claim to coercion is possible. And third, there should be no one who could aid the coerced or intercede with the coercer on the coerced's behalf. Only if the coerced is not able to flee, seek outside help, or appeal to the coercer's conscience can he make a successful coercion claim.[28]

The rest of the conditions have to do with the nature of the coercer's threat. Māwardī outlines seven types of threats. Similar to the normativist contention that the concept of coercion is moralized and depends for its normative force on other moral considerations, Māwardī says that the coercer must seek to coerce through unjust means (*an yakūna mukrihan bi-ʾl-ẓulm*)[29] and characterizes all seven types as involving manifest harm and injury (*al-ḍarar wa-ʾl-adhā ʾl-bayyin*) to the coerced.[30]

The first category consists of threats against life, which Māwardī labels the greatest harm that could afflict a person.[31] This category includes threats not only against the life of the coerced, but also against the lives of bystanders. Māwardī considers the potentially coercive effect of a threat directed against three different categories of bystanders. The first is direct ascendants (father, grandmother, etc.) and descendants (daughter, grandson, etc.). Threats to anyone in this category count as coercive because, according to Māwardī, the extent of the genealogical overlap (*baʿḍiyya*) between the third

[27] Māwardī, *al-Ḥāwī*, 10:231.20. Shīrāzī drops the requirement that the belief of the coerced must be based on empirical signs. He stipulates only that the coerced must believe that in all probability (*yaghlabu ʿalā ẓanni-hi*) the coercer will fulfill his threat.

[28] Ibid., 10:232.6–8. See also Shīrāzī, *al-Muhadhdhab*, 3:4.14, where Shīrāzī simply states that the coercer must be so powerful that the coerced is unable to mount a self-defense. He thus combines the coercer's power requirement with the lack of self-defense requirement on the part of the coerced.

[29] Māwardī, *al-Ḥāwī*, 10:232.9.

[30] Ibid., 10:232.14–15.

[31] Ibid., 10:232.16. Shīrāzī states that any threat that entails harm, such as threats against life or limb, or of severe beating, long imprisonment, or denigration directed against those of high social stature, is coercive, without delving into an extended discussion about bystanders. See *al-Muhadhdhab*, 3:4.15–16.

party and the coerced requires similarity in legal effects (*taqtaḍī tamāzuj fī ʾl-aḥkām*).[32] The second category consists of people who have no direct relation to the coerced. Māwardī gives cousins and complete strangers as two examples of this type of bystander. Threats to the lives of people in this category do not amount to coercion. Māwardī justifies the exclusion by arguing that there is some distant relation (*tanāsub baʿīd*) between all people.[33] Presumably, to admit threats against this set of bystanders would amount to endorsing a coercion standard that was far too liberal. The third category of bystanders consists of relatives whom one is forbidden to marry (*dhū raḥim maḥram*), such as aunts and uncles.[34] Māwardī cites two opinions on whether threats against the lives of this category of bystanders are legally coercive. One opinion holds that such threats are coercive because the law recognizes these people as a legal category, *maḥram*—those whom one is forbidden to marry. The other opinion holds that the threats are not coercive, because of the lack of a sufficient amount of genealogical overlap (*baʿḍiyya*) between the coerced and the bystanders.[35] Māwardī does not indicate which opinion he favors.

The second broad type of legally coercive threat is the threat of severe injury (*al-jarḥ*). Examples of this type include the loss of a limb or injuries involving the spilling of blood. According to Māwardī, these threats are coercive because of the amount of pain involved and the possibility that one could lose one's life.[36]

The third type is the threat of a beating. Such threats are coercive, though Māwardī excludes cases in which the coercer threatens loafers and vagabonds (*ahl al-shaṭāra wa-ʾl-ṣaʿlaka*). He claims that individuals who belong to these social groups actually compete with each other in the amount of pain they can bear, and therefore, empirically speaking, threats of beating directed at them do not coerce.[37]

The fourth type is the threat of imprisonment. Māwardī identifies three types of imprisonment; two of them count as coercive, while the third does not. Imprisonment for a long period of time is coercive, as is imprisonment

[32] Māwardī, *al-Ḥāwī*, 10:232.18–19.
[33] Ibid., 10:232.20–22.
[34] Ibid., 10:232.23–25.
[35] Ibid., 10:232.26–28.
[36] Ibid., 10:233.1–2. See also Shīrāzī, *al-Muhadhdhab*, 3:4.15.
[37] Māwardī, *al-Ḥāwī*, 10:233.3–5.

for an indefinite amount of time. But imprisonment for a short period of time, such as a day, is not coercive.[38]

The fifth type is a threat to destroy property belonging to the coerced. Such threats fall into three categories. The first category consists of threats directed against a substantial amount of property, to the point that if the property were lost, the material well-being of the coerced would be affected. These threats are deemed coercive. By contrast, threats involving an insignificant amount of property—the second category—are not coercive. This leaves the third category: threats against a significant amount of property whose loss would nonetheless not affect the material well-being of the threatened individual because of the latter's vast wealth. Māwardī identifies two opinions on the question of whether such threats constitute coercion. The first view holds that they are coercive because of the amount of property at risk, whereas the second view deems them not coercive because in relation to the overall wealth of the coerced, the harm entailed by the threat is insignificant.[39]

The sixth type of coercive threat is the threat of banishment. Māwardī states that if the threatened banishment would force the coerced individual to leave his family and property behind, the threat is coercive.[40] But if the threatened person has the ability to move his entire household, the coerciveness of the threat of banishment is subject to a difference of opinion. One view denies that it is coercive on the grounds that with respect to the ability of the coerced to meet basic needs, all lands are equal (*li-tasāwī ʾl-bilād kulli-hā fī maqāmi-hi fī-mā shāʾa min-hā*).[41] Another view holds that a threat of banishment is coercive even in these circumstances because banishment is a form of scripturally mandated penalty (*ḥadd*), considered the most severe type of punishment, and because the coerced would suffer harm as a result of being separated from his homeland.[42]

[38] Ibid., 10:233.6–11.See also Shīrāzī, *al-Muhadhdhab*, 3:4.15.

[39] See Māwardī, *al-Ḥāwī*, 10:233.12–18. Shīrāzī gives only the last opinion: threats against the property of someone who would not be affected by the loss are not coercive. Shīrāzī, *al-Muhadhdhab*, 3:4.18.

[40] Māwardī, *al-Ḥāwī*, 10:233.19–20. Shīrāzī claims that banishment that results in one's separation from one's extended family is coercive. See *al-Muhadhdhab*, 3:4.19–20.

[41] Māwardī, *al-Ḥāwī*, 10:233.20–22.

[42] Māwardī, ibid., 10:233.23–24. Banishment is a *ḥadd* penalty because it is a possible punishment for banditry; see Qurʾān 5:33. For banishment as an Islamic legal punishment, see Wizāra al-Awqāf wa al-Shuʾūn al-Islāmiyya, "Nafīyy," in *al-Mawsūʿa al-Fiqhiyya* (Kuwait: Wizāra

The seventh and final type of coercive threat is the threat of public denigration (*istikhfāf*). Māwardī notes that there are two possible types of denigration. One type is coercive; the other is not necessarily so. If the potential denigration is directed at an individual belonging to what Māwardī describes as the rabble (*ruʿāʿ*), people who do not condemn such behavior and among whom insults do not lead to a loss of social position, then the threat does not amount to coercion.[43] There are two opinions on whether threats of denigration directed against the "people of reputation" (*al-ṣiyānāt*) or those educated in proper chivalry (*dhawī ʾl-murūʾāt*) amount to coercion.[44] The first opinion holds that they are, because of the loss of standing that such denigration causes and the resulting pain for the victim.[45] The second opinion holds that they are not, because people know that the targets of the denigration were wronged by it. Māwardī suggests that in order to establish whether the threatened denigration amounts to coercion, an inquiry be made into the background of the target. If she is from the class of those who value worldly fame and status, the threat of denigration is coercive, because it is bound to result in a loss of social position among her peers. If, however, she is from the class of those who have their sights on the hereafter and abjure worldly concerns, the possibility of denigration is not coercive as it does not diminish her social position among her peers and may, in fact, even elevate it.[46]

On the whole, classical Shāfiʿite coercion jurisprudence is much less complicated than its Ḥanafite counterpart. Much of its straightforwardness stems from a less complicated body of positive law governing coercion cases. The Ḥanafites had to expend much energy to generate justifications for their discriminating approach to legal speech. The Shāfiʿites did not have this problem. For them, the vast majority of legal acts, including all varieties of legal speech, were simply invalidated by coercion. The only challenge was defining what was coercive. On this issue, the Iraqi Shāfiʿites of the fifth/

al-Awqāf wa al-Shuʾūn al-Islāmiyya, 1987–2006). On the historical practice of the punishment of banishment in Seljuk society, see Christian Lange, *Justice, Punishment and the Medieval Muslim Imagination* (Cambridge: Cambridge University Press, 2008), 94–97.

[43] Māwardī, *al-Ḥāwī*, 10:233.25–27. [44] Ibid., 10:233.28.

[45] Ibid., 10:234.1–2. See Shīrāzī, *al-Muhadhdhab*, 3:4.17–18, where Shīrāzī claims that a public denigration is coercive only if it is directed against someone of high social stature (*dhawī ʾl-aqdār*) who would suffer diminished social status because of it.

[46] Māwardī, *al-Ḥāwī*, 10:234.3–9.

eleventh century do not evince the same concern for conceptual problems as their Ḥanafite counterparts. There is very little scriptural justification offered for coercion laws, nor is there much of an attempt at formulating metaphors, tests, or legal principles to impose coherence on the inherited positive laws or to encapsulate guiding principles for unprecedented future cases. The Iraqi Shāfiʿites, unlike the Ḥanafites, did not construct a psychological picture of the effect of coercion on choice, contentment, or willingness. In fact, much of Iraqi Shāfiʿite coercion jurisprudence consists of simply enumerating the variety of conditions that must be present for a claim of coercion to be legally effective. The conditions are commonsensical and sensitive to the contextual features of a case of coercion: the coercer must be powerful, the threat must be credible, the coerced must lack recourse to aid against the coercer, and so on. Threats that involve manifest harm or injury are coercive, and the Shāfiʿites listed numerous types of threats that concretize what they meant by this manifest harm. It included not just bodily harm but also psychological harm, such as the loneliness that would ensue from being banished from one's homeland. Some threats are coercive only when directed at certain types of people. Hence the threat of public insult is coercive only if it is directed at a person who would suffer social harm as a result of the insult. The threat of a beating is not coercive if it is directed at people who compete with each other in how much pain they can endure. Therefore, at least for certain types of threats, what is coercive requires an examination of the social status of the target of the threat. It is precisely this flexible, contextualist approach that was criticized by the famous Khurasani Shāfiʿite Imām al-Ḥaramayn al-Juwaynī.

4. JUWAYNĪ, GHAZĀLĪ, AND KHURASANI SHĀFIʿISM ON THE LEGAL DEFINITION OF COERCION

Juwaynī and Ghazālī, whose contributions to Ashʿarī theology were discussed in Chapter 2, were towering figures in classical Islamic thought, and both identify a dispute internal to Shāfiʿism about the correct legal formulation of coercion. Dīb, the editor of Juwaynī's positive law book *Nihāyat al-Maṭlab*, identifies the work as emerging from the Khurasani Shāfiʿite context but, at times, attempting to synthesize the Iraqi and Khurasani strands of the Shāfiʿite tradition.[47] While the Iraqi school seems to have settled on the approach outlined in the previous section,[48] the Khurasani school continued to experience internal divisions. Some Khurasani scholars gravitated toward the Iraqi approach, whereas others, most notably the founder of the Khurasani school, Qaffāl, diverged.

Before giving his own views on the matter, Juwaynī reviews the various positions within Shāfiʿism. At the outset, he admits that "what constitutes coercion is a deep and abstruse issue that the legal scholars (*fuqahā'*) have devoted little attention to."[49] He presents the Iraqi approach first. This approach, according to Juwaynī, considers threats not only against life and limb but also against property to be legally coercive. He adds that the Iraqis hold that "anything that is difficult to bear or is customarily counted as a psychologically compelling cause" could qualify as coercive.[50] By contrast, he says, Qaffāl held that coercion arises only

> if the coercer causes fear by way of [threatening] to cause imminent pain to the [coerced's] body, which the latter cannot bear. For example, if the coercer said, "Kill a certain person (*fulān*); if you do not kill him, I will kill you" or "I will cut off one of your limbs or lash you with a whip or starve you or deny you water or imprison you forever." All of these [threats] are coercive. [But] if the coercer says, "I will do these things to you tomorrow," it is not coercive. If he says, "I will destroy your property or kill your son," it is not coercive, because these are punishments that do not affect the body. If [the coercer] says, "I will slap you in the marketplace," and the coerced is someone of high social stature, this is not coercive, even if bearing it is difficult for the person threatened.[51]

Qaffāl's coercion standard is manifestly different from that of the Iraqis. He explicitly rejects consideration of public humiliation and in general regards only imminent threats of severe harm directed against the body

[47] Juwaynī, *Nihāyat*, 1:149–50.

[48] Indeed, the very fact that Māwardī and Shīrāzī presented substantially the same doctrine is proof of the Iraqis' unanimity. Moreover, Juwaynī's presentation of the Iraqi approach is consistent with the coercion jurisprudence found in the works of Māwardī and Shīrāzī. See ibid., 14:162.

[49] Ibid., 14:161.18–20. [50] Ibid., 14:162.3.

[51] See ibid., 14:162.9–17. Juwaynī quotes this text from one of Qaffāl's students, to whom he refers simply by his title as "the judge." The judge in question was Ḥusayn b. Muḥammad al-Marwazī.

of the coerced as legally coercive. Juwaynī reports that a leading Shāfiʿite scholar after Qaffāl, Ḥusayn b. Muḥammad al-Marwazī (d. 462/1069), modified Qaffāl's standard. He notes that for Marwazī, a legally valid claim of coercion arises when the coercer causes fear through the threat of bodily harm severe enough to make the coercer liable to retaliation (*qiṣāṣ*) for inflicting it. This definition expands the scope of admissible threats to include those of bodily harm that is serious even if not life-threatening. Threats of imprisonment for life are not by themselves legally coercive for Marwazī. However, if the threatened life imprisonment would take place in a dungeon where people routinely die, the threat does count as coercive. Marwazī's formulation attempts to link the coercion standard to something that is already legally recognized: the Qurʾānically mandated rules of retaliation for the direct causation of severe types of bodily harm (*qiṣāṣ*). In the process, he does not substantially change Qaffāl's standard, but he does seek to put it on a more secure epistemic basis by grounding it in a Qurʾānically mandated law.

Qaffāl's and Marwazī's attempts to tighten the coercion standard were not necessarily representative of Khurasani Shāfiʿism. For example, Juwaynī quotes Marwazī's remark that the Iraqis stipulate that the relationship between the demand and the threat made by the coercer is relevant to the evaluation of a legal claim of coercion; so the determination of whether a threat is coercive depends on the nature of the act demanded. Marwazī himself disagrees with the stipulation, but he reports that some other Khurasani scholars hold that coercion is simply what a person is not capable of bearing and that it occurs when the coerced thinks that the coercer will, in all probability, fulfill his threat. Other scholars add that what is coercive is relative to the customs of a particular people, so that the threat of a single slap in public, when directed at a person of high status (*sharīf*), is coercive in that case. These unnamed Khurasani scholars seem to have much in common with the approach of their Iraqi counterparts. On the question of whether a threat against property or against the life of one's son is coercive, Marwazī reports that his own teacher—a student of Qaffāl's named Abū Muḥammad al-Juwaynī (d. 438/1046)—held that what is legally coercive depends on the relationship between the threat and the demand, such that what is coercive in a demand for divorce differs from what is coercive in a demand for homicide. According to Marwazī, Abū Muḥammad preferred the following standard in cases of coerced divorce: what would reasonable people (*ʿuqalāʾ*) choose to subject themselves to in order to avoid having to divorce their wives? His answer was long imprisonment, a painful beating, or an apparent loss in manly honor (*murūʾāt*). Presumably, then, the threat of any of these things by a coercer demanding that the victim divorce his wife produces a legally valid coercion claim, which in turn renders the pronouncement of divorce invalid.

Juwaynī's presentation indicates that the Khurasanis were divided on the issue of coercion. Some preferred a strict standard that admits no contextual considerations, while others upheld a standard that is similar to, if not even more flexible than that of the Iraqis. After discussing the competing approaches within Shāfiʿism, Juwaynī sides with the stricter standard.

Juwaynī criticizes two features of the flexible approach: its contextualism and its desire to correlate the coercer's demand with his threat in determining what is coercive. Juwaynī argues that both features introduce a degree of arbitrariness into legal deliberation that is not suitable for the law (*fiqh*). Considerations of social status, personal wealth, or the individual ability to bear a beating would require inquiry into the specific situation of every potentially coerced individual, and such inquiry is possible only from within that individual's perspective. Juwaynī thus poses the following question: if we admit factors such as the extent of the coerced person's personal wealth into the determination of whether a threat to destroy property is coercive, what is to stop a comparable inquiry into that person's psychological disposition toward wealth? A stingy individual would feel pain at what a generous one would not. This type of inquiry has no discernible nonarbitrary end and falls outside the province of law (*wa-ʾl-kalāmu yakhruju ʿan ḍabṭi ʾl-fiqh*).[52] The same objection applies to the use of a reasonable person standard in deciding what is coercive, which requires comparing the coercer's demand with his threat, in order to determine whether a reasonable person would be justified in succumbing to the coercer's demand. Ultimately, the amount of anxiety or pain that an individual is capable of bearing is reducible to that individual's natural constitution. All of these are considerations that, Juwaynī argues, the law should not admit (*wa-laysa min awzāni ʾl-fiqh*).[53] As for correlating the

[52] Juwaynī, ibid., 14:167.1–14. [53] Ibid., 14:164.13–16.

coercer's demand and threat in order to determine whether a threat is coercive, again the standard is arbitrary. For example, in the case in which a coercer demands a divorce: on one day the coerced may prefer imprisonment over divorce whereas on another day he may not. This variation makes such situations not much different from the normal, everyday choices that individuals make throughout their lives. Indeed, according to Juwaynī, time burdens man with such difficult choices all the time (*fa-qad yurhiqu al-zamānu al-marʾa ilā amthāli-hi*).[54] Acknowledging that a choice is difficult cannot, then, be the foundation of a legal standard for coercion.

Eschewing the arbitrariness of the flexible standard, Juwaynī supports the alternative red line approach to defining coercion: only threats against life or threats of acts that could lead to the loss of life are coercive. He writes:

> The approach of those who have attained the truth is that coercion is that which strips away power and ability to the point that a man is no longer able to either delay or hasten [his choice to act]. He has become like one without choice. This is the case with someone who is threatened with death or with the cutting off of a limb. The coercer's demand is not open to his deliberation or choice.[55]

For Juwaynī, only imminent threats that truly either eviscerate or severely degrade deliberation and choice can legitimately count as coercive. Juwaynī's argument for this standard is twofold. First, he claims that it avoids the potentially arbitrary considerations that the flexible standard admits. And second, he feels that the type of empirical inquiry that the flexible standard requires in order to validate claims of coercion is beyond the disciplinary scope of jurists and judges.

Similar to Juwaynī, Ghazālī notes that previous Shāfiʿite scholars were divided on the proper way to formulate a legal standard for coercion, though he does not correlate the competing approaches with geographical regions. He also departs significantly from the way that Juwaynī presented the root of the dispute. Ghazālī notes one threat that does coerce and does not depend on the method one adopts for validating a legal claim of coercion: the threat against one's life.[56] In Ghazālī's construal of the dispute,

[54] Ibid., 14:165.7. [55] Ibid., 14:165.1–3.

[56] Abū Ḥāmid Muḥammad b. Muḥammad al-Ghazālī, *al-Wasīṭ fī al-Madhhab*, ed. Muḥammad Muḥammad Tāmir, 1st ed., 6 vols. (Cairo: Dār al-Salām li-ʾl-Ṭibāʿa wa al-Nashr wa al-Tawzīʿ, 1997), 5:39.4–5.

the difference between the two methods boils down to whether it is the subjective experience of the individual coerced's that is dispositive in validating a claim of coercion or that of a hypothetical objective reasonable person. In the former method, legal coercion is found when the threat of harm disables the coerced's capacity to deliberate, and therefore makes a choice impossible. Reminiscent of the examples that populated Muʿtazilite theology, he gives the example of one fleeing from a predator, or from a person holding an unsheathed sword. He notes two things about this method. Since it is the subjective experience of the coerced that is the basis for validating a claim of coercion, it allows variation with an individual's capacity to bear the threat—"the weak become scared in such a way that his choice is cancelled, something that would not happen to the strong."[57] Yet, he also notes that any threat that does not involve an immediate harm, such as life imprisonment or starvation, is automatically excluded, because by their nature they do not eliminate the capacity to deliberate.[58] In the second method, claims of coercion are tested against what a reasonable person would have done when confronted with the coercer's threat and demand. For Ghazālī this method emphasizes the relationship between the coercer's threat and demand as an especially relevant feature in validating a coercion claim. For example, while the threat of imprisonment or destruction of one's property would not coerce if the demand is homicide, it would if the demand is divorce.[59]

5. CONCLUSION: THE EMPIRICIST AND RATIONALIST APPROACH OF THE INDEPENDENT-MINDED CLASSICAL SHĀFIʿITES ON DEFINING COERCION

When we compare the respective attempts of the Ḥanafites and the Shāfiʿites to develop a legal definition of coercion, two things stand out. First, the Ḥanafites are much more interested than the Shāfiʿites in providing scriptural justifications for their positions. This interest belies their reputation. Modern scholarship tends to view Ḥanafism as the more rationally oriented and Shāfiʿism as the conservative scripturalist tradition. But when

[57] Ibid., 5:389.9. [58] Ibid., 5:389.5–11. [59] Ibid., 5:389.12–390.2.

it comes to defining coercion, the opposite is the case. Unlike the Ḥanafites, the Shāfiʿites do not offer a single scriptural text or authoritative precedent to substantiate their positions on what is and what is not coercive. Their discussion is entirely empirical and rational.

The second noteworthy point is the relative uniformity of Ḥanafite definitions of coercion. Ḥanafite works do not depart from Shaybānī's positions on the elements needed to make a finding of coercion in various fields of law. Later Ḥanafite thinking thus revolved around elaborating on, clarifying, and supplementing Shaybānī's ideas in a way that was compatible with the core coercion laws of Ḥanafite jurisprudence.

Whereas Shaybānī's judgments were foundational for Ḥanafism, the same is not the case with Shāfiʿī in Shāfiʿism. Shāfiʿī commented briefly on what, empirically speaking, he thought was coercive to the point of altering the normative effects of speech acts. However, not only do these thoughts not serve as a point of departure for subsequent Shāfiʿites; they are not even quoted in later Shāfiʿite works. In fact, the Khurasani Shāfiʿites explicitly contradict Shāfiʿī's thoughts on the matter. While Shāfiʿī claimed that the threat of a severe beating was coercive in the case of speech acts, some Khurasanis disagreed, asserting that only a life-endangering threat is legally coercive. Why did some Shāfiʿites part company with the tradition's founder on this issue? More extensive comparative research on classical Islamic legal texts is needed to explain the predilections of legal scholars belonging to different schools. Existing scholarship on Islamic law suggests two possible explanations. Ahmed El Shamsy identifies a relatively individualistic conception of authority that emphasized deference only to scripture, and not the legal opinions of individual scholars, as a distinctive feature of Shāfiʿism after Shāfiʿī's death.[60] It could be the case that the Shāfiʿītes, because of this self-conception, felt much freer to depart from Shāfiʿī's precedent than the Ḥanafites felt to depart from that of their founding fathers. A second possibility is rooted in Sherman Jackson's observation that the postclassical Mālikite scholar Qarāfī notes explicitly that *taqlīd*, or the duty to defer to the received law of one's school, applies only to the normative rules enunciated

[60] On this, see El Shamsy, "The First Shāfiʿī," and *The Canonization of Islamic Law: a Social and Intellectual History*, chapter 7.

by the tradition's founding fathers.[61] There is no obligation to follow their empirical descriptions. This distinction suggests that it is not primarily an explicit pro-*ijtihād* identity that explains Shāfiᶜite behavior but rather the fact that premodern Shāfiᶜites, and perhaps members of other traditions, did not regard the empirical observations of previous jurists as binding precedents. Thus, finding later Shāfiᶜites ignoring and even contradicting Shāfiᶜī's views on coercion ought not to surprise us.

Regardless of which of these is the correct explanation, one thing is certain: it does not make sense to divide traditions along a rationalism/traditionalism axis, as scholars have habitually done. But if a commitment to rationalism or traditionalism does not explain a given tradition's method of justifying its rules, then what does explain it? The answer to this question emerges from an analysis of jurists' treatment of two specific issues, addressed in the next two chapters: coerced speech and coerced harm to others.

[61] *Islamic Law and State*, 114–116.

5

Coerced Speech Act Jurisprudence in Ḥanafism and Shāfiʿism

1. INTRODUCTION

It is difficult to overstate the centrality of speech in Islamic law. Speech can do a lot of things. It causes divorces and marriages. It concludes contracts of sale and lease. It emancipates slaves. It is through speech, primarily, that one converts to Islam, and it is also through speech that one may apostatize from the faith. Speech is also an important part of some ritual acts. One of the main components of the mandatory daily prayers, *ṣalāt*, is the recitation of a minimal portion of the Qurʾān, without which, the legal scholars say, the performance of prayer is invalid. In short, speech is ubiquitous in Islamic law—and at times it posed formidable problems for legal scholars. Speech is easy, but its legal effects can be momentous. It takes very little effort to utter the words to conclude a marriage or a sale, dissolve a marriage, or emancipate a slave. Yet entering a marriage has a cascade of significant legal effects: it legalizes sex, alters inheritances, and obligates maintenance and sexual availability. The labor involved in contracting the marriage is not proportional to the responsibilities and rights shed and gained.

Given this peculiar character of legal speech, its specific forms and the various accidents that may attend its utterance, such as sleep, insanity, minority, negligence, and indeed coercion, the topic occupied Islamic legal scholars to no end. One could imagine different ways to mitigate the problem of the disproportion between legal speech's labor and its effects. The legal scholars could have stipulated the involvement of duly appointed authorities, such as judges, as an essential condition for the validity of binding pronouncements. Or they could have constructed ornate and onerous formulas that could have marked legal speech as being of a different type, digging a moat between everyday speech and speech acts that transform life. But the jurists did not do either of these. A man could merely say the words, "I divorce Zeynap, I divorce Zeynap, I divorce Zeynap," and his wife Zeynap would be irrevocably divorced and two lives substantially transformed. The central question that the problem of coercion posed to speech acts is whether coercion could invalidate their normal effects.

Of the classical legal traditions, only Ḥanafism preserved the ancient Kufan law that coercion has no effect on pronouncements of divorce and emancipation. By the third/ninth century, all other legal traditions, including non-Sunnite ones, held that coercion invalidates a pronouncement of divorce. Consequently, one of the major burdens of Ḥanafite scholars in the succeeding centuries was justifying the Ḥanafite position in the face of the scriptural and legal arguments developed by rival traditions to criticize the Ḥanafite view. Much of Ḥanafite coerced speech jurisprudence is aimed at accomplishing this objective, and much of it is specifically oriented toward responding to Shāfiʿite criticisms. Likewise, Shāfiʿite coerced speech jurisprudence reflects efforts to defend the tradition against rival traditions' criticisms, albeit to a much lesser extent. Given the relative success of both traditions in the same geographical areas from the fourth/tenth to the sixth/twelfth century, this is not surprising.[1]

Ḥanafite jurisprudence on coerced speech consists of two analytical components. The scriptural component is aimed at showing that the relevant Qurʾān and ḥadīth texts support the Ḥanafite position. This involves two steps: a presentation of the central proof texts that Ḥanafites rely on to justify the laws related to speech acts and an argument for why the proof texts adduced by Shāfiʿites in support of their position do not in fact entail the Shāfiʿite position. The second component involves formulating principles that explain the coherence among the laws that both traditions share and applying those same principles to the laws on which they differ.

[1] The Ḥanafites I examine in this study come predominantly from Iraq, Iran, and Transoxania. In these areas in the fourth/tenth through sixth/twelfth centuries the main competing tradition was Shāfiʿism. On the spread of Shāfiʿism and Ḥanafism in Iran and Transoxania, see Wilferd Madelung, *Religious Trends in Early Islamic Iran*, Bibliotheca Persica (Albany, NY: Persian Heritage Foundation, 1988), 26–38. For an analysis of the at times violent conflict between Shāfiʿites and Ḥanafites in Eastern Iran and Transoxania, see Bulliet, *Patricians*, 28–46.

In addition to demonstrating that their coercion laws are fully reasonable interpretations of scripture and consistent with accepted legal principles, much of Ḥanafite jurisprudence on coerced speech is geared toward generating explanations for two discordant Ḥanafite coercion laws:

1. Life-threatening coercion has no effect on certain speech acts, such as pronouncements of divorce.
2. Minimally coercive threats, such as threats of beating and imprisonment, can invalidate certain other speech acts, such as sales and acknowledgments.

As noted earlier, the Shāfiʿites did not face a similar burden of justification because their position on these issues is much simpler: they held that coercion uniformly invalidates all speech acts without distinguishing between sales, marriages, divorces, emancipations, and acknowledgments. Their coerced speech jurisprudence was therefore unconcerned with establishing coherence among the laws on legal speech: with no perceived discrepancies to justify, the Shāfiʿites felt no need for such elaboration.

Of all the topics examined in this book, it is the jurisprudence on coerced speech that best lives up to the stereotype of Islamic law's dominant method of reasoning—namely, that it consists of scriptural arguments. Yet, the findings of this chapter will demonstrate that the extent and nature of scriptural justifications owes little to belonging to a given tradition. Rather, contingent factors such as the methods of reasoning that came to predominate a given region at a given time explain the types of arguments that take hold across traditions. Another contingent factor that determines how tradition-bound scholars argue with each other is the extent to which the inherited law of a given tradition clashes with the laws of other traditions. The more a tradition's law conflicts with that of other traditions, the more it makes sense for scholars of that tradition to articulate the legitimacy of the law in the most authoritative and canonical shared currency—scriptural interpretation. The fact that Ḥanafites maintained their stance on coerced speech acts in spite of majority opposition, and indeed developed an increasingly sophisticated scriptural defense of it over time, indicates a feature not just of Ḥanafism, but of legal traditions as such: that justifications within the publicly accepted language of a legal system are not necessarily indicative of the actual motivation for preserving a law. That this is the case becomes evident when we look at the history of American jurisprudence on coerced marriages, adoptions, and plea bargains.

2. ḤANAFITE PROOF TEXTS FOR THE VALIDITY OF COERCED DIVORCE

In contrast to commercial exchanges, which require the consent of two or more parties in order for legal consequences to take effect, unilateral speech acts require only the pronouncement of the legally mandated words by the holder of the relevant capacity in order for the legal effects to take place. Ḥanafite authors treat divorce as the paradigmatic instance of a unilateral, irrevocable speech act. Other types of unilateral speech acts are emancipations, vows, and oaths. The Ḥanafites assume that the arguments they adduce to justify the Ḥanafite position on the validity of a coerced pronouncement of divorce apply equally to other speech acts of the same type.

The vast majority of proof texts cited by classical Ḥanafite scholars as the basis for their position on unilateral speech acts stem from Shaybānī's work. The introduction to his book on coercion consists of his citation of one ḥadīth, six reports from the Prophet's companions, and the opinions of several early authorities in favor of the Ḥanafite position on coerced divorce.[2]

Of the five Ḥanafite authors surveyed in this chapter (Jaṣṣāṣ, Qudūrī, Dabūsī, Sarakhsī, and Bazdawī), all but Bazdawī discuss the scriptural evidence for the Shāfiʿite and Ḥanafite positions. Specifically, Jaṣṣāṣ, Qudūrī, and Dabūsī cite portions of the Qurʾānic verses 2:229 and 2:230 as evidence for the validity of the Ḥanafite position. The positive content of these long verses is not important for Jaṣṣāṣ and Dabūsī. They cite the verses only to emphasize the absence of any explicit distinction between coerced and uncoerced pronouncements of divorce in them.

[2] Shaybānī, *al-Aṣl*, 7:298–302.2. The number of proof texts collected by Shaybānī on this topic exceeds the amount of textual evidence he usually gives in support of Ḥanafite positions. I think this is an indication that already in Shaybānī's time, the Ḥanafite position on coerced divorce had become a minority one.

Jaṣṣāṣ categorizes the verses as a type of justification that relies only on the verses' apparent meaning (*fa-amma ʾl-dalīl ʿalā ṣihhati qawli-nā min jihati ʾl-ẓāhir*). He notes that the general sense of the verses' phrasing requires that one affirm the validity of a coerced pronouncement of divorce (*wa-ʿumūmu-hu yūjib wuqūʿa ṭalāq al-mukrah*) because it does not specifically distinguish between coerced and uncoerced pronouncements.[3] Dabūsī makes the same argument.[4]

Qudūrī entertains the objection that the aim (*qaṣd*) of the verses is to clarify the laws regarding the revocability of two pronouncements of divorce and the prohibition of remarriage after the third. The implication of the objection is that the verses are not trying to establish conditions of validity for divorces, and hence they cannot serve as an argument for why coerced divorces are valid. To this, he responds that what is of primary relevance for the construction of laws is not the aims the speaker seeks to accomplish through speech but the generality of the language used,[5] and since the generality of the language in these verses makes no explicit distinction between coerced and uncoerced divorces, the legal presumption must be that coercion is irrelevant to a divorce's effectiveness.

In addition to the Qurʾānic verses, Jaṣṣāṣ, Qudūrī, and Dabūsī cite ḥadīth texts. For Sarakhsī, the ḥadīth texts, along with reports from companions and their successors, are the main proof texts in coerced speech jurisprudence. In one ḥadīth, the Prophet is confronted with the case of a woman who climbs on top of her husband while he is sleeping, holds a knife to his neck, and demands a divorce. The husband complies, then presumably later complains to the Prophet. The Prophet replies, "There is no rescission in divorce" (*lā qaylūla fī ʾl-ṭalāq*).[6]

[3] Jaṣṣāṣ, *Sharḥ*, 5:6.1–3.

[4] See Dabūsī, *Asrār*, 997.22, though unlike Jaṣṣāṣ, Dabūsī does not reference either the apparent or the general sense of the verses.

[5] Qudūrī, *al-Tajrīd*, 10:4912.3–7.

[6] Jaṣṣāṣ, *Sharḥ*, 5:6.7–13; Dabūsī, *Asrār*, 997.26; Qudūrī, *al-Tajrīd*, 10:4913.8–4915.5; Sarakhsī, *al-Mabsūṭ*, 24:50.13–16. Exactly what the Arabic word *qaylūla* means is debated in the legal community. Jaṣṣāṣ assumes that the word is a synonym for *iqāla*, which means cancellation or rescission. On the debate regarding the term's meaning, see Māwardī, *al-Ḥāwī*, 10:229.26–29. Sarakhsī notes that the term can mean either rescission or a midday nap. Either way, he interprets the ḥadīth as justifying the Ḥanafite position. With the latter meaning, the Prophet was merely saying that the man had been tried by the ordeal of falling asleep at that time, and that this did not cancel the legal validity of his pronouncement of divorce. I should point out that the published version of Sarakhsī's text should probably be emended from the existing *bi-hādha*

A companion report alternately attributed to ʿAlī and to Ibn ʿAbbās declares, "Every divorce is valid except that of the minor (*al-ṣabī*) and the partially insane (*al-maʿtūh*)."[7] Following Shaybānī's core argument,[8] later Ḥanafites construe this report as establishing that *only* minority and insanity invalidate a pronouncement of divorce. Sarakhsī further argues that someone who is coerced to pronounce a divorce is not in the same class as a minor or an insane person, because in his case moral agency and the status of being under moral obligation persist despite the coercion (*li-baqāʾi ʾl-ahliyya wa-ʾl-khiṭāb maʿa ʾl-ikrāh*), whereas they do not for minors and the insane.[9]

Another important proof text for the Ḥanafite position on coerced legal speech acts is a ḥadīth attributed to the Prophet in which he equates the legal effects of serious and jestful speech in three specific matters: marriage, divorce, and manumission.[10] The Shāfiʿite Māwardī interpreted this text narrowly to assert that only the excuse of jest would not invalidate the legal consequences that follow from pronouncing a divorce, consenting to a marriage, or manumitting a slave.[11] The Shāfiʿites held that the effect of the ḥadīth was to establish that one cannot pronounce a divorce and then claim that one had been just joking in order to invalidate it. Jaṣṣāṣ, on the other hand, interprets the text in the following way:

> The Prophet equated the legal effects of the one who is serious and the one who jests, even though one of them intended the legal consequence of the utterance while the other did not. This indicates that the legal consequence is binding on anyone who utters a divorce, and that the absence of will [for it] has no effect in lifting the legal consequence of his utterance.[12]

li-ajli yawm al-qaylūla to *bi-hādha li-ajli nawm al-qaylūla*. Incidentally, in contrast to Dabūsī, Jaṣṣāṣ cites complete chains of transmission for each of the ḥadīths he uses. Qudūrī also cites this ḥadīth as an argument against an objection that sought to emend the text of the ḥadīth in such a way as to render Ḥanafite reliance on it mute. Qudūrī cites the authority of the Basran scholar of Arabic Ibn Jinnī (d. 392/1002) and Abū Zayd al-Anṣārī (d. 214/830) to resist the emendation.

[7] For Qudūrī's citation of the report, see Qudūrī, *al-Tajrīd*, 10:4926.1–2.

[8] Shaybānī, *al-Aṣl*, 7:301.9–11. Shaybānī attributes it to ʿAlī alone.

[9] Sarakhsī, *al-Mabsūṭ*, 24:52.16–19. Sarakhsī attributes the report to ʿAlī as well as Ibn ʿAbbās.

[10] Jaṣṣāṣ, *Sharḥ*, 5:7.5–8; Dabūsī, *Asrār*, 998.1–2; Sarakhsī, *al-Mabsūṭ*, 24:51. Unlike the other two, Jaṣṣāṣ cites the entire chain of transmission for the ḥadīth. Sarakhsī additionally cites reports attributed to ʿUmar, ʿAlī, and Ibn al-Musayyib containing substantially the same idea.

[11] See, for example, Māwardī, *al-Ḥāwī*, 10:230.22–25.

[12] Jaṣṣāṣ, *Sharḥ*, 5:7.9–12.

Qudūrī and Dabūsī go beyond using the ḥadīth to defend the validity of the Ḥanafite position on coerced divorce. They use it to establish features of speech acts that are mutually exclusive: all speech acts are either serious or jestful, and in the cases of marriage, divorce, and emancipation, performing a speech act in jest has no vitiating effect on the legal consequences of the act.[13] Factually speaking, Dabūsī argues, a coerced speech act is a serious one; therefore its legal consequences are valid. He writes:

> The speech of the coerced is serious, because he is coerced to adopt the serious mood, and he has obeyed what was demanded of him [by the coercer], except he did not do it while being satisfied with his choice. This is because nothing else occurred to the mind of the [coerced] agent [when the coercer demanded the pronouncement] and he responded in a serious mood, though he acted out of fear.[14]

Sarakhsī makes substantially the same argument as Dabūsī, adding that contentment and coercion are mutually exclusive categories. Coercion negates contentment, but according to the law, the validity of these speech acts does not depend on contentment, and therefore coercion has no effect on their validity.[15]

3. SHĀFIʿITE PROOF TEXTS FOR THE INVALIDITY OF COERCED DIVORCE

As we saw in Chapter 4, Shāfiʿī gives two scriptural arguments for his position that coercion invalidates legal speech acts such as divorce. He cites the Qurʾānic verse 16:106 and notes that if coercion can cancel the normative effects of as serious a sin as uttering disbelief, then a fortiori it can cancel the effects of all other speech acts.[16] In addition, he cites the Prophetic ḥadīth

[13] See Qudūrī, *al-Tajrīd*, 10:4915.5–9. Dabūsī argues that the serious/jestful dichotomy as applied to speech acts is similar to the true/false dichotomy as applied to legally relevant factual statements. In both cases the categories are mutually exclusive. See Dabūsī, *Asrār*, 998.16–17.

[14] Dabūsī, *Asrār*, 998.7–8.

[15] Sarakhsī, *al-Mabsūṭ*, 24:51.27–52.5.

[16] The fifth/eleventh-century Shāfiʿite Ibn al-Maḥāmilī (d. 415/1024) also cites this verse as proof for the Shāfiʿite position. See Aḥmad b. Muḥammad Ibn al-Maḥāmilī, *al-Lubāb fī al-Fiqh al-Shāfiʿī*, ed. ʿAbd al-Karīm b. Ṣunaytān Amrī, 1st ed. (Medina: Dār al-Bukhārī, 1416[/1995]), 370.7–371.3.

that says, "Mistaken acts, forgetful acts, and what one is forced to do are lifted from my community." Māwardī and Shīrāzī also cite this ḥadīth, though neither reproduces the a fortiori argument based on Qurʾān 16:106. Māwardī adds a ḥadīth in which the Prophet declares that there is "no divorce in the case of closure (*ighlāq*)." He points out that there are two different ways to interpret the legal significance of the term "closure" (*ighlāq*) used in the ḥadīth and refers to the philological authority of Abū ʿUbayd (d. 224/838), who glosses the term as referring to coercion, "because the choice of the coerced is as if closed in."[17]

4. ḤANAFITE TREATMENT OF SHĀFIʿITE PROOF TEXTS AND SHĀFIʿITE RESPONSES

Ḥanafite scriptural justification needed not only to show how proof texts justify a positive law in their tradition, but also to defend that law against the scriptural justifications produced by legal traditions with conflicting laws on the same case. The Shāfiʿites held that coercion invalidates all speech acts, including acts such as divorce. Many of their justifications relied on entirely different proof texts than those used by the Ḥanafites. The Ḥanafite jurists sought to show why these proof texts did not commit them to the Shāfiʿite law. The most important of these proof texts was a ḥadīth cited by Shāfiʿī that states, in one version, "Mistaken acts, forgetful acts, and what one is forced to do are lifted from my community."[18]

4.1 "Mistaken acts, forgetful acts, and what one is forced to do are lifted from my community"

That this was one of the most important proof texts against the Ḥanafite position on coerced speech is evident from the fact that even the third/ninth-century Ḥanafite Ṭaḥāwī devotes a chapter to explaining why it does not undermine the Ḥanafite position on coerced speech acts. Ṭaḥāwī notes that

[17] Māwardī, *al-Ḥāwī*, 10:228.27–229.2.

[18] There are actually several different versions of this ḥadīth. For an analysis of the versions, their dating, and the authenticity of the ḥadīth, see Syed, "Coercion in Classical Islamic Law and Theology," 42–7.

two groups, which he does not name explicitly, interpret the ḥadīth in different ways. One group reads the ḥadīth to establish the law that coercion invalidates marriages, oaths, emancipations, and divorces. The second group holds that the text refers only to the effect of coercion on the legal and moral effects of apostasy. For the latter, the ḥadīth addresses the same historical context and issue as Qurʾān 16:106—namely, coerced apostasy. Ṭaḥāwī admits that the text can support both interpretations and offers an argument that tips the balance in favor of the second camp. He points out that everyone agrees that if a man distractedly utters the divorce formula regarding his wife, the divorce is effective and not undermined by his forgetfulness. No one thinks that the ḥadīth applies to this case, even though forgetfulness is one of the specific features mentioned in the ḥadīth. Similarly, the ḥadīth does not automatically require the invalidity of coerced divorces, emancipations, vows, and marriages.[19]

Jaṣṣāṣ adopts an entirely different strategy. He dismisses the legal value of the ḥadīth by citing the opinion of the ḥadīth scholar Aḥmad b. Ḥanbal (d. 241/855) that only versions of the ḥadīth that have al-Ḥasan al-Baṣrī transmitting directly from the Prophet (classified as *mursal*) are historical. According to Ibn Ḥanbal, all the other versions are fabricated. Jaṣṣāṣ concludes that since the opponents of the Ḥanafites make it a policy not to rely on ḥadīth with *mursal* chains of transmission, they cannot use this ḥadīth as proof for their legal positions.[20]

Jaṣṣāṣ adds that even if one were to assume that the ḥadīth is authentic, it still does not support the law that coercion invalidates a pronouncement of divorce. He argues that relying on the literal sense of the ḥadīth to construct the law would imply the negation of the actual occurrence of the coerced act, because the ḥadīth literally says, "Coerced acts are lifted from my community" (*rufiʿa ʿan ummatī mā istukrihū ʿalay-hi*). But coerced acts do in fact take place and can be seen with the naked eye. Therefore, this interpretation is absurd. Since this is the case, Jaṣṣāṣ concludes that the Prophet's intended message is not fully expressed by the actual words of the ḥadīth, and it must

[19] Aḥmad b. Muḥammad al-Ṭaḥāwī, *Sharḥ Maʿānī al-Āthār*, ed. Muḥammad Zuhrī al-Najjār and Muḥammad Sayyid Jād al-Ḥaqq, 1st ed., 5 vols. (Beirut: ʿĀlam al-Kutub, 1994), 3:96.1–10.
[20] Jaṣṣāṣ, *Sharḥ*, 5:9.6–16.

be read elliptically. Comprehending the real meaning of the ḥadīth requires supplying the missing words that will generate the full meaning of the ellipsis.[21]

According to Jaṣṣāṣ, there are two possible ways to establish the legal intent of the ḥadīth. We can either attempt to identify the missing element in the text or regard the phrasing of the text as metaphorical. If we pursue the former strategy, we should keep in mind that legal presumptions about the attributes of a text, such as its specificity or generality, can be made only about the actual words of the text, not the missing element. If we pursue the latter possibility, we should recognize that we can use a text metaphorically only if we have some kind of evidence that justifies disregard of the text's apparent meaning. Though Jaṣṣāṣ does not explicitly say so, the latter possibility is unjustified, since in his view we lack the evidence that would warrant such a move. We are thus left with the former possibility.[22]

Jaṣṣāṣ identifies two possible candidates for the missing element. The meaning of the ḥadīth could be either "*the legal effects of* coerced acts are lifted from my community" or "*the sinful effects of* coerced acts are lifted from my community." It cannot, in Jaṣṣāṣ's view, be both, given his argument that legal presumptions about the generality of a text can be made only about the text's actual phrasing. Therefore, it cannot be assumed that the text covers both legal consequences in this world and the effects of sin in the next. We must choose one of the two constructions, but this choice cannot be arbitrary. In order to decide which of the two constructions to favor, we need evidence external to the text, perhaps from other texts. Jaṣṣāṣ asserts that the missing element must be "the sinful effects," because the prima facie sense of phrases such as "God forgives John" or "God pardons John" is that God negates the sinful, otherworldly consequences of the offending act. Moreover, the fact that all jurists hold that mistaken or forgetful pronouncements of divorce are nonetheless binding indicates that the ḥadīth must refer to the removal of an act's sinful effects rather than its legal ones. For these reasons, Jaṣṣāṣ argues that the ḥadīth cannot negate the legal consequences of coerced divorce.[23]

[21] Ibid., 5:10.4–10. [22] Ibid., 5:10.7–16. [23] Ibid., 5:10.15–11.11.

Dabūsī adopts a strategy similar to that of Jaṣṣāṣ. He notes that both Shāfiʿites and Ḥanafites admit that in *some* cases neither coercion nor lack of intent invalidates the legal consequences of a coerced or mistaken act. Given this agreement, Dabūsī argues that the ḥadīth ought not to be construed as a global law on the impact of coercion on the legal consequences of a particular act; rather, it ought to be read in a modified sense. What is this modified sense? The apparent meaning of the ḥadīth's wording is insufficient to support a law. In order to construct a law, we must, therefore, read into the text what it inferentially requires (*iqtiḍāʾ*). According to Dabūsī's legal hermeneutics, the ḥadīth requires the addition of elements to the scriptural text in order to complete the meaning necessary for the construction of a legal or moral norm.[24] As linguistic inferences go, Dabūsī considers this hermeneutical technique to have the most tenuous connection to the scriptural text.[25] When the connection is weak, the scope of the law's application must be construed as narrowly as possible. In the case of the ḥadīth referring to "lifted" liability, Dabūsī comments that this means that "only the judgment of sin has been negated (*wa-qad intafā ḥukm al-ithm*)" from an agent who has committed a mistaken, forgetful, or—for our purposes—coerced act.[26] Being coerced cancels the agent's moral, otherworldly liability for the act before

[24] Importantly, the authority of the legal or moral norm is still conceived of as depending upon the text from which it is derived. Despite the fact that Dabūsī's method requires information external to the text, he still insists that the resulting law be attributed to the text (*ḥukm al-muqtaḍā muḍāf ilā ʾl-naṣṣ*). See Abū Zayd ʿAbd Allāh b. ʿUmar al-Dabūsī, *Taqwīm Uṣūl al-Fiqh wa Taḥdīd Adillat al-Sharʿ*, ed. ʿAbd al-Jalīl ʿAṭā, 1st ed., 2 vols. (Damascus, Syria; Tripoli, Lebanon: Dār al-Nuʿmān li-ʾl-ʿUlūm; Dār al-Imām Abī Ḥanīfah, 2005), 1:314.9–11. While there was widespread agreement on the validity of "inferred requirement" as a linguistic operation, there was disagreement about whether the weakness of the operation had an effect on the resulting law's scope of application. According to Dabūsī, the Ḥanafites regarded the hermeneutical operation as downgrading the presumptive generality of the law, whereas the Shāfiʿites held the position that the operation has no effect on its scope and that the law derived from the text retains the same level of generality. For a theoretical exposition of the hermeneutical technique of inferential requirement, see ibid., 1:314–321. For scholarship on it, see Zysow, *The Economy of Certainty: an Introduction to the Typology of Islamic Legal Theory*, 57, who, relying on later Central Asian Ḥanafites, defines the inferential requirement as "the legal background necessary for the text to take effect." See also Kamali, *Principles of Islamic Jurisprudence*, 128–30.

[25] The other three categories, in order of decreasing strength, are the plain expression of the text (*ʿibārat al-naṣṣ*), the indication of the text (*ishārat al-naṣṣ*), and the allusion of the text (*dalālat al-naṣṣ*). For this, see Dabūsī, *Taqwīm*, 300–26. For contemporary scholarship on these categories in Muslim legal theory more generally, see Kamali, *Principles of Islamic Jurisprudence*, 124–48, and Zysow, *The Economy of Certainty: an Introduction to the Typology of Islamic Legal Theory*, 55–58.

[26] See Dabūsī, *Asrār*, 1001.16–19.

God. But the text does not imply anything about the legal consequences of the act in this world. For all of these reasons, Dabūsī concludes, the "lifted" ḥadīth cannot be read as supporting the Shāfiʿite law.

4.2 "Actions are [judged] by intentions"

Ṭaḥāwī and Dabūsī take aim at the interpretation of another famous ḥadīth used to justify the position that coercion invalidates all speech acts, including divorces. The ḥadīth in question begins with the statement that "actions are [judged] by intentions." Countering what he describes as the Shāfiʿite view, Ṭaḥāwī denies that the ḥadīth establishes the principle that the appropriate intention must accompany a speech act for the act to be deemed legally valid. He reinterprets the ḥadīth as confirming simply that Divine reward in the hereafter for a given action correlates with the agent's intention in performing the action.[27] But, he claims, the ḥadīth has no legal effect on the issue of coerced divorce.

Dabūsī interprets the "intentions" ḥadīth in the same way in which he interpreted the "lifted" ḥadīth. He asserts that since both the Ḥanafites and the Shāfiʿites evaluate the validity of at least some actions without considering intention, the ḥadīth must be interpreted in light of what is inferentially required to establish a law different from the one that the Shāfiʿites base on it. Just as he argued for limiting the scope of the "lifted" ḥadīth to moral consequences in the hereafter, so he also argues that the "intention" ḥadīth must be construed to refer only to rewards in the hereafter. The function of the ḥadīth is merely to notify the believers that God rewards them according to what they intended by their acts (*wa-qad taʿallaqa bi-ʾl-niyyati ḥukmu al-thawābi fa-lam yuthbat mā siwā-hu*).[28] Through this argument, Dabūsī seeks to eliminate considerations of intention in assessments of the legal validity of coerced legal speech, especially those statements that, once uttered, are irrevocable. Interestingly, though Ḥanafite authors treat this ḥadīth as a putative proof text for the Shāfiʿite law, none of the Shāfiʿites analyzed in this book actually cites it in support of his position.

[27] Ṭahāwī, *Sharḥ Maʿānī al-Āthār*, 3:96.12–97.1.

[28] Dabūsī, *Asrār*, 1001.18–19.

4.3 "No divorce in the case of closure"

A third ḥadīth claimed as proof for the position that coercion invalidates a pronouncement of divorce is the ḥadīth "No divorce in the case of closure," mentioned earlier in the chapter. Māwardī cites Abū ʿUbayd's interpretation of "closure" as coercion, because coercion closes off choice.[29] Dabūsī refers to the ḥadīth as a Shāfiʿite proof text but does not attempt to reinterpret it.[30] Jaṣṣāṣ argues that "closure" refers not to coercion but to insanity, because when "a person's door is closed in on him, he is prevented from [legally] engaging in all types of legal acts." Only insanity, not coercion, legally cancels the validity of *all* types of legal acts, and therefore the ḥadīth must refer to insanity.[31]

Qudūrī reproduces the argument offered by Jaṣṣāṣ, remarking that it is the standard response of his colleagues.[32] In addition, he denies that Abū ʿUbayd had anything to say about this ḥadīth and asserts that the gloss quoted by Māwardī was attributed to him by Ibn Qutbī, who does not specify where his information comes from and who is himself not an authority for experts of the Arabic language (*wa-laysa huwa ḥujjatan ʿinda ahl al-ʿarabiyya*). Based on the usage of the related verb *ghalaq* in poetry, Qudūrī proposes that the meaning of the phrase is that "a man who is truly in love with his wife or slave is in a state of *ighlāq* or closure to the extent that he cannot divorce or emancipate her."[33] Hence the Prophet is not prescribing a law in this ḥadīth but rather describing the reality of romantic love—it fundamentally prevents one from letting go of the object of one's love.

The Ḥanafites used one nonscriptural argument in support of their position on coerced speech acts that did not stem from concerns about the internal coherence of their corpus juris. Both Sarakhsī and Bazdawī argued that one cannot regard coercion as simply erasing the moral or legal consequences of an act. Just as coercion does not eliminate moral agency or

[29] Māwardī, *al-Ḥāwī*, 10:229.1–9.
[30] Dabūsī, *Asrār*, 996.12.
[31] Jaṣṣāṣ, *Sharḥ*, 5:8.8–9.5.
[32] Qudūrī, *al-Tajrīd*, 10:4920.1–4.
[33] For Qudūrī's linguistic analysis and evidence, see ibid., 10:4922.6–4924.6. For a summary of his analysis and interpretation of the report, which requires emendation of the key term *ighlāq* to *ghilāq*, see ibid., 10:4923.4–7. For essentially the same interpretation but without requiring emendation, see ibid., 10:4924.1–5.

choice, it also does not eliminate an act's consequences as if the act never happened,[34] something Bazdawī describes as a fundamental principle of Shāfiʿite coercion jurisprudence. As an alternative to legal elimination, Sarakhsī holds up the idea of transference, but only for those acts that pass the instrument test. For Sarakhsī, coercion does not eliminate moral responsibility, but it does have the effect of transferring legal consequences for acts that pass the instrument test. Since speech acts fail the instrument test and their legal consequences cannot simply be erased by coercion, the Ḥanafites are left with only one possible position, which they readily acknowledge as a fundamental principle of their coerced speech jurisprudence: as a legal presumption, one must acknowledge the prima facie validity of any act performed by an agent who has the legal competence to engage in it and the appropriate legal relationship to the object of the act (*taṣarruf min ahli-hi fī maḥalli-hi*).[35] This idea is first spelled out by Dabūsī,[36] and Sarakhsī claims that it is implicit in the legal precedents (ḥadīth, companion statements, and legal doctrines of the early authorities) cited at the beginning of his chapter on coercion.[37] The Ḥanafites shift the focus of analysis from whether a particular speech act was willed or intended by the agent to whether the agent had the capacity to engage in that act. Even if a person coerced to divorce a wife or to manumit a slave may not have intended to do so, the Ḥanafites thought that the mere presence of the capacity to form intentions was sufficient to establish the effectiveness of these unilateral speech acts.

5. ḤANAFITE CASE ARGUMENTS

We can divide the justifications offered by classical Ḥanafites for their coercion jurisprudence into two main types: scriptural and legal. Scriptural

[34] The Arabic term that is most commonly used to denote the concept of elimination in Ḥanafite texts is *ihdār*. Another common term is *ilghā*ʾ. The rejection of the concept of legal elimination is given as a fundamental principle of coercion jurisprudence first by Sarakhsī and later by Bazdawī. See Sarakhsī, *al-Mabsūṭ*, 24:87.21–22, 24:173.28–174.2, and Bazdawī, *al-Kāfī*, 5:2432.1–2. For the germs of the argument in Dabūsī's work, see Dabūsī, *Asrār*, 998–1000.

[35] Sarakhsī, *al-Mabsūṭ*, 24:68.27–28.

[36] Dabūsī, *Asrār*, 998.22–23.

[37] Sarakhsī, *al-Mabsūṭ*, 24:68.27.

arguments seek to show that a scriptural proof text supports the law that the tradition upholds. Such arguments are aimed at bridging the gap between a proof text and a law and at reconciling the two. Scriptural arguments can also be deployed to explain why a given proof text does not support a law that contradicts the one to which the tradition is committed. Such arguments are used in an attempt to prove that a gap exists between a proof text and a law. Ḥanafite coercion jurisprudence also employs another type of argumentation, which I call legal analysis. Legal analysis consists, among other things, of invocation of substantive legal principles as justifications for existing laws and as guidelines for the discovery of new laws. The epistemic origin of these principles varies. Sometimes they are derived from scriptural sources. Other times they represent in abstract form the common features of different laws within a tradition or of laws shared by multiple traditions. And other times still they are succinct metaphors or tests that encapsulate the values that jurists see as governing jurisprudence in a given field. The instrument test is an example of this type of legal analysis. Legal analysis can also consist of a search for coherence among laws pertaining to different cases. In such analysis, the dispute between traditions committed to conflicting laws on a given case revolves around other relevant cases that can be called upon to support a tradition's position. This approach often involves responding to charges of unprincipled or arbitrary reasoning posed by scholars of rival traditions who claim that the two cases are not in fact governed by the same principle.

Legal analysis in Ḥanafite jurisprudence on coerced speech centers on three major threats to the internal coherence of the Ḥanafite corpus juris posed by their commitment to their position on coerced unilateral speech. If intention is not a valid legal criterion for invalidating irrevocable coerced speech, then what justifies the Ḥanafite positions on the invalidity of the legal speech acts of minors, the invalidity of coerced acknowledgments (*iqrārāt*), and coercion's capacity to create at least defective, and thus ex post facto voidable, commercial transactions, even though these are also a type of speech act?

5.1 The Speech Acts of Minors and the Shāfiʿite Intention Principle

Both Ḥanafite and Shāfiʿite scholars agree that minors are not legally responsible for their acts. Dabūsī notes that the reason minors are not held responsible for their actions is that they lack the requisite intellectual and physical capacity to willingly undertake obligations.[38] But in Dabūsī's account, his Shāfiʿite interlocutors go a step further.[39] They argue that what the insane, the sleeping, and minors have in common is their lack of an intention when performing a speech act. It is this absence, they claim, that accounts for both traditions' invalidation of the consequences of any speech acts undertaken by these types of agents.[40] They further point out that minors lack the specific capacity of discerning the particular meanings of words and therefore of forming a particular intention in their use.[41] If it is the lack of a valid intention behind a speech act or the lack of the very capacity to form an intention that blocks the legal consequences of a minor's legal speech act, then can the same argument not be made for the coerced? A coerced agent performs the demanded speech act not to express an intention but rather to repel the harm that the coercer threatens to inflict.

Dabūsī attempts to neutralize this argument by asserting that laws and legal judgments can be based only on what is empirically accessible, which intentions are not. In an argument that Sarakhsī reproduces, Dabūsī claims that although it is true that the possession of relevant capacities is necessary for full legal and moral competence, the point at which individuals actually acquire those capacities is "an internal matter regarding which people vary"

[38] See Dabūsī, *Asrār*, 999.1–8, where Dabūsī notes that revelation makes the full maturation of the intellect a proxy for the balance of the various types of capacities needed to accomplish the duties owed to God. Dabūsī notes that this is an act of mercy on the part of God (*al-sharʿu aqāma ʾl-bulūgha ʿan ʿaqli fī tawajjuhi al-khiṭābi maqāma iʿtidāli ʾl-asbābi allatī yabtanī ʿalay-hā ʾl-khiṭābu min anwāʿi al-qudrati li-iqāmati mā khūṭabu taysīran ʿalay-nā*), for had God made the acquisition of the actual capacities to discharge the duties owed to Him a condition for moral agency, human beings would have faced much hardship (*fa-innahu law banā-hu ʿalā adnā ʾl-qudra la-aḥarajna fī iqāmati-hi*). Dabūsī echoes the same sentiments in his work of legal theory, the *Taqwīm*. For this, see Dabūsī, *Taqwīm*, 2:894.

[39] I have not found these arguments in Shāfiʿite sources.

[40] Dabūsī, *Asrār*, 996.15–16.

[41] In ibid., 996.16–17, Dabūsī writes, "He has no discernment through which he might intend [the] predetermined [meanings] of words" (*lā tamyīza la-hu li-yaqṣida bi-ʾl-tamyīzi mā wuḍiʿa ʾl-kalāmu la-hu*).

(*amrun bāṭinun yatafāwatu fī-hi ʾl-nās*)[42] and thus an "impossible matter to ascertain" (*fa-yataʿadhdharu ʾl-wuqūfu ʿalay-hi*)[43] for the purpose of establishing moral and legal competence. In fact, it is precisely for this reason, says Dabūsī, that the Divine law fixes the age of majority as the moment after which individuals can be held morally and legally responsible.[44] He asserts that the only consideration in determining the validity of a speech act "is whether it is uttered by someone who has the competence to form an intention, not the reality of the intention" (*tubnā ʾl-aḥkāmu ʿalā kawni ʾl-fāʿili min ahli ʾl-qaṣdi dūna ḥaqīqati al-qaṣd*).[45] Again, the reason for this limitation is that forming an intention is an internal act. Dabūsī gives a hypothetical example to demonstrate his point:

> A man says to his wife: if you love me, you are divorced. His wife, angry, says, "I love you." She is considered divorced even if the husband denies [that she loves him]. This is because love exists in the heart. [From a legal perspective] it is impossible to depend on its reality in assessing legal consequences. The consequences are connected to the cause that customarily indicates [the reality], which is the testimony of the tongue.[46]

In addition to denying that legal judgments regarding the validity of speech acts are dependent on the integrity of intention, Dabūsī also denies the Shāfiʿite claim that intention is vitiated by coercion, arguing that

> the coerced acts with discernment and perceptiveness because he knows the two evil options [before him], distinguishes the lesser evil, and chooses it. He is, however, forced to do it unwillingly, not desiring it willingly.[47]

The coerced fully intends the act he performs. It is not intention that is compromised by coercion but willingness, and Dabūsī disputes the contention that willingness (*ṭawāʿiyya*) is essential to the validity of speech acts by invoking the case of the insane (*majnūn*). An insane person, he points out, speaks willingly, but the law regards that speech as nonsense (*laghw*) because such a person has no discernment (*tamyīz*) nor reason (*ʿaql*).[48]

[42] Ibid., 999.4–5. [43] Dabūsī, ibid., 999.5–6.
[44] See ibid.: "Thus, revelation has established the full maturation of the intellect as majority, which, customarily, is the cause of the equanimity of the intellect" (*fa-aqāma al-sharʿu ʾl-bulūgha ʿan ʿaql alladhī huwa sababu iʿtidāli ʾl-aqli ʿādatan*). See also Sarakhsī, *al-Mabsūṭ*, 24:69.5–7.
[45] Dabūsī, *Asrār*, 999.28. [46] Ibid., 999.28–30. [47] Ibid., 999.8–9.
[48] Ibid., 999.8.

Moreover, Dabūsī argues that the burden of proof is on those who make willingness a criterion for the validity of speech acts, "because it [willingness] is a hidden attribute, one of the attributes of the heart, and therefore it is impossible to base assessments of validity on it" (*wa-li-anna al-ṭawʿa ṣifatun bāṭinatun min ṣifāti ʾl-qalbi fa-yataʿadhdharu bināʾu al-ṣiḥḥati ʿalay-hi*).[49] Willingness "can cease to exist through hidden reasons known only to the agent" (*fa-inna-hu yazūlu bi-asbābin khafiyyatin lā yaʿrifu-hā ghayr ʾl-mutaṣarrif*).[50] It is "even less accessible to knowledge than equanimity of intellect" (*wa-inna-hu akhfā min maʿrifati Al-ʿaql*),[51] the underlying cause of majority.

Sarakhsī provides a similar description of what, exactly, someone coerced to pronounce a divorce is doing. He, too, asserts that coercion does not eliminate intent or choice:

> This is because the coerced knows of two evils and chooses the lesser one. This is evidence of the correct functioning of his choice. How could [coercion] eliminate his choice when he intends to do a particular action in order to repel evil from himself? He cannot accomplish this goal without pronouncing the divorce. Something that can only be accomplished through a given means then becomes as if a goal itself. Therefore, we know that he chooses and intends, but not for an intrinsic reason. On the contrary, [he does it] to repel harm from himself. He has the same status as a jester who intends an utterance, choosing it not for its legal consequences but for something else. A divorce uttered by the jester is [nonetheless] valid. Through this case, it becomes clear that [an agent's] contentment with the legal consequence [of an act] once he has intended [the act] and chosen the legal cause is not a legal consideration.[52]

This passage encapsulates in summary form the Ḥanafite strategy on coerced speech. In accordance with their overall empirical description of the effect of coercion on choice, the Ḥanafites maintain that the coerced pronouncer of divorce (or manumission) still chooses to utter the formula of divorce (or manumission). The most important proof text that the Ḥanafites think relevant to the case of coerced speech is the Prophetic ḥadīth that affirms the validity of speech acts uttered in jest. The Ḥanafites argue for the similarity

[49] Ibid., 999.10–11. [50] Ibid., 999.11. [51] Ibid.
[52] Sarakhsī, *al-Mabsūṭ*, 24:69.11–17.

of a coerced pronouncement of divorce and a pronouncement made in jest because all of the Sunnite legal traditions uphold the validity of a divorce pronounced in jest.

Ḥanafite coercion jurisprudence had to respond not only to the position adopted by the other legal traditions that coercion invalidates all speech acts, but also the potential inconsistency between their own laws: the Ḥanafites held that coercion does in fact invalidate legal acknowledgments and creates an option of cancellation for commercial exchanges. Both of these acts are types of legal speech. The discrepancy, of course, invited charges of inconsistency and forced the Ḥanafites to make efforts to show why legal acknowledgments and commercial exchanges were different from divorces and manumissions.

5.2 Coerced Acknowledgments (*Iqrārāt*)

A legal acknowledgment is the explicit recognition of certain facts that in some way affect the legal status of the acknowledger. One of the most important types of acknowledgment in Islamic legal thought is the admission of a debt owed to someone else. The difference between an acknowledgment and a speech act is that speech acts create a new set of legal rights and obligations. A pronouncement of divorce, for example, creates the duty to pay off the marriage gift (*mahr*) and eliminates the duty of maintenance. An acknowledgment does not by itself create new rights and duties; rather, it legally confirms the historical event that created a new legal situation in the past. An acknowledgement of a divorce does not create the duty to pay off the marriage gift, but legally confirms its existence as a debt, if it has not already been paid off.

The challenge facing the Ḥanafite jurists was to explain why coercion would render acknowledgments invalid but would not do the same to legal speech acts. At a basic level, both involve legally relevant speech. If coercion has no effect on a pronouncement of divorce, why can it invalidate an acknowledgment of a past divorce? Why does an acknowledgment not fail the instrument test?

Qudūrī, Dabūsī, and Sarakhsī assert that what distinguishes acknowledgments from coerced speech acts is that the central criterion for determining the validity of an acknowledgment is whether it is true.[53] An acknowledgment is simply declarative speech (*ikhbār*) about a past event.[54] Here Qudūrī and Dabūsī make a distinction between speech acts, which create legal consequences by their very performance, and declarations, which rely on correspondence to some external past state of affairs in order to validate the established legal consequences of that past event. The former, as speech acts, create legal rights and responsibilities. The latter, as declaratives, must conform to a past event in order to affirm legal rights and responsibilities. The fact that declaratives, in contrast to speech acts, purport to be about some past event changes the relationship between validity and willingness. As seen earlier, Dabūsī refused to countenance the possibility that coercion's vitiation of willingness could invalidate a speech act. However, in the case of acknowledgments, Dabūsī argues that coercion's effect on the willingness of an acknowledgment can lead to its invalidation by tipping the scale in favor of finding the acknowledgment false. Dabūsī notes:

> We take his condition of willingness as an indication of truth. Willingness (*ṭawʿ*) is taken to indicate that he is not lying about himself. We take coercion as an indication of a lie. It is apparent that he says what he does to repel harm, not to make what actually happened manifest [in speech].[55]

It is important to note that it is not the agent's unwillingness itself that invalidates the acknowledgment. Rather, the unwillingness of the coerced agent to perform the acknowledgment tips the balance in favor of judging it to be false, and a false acknowledgment is invalid.

[53] Dabūsī, *Asrār*, 1000.6–10; Qudūrī, *al-Tajrīd*, 10:4927.3–4; Sarakhsī, *al-Mabsūṭ*, 24:61.13–14. For Dabūsī, an acknowledgment may be invalidated "because it is a lie, not because it is coerced speech. The invalidity of a lie stems from the lie's connection to something other than what it purports to be about" (*li-anna-hu kidhbun lā anna-hu kalāmu mukrahin wa-fasādu ʾl-kidhbi li-anna-hu iḍāfatun ilā ghayr maḥalli-hi*)."

[54] Dabūsī, *Asrār*, 1000.9–10; *al-Tajrīd*, 10:4927.3–6. Qudūrī writes: "The central principle in the case of acts of reporting on a past event is that the reports may either be true or false. If one makes an acknowledgment voluntarily, it is presumed to be true, because a reasonable person (*ʿāqil*) lies only to gain a benefit or to prevent a harm, and these are not applicable in the previous case. If, however, coercion is present, the presumption is that the agent made the acknowledgment in order to save himself from a beating. This presumption prevents consideration of the statement as true, and therefore it does not validate a divorce." Dabūsī says similarly that "the legal purpose of an acknowledgment is [to act] as a stand-in for that which the report is about before the agent's act of declaring it" (*li-anna maḥalla ʾl-ikhbāri qiyāmu ʾl-mukhbir ʿan-hu sābiqan qabla ikhbāri-hi*).

[55] Dabūsī, *Asrār*, 1000.8–9.

Sarakhsī's analysis of this problem is substantially similar to those of Qudūrī and Dabūsī. Sarakhsī's justification for why coercion invalidates acknowledgments but not speech acts is related to his justification for why coercion invalidates the legal consequences of an act of apostasy. Specifically, apostasy is an acknowledgment or a factual report about the apostate's theological beliefs. For Sarakhsī, "the coerced speaks, giving a report about his beliefs."[56] The judicial presumption before taking account of any positive evidence in favor of or against any given acknowledgment's validity is to suspend judgment about its truth or falsehood.[57] One indication that favors the truth and therefore the validity of the acknowledgment is the willingness of the acknowledger to utter the acknowledgment. According to Sarakhsī, "in the case of the coerced, the fact that there is a sword over his head is evidence that [the acknowledgment] is a lie. The fact that the declarer made the choice to utter the acknowledgment does not make it a reality."[58] In this way, coercion invalidates an act of apostasy just like it does all other acknowledgments.

5.3 Acknowledgments and the Case of Breast Milk Relationships (*Riḍā*ᶜ)

The Ḥanafites were not confined to a defensive posture on the threat that their position on coerced acknowledgments posed to their position on coerced divorce. There was one particular case that in fact demonstrated their point that being coerced to acknowledge a given act has different legal consequences than being coerced to do the act itself. This was the case of the generation of prohibitions on whom one may marry by the act of breastfeeding, and the Ḥanafites used it to push their Shāfiᶜite colleagues to accept the Ḥanafite position. Understanding how the invocation of this case could serve as an argument for the Ḥanafite position requires awareness of the basic logic underpinning the legal effects of breastfeeding on the generation of marriage prohibitions.[59] Let us take the example of two

[56] Sarakhsī, *al-Mabsūṭ*, 24:69.21.
[57] See this sentiment also in ibid., 24:61.13.
[58] Ibid., 24:69.19–20.
[59] On this topic generally, see Wizāra al-Awqāf wa al-Shuʾūn al-Islāmiyya, "Riḍāᶜ," in *al-Mawsūᶜa al-Fiqhiyya* (Kuwait: Wizāra al-Awqāf wa al-Shuʾūn al-Islāmiyya, 1987–2006).

individuals, Zeynap and ʿAmr. They are unrelated in the sense that they could marry each other; there is no blood relationship between them that would make the relationship legally incestuous and therefore prohibited. But let us assume that it was discovered that Zeynap's mother breastfed ʿAmr several times when he was a child. According to both Ḥanafites and Shāfiʿites, this would make ʿAmr and Zeynap "milk" siblings, and they could not, therefore, marry each other. How does this case relate to the arguments about coercion and acknowledgments? Both Ḥanafites and Shāfiʿites agree that the prohibitions that would normally arise from voluntary breastfeeding would arise even if Zeynap's mother had been coerced to breastfeed ʿAmr. The fact of coercion in no way cancels the normative effects of the breastfeeding. On the other hand, if Zeynap's mother credibly claims that she was coerced to acknowledge her past breastfeeding of ʿAmr, the fact of coercion invalidates the acknowledgment and the normative effects are canceled; Zeynap and ʿAmr are free to marry each other. Both Ḥanafites and Shāfiʿites make this distinction between coerced breastfeeding (on which coercion has no effect) and coerced acknowledgment of breastfeeding (on which coercion has an effect). The Ḥanafite Qudūrī points to this case to argue that since the Shāfiʿites distinguish between the coerced acknowledgment of an act and the act itself in the case of breastfeeding, the Ḥanafite distinction between coerced acknowledgments and coerced divorce is not arbitrary.[60]

Māwardī counters this argument by insisting that the ingestion of breast milk is a bodily act as opposed to an acknowledgment, which is an act of speech. In the case of bodily acts, considerations of intent (*qaṣd*) are legally immaterial—the normative consequences are the same whether one is coerced to ingest breast milk or does so voluntarily. But in the case of coerced acknowledgments, the normative effects are different, because an acknowledgment is a type of speech, and for speech acts considerations of intent are legally relevant. Māwardī presents the hypothetical case of an insane woman who breastfeeds a child. Despite the fact, affirmed by the Ḥanafites, that insanity completely impedes moral agency, the normal prohibitions relating to marriage still follow. But if

[60] Qudūrī, *al-Tajrīd*, 10:4927.1–2.

she merely makes an acknowledgment of the act of having breastfed the child, they do not.[61]

5.4 Coerced Commercial Transactions

Commercial transactions are speech acts, like divorces and emancipations; yet the Ḥanafites hold that in the former case, coercion has the effect of creating a defective contract that the coerced has the option of either canceling or confirming after the coercion has ceased. In fact, not only do the Ḥanafites allow coercion to modify the consequences of a commercial transaction; they also admit the least severe type of threat to cross the threshold of legal coerciveness in such cases: the threat of a beating, for example, suffices. How do the Ḥanafites justify this differential attitude, since both divorces and sales are speech acts?

The authors of the legal handbooks provide one explanation for why commercial transactions are different from unilateral speech acts: the existing positive Ḥanafite laws recognize a right of rescission in the case of commercial transactions but not in the case of speech acts such as marriage, divorce, and vows. Presumably, since Ḥanafite positive law already contains a right of rescission in the context of commercial dealings, it can easily be argued that coercion, too, has the potential to render a transaction defective and thus rescindable.

Starting with Jaṣṣāṣ, Ḥanafite scholars start to say, along with the rescission argument, that contentment (*riḍā*) is a relevant psychological category for the validity of commercial transactions.[62] Threats against life or limb as well as threats of lesser harm, such as imprisonment, vitiate contentment and therefore create the option of rescission. Contentment is thus a necessary condition for the full legal validity of a commercial transaction.

[61] Māwardī, *al-Ḥāwī*, 10:229.21–23. Qudūrī responds to this Shāfiʿite argument by arguing that coercion does in fact have a normative effect on certain types of bodily acts. A person who is coerced to drink wine is not punished, nor is one who is raped. Also, even Shāfiʿites admit that in some cases coercion has no effect on the normative consequences of speech. For example, the Shāfiʿites hold that the coerced conversion of a non-Muslim enemy combatant (*ḥarbī*) is valid in spite of the coercion. Qudūrī's point is that the relationship between coercion and the distinction between bodily acts and speech acts is not straightforward, even according to Shāfiʿite laws. See Qudūrī, *al-Tajrīd*, 10:4917.6–8.

[62] See Jaṣṣāṣ, *Sharḥ*, 8:438.6–10. See also, similarly, Qudūrī, *al-Tajrīd*, 10:4928.14–18.

But why is contentment considered only in this context, and not in the case of other types of speech acts? Only Dabūsī ventures a justification of this differential treatment of legal speech. He offers a scriptural argument based on the central Qurʾānic verse regulating commercial exchanges, "O believers, do not devour one another's possessions wrongfully. But let there be trade between you through mutual consent (*ʿan tarāḍin*)."[63] He construes the verse as positively stipulating "mutual contentment" as a condition for the full effectiveness of all commercial exchanges. Dabūsī infers that "since the exceptional clause is [described] by the attribute of mutual contentment, it is known that what is specifically excepted is the opposite of mutual contentment, which is coercion" (*wa-lammā kāna ʾl-istithnāʾu bi-ṣifati ʾl-tarāḍī ʿulima anna ʾl-mustathnāʾa min-hu bi-khilāfi ʾl-tarāḍī wa-huwa ʾl-kurh*).[64] In fact, Dabūsī asserts, had it not been for this scripturally based provision, commercial legal speech acts would be treated the same way as divorces.[65] He makes the provocative suggestion that had there been no scriptural text addressing the matter, any sale would be completely valid as long as the seller was categorized as legally competent to undertake it (i.e., being in possession of majority, rationality, etc.) and had a legitimate connection to the object sold (e.g., by being its owner).[66] For Dabūsī, the paradigmatic rational case seems to be irrevocable legal speech acts such as divorce. Scripture qualifies this law with respect to commercial transactions by adding an extra condition (namely, mutual consent) for their full effectiveness.[67]

[63] Qurʾān 4:29. [64] Dabūsī, *Asrār*, 1002.1–3.

[65] See ibid., 1002.8–10, where Dabūsī basically says that coerced sales "would have been effective just like divorce" (*fa-kāna yanbaghī an yanfudh ka-ʾl-ṭalāq*).

[66] Ibid., 1002.9–10.

[67] This statement seems to suggest that there are positive legal laws accessible to reason and independent of God's revelation, and that these have a basic normative structure that is subsequently modified by revelation. Dabūsī seems to think that, in a sense, God uses equity reasoning (*istiḥsān*) to modify the rational laws in order to meet certain public policy considerations. In the context of Islamic legal history, this is a fairly bold move, and it strengthens Bedir's characterization, based on a reading of Dabūsī's work of legal theory, the *Taqwīm*, of Dabūsī as committed to the idea that "reason constitutes the fundamental structure of morality and law while revelation makes additional adjustments over that structure." See Murteza Bedir, "Reason and Revelation: Abū Zayd al-Dabbūsī on Rational Proofs," *Islamic Studies* 43 no. 2 (2004): 240.

6. SHĀFIʿITE CASE ARGUMENTS

Thus far we have looked at Ḥanafite and Shāfiʿite interpretations and counterinterpretations of scriptural proof texts. We have also seen how the Ḥanafites dealt with arguments that derive their force from concerns about coherence among laws. Now let us take a brief look at Shāfiʿite case arguments. Māwardī offers five nonscriptural arguments that criticize the Ḥanafite position and seek to substantiate the Shāfiʿite position on coercion and unilateral speech acts. All of the arguments involve the citation of specific cases and the legal principles they exemplify to establish the superiority of the Shāfiʿite position. Two of these arguments will suffice as examples.

In one argument, Māwardī promotes the idea that coercion ought to be treated like insanity, minority, and sleep. Just as, for example, a divorce uttered by a person in any of these states is considered ineffective, as the Ḥanafites would agree, so ought the utterance of a divorce by someone who is coerced.[68]

In the second argument, Māwardī urges assimilation of the case of coerced divorce to the case of apostasy. Normally, one of the normative consequences of voluntarily uttering words of disbelief is the automatic and irrevocable dissolution of the marital bond with one's spouse. Yet both the Ḥanafites and the Shāfiʿites agree that the presence of coercion prevents this consequence. Māwardī generalizes from this case to the principle that any forced utterance that would result in dissolution of the marital bond ought to be regarded as invalid. This principle would naturally include coerced divorce under its purview.[69]

[68] Māwardī, *al-Ḥāwī*, 10:230.7–8.

[69] Ibid., 10:230.9–10. Qudūrī's response to this Shāfiʿite argument is to assert that the utterance of words of disbelief is not by itself sufficient to cause the dissolution of the marriage. Rather, the dissolution follows believing in and intending the disbelief. In support, he cites the claim that if a person internally intends or assents to disbelief but does not express it, the marriage is considered dissolved, and if he resolves internally to disbelieve in twenty years' time, he has disbelieved in the present; but if he intends a divorce internally without expressing it, no divorce has occurred. Qudūrī's aim is to distinguish the two cases, apostasy and divorce, as different and thus resistant to the assimilation that Māwardī presses on his Ḥanafite colleagues. See Qudūrī, *al-Tajrīd*, 10:4928.5–7.

7. WHY DID THE ḤANAFITES NOT SIMPLY CHANGE THEIR MINDS?

It should be clear by now that the classical Ḥanafite jurists spilled much more ink on the subject of coerced speech jurisprudence than did their Shāfiʿite counterparts. What explains the difference in coverage? One reason probably lies in the fact that the Ḥanafites had the burden of explaining away the perceived discordance between their position on coerced speech acts and their other laws. The Shāfiʿites simply did not face this problem. Another probable reason is the fact that the Ḥanafites stood alone on this issue. All the other Sunnite and non-Sunnite schools held that coercion invalidates unilateral speech acts. Finding themselves starkly in the minority, the Ḥanafites perhaps felt an extra burden to prove the scriptural legitimacy of their position and the coherence of their corpus juris in a way that the Shāfiʿites did not. But this raises another question. Presumably, the Ḥanafites could have avoided this problem entirely by simply changing their minds and adopting the position of their Shāfiʿite rivals. They did not do so. Why?

There are at least three possible answers to this question. One answer has to do with the nature of laws. In his diachronic analysis of the structure of legal reasoning in Ḥanafite legal texts dealing with the issue of women and public prayer, Behnam Sadeghi found that the justifications for laws change at a much faster rate than the laws themselves. In fact, once a law has been accepted as part of the corpus juris of a given tradition, it hardly ever changes. A law changes only if, for one reason or another, it becomes socially or politically intolerable. The cause of change in laws has little to do with the principles and scriptural interpretations cited by the jurists who justify the laws. Laws change for social reasons, and justifications emerge to smooth over that change. Relying on the scholarship of Alan Watson, Sadeghi terms the persistence of laws over time legal inertia. Given the fact of legal inertia, no explanation is needed for why a given law persists over time. It does so because it is recognized as the law. Once the coerced divorce law was recognized as part of the Ḥanafite corpus juris, its perpetuation and justification by Ḥanafites could be assumed, and since all three of the founding fathers of Ḥanafism agreed on the law, its place in the Ḥanafite corpus juris was assured.[70]

[70] Sadeghi, *The Logic of Law Making in Islam*, 30–32.

A second possible explanation for why the Ḥanafites did not change their minds has to do with the nature of the social practices that the laws govern. Baber Johansen has argued that the reason why the Ḥanafite laws regulating commercial contracts differ from those regulating marriages, divorces, and manumissions reflects the differences in the objects being exchanged in these social transactions. People engage in commercial contracts in order to exchange commodities. The laws governing such exchanges impose few if any conditions on who may engage in these transactions. Any legally competent agent can enter into a commercial contract and be assured of equal treatment regardless of whom that agent is transacting with. Furthermore, the laws allow for a variety of ways in which the people engaging in these transactions can opt out of them, and as seen earlier, Ḥanafite jurists held that coercion renders commercial transactions automatically voidable. By contrast, marriages, divorces, and manumissions entail substantial modifications to households. As a consequence, the Ḥanafite laws encourage, for example, equality of familial standing in marriage contracts but not in commercial contracts.[71] Johansen notes that unlike the laws regulating the validity of commercial transactions, those regulating marriage, divorce, and emancipation

> follow the principle of a strict formalism which leaves very little place for intent, purpose, and knowledge of the parties concerned. Social exchange is a very serious business in which room for maneuvering is restricted to the utmost in order to avoid the disruptive effects of frustrated hopes and expectations and of negative classification.[72]

The laws on coerced divorce, marriage, and manumission are merely an extension of the formalist logic of the laws that decree how these social transactions ought to be concluded. The difference in the regulation of commercial and social transactions stems from the diverging social attitudes toward the respective objects being exchanged in the two types of transaction. Given the substantial domestic effects of divorces, marriages, and emancipations, the Ḥanafites would presumably want to inject as much predictability and certainty into these transactions; they had a lot riding on

[71] See Baber Johansen, "The Valorization of the Human Body in Muslim Sunni Law," *Interdisciplinary Journal of Middle Eastern Studies* 4 (1996): 71–73.

[72] Ibid., 74.

them. For this reason, they adopted a strictly formalist approach in these areas of the law. The reason why these laws persist as part of the Ḥanafite corpus juris is that the social attitudes regarding the nature of the transactions in question persist.

There is certainly something to Johansen's observation that the differences in the Ḥanafite treatment of commercial versus social transactions derive from the difference in the types of objects being exchanged. Yet these social attitudes were presumably not limited to Ḥanafite jurists nor to Ḥanafite-majority societies. Rather, they were held by non-Ḥanafites as well, and non-Ḥanafite jurists nonetheless held that coercion invalidates divorces, marriages, and emancipations.

There is one other potential explanation for the generation and persistence of the Ḥanafite laws on coerced unilateral speech acts. Some modern scholars regard membership in a legal tradition to consist of commitment to a certain set of legal principles or a particular legal philosophy. These scholars see the laws that make up a tradition's corpus juris as an expression of such a transhistorical set of values. For example, Brinkley Messick argues that what explains the strict formalism of Islamic divorce law as opposed to the relative flexibility of Islamic contract law is the fundamentally different role that intentions play in the two types of practices. Since more than one intention is involved in contracts, a more flexible approach to the obligations to which contractual agreements give rise is needed. But this is not the case for unilateral speech acts such as divorce, in which only the intention of the speaker is at issue. Moreover, Messick claims, the Ḥanafite treatment of unilateral speech is thus an accurate expression of Islamic law's foundational theological preoccupation: divining Divine intent through the analysis of manifest expressions of speech.[73]

The problem with this explanation is similar to that which afflicted Johansen's approach: it does not explain all the data. The Shāfiʿites were also committed to the theological project of discovering Divine intent through the analysis of scripture's manifest language, but held that coercion does

[73] Brinkley Messick, "Indexing the Self: Intent and Expression in Islamic Legal Acts," *Islamic Law and Society* 8, no. 2 (2001).

invalidate a pronouncement of divorce. One of the justifications they gave is that it renders the coerced agent's intent defective. The Shāfiʿites do not, therefore, adopt strict formalism in this case, even though divorce is the paradigmatic instance of a unilateral speech act.[74] All explanations of laws within a tradition that rely on commitments to higher-order principles suffer from this problem. Their weakness is rooted in their mistaken view of how laws and traditions relate to principles, especially in the context of Islamic legal thought, and in their inadequate distinction between two different types of phenomena in legal history, which require different explanations. The factors that explain the creation of a law are different from those that explain its persistence over time. A jurist's articulation of a new law could in fact be caused by any number of different factors: social and economic circumstances, political favoritism, the jurist's perception of what a given higher-order principle requires, her assimilation of a particular case to an existing law addressing a different case, her reading of a scriptural text, or some combination of the above. The variables are so numerous and nonhierarchically related as to render the chances of accurately predicting the resulting law exceedingly remote. From a purely conceptual point of view, the jurist is not really very constrained by scripture, hermeneutical philosophy, or substantive moral or legal principles. To put it in Sadeghi's terms, she has maximal hermeneutic flexibility. The anatomy of the debate between the Shāfiʿite and Ḥanafite scholars on the issue of coerced speech is a perfect demonstration of this phenomenon. The scholars belonging to each camp had a ready supply of arguments and counterarguments that proved, at a minimum, the reasonableness of the position they favored.

The final approach to explaining the persistence of the Ḥanafite position on coerced speech acts is to emphasize the intellectual function of the classical positive law texts and to recognize that the laws in Ḥanafite books do not necessarily prevent Ḥanafite jurists from adopting legal positions outside of the tradition when intolerable social harm would attend the application of their own laws. While it may be true that once a law is accepted

[74] Powers makes the same criticism of this approach; see Paul R. Powers, *Intent in Islamic Law* (Leiden: Brill, 2006), 166–67.

as part of the corpus juris of a tradition it tends to persist over time, this does not mean that the law of the books is automatically applied by judges and muftis. Just as scripture or commitment to a legal philosophy does not determine the tradition's law, similarly the tradition's law does not necessarily determine its application in practice. At least in the post-classical period, Ḥanafite judges authorized, from time to time, judges of other traditions to apply the laws of those other traditions, and Ḥanafite muftis relied on the doctrines of other legal traditions in those cases in which the application of the Ḥanafite law would have caused undue social harm.[75] For example, the Indian Ḥanafite Ashraf ʿAlī Thānawī (d. 1362/1943) drew on the Mālikite doctrine on the waiting period that women whose husbands were missing had to observe before remarriage to argue for a law that contravened the Ḥanafite law, and he in fact urged the former's adoption as state law in India.[76] Even more relevant for our discussion, the tenth/sixteenth-century Ḥanafite Ibn Nujaym (d. 970/1563) is recorded in a collection of fatwas as holding that coercion does in fact invalidate a pronouncement of divorce, even though in his work of positive law he defends the traditional Ḥanafite law that coercion has no effect on the legal consequences of a divorce.[77]

Given the fact that the positive law works did not necessarily constrain muftis to issue fatwas according to their school's doctrine or judges to decide cases based on it, what, then, is the function of the positive law works? In short, their authors sought to provide as convincing a justification as they could for each individual legal opinion that fell within the aegis of the tradition. They sought to validate the legitimacy of the laws that make up the tradition as a comprehensive starting point for legal inquiry and analysis.

[75] See Rudolph Peters, "What Does it Mean to be an Official Madhhab? Hanafism and the Ottoman Empire," in *The Islamic School of Law: Evolution, Devolution, and Progress*, ed. P.J. Bearman, Rudolph Peters, and Frank E. Vogel (Cambridge, MA: Islamic Legal Studies Program Distributed by Harvard University Press, 2005), 155–57.

[76] Muhammad Qasim Zaman, *Ashraf ʿAli Thanawi: Islam in Modern South Asia*, Makers of the Muslim World (Oxford: Oneworld, 2008), 62–65.

[77] For the fatwa, see Zayn al-Dīn b. Ibrāhīm Ibn Nujaym and Dāwūd b. Yūsuf al-Khaṭīb, *al-Fatāwā al-Ghiyāthīyya*, 1st ed. (Cairo: al-Maṭbaʿa al-Āmīrīyya, 1321[/1903]), 169, and for the work of positive law, see Zayn al-Dīn b. Ibrāhīm Ibn Nujaym, *al-Baḥr al-Rāʾiq*, ed. Zakariyya ʿUmayrāt, 1st ed., 6 vols. (Beirut: Dār al-Kutub al-ʿIlmiyya, 1418[/1997]), 3:428.

In the process, they communicated to their pupils the techniques of reasoning that reconciled the laws with the scriptural sources as well as the substantive principles that demonstrated the overall coherence of the laws. More than anything, the positive law works were intellectual products, and their relationship to the norms being applied in the courts or offered as fatwas was more tenuous than has been considered. The fact that the coerced divorce law persisted and that it elicited repeated justification over the history of Ḥanafism cannot therefore be explained by reference either to historical facts external to the workings of Ḥanafism as an intellectual tradition or to external social values.

8. CONCLUSION: THE POWER OF THE CONTINGENT FEATURE OF REGION IN EXPLAINING TRADITIONS' RATIONALITY ON COERCED SPEECH

The analysis of Ḥanafite and Shāfiʿite coerced speech jurisprudence yields many insights into the nature of reasoning in legal traditions. It clarifies the function of legal principles in Islamic legal thought as represented in classical positive law texts. It shows that regionalism influences the character of reasoning in these texts. In contrast to stereotypical understandings of Ḥanafism as more rationalist and Shāfiʿism as more scripturalist, it suggests that what determines the content of justification in classical positive law texts is determined by factors such as the extent to which a tradition's position clashes with those of others.

Besides competing interpretations of scriptural texts, the intertradition argumentation in coerced speech jurisprudence plays out as a conflict between the principle that intentions are essential elements in judging the normative effects of actions, the principle that the law can only rely on judgments that are empirically accessible, and the principle that an action undertaken by a person that has the capacity for it is presumptively responsible for its legal and moral effects. The proponents of the Shāfiʿite position as depicted in Ḥanafite sources urged application of the principle that intentions are integral to judging the legal validity of specific speech acts. Since coercion vitiates intention, the Shāfiʿite interlocutors argued, coerced speech acts must be invalid. The Ḥanafites, by contrast, promoted the principle that speech acts ought to be judged by whether the speaker possesses the relevant capacity to legally perform the act. If he does, then the law must presume the act to be valid. Furthermore, the principle that the legal validity of acts is based on empirically available information precludes recourse to private intentions in establishing a speech act's validity. The Ḥanafites combined the latter two principles to defend the Ḥanafite law that coerced speech is nonetheless legally effective, at least in the context of acts such as divorces.

A surface reading of this debate might suggest that what explains the difference between Ḥanafism and Shāfiʿism is the relative strength of commitment to these competing principles. Shāfiʿites placed more importance on intentions—that is what explains their coerced speech jurisprudence. Ḥanafites placed more importance on the public aspect of the performance of acts, which would explain their coerced speech jurisprudence. This view would surmise that it is a tradition's commitment to different principles that determines its laws. Yet, a deeper examination reveals that it is not usually the case that a given tradition avows commitment to only a limited set of unique principles, disavowing others. For example, contrary to what we might expect from the analysis of the Shāfiʿite position on coerced speech acts, it is not the case that the Shāfiʿites always allowed considerations of intention to trump the prima facie sense of an uttered speech act. In fact, for the Shāfiʿites, divorces pronounced in jest were still fully effective, despite the fact that the jester did not intend the divorce. Nor is it the case that the Ḥanafites consistently excluded considerations of intention in all areas of the law and relied only on empirical sources to assess the legal and moral effects of acts. Simply put, legal principles do not determine the laws of a tradition because traditions retain commitment to a host of seemingly conflicting principles and choose rather to discretionally deploy them as justification for laws governing different cases.

Instead of regarding a tradition's rationality as a highly structured legal philosophy that influences tradition-bound jurists to elaborate the tradition's laws in a given direction, it is more useful to think of it as a non-hierarchically organized toolbox. A toolbox that contains scriptural texts, hermeneutical principles, legal and moral principles, theological premises, and the history of interpretation that precedes the jurist in time. The jurist will pick the tool most appropriate to the discursive task at hand. The appropriateness of a tool has little to do with a tradition's legal philosophy and more to do with the conceptual demands of the legal and moral problem at hand (domain-specific constraints), the actual constraints imposed by tradition membership on the jurist (internal constraints), the discursive context of other competing traditions (external constraints), and contingent historical factors, such as the extent to which a tradition ends up adopting a minority position on a given issue or the methods of reasoning that have come to predominate the intellectual culture of a given place at a given time.

Though both Islamic religious scholars and Western Islamicists have emphasized the role of region in explaining the character of Islamic legal thought in the formative period of Islamic legal history, it is almost absent in the analysis of the post-formative period. Yet regionalism explains the character of reasoning across traditions in the classical period. Of all the authors discussed in this chapter, the two scholars who offer the most detailed presentations of the respective arguments put forward by the two traditions are Māwardī on the Shāfiʿite side and Qudūrī on the Ḥanafite side. In fact, both authors, at times, reproduce the exact same arguments.[78] This is not surprising, given that both Qudūrī and Māwardī were Baghdadi scholars. According to historical reports, Qudūrī participated in several public debates with Abū Ḥāmid al-Isfarāʾīnī, Māwardī's teacher and the leading Shāfiʿite in his day.[79] This geographical correlation suggests that, contrary to current Islamic legal historiography, regionalism did not end with the rise and institutionalization of the legal traditions in the fourth/tenth century. While the contingent fact of regionalism by Māwardī's and Qudūrī's time no longer explained the patterns of jurists' commitment to concrete laws, it still explained similarities in the methods and styles of justification used to defend a legal tradition's inherited laws. There seems to be a definite Iraqi way

[78] For the citation of the grammarian Abū ʿUbayd's gloss on a ḥadīth, see Qudūrī, *al-Tajrīd*, 10:4919.16 and Māwardī, *al-Ḥāwī*, 10:229.1. For the citation of the companions' consensus on coerced divorce, see Qudūrī, *Mukhtaṣar*, 10:4925.5–6 and Māwardī, *al-Ḥāwī*, 10:229.4–5. On the citation of an alternative version of the "lifted" ḥadīth, see Qudūrī, *al-Tajrīd*, 10:4918.9–10 and Māwardī, *al-Ḥāwī*, 10:229.19–20. These examples do not exhaust the similarities.

[79] M. Ben Cheneb, "al-Ḳudūrī, Abu ʾl-Ḥusayn/al-Ḥasan Aḥmad," in *Encyclopedia of Islam, Second Edition*, ed. P. Bearman, et al. (Leiden: Brill, 1980–2004).

of reasoning that transcends tradition boundaries. Regardless of tradition affiliation, both the Iraqi Shāfiʿites and the Iraqi Ḥanafites relied extensively on scriptural interpretations in justifying the laws of their own tradition and criticizing those of the opposing tradition. The Khurasani Shāfiʿites and the Central Asian Ḥanafites, on the other hand, used predominantly two different types of justification: invocation of moral or legal principles that required adherence to a certain law, and casuistry.

The findings of this chapter also contradict stereotypical characterizations of the two traditions in Islamic and contemporary Western legal historiography. Of the four Sunnite traditions, Ḥanafism is supposed to be the most reliant on nonscriptural modes of legal reasoning, whereas Shāfiʿism's hallmark is its call for reliance on isnād authenticated ḥadīth as justification for laws. The evidence discussed here, though not exhaustive, does not bear these claims out. The Baghdadi Ḥanafites show a much greater interest than their Shāfiʿite peers in a ḥadīth's chain of transmission as a feature relevant to the authority of a law, evident in, for example, Jaṣṣāṣ's appeal to Aḥmad b. Ḥanbal's judgment on the "lifted" ḥadīth. They also engage much more comprehensively with the relevant ḥadīth texts.

Beyond regionalism, there is another factor that explains the relatively scripture centric characteristic of Ḥanafite coerced speech jurisprudence. The arguments made by both the Ḥanafites and the Shāfiʿites on the subject of coerced speech consisted, to a large degree, of interpretations of scriptural texts (Qurʾān and ḥadīth). By contrast, Ḥanafite and Shāfiʿite jurisprudence on coerced harm to others (discussed in detail in the next chapter) almost entirely lacked reference to scriptural arguments. This difference reflects the differing positions of the traditions' particular laws vis-à-vis the Sunnite mainstream. Since the Ḥanafites held the lone minority position on the issue of coerced unilateral speech acts, it stands to reason that they would couch their analysis in terms of an authority that all of the classical legal traditions shared—namely, commitment to the Qurʾān and the Sunna as the sources of legal norms. Given that Ḥanafite argument for their coerced speech jurisprudence was articulated on largely scriptural grounds, it makes sense why the Shāfiʿites, their competitors, would couch their criticisms of the Ḥanafite position in similar terms. But in the case of coerced harm jurisprudence, neither the Ḥanafites nor the Shāfiʿites represented a lone minority position.

In fact, both traditions preserved conflicting opinions on how to distribute moral and legal responsibility among the relevant agents. Hence, both sides' argumentation for the various opinions proceeded mostly on nonscriptural grounds.

9. THE YIELDS OF COMPARISON: ḤANAFITE COERCED SPEECH AND AMERICAN COERCED MARRIAGES, ADOPTIONS, AND PLEA-BARGAINS

The Ḥanafites had different standards for coerciveness in different fields of law. For commercial transactions, a threat of imprisonment or severe beating was sufficient to grant the coerced party the option of rescission. But this same threat would not suffice to lift the consequences of a coerced act if the act involved harming another person, either bodily or financially. While a threat against one's life was sufficient to deter the criminal penalty for homicide or rape, it could not invalidate a pronouncement of divorce. The fact that the Ḥanafites defined coercion differently for different legal acts meant that determining what is legally coercive was not simply an empirical matter. This way of treating coercion is not unique to the Ḥanafites: American coercion jurisprudence displays similar features. What is legally coercive in contracts is not the same as what is legally coercive in marriages, adoptions, and plea-bargains, for example. In fact, until very recently, courts routinely held that pressures that would normally render a contract voidable do not have the same effect on a marriage. Shotgun weddings thus resulted in legally valid marriages. Accordingly, a 1952 New York court approved the use of pressure as "the right and proper course," arguing that "to accede to the suggestion of duress would destroy a time honored method long used by society as a means of protecting itself against the evils of illegitimate children, unmarried mothers and 'ruined' womanhood."[80] The courts thus raised the threshold of what they considered coercive in marriage in response to certain public policy interests. Similarly, the courts were unwilling to rescind a biological mother's surrender of a child to adoptive parents even if she had

[80] The case is cited in Wertheimer, *Coercion*, 76.

been forced into the surrender by environmental or emotional stress. The courts considered the finality and irrevocability of the adoption process to be in the best interests of the child, and they were therefore unwilling to consider arguments regarding the quality of the biological mother's volition in order to invalidate the adoption.[81] Finally, despite the fact that choices offered to defendants in plea-bargains would count as coercive if offered in the case of commercial contracts, American courts continue to uphold the practice, and insist that they are not in fact coercive. It seems to be clear that the judges rule that the practice of plea-bargaining is not coercive in the relevant sense, because they fear undermining a widely used and deeply institutionalized practice in the legal system.[82]

[81] See ibid., 77–84. [82] Ibid., 122–43.

6

Coerced Harm Jurisprudence in Ḥanafism and Shāfiʿism

1. INTRODUCTION

Consider the following two scenarios. In the first scenario, Zayd threatens ʿAmr's life. He says, "If you don't rape Zeynap, I'll kill you." In the second scenario, Zayd threatens to kill ʿAmr unless ʿAmr kills Zeynap. These two paradigmatic cases represent the starting point of medieval Ḥanafite and Shāfiʿite coerced harm jurisprudence. Both cases involved two core questions. What should ʿAmr do? And if ʿAmr complies with Zayd's demand and causes harm to Zeynap, how should the legal and moral responsibility for the act of harm be distributed among the three agents—Zayd, the coercer; ʿAmr the coerced; and Zeynap, the victim? The Ḥanafite and Shāfiʿite response to the first question was unanimous: ʿAmr should resist Zayd's demand, even to the point of dying; if he suffers harm to avoid causing an innocent bystander harm, he merits Divine reward. The fact of coercion would not excuse ʿAmr's sin of causing Zeynap harm, whether by raping or murdering her. Accordingly, this aspect of both Ḥanafite and Shāfiʿite jurisprudence consists of justifications to explain why ʿAmr's moral obligation to refrain from harming Zeynap persists despite Zayd's coercion. But in contrast to their unanimity on ʿAmr's moral obligation to refuse Zayd's demand even if he himself is killed as a result, the founding jurists of the two traditions were internally divided regarding the proper distribution of this worldly liability for ʿAmr's act of coerced rape or murder. This aspect of the two traditions' coerced harm jurisprudence thus consists of justifying the various positions taken by the founding fathers.

In contrast to coerced speech jurisprudence, where the two legal traditions adopted broadly opposing positions, in coerced harm jurisprudence, they adopted broadly similar laws, and articulated the reasoning for those positions in broadly comparable ways. In fact, the parallel ways in which Ḥanafites and Shāfiʿites struggled with the correct legal and moral position on coerced murder is found also amongst the ways that Anglo-American philosophers and judges grappled with the same issue. This similarity is the clearest evidence of constraints that originate not from commitment to a given tradition, or contingent contextual factors, but in consideration of a given moral and legal problem itself (such as coerced murder), or as I call them, the constraints that are specific to a given domain of inquiry.

2. RAPE

2.1 Ḥanafites on Rape

Understanding the rules defining the distribution of moral and legal responsibility for rape requires an appreciation of how the jurists conceived of sexual morality more broadly. In Islamic law, heterosexual activity is permitted only within two types of relationships: marriage and concubinage. Sex outside the context of these two relationships is not only immoral but illegal, meaning that it is a corporally punishable offense. Broadly speaking, the scripturally mandated punishment (*ḥadd*) for sexual intercourse committed by a man or a woman who has never been married is a hundred lashes of the whip. The scripturally mandated punishment (*ḥadd*) for married or previously married offenders is stoning to death.[1] The punishment is applied to both parties to the sexual act. While the punishment is undoubtedly gruesome, the standard of proof required to establish the crime is high, exceeding that required for most other crimes; according to both Ḥanafite and Shāfiʿite doctrine, illicit

[1] For a brief outline of classical legal doctrines on illegal sexual activity (*zinā*), see Rudolph Peters, *Crime and Punishment in Islamic Law: Theory and Practice from the Sixteenth to the Twenty-first Century* (Cambridge, UK: Cambridge University Press, 2005), 59–62.

intercourse is proven only through either confession or eyewitness testimony of the act of penetration by four adult Muslim male witnesses with reputations of probity.[2] Assuming that this stringent standard of proof is met, the one central question in legal discussions of coerced rape is what effect coercion has on the liability for the physical rapist's punishments of lashing and stoning.

As noted in Chapter 3, three different opinions are attributed to the founding fathers of the Ḥanafite tradition on the issue of the penalty for coerced rape. Two of these are associated with Abū Ḥanīfa. According to his first opinion, coercion cannot in any way excuse rape, and therefore a rapist who is coerced to commit it is nonetheless held liable for the full corporal punishment (*ḥadd*). Abū Ḥanīfa later modified his opinion, adding an exception: if the person doing the coercing is the ruler, the coerced rapist is not liable for punishment. The third Ḥanafite position is attributed by different authors to different founding fathers. According to this position, if the coercer is capable of coercing in the same way as a ruler, the distinction between a ruler and a non-ruler is immaterial: the coerced rapist is not punished.

Shaybānī deals extensively with the issue of coerced rape in his book on coercion. His analysis forms the basis of later Ḥanafite thinking on the issue. He is likely the main, if not the only, source of later Ḥanafites' knowledge of Abū Ḥanīfa's two opinions on the matter. In his book, Shaybānī attributes a third position to Abū Ḥanīfa, which subsequent Ḥanafites identify as Shaybānī's. This opinion extends the logic of Abū Ḥanīfa's second position, which cancels the liability of a rapist who is coerced by the ruler, to cases in which the coercer is not the ruler but the coercion takes place outside an urban center or in a place in which it is impossible for the coerced to seek help.[3] In those opinions where coercion mitigates the coerced rapist's *ḥadd*

[2] On the evidence required for the punishments, see ibid., 14–16. For an in-depth analysis of Ḥanafite laws of evidence and procedure for rape, see Azam, *Sexual Violation in Islamic Law*, 170–200, especially 199–200. Azam trenchantly concludes: "The overall structure of substantive, evidentiary, and procedural aspects of Ḥanafī *fiqh* as regards *zinā* generally, and as regards rape in particular, thus highlights the way that principles that were highly effective in protecting personal sexual privacy in consensual situations became obstructionist and detrimental in coercive situations. The Ḥanafī jurists do not seem to have recognized in any meaningful way that sex itself could be an instrument of harm."

[3] Shaybānī, *al-Aṣl*, 7:343.7–11.

punishment, Shaybānī specifies that only a threat against life or limb has the ability to cancel his liability.[4]

An act of rape has another possible legal consequence: it could create a duty to compensate the victim by an amount that is the equivalent of the bridal gift she would customarily receive for marriage. Abū Ḥanīfa held that if the rapist avoids the *ḥadd* penalty because he was coerced, he is still personally liable for the compensation owed to the victim, and he cannot recover its value from the coercer. But if, for whatever reason, he does not avoid the *ḥadd* punishment, then he is not liable for the bridal gift. Shaybānī articulates Abū Ḥanīfa's position as follows:

> When the *ḥadd* is avoided, the bridal gift becomes obligatory. When the *ḥadd* is obligatory, the bridal gift is invalidated. The *ḥadd* and the bridal gift cannot be combined in one act of coitus, and there is never a case of [illegal] coitus without there being either a bridal gift or a *ḥadd* punishment.[5]

While coercion may allow the coerced agent to escape the *ḥadd* punishment in this world, this does not mean that the rapist has not sinned. In contrast to the effect of coercion on the consumption of illicit foods, in the case of rape coercion does not render the demanded act permitted: the rapist, though coerced and perhaps not liable for the *ḥadd* punishment, sins when he undertakes the act. In fact, if he resists the coercer's demand to the point of being killed or suffering bodily harm, he will be rewarded in the next life.[6] In addition, only threats that would result in the loss of life or limb cancel the rapist's *ḥadd* punishment. Threats of imprisonment or enchainment do not have this effect. If the coercer makes these latter types of threats and the coerced complies with the demand and commits the rape, he is fully liable for the *ḥadd* penalty for having engaged in illegal sexual intercourse.[7] But a rape victim avoids punishment even if she (Shaybānī simply assumes the victim is a woman) is threatened with only imprisonment.[8] Moreover, when a potential

[4] Ibid., 7:400.9–14. He explicitly notes that this position is a departure from the rule required by strict legal reasoning (*qiyās*) and justified only by the more flexible equity type of reasoning (*istiḥsān*). For an analysis of Shaybānī's use of legal reasoning and equity reasoning in the *Aṣl* and other works, see Boynukalın's introduction to his edition of the *Aṣl*: Boynukalın, *al-Aṣl: al-Muqaddima*, 211–23.

[5] Shaybānī, *al-Aṣl*, 7:343.4–6. This principle became an object of contention and dispute between later Ḥanafites and Shāfiʿites. For a keen analysis of what motivated its articulation in coerced rape jurisprudence, and its effects on other issues, see Azam, *Sexual Violation in Islamic Law*, 154–69.

[6] Shaybānī, *al-Aṣl*, 7:400.11–13. [7] Ibid., 7:343.18–20. [8] Ibid., 7:401.1–2.

rape victim is threatened with death if she does not consent to intercourse, the rape victim is fully permitted to comply, with the implication that she does not sin by doing so.[9] Shaybānī, using reasoning repeated and elaborated by later Ḥanafites, justifies the differential treatment of men and women in this context by arguing that "the man cannot have an erection except through pleasure (*ladhdha*), and he is the physical agent of the act, whereas the woman is [simply] the object of the act."[10]

Shaybānī considers one other variation of a coerced rape case. If the intended victim consents to illegal sexual intercourse with the coerced, does this consent have any effect on the morality of the act or on the coerced rapist's liability for punishment? Shaybānī holds that it makes no difference and adds that it is impermissible for the victim to give consent. The coerced rapist still sins if he carries out the act, regardless of whether the victim consents, and it is still an act of injustice against her.[11]

Later Ḥanafite discussions on coerced rape uphold and elaborate on the central features of Shaybānī's analysis: they note disagreement on the liability of the coerced rapist, maintain that he has sinned even if he escapes punishment, and discuss why and under what circumstances the victim is not guilty of sin. The discussion on the coerced rapist's liability for the *ḥadd* penalty involved reconstructing the legal and moral reasoning that might have motivated the discordant opinions of the founding fathers.

One question in particular animated later Ḥanafite scholars: why does Abū Ḥanīfa make a distinction between rulers and nonrulers in considering the coerced rapist's liability for the *ḥadd* punishment? Jaṣṣāṣ reproduces the reasoning of his teacher, the Baghdadi Ḥanafite Abū ʾl-Ḥasan al-Karkhī (d. 340/952). Karkhī reasons that if the caliph orders someone to commit rape (an illegal sexual act), he has effectively disqualified himself from the office on moral grounds. He has coerced someone to commit a sin and thereby himself become a sinner (*fāsiq*). Under these circumstances, the coerced rapist's punishable act takes place in a situation in which there is no legitimate head of state. Since the *ḥadd* punishments may be applied only when a legitimate government exists, the coerced rapist escapes the *ḥadd* penalty. The case of coerced rape is similar to other cases in which *ḥadd* punishments are suspended because there is no

[9] Ibid., 7:416.18–21. [10] Ibid., 7:401.2–4. [11] Ibid., 7:343.11–13.

ruler at all or because the crime has been committed outside of Islamic legal jurisdiction (*dār al-ḥarb*). In fact, the ruler himself is not punished for offenses that would ordinarily merit a *ḥadd* penalty, because when he commits such a crime, he disqualifies himself from office, and is thus committing an act in the absence of a ruler with the authority to implement the punishments.[12]

Sarakhsī does not offer either one of these arguments as an explanation for Abū Ḥanīfa's distinction between rulers and nonrulers. He records internal disagreement among Ḥanafites regarding the reason for Abū Yūsuf's and Shaybānī's departure from Abū Ḥanīfa's first opinion—the opinion that distinguished between coercion by the ruler and that by a nonruler. According to Sarakhsī, one explanation held that in the time of Abū Ḥanīfa, the ruler—that is, the holder of the highest executive office—was factually the most powerful person in the land and commanded the obedience of all people, and therefore he counted as the only person who could truly coerce. But by the time of Abū Ḥanīfa's students, Abū Yūsuf and Shaybānī, the historical circumstances had changed: local powers had emerged that could also exert coercive force within their particular regions. Abū Yūsuf and Shaybānī consequently modified Abū Ḥanīfa's opinion by obliterating the distinction between rulers and nonrulers, arguing that if one's life is threatened, regardless of the political identity of the threatening coercer, one is not liable for the *ḥadd* punishment for a coerced act.[13] In support of this view, Sarakhsī adds the following empirical argument: Because a ruler knows that he is not likely to simply disappear one day, he is full of confidence in his commands and does not consider himself to be in danger if he does not actually fulfill all the threats that he makes. Nonrulers, on the other hand, are hasty. They are not as confident about the prospects of their power, and they are therefore less likely to refrain from fulfilling their threats.[14] Sarakhsī himself seems to disagree with the explanation that roots Abū Ḥanīfa's distinction between rulers and nonrulers in the political reality of the ruler's coercive power in Abū Ḥanīfa's time. Rather, he argues that the distinction is motivated by the

[12] Ibid., 8:455.18–456.1. The same arguments are largely reproduced by Qudūrī. See Qudūrī, *al-Tajrīd*, 11:5896.10–11 and 11:5897.9–10.

[13] Sarakhsī, *al-Mabsūṭ*, 24:104.17–19. Sarakhsī also notes that Abū Yūsuf and Shaybānī further held that though he is not liable for the *ḥadd*, he has still sinned, and that the rape victim has neither sinned nor committed an act of illicit intercourse.

[14] Ibid., 24:104.23–26.

fact that a coerced individual can always seek the aid of the ruler against an unjust threat made by a nonruler, but such recourse is not available if the coercer is the ruler himself.[15]

How do later Ḥanafites explain Abū Ḥanīfa's "early" view that coercion makes no difference at all for the rapist's legal liability: the physical rapist is still liable for the *ḥadd* punishment? It comes down to the meaning of an erection. Echoing Shaybānī, Sarakhsī says that "a man's erection is inconceivable without pleasure (*ladhdha*). Pleasure is evidence of willingness. Erections do not occur in the presence of fear."[16] For Sarakhsī, the fact that the rapist is physically able to carry out the rape is an indication that he is not in fact coerced. Rather, his erection proves that he is a willing perpetrator of the crime, and thus deserves the *ḥadd* penalty.

But what, then, to make of Abū Ḥanīfa's second opinion, according to which the coerced rapist's liability depends on whether the coercer is the ruler? Even in this case, the coerced would presumably still require an erection to commit the rape. The Ḥanafites imply that Abū Ḥanīfa must have changed his mind about what the erection signifies. An erection does not necessarily indicate willingness to commit the rape or the absence of fear of the coercer's threat against his life. Sarakhsī, in the course of justifying Abū Ḥanīfa's second opinion, writes:

> An erection is not evidence of the absence of fear. An erection sometimes occurs naturally [without choice] because of the strength of the sexual desire that God implanted in men, and sometimes it occurs through volition. Note that someone who is asleep may have an erection naturally, without his choosing or intending it.[17]

With the exception of Ṭaḥāwī, who sided explicitly with Abū Ḥanīfa's first opinion, it is not clear where the later Ḥanafites themselves stood on this issue. Jaṣṣāṣ merely notes the various opinions and the possible reasoning behind them.[18] Dabūsī does the same in summary fashion.[19] Sarakhsī

[15] Ibid., 24:104.27–24:105.4. This view does not explain why Abū Yūsuf and Shaybānī departed from Abū Ḥanīfa's first opinion.

[16] For this, see ibid., 24:103.21–22. See also Jaṣṣāṣ, *Sharḥ*, 8:455.5–8, where Jaṣṣāṣ notes that erections cannot occur without desire (*shahwa*) and they therefore indicate willingness (*ṭawʿ*) and contentment (*riḍā*). See also Dabūsī, *Asrār*, 1007.17–18.

[17] Sarakhsī, *al-Mabsūṭ*, 24:104.10–12.

[18] See Jaṣṣāṣ, *Sharḥ*, 8:454–456.

[19] See Dabūsī, *Asrār*, 1007.17–19.

provides additional arguments in favor of Abū Yusuf's and Shaybānī's opinion whereas he simply recites the received reasoning behind the other opinions, so it seems that he favored the former opinion.[20]

Three further questions related to the issue of rape remain: Is the coercer liable for punishment? Is the rape victim? And what is the moral status of the act and of the three agents involved (the coercer, the coerced, and the victim)?

Sarakhsī dispenses with the first question easily: the coercer is not liable for any criminal penalty. The reason has to do with the instrument test. Sarakhsī asserts that in cases of rape, "it is inconceivable that the coerced can become a tool of the coercer."[21] Rape thus fails the instrument test, and the legal consequences for the act cannot be transferred to the coercer. The Ḥanafites construed the instrument test very strictly. The instrument test succeeds in transferring legal consequences from the coerced to the coercer only if the coercer can forcibly use the body of the coerced to cause the harm in a literal sense.

That premodern scholars would raise the question of the legal liability of the rape victim is due to the way in which they conceptualized rape—namely, as an act of forced fornication.[22] Since fornication involves potential liability for both participants, the question of the coerced partner's liability would also naturally arise. However, all of the legal traditions held that a rape victim is not held liable for punishment.[23] In fact, both Sarakhsī and Bazdawī

[20] See Sarakhsī, *al-Mabsūṭ*, 24:103.19–105.5. The citation of multiple opinions without identification of the correct one is a feature of the reasoning found in books of positive law. There is often no attempt to tip the balance in favor of one rule over another. Wheeler, in an attempt to explain this feature, argues that classical scholars reconstructed the reasoning behind the opinions of the founding fathers to demonstrate that they are reducible to different applications of principles that all share in common; see Wheeler, *Applying*, 150. Calder makes the case that the reconstruction of arguments for competing positions is partly the result of the text's pedagogical function in classical legal academia. (Wheeler makes a similar claim.) See specifically Norman Calder, *Islamic Jurisprudence in the Classical Era*, ed. Colin Imber (New York: Cambridge University Press, 2010), 55 for comments on Sarakhsī's style and contribution to the Ḥanafite tradition in the *Mabsūṭ*. See also Wheeler, *Applying*, 164–65.

[21] Sarakhsī, *al-Mabsūṭ*, 24:104.4–6; Bazdawī, *al-Kāfī*, 5:2455.4–2456.1.

[22] On the treatment of rape in formative Islamic law and the classical Ḥanafite and Mālikite traditions, see Azam, *Sexual Violation in Islamic Law*.

[23] In all of the legal works that I have consulted, the jurists presume that the victim is a woman.

stress that a woman is not to be punished for being raped even if the coercer's threat is merely of imprisonment. In contrast to the coercer's threat to the coerced rapist, the threat to the victim does not have to be compelling in order to create a legal doubt that subverts her punishment and if the threat is compelling, she is fully excused. Part of the reason she is excused lies in the nature of her physical role in the rape. For Sarakhsī, while she functionally enables (*tamkīn*) the act to take place in the sense that the rape could not happen without her, she is not an active agent in it. She is not the physical author of the act of rape (*laysa min jihati-hā mubāshiratun lil-fiʿl*).[24] She is merely the object (*fa-hiya mafʿūlun bi-hā*)[25] or the recipient of the act (*maḥall al-fiʿl*).[26] As further proof of the victim's passive role in the rape, Sarakhsī notes that a woman could also be involved in an act of fornication while asleep or otherwise not fully aware, with the clear implication in these cases being that she is not held legally or morally responsible for the act.[27] Bazdawī adds that if the coercion is compelling, the victim is fully excused for her participation in the intercourse that constitutes the rape: since she, unlike the rapist, causes no harm to anyone else, the prohibition that her act violates resembles the prohibitions associated with duties owed to God,[28] such as not uttering words of disbelief. As such, if she perseveres in the face of the threat by refusing to submit to the coercer's demand, she is rewarded, and if she submits, she is excused. Meanwhile, noncompelling coercion, while it does not morally excuse the act, is sufficient to create a legal doubt (*shubha*) that subverts her legal punishment in this world.[29]

[24] Sarakhsī, *al-Mabsūṭ*, 24:158.17–18. [25] Ibid. [26] Ibid., 24:103.23–24.
[27] Ibid., 24:103.25–26. [28] Bazdawī, *al-Kāfī*, 5:2470.3–4.
[29] Ibid., 5:2470.5–7. There seems to have been some disagreement about whether a rape victim can clearly object to her rape within the Ḥanafite school. Azam discusses the views of Qudūrī and the later Ḥanafite Burhān al-Dīn al-Kāsānī (d. 593/1197), who both cite the "semi-compliance" of the rape victim as a justification for different aspects of Ḥanafite rape law. Qudūrī cites it to justify why the rape victim does not deserve monetary compensation, when the physical rapist is given the *ḥadd* punishment (the standard Ḥanafite doctrine) and Kāsānī cites it to throw doubt on the accepted Ḥanafite position that cancels the *ḥadd* penalty from the rape victim. Based on these two cases Azam characterizes classical Ḥanafite doctrine on rape in the following way: "These passages demonstrate the manner in which the substantive doctrine of the school, and the particular ways in which this doctrine was theorized, resulted in a juristic architecture that granted little legal significance to whether or not a woman consented or objected to sexual encounters. The interrelationship between *zinā* and *mahr*, and the perceived antithesis between the two, thus resulted in a doctrine that invalidated female volition in sexual matters in all but the narrowest circumstances." Azam, *Sexual Violation in Islamic Law*, 169.

Sarakhsī and Bazdawī assert that the distribution of moral and legal responsibility of the coerced rapist is not the same as that of the woman.[30] Although some of the Ḥanafite masters whom Sarakhsī cites hold that coercion subverts the legal liability of the rapist, it has no effect on the moral status of his act. Sarakhsī writes:

> If the coerced performs the act [of rape], he has committed an injustice. The prohibition against injustice is eternal. This is the case even if [the victim] gave him permission. Her permission is not given legal consideration [for determining his moral responsibility]. Moreover, the prohibition against fornication is eternal. It admits no exception. In no case is it ever permitted, in contradistinction to the prohibition against [consumption of] carrion or pork.[31]

Sarakhsī gives two reasons for why the prohibition against rape never ceases. One is that in contrast to prohibitions dealing with the consumption of forbidden foods, rape is an act of injustice. As such, it involves the violation of the rights of other human beings. The prohibition against injustice does not admit exceptions or suspensions. The second difference is that the Divine texts themselves *specifically* suspend the prohibitions against carrion and pork in cases of dire necessity, but make no such exemption for either rape or murder. Bazdawī adds a third reason:

> Fornication, like homicide and injury, is an act that coercion can neither permit nor excuse, because the indication for [the existence] of an excuse is fear of loss [of life or limb], and in this respect the coerced and the person whom the coerced would violate are equal. Coercion is [legally and morally] eliminated in cases dealing with the life of the person whom the coerced would violate because of conflict (*taʿāruḍ*) [between the values of equal lives].[32]

Bazdawī argues that there is no nonarbitrary way to weigh the harm that would be suffered by the coerced against the harm that would be suffered by the person whom the coerced would harm. All are equal before God, and therefore the prohibition stands despite the coercion.[33]

[30] See Sarakhsī, *al-Mabsūṭ*, 24:158.15, where he explicitly notes "we differentiate between the side of the man and that of the woman in the case of coercion involving threats against life." See similarly Bazdawī, *al-Kāfī*, 5:2470.6–7.

[31] Sarakhsī, *al-Mabsūṭ*, 24:105.19–21.

[32] Bazdawī, *al-Kāfī*, 5:2463.4–6.

[33] Bazdawī adds a further harm in the case of rape. If the rape results in pregnancy, it undermines the attribution of paternity for the child (*fasād firāsh*) because the pregnancy occurs within a relationship not sanctioned by the law. Ibid., 5:2463.6–2464.1.

For these reasons, the prohibition against coerced fornication is firm, especially for the rapist. Because of the passive nature of a woman's role in a rape, the jurists do not conceive of her as actively harming another individual. In the eyes of Sarakhsī, she is not committing an act of injustice. Since she is not harming anyone else, the conditions that must be met for her responsibility for the act of fornication to be diminished or canceled are less stringent.

Recall that while compelling coercion does not, in the Ḥanafites' view, eliminate or alleviate the coerced rapist's moral responsibility, it does, according to one opinion within the tradition, avert legal punishment in this world. Why does moral liability remain undiminished even as a legal punishment is canceled? Sarakhsī starts his explanation by explicitly noting that threats of imprisonment cannot result in the suspension of punishment. If a coercer threatens imprisonment or enchainment and demands that a man commit rape, and the man complies, he is to be punished.[34] But if the threat is compelling—that is, directed at the man's life or limb—he is not punished. The suspension of the punishment is not due to the act's being morally justified; rape remains unlawful. But like in the case of a woman who submits to rape when threatened with imprisonment, the coercion creates a legal doubt (*shubha*). In Islamic criminal law, legal doubts have the function of suspending punishments.[35]

Thus far the coerced rape case assumes a scenario where the coerced complies with the coercer's demand that he rape an innocent bystander. But what if the coerced man refuses to rape the bystander, and the coercer kills him as a result? On this, Sarakhsī writes:

> If he refuses to perpetrate rape and is killed as a consequence, he is [Divinely] rewarded for it, because he has refused to commit a prohibited act. He has striven to obtain God's pleasure by desisting from violating the limits of religion and by striving not to overstep them, even in cases in which he would have been justified in doing so, such as in uttering words of disbelief [when coerced]. We explained in that case that if he refuses to comply to the point of being killed,

[34] Sarakhsī, *al-Mabsūṭ*, 24:105.24–27.

[35] On the history and conceptual structure of this legal maxim, see Rabb, *Doubt in Islamic Law: a History of Legal Maxims, Interpretation, and Islamic Criminal Law*, especially 136–56 for early Ḥanafite jurisprudence.

> he is rewarded. This is even more the case where there is no excuse [such as in rape].[36]

The coerced is rewarded for resisting the coercer's demand. If the coercer threatens his life and he acquiesces with the coercer's demand, he avoids the punishment in this world, but not liability in the hereafter. If the threat made is not against his life, but he nonetheless does what the coercer requests, he is held both morally and legally liable. This divergence between the demands of morality and the requirements for applying this-worldly legal punishment is also a central tension in coerced murder jurisprudence, discussed later in this chapter, and in fact constitutes one of the core problems that Ḥanafite jurists grappled with.

2.2 Shāfiʿites on Rape

In his writings, Shāfiʿī does not address the question of the legal and moral responsibility of a person who is coerced to rape, but he does discuss the general issue of rape. His position on the respective moral and legal responsibilities of the rape victim and the rapist is very similar to that of the Ḥanafites, with one important difference. Like the Ḥanafites, Shāfiʿī holds that the victim is not held morally or legally responsible for the act of illegal sexual intercourse. The rapist, however, is liable for the *ḥadd* punishment. Moreover, the rapist is also responsible for compensating the victim in the amount of the customary bridal gift. In contrast to the Ḥanafite position, this obligation to compensate holds even if the rapist avoids the *ḥadd* punishment for legal reasons.[37]

The later classical Shāfiʿites Māwardī, Juwaynī, and Ghazālī address the specific issue of a coerced rapist's liability for punishment. Like within Ḥanafism, there was internal disagreement on this issue within the Shāfiʿite tradition, though all three jurists identify one and the same position as the opinion that they uphold and then cite a minority opinion, which they explicitly describe as not representative of the tradition.[38] The opinion

[36] Sarakhsī, *al-Mabsūṭ*, 24:105.24–27.

[37] Shāfiʿī, *al-Umm*, 7:392.20–23.

[38] See Māwardī, *al-Ḥāwī*, 17:84.21–85.15; Juwaynī, *Nihāyat*, 14:460.917 and 16:114.1–10; Ghazālī, *al-Wasīṭ fī al-Madhhab*, 6:446.4–5.

that they endorse and identify as dominant holds that coercion cancels the coerced rapist's liability for the *ḥadd* punishment. The weak opinion, which some jurists liken to one of Abū Ḥanīfa's opinions, holds that the coerced rapist does not avoid the *ḥadd* punishment. Their reasoning underpinning the latter opinion is similar to classical Ḥanafite reconstructions of Abū Ḥanīfa's reasoning for his first position: it interprets the rapist's erection as implying the presence of desire and choice. Juwaynī is the only Shāfiʿite jurist to address explicitly the coerced rapist's moral responsibility (the others most likely did not mention it only because they assumed their readers knew it was sinful). According to Juwaynī, "Even if coercion is conceivable [in the case of being coerced to rape], it [the rape] is not permitted. Its prohibition stands, for it involves the violation of a grave prohibition."[39]

Of the three classical jurists, Māwardī is the only one to record three criticisms of Abū Ḥanīfa's positions on coerced rape. As a criticism of Abū Ḥanīfa's early opinion, he denies that jurists ought to construe the presence of an erection as a sign of choice and willingness to engage in the rape. Mirroring Ḥanafite explanations of why Abū Ḥanīfa changed his mind and adopted his second opinion, Māwardī writes:

> Desire is located in [a human's] natural impulses (*al-shahwatun markūzatun fī ʾl-ṭibāʿ*), which cannot be repelled. All that a person can do is refuse to give way to them. Therefore, the coercion is applied to the act and not the desire, and the *ḥadd* punishment is due only on the act and not the desire.[40]

By depicting an erection as a natural reaction to stimuli, Māwardī thus denies that it is an indication of a coerced individual's willingness and choice.

Māwardī presents two other arguments against the later Ḥanafite interpretation of Abū Ḥanīfa's second opinion, which averts the rapist's *ḥadd* punishment if the coercer is a holder of political power (*sulṭān*). The later Ḥanafites justified this opinion by pointing out that *ḥadd* punishments can be carried out only when the highest executive office of the land is occupied. In the absence of political authority, a criminal may legally deserve the *ḥadd* punishment, but a procedural impediment, the lack of a legitimate

[39] Juwaynī, *Nihāyat*, 16:114.9–10.
[40] ʿAlī b. Muḥammad al-Māwardī, *al-Ḥāwī al-Kabīr*, ed. Maḥmūd Maṭarjī, 1st ed., 24 vols. (Beirut: Dār al-Fikr, 1994), 17:85.7–9.

ruler, suspends the obligation to carry it out. Māwardī counters this argument by pointing out that the offices of the *sulṭān*, presumably the holder of political power, and the *imam*, the holder of legitimate authority, can be distinct. So even if the *sulṭān* forces someone to commit a gross act of iniquity, illegal sexual intercourse, and thereby disqualifies himself from office, the *imam*'s legitimacy remains intact.[41] In a second argument, Māwardī simply denies that legitimate political authority is needed in order to carry out *ḥadd* punishments. He argues that just as the absence of an *imam* does not legalize *ḥadd* crimes, it also does not require the cancellation of the *ḥadd* punishments themselves.[42]

3. MURDER

The discussion of coerced homicide in the classical sources revolves around the correct distribution of legal and moral responsibility between the coercer and the coerced. At the moral level, the question was whether the coerced agent sins by acquiescing to the coercer's demand to kill another person. On this question, both the Ḥanafites and the Shāfiʿites were unanimous: coercion is no excuse for homicide. But the issue of the respective legal liability of the coercer and the coerced for the act of killing generated much internal disagreement within each of the traditions. Part of the reason for this disagreement lay in the fact that the Islamic laws regulating intentional and unlawful killing give the legal heirs of the victim many options in deciding how to proceed against a person convicted of homicide. The heirs have the right to seek the killer's execution. Alternatively, they may accept financial compensation, or even pardon the offender.[43] Given the multiplicity of possible legal responses to homicide, the question of legal liability for this crime was a bit more complicated than that for rape. In the case of rape, the central issue was whether or not coercion suspended the coerced rapist's punishment for the crime. In the case of homicide, because there are essentially two possible punishments, execution and financial compensation, juristic

[41] Ibid., 17:85.12–13. [42] Ibid., 17:85.14–15.
[43] For an account of the main principles and laws regulating homicide according to classical doctrine, see Peters, *Crime*, 38–53.

disagreement centered on whether the fact of coercion can take execution as an option off the table, and whether this applies to the coercer or to the coerced.

3.1 Ḥanafites on Murder

Much as in the case of Ḥanafite jurisprudence on coerced speech and rape, Shaybānī's discussion of the issue of coerced homicide provides the essential building blocks for later Ḥanafite thinking on the matter. Shaybānī constructs the coerced homicide case as follows:

> [Assume that] the caliph sends an agent [to take responsibility] over a given region, such as Khurasan or some other place. [The agent] assaults a man and commands him to kill another person illegally (*ẓulman*). The man refuses to obey the command, to which the agent responds: "Either you kill him with a sword or I kill you." The man kills the other person.[44]

Leaving aside the curious fact that Shaybānī frames a government agent in the role of the coercer, we are told that there are two different opinions on the legal solution to this problem. Abū Ḥanīfa held that the coercing agent and not the coerced killer is solely liable to the full legal sanction for homicide. By contrast, Abū Yūsuf excluded execution as an option in this situation and argued that the most the coercer can be held liable for is financial compensation to the heir(s) of the victim. Shaybānī quotes Abū Yūsuf as saying that he used juristic preference (*istiḥsān*) to arrive at his position, the implication being that a straightforward analogy would yield Abū Ḥanīfa's position instead.[45] Shaybānī endorses Abū Ḥanīfa's position as the correct one.[46] He justifies it by reference to the precedent of the first caliph, Abū Bakr (d. 13/634). According to the relevant part of the report, Abū Bakr threatened to impose corporal punishment or retaliation on a government agent who, he suspected, had illegally ordered the amputation of the hand of a boy he employed. Shaybānī interprets Abū Bakr's act as legitimating the possibility

[44] Shaybānī, *al-Aṣl*, 7:322.5–7.

[45] See ibid., 7:322.9. Shaybānī quotes Abū Yūsuf directly as saying, "I used juristic preference to oblige the coercer to pay financial compensation as opposed to killing him" (*astaḥsinu an ajʿala ʿalā ʾl-āmiri ʾl-diya wa-lā aqtalu-hu*).

[46] Ibid., 7:322.8.

that the issuer of a coercive command be held personally liable to the fullest extent for illegal commands that lead to harm to others.[47]

Shaybānī acknowledges, however, that Abū Ḥanīfa's position is not without its weakness. He quotes an anonymous interlocutor as asking, "How can you execute the person who issued the command when he has not killed with his own hand?"[48] Shaybānī offers two different arguments in response. First, he points to the law governing cases of brigandage (*qatʿ ṭarīq*), which authorizes the execution of criminals even if they did not themselves physically kill anyone.[49] Since all jurists accept this law as legitimate, Shaybānī argues, the fact that a coercer does not physically kill the victim cannot categorically exclude the possibility that he be held fully responsible for the crime. Second, Shaybānī cites the opinion of a prominent early authority, al-Ḥasan al-Baṣrī (d. 110/728), on a different case. Al-Ḥasan al-Baṣrī held that a witness whose testimony led to the execution of an adulterer could himself be executed if he retracted his testimony after the adulterer's punishment had been put into effect.[50] The underlying logic is the same as in the previous argument: if al-Ḥasan al-Baṣrī thought it legitimate to execute a witness whose retracted testimony caused an unjustified death despite the fact that the witness did not himself kill the convict, then as a general rule being the physical agent of the killing is not a requirement for execution.

As in the case of rape, although the coerced perpetrator may avoid legal punishment in this world, he has nonetheless committed a moral offense. Shaybānī writes:

> The commanded individual sins (*āthim*) when he kills, even if he is coerced. He must not kill on the coercer's command even if the coercer will kill him or order someone else to kill him if he refuses. This is because this [the act of killing] is a deeply unjust interpersonal act (*maẓālim al-nās*). A person must not commit such an injustice even if he is threatened with death.[51]

Shaybānī's justification for holding the coerced killer still in some way morally responsible for the act even if not liable to the legal punishment is based on the interpersonal nature of the injustice. He adds that it would be similarly unjust for the coerced individual to obey a coercer who demands, on

[47] See ibid., 7:302.3–17. [48] Ibid., 7:322.11. [49] Ibid., 7:322.12–13.
[50] Ibid., 7:322.14–15. [51] Ibid., 7:323.6–9.

pain of death, that the former not kill the victim but rather pluck out the victim's eye or amputate her hand. If the coerced complies, he has sinned. But it is the coercer who is held legally responsible to the fullest extent—he is liable for retaliation. Shaybānī adds, however, that the caliph may subject the coerced person, if he complied with the coercer's demand, to a discretionary punishment (*taʿzīr*).[52] The same applies if the coercer gives the coerced the choice to kill one of two people, or the choice to either kill one person or rape another. If the coerced kills one of the two possible victims, the coercer is liable for the full legal penalty while the coerced avoids legal liability, though he has sinned. If the coerced chooses to commit a rape, the fact of coercion suspends his punishment for fornication, but he remains liable for monetary compensation to the victim. In these cases, too, Shaybānī urges the government to subject the coerced perpetrator to the discretionary punishment.[53] Shaybānī also considers the case in which the coercer does not issue an explicit verbal threat when demanding an illegal homicide. Shaybānī says that if there is no way for the coerced to refuse the demand to kill, and she fears for her life if she does not comply with it, the coercer is held fully responsible for the crime.[54] However, if the coerced fears something less than the loss of life, such as imprisonment, and goes ahead with the homicide, she is fully liable for punishment.[55]

Shaybānī's elaboration and justification of the coerced homicide laws form the main elements of later Ḥanafite jurisprudence on coerced homicide. An additional element that is not found in Shaybānī's work but is recorded by later Ḥanafite scholars is Zufar's distinctive opinion on the issue. His view was the most stringent: the coerced killer alone is held fully responsible for the murder, and he is liable for the highest possible punishment. Classical Ḥanafite jurisprudence thus unfolds through the reconstruction of justifications that support the three early opinions—those of Abū Ḥanīfa/Shaybānī, Abū Yūsuf, and Zufar, respectively—along with the elaboration of justifications for other, unanimously held aspects of Ḥanafite doctrine.

Just as Shaybānī insisted that even a coerced agent sins if he commits murder, Jaṣṣāṣ affirms the position that coercion can never permit murder or

[52] Ibid., 7:323.9–12. [53] Ibid., 7:400.9–23. [54] Ibid., 7:324.16–325.3.
[55] Ibid., 7:324.9–11.

rape because these acts constitute a transgression against the rights of other people. The principle of equality of security from harm against one's person precludes lawful preference for one life over another without just cause.[56] Likewise, all the other Ḥanafite scholars either imply or state explicitly that coercion has no effect on the moral status of killing another person. But their unanimity on the moral prohibition against homicide did not translate into an equally unanimous response regarding the legal consequences of the act in this world. In fact, much of Ḥanafite coerced homicide jurisprudence is devoted to explaining why, according to the dominant opinion in classical Ḥanafism, the coerced killer is not held legally responsible for the act even though he sins when he commits it.

Even though most Ḥanafites endorsed Abū Ḥanīfa's and Shaybānī's position, Dabūsī and Sarakhsī made attempts to reconstruct the reasoning behind Zufar's and Abū Yūsuf's positions. The basic structure of both reconstructions of Zufar's argument is to reason from the classical Ḥanafite consensus that the coerced sins by killing to the conclusion that she ought to be held fully liable for the crime. Dabūsī uses the logic of the instrument test to demonstrate the viability of Zufar's position. He reasons that if coercion truly turns the coerced into an instrument, such that the legal consequences of the act are transferred to the coercer, then it ought also to invalidate the coerced agent's choice of becoming an instrument in the first place.[57] But if coercion invalidates the choice to become an instrument, the coerced killer ought not to be considered a sinner at all. This is a claim that no Ḥanafite was willing to make: all classical Ḥanafites seem to have held that the coerced indeed sins by killing, no matter how severe the coercion, and Zufar's position simply draws the logical conclusion that the coerced killer then ought to be held legally responsible for the sinful act and suffer the appropriate punishment.

Sarakhsī's reconstruction of Zufar's justification offers four additional arguments:

1. Interpretation of scripture
2. Invocation of the equality between the coerced and the victim

[56] Jaṣṣāṣ, *Aḥkām*, 3:251.23–26. [57] See Dabūsī, *Asrār*, 1006.7.

3. An analogy to the case of starvation
4. The principle of self-defense.

According to Sarakhsī, Zufar's position is based on the interpretation of Qurʿān 17:33, which reads, "And if anyone is killed unjustly, We have given his next of kin a certain authority"—that is, the authority to seek retaliation against the killer. The question is who qualifies as the killer, the coercer or the coerced. For Zufar's position, the coerced individual is the real killer. Sarakhsī explains that since murder is an empirically perceivable act (*fiʿl maḥsūs*), and the empirical killer is the coerced, he is to be held liable for the act.[58] The second argument offered by Sarakhsī for Zufar's position asserts that "whoever kills someone who is his equal in order to save himself has intentionally [violated] a compensable right (*ḥaqq maḍmūn*). Therefore, the full legal sanction (*qawad*) is required for him."[59] This claim emphasizes that the coerced acted on a preference for one life over another in an area in which he had no right to do so. In the third argument, Sarakhsī notes that someone who is coerced to kill is in a position analogous to that of someone who is compelled by starvation to kill and eat the flesh of another human being. In this case, as all Ḥanafites would accept, the killer, even if compelled by extreme hunger, is still held legally responsible for the act of homicide. The same reasoning should apply to the case of coerced homicide.[60] Finally, the very fact that the victim of an attempted coerced murder has a legitimate right to kill the coerced attacker in self-defense indicates that the law holds the coerced responsible for the attempted homicide. Otherwise, it would not have been wholly permissible for the victim to defend himself to the point of killing the coerced.[61]

How do the later Ḥanafite scholars justify the remaining two opinions, those of Abū Yūsuf and Abū Ḥanīfa/Shaybānī? Recall that Abū Yūsuf held that neither the coerced nor the coercer is held liable for the full legal punishment of retaliation (*qiṣāṣ*). The coercer is, however, responsible for the payment of the appropriate amount of blood money (*diya*) from his personal property to the heirs of the victim within three years of the murder.[62] Why

[58] See Sarakhsī, *al-Mabsūṭ*, 24:85.13–15.
[59] See ibid., 24:85.11–12. [60] Ibid., 24:85.18–24.86.2. [61] Ibid., 24:85.16–19.
[62] The stipulation that the coerced killer should pay out of his own pocket emphasizes that the victim's clan (*ʿāqila*) is not financially responsible for the crime.

does Abū Yūsuf exclude the option of retaliation for both the coercer and the coerced? According to Dabūsī, the physical act of killing can be attributed only to the physical agent of the act.[63] Presumably for this reason, the coercer cannot be held liable for retaliation. As for the coerced, Dabūsī notes that for Abū Yūsuf, the existence of legal doubt impedes the application of the penalty of retaliation.[64] The penalty of retaliation is applied only when the murder is committed *intentionally* and there are no legal doubts about its commission. It is for this same reason, for example, that a person who unintentionally causes the death of another is not liable for retaliation. Because a coerced killer, similarly, does not intend the victim's death, he is not subject to retaliation: he "did not [truly] intend to kill, but rather intended to save his own life."[65] The lack of malicious intent creates a punishment-averting legal doubt. Precisely the same legal reasoning underpins the Ḥanafite law on rape.[66] In both cases, the coerced, when compelled into an act by a threat against life or limb, escapes the *ḥadd* punishment because of the presence of a legal doubt.

Sarakhsī's arguments for Abū Yūsuf's position are substantially similar, though he addresses only the question of why the coercer is not held fully liable. He says that the fact that the coerced is still regarded as having sinned is evidence that the "entirety of the act cannot be attributed to the coercer."[67] Furthermore, retaliation is incumbent only in the case of direct physical action. Since the coercer is not the physical agent of the murder, the retaliation cannot be directed against him.[68]

The third Ḥanafite opinion on coerced homicide discussed in the classical literature is that shared by two of the founding fathers of the tradition, Abū Ḥanīfa and Shaybānī, and by all indications considered the preferred opinion by later authors. Both jurists held that only the coercer is held fully liable for the act of homicide. Most Ḥanafite writings on coerced homicide are devoted to answering two questions that emerged from this position: What justifies it? And why, if the coerced killer is absolved of legal responsibility, is she nonetheless considered to have committed a sin? Jaṣṣāṣ begins his

[63] See Dabūsī, *Asrār*, 1006.14–15. [64] Ibid. [65] Ibid., 1006.15–16.
[66] Ibid., 1006.16. [67] Sarakhsī, *al-Mabsūṭ*, 24:88.16–17.
[68] Ibid., 24:88.17–18.

analysis by noting that the law on the coerced destruction of property holds the coercer and not the coerced responsible for paying financial compensation to the owner of the destroyed property.[69] The fact of coercion transfers legal responsibility for the act of destruction from the coerced to the coercer. Jaṣṣāṣ argues that the same logic applies in the case of coerced homicide. Furthermore, in another version of the self-defense argument seen earlier, Jaṣṣāṣ points out that the very fact that the coerced person and the intended victim may legitimately band together in order to kill the coercer without fear of the moral or legal consequences is an indication that coercion has an effect on the coercer's legal responsibility. The legitimacy of self-defense against the coercer also shows that the act of coercion has the effect of rendering the spilling of his blood permissible.[70] The implication is that if spilling his blood is permissible in self-defense, it is also permissible to shed his blood through execution.

But how does Jaṣṣāṣ respond to the argument that the legal consequences should follow the moral consequences of the coerced act? The reasoning underlying Zufar's position was that the coerced agent sins in killing an innocent person and thus ought to be held legally responsible for the act. To this argument, Jaṣṣāṣ responds with three other examples of cases in Ḥanafite legal thought in which the commission of a sin does not necessarily require legal responsibility. In view of these cases, he concludes, there is no necessary concomitance between the two forms of responsibility (moral and legal). The first of the three cases involves a Muslim who is given a guarantee of safe passage (*amān*) by a non-Muslim sovereign. If the recipient of the guarantee then kills another Muslim while outside of Islamic legal jurisdiction, he has committed a sin but is not liable for the *ḥadd* punishment for murder, because he committed the act outside of the Muslim state's jurisdiction.[71] In the second case, a person living outside of Islamic legal jurisdiction converts to Islam and then kills another Muslim. Again, she has committed a sin but is not subject to any of the legal penalties for homicide, because the act occurred beyond the state's jurisdiction.[72]

[69] Jaṣṣāṣ, *Sharḥ*, 8:451–2. Dabūsī notes that the position of Abū Ḥanīfa and Shaybānī on coerced homicide is the result of an analogy drawn on the case of coerced property destruction. Dabūsī, *Asrār*, 1006.23–24.

[70] Jaṣṣāṣ, *Sharḥ*, 8:452.6–11.

[71] Ibid., 8:453.11–13.

[72] Ibid., 8:453.14–16.

The third case relates to the way in which retaliation is exacted on a person convicted of homicide. The Ḥanafites hold that the criminal is to be executed only by use of a sword. If the executioner carries out the punishment by the use of fire, he has sinned, but he is not held legally responsible for undertaking the execution in an illegal way.[73] Jaṣṣāṣ's point is to demonstrate to other Ḥanafites who might be sympathetic to Zufar's position (such as Ṭaḥāwī) that Ḥanafite laws do not always require legal consequences to follow from moral culpability. If in these cases a person can be a sinner, liable to God's accountability in the next world, without being held accountable in this world, then there is no a priori reason why this would not be possible in the case of coerced murder.

Dabūsī, in his analysis of the Abū Ḥanīfa/Shaybānī position, uses the instrument test to demonstrate the transfer of legal consequences from the coerced to the coercer. The instrument test stipulates that compelling coercion results in transference only in cases in which it is empirically conceivable that the coercer could have physically used the body of the coercer as an instrument. Since it is possible that the coercer could grab the arm of the coerced and literally use it as an instrument to kill the intended victim, the application of the instrument test yields a successful transference result in the case of coerced murder.[74] In this case, Dabūsī notes that it is specifically a threat against life (*bi-waʿīd al-qatl*) that constitutes compelling coercion.[75]

Dabūsī then explains why the coerced is still considered a sinner even though he is not responsible for any of the legal consequences of his act. Dabūsī introduces the case of a *muḥrim* (someone who has entered a state

[73] Ibid., 8:453.17–18. Peters notes that while the Ḥanafites and the Shīʿites stipulate that the execution must take place by the sword, other schools hold that retaliatory death should be inflicted in the same way in which the victim was killed. In this case, the Ḥanafites imagine a situation in which the Ḥanafite law on execution is violated. It is possible that even those schools that admitted execution with whatever method the killer had used, ruled out execution by fire because of its particularly cruel nature. In either case, the executioner has violated an ethical norm, but one that does not have legal consequences. See Peters, *Crime*, 37.

[74] Dabūsī, *Asrār*, 1006.23–24.

[75] Ibid., 1006.24–26. In previous cases Dabūsī defined compelling coercion as threats against life or limb. It is not clear whether the omission of threats against limb is intentional. But it is likely that since the coercer's demand is the life of the victim, in order for the threat to count as compelling, it would have to be commensurate with the demand. Only a threat against the life of the coerced can thus justify transference. This idea is not found in Dabūsī's writings, though it is found in Sarakhsī's work. For Sarakhsī likewise omitting reference to threats against limb as legally coercive in the case of coerced homicide, see Sarakhsī, *al-Mabsūṭ*, 24:86.29–87.1.

of ritual consecration during the pilgrimage) who is coerced to kill prey (which is normally prohibited when in a state of consecration) to analyze the nature of the sin that the coerced commits in the case of homicide. A valid performance of the pilgrimage requires that a person enter a state of ritual consecration. Practically speaking, this involves the observation of specific proscriptions above and beyond those that are in effect outside the state of consecration. One such proscription requires *muḥrims* to refrain from hunting. If a *muḥrim* violates this proscription, he renders his state of consecration defective. In order to restore it, he must perform certain acts of expiation. In the case of the coerced *muḥrim*'s killing of an animal, the question that coercion raises is whether it is the coerced or the coercer who is responsible for the required act of expiation. Dabūsī's presentation of the case adds a further complication: What if the animal is not wild but is rather owned by a third party? Who is responsible for paying financial compensation to the owner of the animal? The commonly accepted Ḥanafite view is that in this case, despite the presence of coercion, it is still the *muḥrim* who must perform the acts of expiation to restore his state of consecration, but the coercer is held financially liable for compensation for the killed animal if it belongs to someone. Dabūsī explains that the application of the instrument test to this scenario fails to transfer the legal consequences of the coerced act with respect to expiation, but succeeds with respect to financial compensation.[76] Part of the reason for its failure is that the object of the transgression is the *muḥrim*'s personal state of consecration (*jināya ʿalā ʾl-iḥrām*), not an external object belonging to someone else.[77] Hence the coerced is still responsible for the expiation. The same reasoning applies to the Ḥanafite requirement that someone who is coerced to break her fast or her prayer is still obliged to make up the fast or the prayer, because these are actions that pertain to a person's observation of religious proscriptions (*jināya ʿalā ḥudūd dīni-hi*) and therefore do not admit transference. Similarly, the coerced murder in fact constitutes a transgression against two objects. It is not only a transgression against the victim's person (*jināya ʿalā ʾl-maqtūl*);[78] it is also a transgression

[76] Dabūsī, *Asrār*, 1007.1–2. [77] Ibid., 1007.8–10.

[78] Ibid., 1007.9–11. Dabūsī is not claiming that the coercer does not sin. Insofar as the instrument test transfers the attribution of the legal consequences of the homicide to her, she is regarded as the one who intended to kill the victim. In doing so, she has committed a wilful act of supreme harm against the victim. This is a sin, and she is obliged to do expiation if the

that violates the coerced killer's personal religious duties. The instrument test succeeds in validating transference of the legal consequences associated with the transgression against the victim's person, but it fails in transferring the coerced's transgressions against his own personal religious obligation to not kill. By invoking the accepted logic of the effect of coercion in the case of the *muḥrim*, and the one who fasts and prays, Dabūsī demonstrates why the coerced sins when he kills but why, at the same time, he avoids the legal consequences of his act.

Sarakhsī reproduces variations of Jaṣṣāṣ's and Dabūsī's justifications for the Abū Ḥanīfa/Shaybānī position on coerced homicide. Like Jaṣṣāṣ, he asserts that the fact that the coerced sins does not necessarily mean that he ought to be held legally responsible for the act.[79] Sarakhsī notes that if a man gives someone else permission to cut off his hand, the amputator sins in committing the act but cannot be held legally responsible for it.[80]

Sarakhsī's explanation of the nature of the coerced murderer's sin mirrors Dabūsī's analysis. He states that while coercion can change the attribution of the act, it cannot change the nature of the object that the act is directed toward. In the case of coerced murder, there are two such objects. The first is the person of the victim, whose killing constitutes a violation of a compensable right (*fa-amma fī ḥaqqi ʾl-ḍamāni fa-maḥallu ʾl-jināyati nafsu al-maqtūl*).[81] The legal consequences of the act of murder originate in the violation of this right, regardless of whether the act is attributed to the coerced or the coercer. The instrument test can validate the transference of legal consequences originating in this object from the coerced to the coercer. But the second object is the religious proscriptions that apply only to the person of the coerced. Sarakhsī writes:

> When we say that the coerced is a sinner and that in the case of sin the act is attributed to him, it is because it is a transgression against his religion (*jināya ʿalā dīni-hi*). He commits an act that is purely prohibited (*ḥarām maḥḍ*).[82]

victim's heirs choose to either pardon or demand blood money from her. For all of this, see ibid. For substantially the same argument, see also Bazdawī, *al-Kāfī*, 5:2460.1–2461.6.

[79] Sarakhsī, *al-Mabsūṭ*, 24:87.7. [80] Ibid., 24:87.8–9. [81] Ibid., 24:87.16–17.

[82] See ibid. In the same passage, Sarakhsī describes the sin as consisting of a "transgression against the bounds of his personal religion" (*al-jināya ʿalā ḥadd dīni-hi*).

The nature of this object does not admit transference. In the violation of the coerced's religious duty, it is not conceivable that the coerced can serve as the mere instrument of the coercer.[83]

3.2 Shāfiʿites on Murder

The founding fathers of Ḥanafism, Abū Ḥanīfa, Abū Yūsuf, Shaybānī, and Zufar, disagreed profoundly on the proper distribution of responsibility in a case of coerced homicide. Much of classical Ḥanafite jurisprudence on coerced homicide was inspired by the search for the reasons behind these disparate opinions. The situation is similar, though not identical, in Shāfiʿism. Shāfiʿī himself bequeathed to later Shāfiʿites two different opinions on whether coercion eliminates a coerced killer's liability for the penalty of retaliation. Most classical Shāfiʿites explicitly identified Shāfiʿī's more stringent opinion (that coercion does not eliminate the coerced's liability to retaliation) as correct. However, while there was relative uniformity in the identification of the preferred position on the issue within the tradition, there was quite a bit of diversity in the conceptual frameworks within which classical Shāfiʿites embedded their discussions of coerced homicide. Shāfiʿī himself discusses the case of coerced homicide within a larger discussion of the problem of a superior issuing an illegal order to a subordinate to kill another human being. This way of framing coerced homicide is retained and expanded by Māwardī, only to be discarded and criticized by Juwaynī. Ghazālī adopts an entirely different framework. He links culpability for homicide to causality, and his discussion of coerced homicide takes place within this broad conceptual framework.

The case of a superior's order to kill someone illegally involves questions about who legitimately qualifies as a superior and who is held legally responsible for the illegal act. Shāfiʿī asserts that if the order to kill is issued by a legitimate ruler, the ruler is held responsible for the illegal homicide. He bases this law on the same precedent that Shaybānī identified as foundational for the case of coerced homicide, involving the first caliph, Abū Bakr.[84]

[83] Ibid., 24:87.19–20. For substantially the same argument, see Bazdawī, *al-Kāfī*, 5:2461.3–4.
[84] Shāfiʿī, *al-Umm*, 7:106.16–107.1.

Shāfiʿī interprets the report of the case as substantiating the fundamental law that a superior is culpable for unjustly commanding a subordinate to do harm to someone else. His occupation of political office does not grant him immunity from the highest legal penalty, if his order to harm another was illegal and resulted in actual harm to that person through the agency of the subordinate to whom he issued the order. But what about the subordinate's legal liability?

On this question, the material issue for Shāfiʿī is whether the subordinate knew of the illegality of the superior's command to kill.[85] If the subordinate did not know that the command was illegal, she is excused for the crime and the superior is held fully liable, although Shāfiʿī expresses the preference that the subordinate still undertake the requisite expiation (*kaffāra*) for the crime. But if the subordinate knew that the command was illegal, *both* he and the ruler are held fully liable for the crime. In both cases, the ruler is held fully responsible. But what happens if the subordinate knew that the command was illegal but was coerced by the superior to obey it anyway?[86]

Shāfiʿī notes two positions that presumably circulated in the legal circles of his day on the legal and moral responsibility of the coerced killer,[87] without indicating a preference for either one.[88] One position holds the coerced fully responsible, on the grounds that the coerced violated the prohibition against wrongful killing and that coercion nullifies only the legal and moral effects of acts that do not involve harm to others.[89] The second position holds that the coerced is not liable for the full legal sanction because the existence of coercion counts as a legal doubt (*shubha*), which often impedes the application

[85] Shāfiʿī, ibid., 7:107.6–8.

[86] In fact, Shāfiʿī extends the financial liability of the ruler (*sulṭān*) for homicide in two other cases that involve coercion but not necessarily an intent to kill on the part of the ruler. In the first, the ruler coercively orders that either a cyst/tumor (*silaʿa* or *akila*) on someone else's body, or the limb on which the cyst resides, be removed (*qaṭʿ*). If the subject dies as a result of the operation, the ruler is held liable. In the second case, the ruler coerces someone to climb up or go down (e.g., into a well); if the climber slips, falls, and dies, the ruler is liable for the blood money. Shāfiʿī adds that the same judgment applies to all cases similar to the latter case. On another occasion, Shāfiʿī enunciates an even more general legal principle: if the ruler coerces a man into obeying any order that is not in the best interests of Muslims, and the man dies as a result, the ruler is financially liable for his blood money. For these arguments, see ibid., 7:218.1–219.1.

[87] Ibid., 7:107.8–9.

[88] This is probably the reason why later Shāfiʿites attribute two opinions to him on this issue.

[89] Shāfiʿī, *al-Umm*, 7:107.10–11.

of punishments in Islamic jurisprudence.[90] The coerced is, however, held responsible for payment of half of the blood money to the victim's heirs, and he must do expiation (*kaffāra*) for the act.[91] That said, the determination of whether the coerced is liable for the legal penalty of retaliation is not connected to the moral value of the act. Shāfiʿī asserts that while coercion can, generally speaking, render some prohibited acts permitted, it cannot have that effect if the coerced act involves harming others (*lā yaḍurru aḥadan*).[92] While coercion may impede the application of the punishment of retaliation on the coerced, the coerced has still committed an impermissible act.

In these cases, Shāfiʿī assumes that the superior issuing the illegal order is either the ruler himself or one of his supreme executive aides—that is, someone vested with legitimate political authority. Since not all holders of power are legitimate political authorities, Shāfiʿī then turns his attention to the question of whether the nature and basis of a power holder's power have any effect on the distribution of responsibility between the coercer and the coerced. Shāfiʿī considers the following three variants of a superior: an illegitimate provincial governor, the leader of a band of criminals, and a village strong man. If the superior is a provincial governor (*al-wālī al-mutaghallib wa-ʾl-mustaʿmal*) who has illegitimately usurped power (*idhā qahara fī mawḍiʿi-hi*) over an area and commands a subordinate to carry out an illegal killing, Shāfiʿī holds that the superior is held responsible for the homicide. He adds that this is the case regardless of the length of his tenure in the position.[93] If the superior's power is based on the following of a band of thieves or some other type of social solidarity (*al-rajul al-mutaghallib ʿalā ʾl-luṣūṣiyya aw al-ʿaṣabiyya*), and he wields such power over the subordinate that the latter cannot refuse the command (*idhā kāna qāhiran lil-maʾmūr lā yastaṭīʿ al-imtināʿ min-hu*), both the superior and the subordinate are held fully responsible for the crime.[94] In the third variant

[90] Rabb, *Doubt in Islamic Law: a History of Legal Maxims, Interpretation, and Islamic Criminal Law*, especially 167–84 for its function in early Shāfiʿite criminal law.

[91] Shāfiʿī, *al-Umm*, 7:107.12.

[92] Ibid., 5:701.17–702.3. Specifically, he writes, "If someone is coerced to kill another, it is not permitted that he do that."

[93] Ibid., 7:107.12–13.

[94] Ibid., 7:107.14–16. This position seems to imply that if the coerced can be judged to have been capable of refusing the command, the issuer of the command evades liability for the murder.

scenario, the superior is a village strong man who has not established domination over everyone in the village; but, he does dominate the subordinate in question, though not to the point that the latter is unable to refuse the superior's command through resisting, fleeing, or seeking aid from some other group. Under these circumstances, the subordinate alone is held fully liable for a murder ordered by the superior, though Shāfiʿī holds the superior liable for discretionary judicial punishment (*ʿuqūba*).[95] But if the superior's power is such that the subordinate is not able to refuse, then both are liable for the full penalty.[96]

In all of these cases, the material issue at stake for Shāfiʿī is whether the superior, in addition to the coerced subordinate, is held responsible for the coerced crime. In cases in which the superior is not the legitimate political authority, Shāfiʿī's operating principle in determining his responsibility is the extent of his power over the subordinate. Is it so overwhelming that the subordinate cannot refuse his commands? If so, then the superior is also held responsible. Only in the case that the superior acts in the capacity of a legitimate political authority does Shāfiʿī entertain the possibility that coercion could mitigate the coerced subordinate's responsibility, and he is content to note disagreement on the issue.

Later Shāfiʿites do not stop at simply recording the disagreement. While they ascribe two conflicting opinions to Shāfiʿī on whether the coerced is held fully responsible in such situations, the majority of them specifically identify the more stringent opinion as correct. All hold that coercion does not excuse the coerced's act of homicide and that both the coercer and the coerced are fully liable for the maximum penalty.

Among the later Shāfiʿites, Māwardī's discussion of coerced homicide is an elaborate expansion of Shāfiʿī's basic framework. Like Shāfiʿī himself, Māwardī embeds the issue of coerced homicide within a larger discussion of illegal superior orders. The discussion proceeds in much the same way as it did in Shāfiʿī's work. Briefly, the commanded subordinate (*al-maʾmūr*) is excused for carrying out an execution ordered by his superior if he did not know that the execution was unjust and believed that the ruler would only

[95] Ibid., 7:107.17–108.1. [96] Ibid., 7:108.2–3.

order only killings that were legal.[97] Only the ruler himself is held liable to the full extent of the legal sanction for the crime. If, on the other hand, the subordinate knew that the command was illegal, there are two alternatives: either he executed the illegal command out of his own free will (*mukhtār*) or he was coerced into obeying.[98] If the former, according to Shāfiʿī's predominant opinion (*ẓāhir min madhhab al-Shāfiʿī*) and the position of the majority of Shāfiʿite jurists, the subordinate, and not the ruler, is regarded as the killer, and he alone is held liable for the full sanction (*qawad*).[99] If the command was accompanied by a coercive threat, then the commander becomes liable to the full legal sanction for homicide. There are two views on whether the subordinate is likewise liable in this situation. The first view, which Māwardī endorses, holds both the commander and the coerced commanded (*al-maʾmūr al-mukrah*) equally and fully liable.[100] In this view, the subordinate, despite the exigent circumstances, is held fully responsible.

Shāfiʿī's justification for this view consisted of merely noting that killing is never permitted and that coercion cannot allow a person to harm another. Māwardī's justification is much more extensive and forms part of his discussion of the Ḥanafite Abū Yūsuf's contrary position that held neither the coerced nor the coercer liable for the full legal penalty of retaliation. Māwardī's first argument against Abū Yūsuf's position and in support of the Shāfiʿite position involves the interpretation of the Qurʾānic verse 17:33, a foundational text for the law of homicide: "And if anyone is killed unjustly, We have given his next of kin a certain authority." Māwardī argues that the verse requires that the victim's heirs be given the authority to decide on the murderer's fate. He accuses Abū Yūsuf's position of suppressing this

[97] However, both Māwardī and Shīrāzī cite Shāfiʿī's position that it is recommended (*yustaḥabb*) that the subordinate perform expiation (*kaffāra*), as he was the direct physical cause (*mubāshir*) of the death. See Māwardī, *al-Ḥāwī*, 12:72.3–4.

[98] Ibid., 12:72.10–13.

[99] However, Māwardī does not let the ruler completely off the hook. The ruler (*imām*) is still sinning (*āthim*) even though he is not liable for any legal sanction, whether in the form of retaliation (*qawad*), blood money (*diya*), or expiation (*kaffāra*). He does note some disagreement on this issue among his colleagues, some of whom held the superior equally liable for the full legal sanction purely for his illegal command. Māwardī concedes that from the perspective of public welfare (*maṣlaḥa*) and the need to restrain the enmity of rulers, this view has its strong points, even if it is weak from the perspective of analogical reasoning. See ibid., 12:72.14–22.

[100] Ibid., 12:72.23–73.3. Māwardī wrongly attributes this view to the early Ḥanafite jurist Zufar.

authority, even though an unjust action has occurred.[101] In addition, whereas the absence of an intent to kill may protect a killer from the punishment of retaliation, making the case not one of intentional homicide but rather one of manslaughter, this does not apply to coerced homicide. The coerced fully intends to kill, and to kill wrongfully, if only to save himself. The fact that he kills in order to save himself does not avert the penalty of retaliation.[102] Along with these scriptural arguments, Māwardī cites laws governing three similar cases to support the conclusion that coercion does not absolve the coerced of the full legal sanction. The first of these three is the case of a starving person who is compelled by her hunger to kill a bystander in order to eat the victim's flesh and thus stave off her own demise. Despite the compelling circumstances, the killer is still subject to retaliation. The second case is that of a group of people who throw an individual off a sinking boat in order to save themselves. In this case also, retaliation is applicable to those who threw the poor soul off the ship. Likewise, someone who encounters a predatory animal and pushes a bystander into the animal's path to save himself at the bystander's expense is also liable for retaliation. Māwardī extends the reasoning of these agreed-upon cases to coerced homicide:

> The case of the coerced who saves himself by [sacrificing] another is similar, because there is no excuse for someone who saves his own life by killing another. The sanctity of another person's [life] is equal to the sanctity of his own [life]. Saving himself by sacrificing another is no more appropriate than sacrificing himself to save another. The two [lives] are equal.[103]

Shāfiʿī's second view on the legal liability of a killer acting under a coercive threat holds that only the ruler (*imām*) and not the coerced killer is liable for retaliation.[104] Māwardī notes that those of his colleagues who support this second view disagree on its basis. One group, whom he identifies as the Baghdadis, hold that the cause for the nonapplication of the sanction to the coerced is the fact that coercion is a type of legal doubt (*shubha*).[105] Thus, through the generally accepted legal principle that doubts impede the application of punishments, the punishment for the homicide is lifted from

[101] Ibid., 12:73.15–17. [102] Ibid., 12:74.21–22.
[103] See ibid., 12:74.27–29. [104] Ibid., 12:72.4.
[105] As we saw, Shāfiʿī cited the same reasoning as justification for this position.

the coerced. Categorizing coercion as a type of legal doubt, however, does not necessarily lead to full moral and legal exculpation. The Baghdadis hold that although the coerced is no longer liable to the corporal punishment of retaliation (*qawad*), he can still be held liable for half of the blood money (*diya*).[106]

The other group, the Basrans, employ legal reasoning similar to that of the Ḥanafites in their defense of the legal opinion that a coerced killer should not be held legally responsible for a homicide. They hold that the legal basis for the complete cancellation of the killer's liability is the fact that coercion is a type of compulsion (*iljāʾ*) and necessity (*ḍarūra*) that results in the transfer of the act's attribution from the physical agent (*mubāshir*) to the person who commanded it (*al-ikrāhu iljāʾun wa-ḍarūratun tanqulu ḥukma ʾl-fiʿli ʿan ʾl-mubāshiri ilā ʾl-āmir*). The coerced agent should not, therefore, be held legally responsible for the crime and is not liable for the corporal sanction (*qawad*), blood money (*diya*), or expiation (*kaffāra*). The Basrans compare this case to that of a judge who convicts a defendant of the crime of homicide on the basis of false testimonies (*shuhūd al-zūr*) and sentences him to execution. The implication of the Basrans' position, as depicted by Māwardī, is that no jurist would regard the judge as the killer of an innocent person. Rather, the responsibility for the wrongful conviction would rightly fall on the person who knowingly gave false testimony.[107] The Basrans urge a similar conclusion in the case of coerced homicide.

Māwardī notes another internal disagreement within the camp that was willing to recognize coercion as an excuse in the case of homicide. Does the fact that the demanded act is murder change what threats can establish a legally successful claim of coercion? One view denies that there is any relationship between what the coercer demands and what he threatens in determining whether coercion has any effect in the case of homicide. The threatened act could be killing, maiming, confinement, or destruction or usurpation of property. According to this view, what is legally coercive in the case of a demand to commit murder is the same as what is legally coercive when the demand is to pronounce a divorce. The alternative view holds that

[106] Māwardī, *al-Ḥāwī*, 12:73.5–8.
[107] Ibid., 12:72.8–11. Māwardī correctly attributes this view to Abū Ḥanīfa and Shaybānī.

only when one is threatened with death can coercion serve as a legal excuse for committing homicide. The jurists who hold this position argue that the inviolability (*ḥurma*) of lives ranks higher (*aghlaẓ*) than the inviolability of property, which means that the threatened action that would constitute the exculpatory coercion must be equally as severe as the act being demanded.[108]

Shāfiʿī began his discussion of coerced homicide with the assumption that the coercer was either the legitimate ruler or his agent, and then considered the question of whether the distribution of responsibility is altered if the coercer is instead an illegitimate political usurper, a gang leader, or a village strong man. He seemed to grant a political usurper the same status as the legitimate political authority. If we accept Shāfiʿī's less stringent position (that a coerced killer is not liable for retaliation), then someone coerced to kill by an usurper could presumably use this coercion as an excuse to avoid the punishment of retaliation. But according to Shāfiʿī, this option was not available when the coercer was a gang leader or a village strongman. Māwardī makes Shāfiʿī's concrete, case-by-case discussion more abstract and explicit. He considers two different types of superiors: legitimate power holders and illegitimate power holders. The legitimate power holders are those identified by Shāfiʿī: the ruler (*imām*) and any of his agents. But his discussion of the second type is interesting. Māwardī divides illegitimate power holders into two general types: rebel rulers and brigands. He assimilates the case of power holders who claim that their exercise of power is legitimate to the case of rulers who coerce their subjects to commit homicide. This is especially the case when the coerced subordinate conscientiously believes that the power holder is the legitimate ruler. Part of Māwardī's reasoning relies on a Shāfiʿite legal position that validates rebel court judgments and their collection of taxes (*zakāt* and *kharāj*). The fact that the Shāfiʿītes accepted the legitimacy of rebel legal actions implied, for Māwardī, that they could be assimilated to the category of legitimate rulers in the case of coerced homicide. But what about a power holder who makes no claim to legitimate rule, such as a brigand? Is the case of the brigand comparable to that of the legitimate ruler? Māwardī reports two different views on this question among the Shāfiʿites. One view considers the two equivalent, because the ruler's

[108] Ibid., 12:75.23–76.3.

coercion is exactly the same as that of the brigand. According to this view, the only thing that matters in judging how to distribute legal liability between the coercer and the coerced is whether the coercer's threat amounts to coercion, not the legitimacy of his power. The second view differentiates the case of the brigand from that of the legitimate ruler in two ways. First, when the brigand orders an illegal homicide, the recipient of the order can easily escape the small amount of territory under the brigand's power. This is not the case when the commander is a legitimate ruler. Second, there is a prima facie duty to obey the commands of a legitimate ruler: as long as his commands are legal, his subordinates are under a moral obligation to fulfill them. But no such duty exists when the commander is a brigand.[109]

This internal Shāfiᶜite dispute mirrors a dispute among modern Western coercion theorists, who are divided on the nature of the relationship between coercion and responsibility. One camp holds that the challenge in determining coercion's effect on responsibility essentially boils down to formulating a standard for identifying when coercion has occurred. For this camp, a finding of coercion automatically generates a change in the distribution of responsibility between, for example, the person who commands an illegal homicide and the person to whom the command to kill is directed. The other camp denies that the relationship between coercion and responsibility is so straightforward; in their view, coercion is one of many potential moral considerations, and a judgment about whether it affects responsibility for a particular act must be made in conjunction with these other considerations. This same reasoning is reflected in the second Shāfiᶜite opinion, which insists that the prima facie duty to obey a legitimate ruler interacts with the fact of coercion to change the distribution of responsibility for an illegal homicide: coercion is not a foundational or monopolistic ethical value. When the power holder is a brigand, there is no prima facie moral duty to obey, and hence there is no change in the distribution of responsibility for the illegal homicide despite the presence of coercion.

Māwardī's presentation of the coerced homicide issue is fairly exhaustive. He continues Shāfiᶜī's practice of discussing coerced murder within the issue of illegal superior orders. He reproduces both of Shāfiᶜī's two opinions on the

[109] Ibid., 12:77.13–20.

liability of a coerced killer and provides extensive justification for them even as he identifies one as more consistent with the tradition's core principles. By contrast, Juwaynī's presentation of the coerced homicide issue represents a departure from Māwardī in several respects. Unlike Māwardī, Juwaynī is uninterested in the justification for the core coerced homicide laws. Like Māwardī, he identifies the more stringent Shāfiʿite position—the one that held the coerced and the coercer fully responsible for the homicide—as correct. He provides one new argument for the stringent position: the reason both are held equally responsible is that they are seen as partners in crime.[110] The coercer "is the compeller who uses the strongest of causes, which preponderantly causes the homicide,"[111] while the coerced is the actual physical killer.[112] Seen as partners, both the coercer and the coerced deserve the full penalty for murder. This is about the only argument Juwaynī makes for the position he favors.[113]

Although Juwaynī does not explicitly consider variations in the institutional identity of the coercer (legitimate ruler vs. rebel ruler vs. brigand) as Shāfiʿī and Māwardī did, he does discuss the issue of a legitimate ruler's illegal command to kill. His framing assumptions are exactly the same as those posited by previous Shāfiʿites: if the executioner charged with a killing does not know of the command's illegality, he has no liability for punishment of any kind. Juwaynī gives a consequentialist argument that prioritizes political order to justify this position: "If we connect liability [for an execution] to the executioner, then administration of politics will not be ordered (*la-mā ʾntazimat al-siyāsāt*), for everyone who kills [on orders] will fear the [legal] consequences [of his act]."[114]

110 Juwaynī says that he offers an exhaustive examination of the coerced homicide issue in a separate, now lost work, *al-Masāʾil waʾl-Asālīb*. Juwaynī refers to the partnership analogy at least two times in his discussion on coerced homicide. See Juwaynī, *Nihāyat*, 16:115.19 and 16:119.15.

111 Presumably, the psychological response generated by a threat against one's life is what Juwaynī has in mind, when he is talking about the "strongest of causes."

112 Juwaynī, *Nihāyat*, 16:115.18–21. When discussing a scenario involving a minor coercing an adult to commit homicide, Juwaynī again describes the logic for the paradigm case of obliging full punishment on the coerced as the result of interpreting him as a partner.

113 His subsequent discussion takes the position for granted and moves on to an exploration and elaboration of other aspects of coerced homicide scenarios: how the blood money obligation is to be divided up between the coerced and the coercer, and whether the coerced is obliged to do expiation for the act.

114 Juwaynī, *Nihāyat*, 16:121.7–8.

Ghazālī also departs from Shāfiʿī's and Māwardī's framing of the coerced homicide issue. He does not embed the issue in a discussion about illegal orders. Rather, he connects the moral and legal liability for the crime of homicide to the efficacy of an agent's action in causing the death of another. For Ghazālī, there are three general types of cause: a direct physical cause (*ʿilla*), a necessary condition (*sharṭ*), and an ultimate cause (*sabab*). Each of these types of cause bears on the agent's liability for the full penalty of retaliation. Examples of a direct physical cause include the making of an incision into another person's jugular vein, which causes the victim's subsequent death, and the throwing of a spear that causes an injury resulting in death. The agent who is the direct physical causer of the injury that leads to death is liable for retaliation. The liability does not extend to a person whose causal role is that of providing a necessary condition for the occurrence of death—the second type of cause. Ghazālī's example of this type consists of a scenario in which ʿAmr digs a ditch, and Zeynap pushes Zayd into it. The fall causes Zayd's death. The digging of the ditch was a necessary condition for Zayd's death; Zayd would not have died had the ditch not existed. Yet for Ghazālī, ʿAmr's action was not causally efficacious enough to warrant imposing the penalty of retaliation on him.

If acts that constitute direct physical causes are liable for retaliation, and acts that merely supply necessary conditions are not, acts that represent ultimate causes occupy an ambiguous middle ground. The classification of an act as an ultimate cause does not immediately produce a judgment on the agent's liability for retaliation. Ghazālī categorizes coercion to commit murder as an ultimate cause, but he adds that "it has a strong resemblance to the direct physical cause, because it preponderantly causes the motivation to kill in the coerced."[115] For this reason, argues Ghazālī, the coercer, the ultimate causer of the homicide, is liable for retaliation. Ghazālī thus endorses the inherited Shāfiʿite position.

What about the legal liability of the coerced? On this issue, Ghazālī follows the lead of previous Shāfiʿītes, noting the existence of two opinions but explicitly identifying the position that holds the coerced liable for retaliation as the stronger one.[116] The difference between Ghazālī and his predecessors

[115] Ghazālī, *al-Wasīṭ fī al-Madhhab*, 6:259.7–8.

[116] Ibid., 6:263.2–3.

lies in the conceptual framework within which Ghazālī discusses the position. Within Ghazālī's causal framework, the problem of coerced homicide represents the conjunction of two different types of cause: the act of the coerced is the direct physical cause, and that of the coercer is the ultimate cause. The legal question is how the conjunction of the two types of cause affects the two agents' liability. Ghazālī discusses three cases that typify different degrees of conjunction between direct physical and ultimate causation. The case of false testimony that leads to a wrongful execution is one in which the ultimate causers (witnesses who give false testimony) act in conjunction with the legal system (a judge who gives a verdict and an executioner) to cause a homicide. In this case, Ghazālī identifies the ultimate cause as preponderant over the physical cause in the resultant homicide and therefore holds the witnesses who gave the false testimony liable for retaliation.[117] This case contrasts with a second case, in which ʿAmr throws Zeynap down the side of a hill. Zayd, who is at the bottom of the hill, slices Zeynap in half as she falls, killing her. Ghazālī identifies ʿAmr as the ultimate cause and Zayd as the physical cause and says that in this case the physical cause is preponderant over the ultimate cause in bringing about the resulting death. Consequently, Zayd is liable for retaliation whereas ʿAmr is not.[118] The case of coerced homicide is one in which Ghazālī thinks the ultimate cause (the coercer's demand) is equal to the physical cause (the coerced's act of murder). Again, Ghazālī frames the issue of the physical causer's liability for retaliation in terms of the causer's causal efficacy. He asks rhetorically: "Does the [ultimate cause] dominate the direct physical action in such a way that retaliation is not required of the coerced?"[119] He merely notes the existence of two opinions on the issue.[120]

This causal framework is not present in Ghazālī's discussion of the issue of superior orders and whether a ruler's command is itself a form of coercion. There are two ways of conceiving the issue, and the tension that characterized Māwardī's discussion of it resurfaces in Ghazālī's: Is the judgment of coercion's effect on the coerced's responsibility a purely empirical judgment? Or does the judgment depend on its interplay with a prima facie duty

[117] Ibid., 6:262.4–7. [118] Ibid., 6:262.8–10. [119] Ibid., 6:262.8.
[120] Ibid., 6:262.2–3.

to obey a legitimate ruler? If one considers it solely an empirical matter, then what is relevant to deciding whether a ruler's command is by itself coercive is whether "it is known from the ruler's habits that he assaults those who disobey him, even without explicit threats."[121] According to Ghazālī, from this perspective the inherent coerciveness of a ruler's command also potentially applies to the commands of power holders who are not rulers. But is there something morally different about obeying the commands of a legitimate ruler, such that the command of a ruler is categorically different from the commands of other power holders? If it is, then only a ruler's command may be classified as coercive in the absence of an explicit threat and consequently may alter the normative consequences of an illegal act for the coerced; the commands of other power holders may not do so. Ghazālī does not explicitly endorse this second way of thinking about rulers' commands, but it seems that this is the position that he is committed to.

But why is the ruler's command morally different? Ghazālī claims that "all things being equal, there is a duty to obey the ruler (*anna ṭāʿata al-sulṭāni wājibatun ʿalā ʾl-jumla*), so that disobedience to him does not lead to civil strife."[122] In fact, the avoidance of civil strife is also the reason behind the position that says that a ruler should not be deposed even if he commits a grossly immoral act (*fisq*). Ghazālī argues that if taking action to replace such an immoral ruler would incite civil strife, it should not be attempted.[123] Given the intimate connection between obedience to the ruler and the prevention of civil strife, Ghazālī elegantly describes the morality of disobedience to the ruler's commands as one in which "obligation and prohibition are in competition over the act" (*fa-tazāḥama ʿalā ʾl-fiʿli mūjibun wa-muḥarrimun*).[124] This being the case, if disobedience is not permitted, then coercion, in the form of the ruler's illegal command, constitutes a viable excuse. Ghazālī's framing of the issue thus has the effect of validating coercion as a potential excuse. The existence of the duty to obey the ruler serves as an additional complicating feature that obscures the subordinate's ability to determine the legality of the command. That Ghazālī sees the duty as specific to the ruler becomes apparent in his discussion of the case of a slave owner's illegal command

[121] Ibid., 6:263.13–14. [122] Ibid., 6:264.2–3. [123] Ibid., 6:264.3.
[124] Ibid., 6:264.4.

to his slave to kill someone. In this case, the slave is required to disobey the order, because there is no danger that his disobedience will incite civil strife. Theoretically, the slave has recourse to an authority higher than his master—namely, the ruler—to escape the consequences of deciding to disobey the slave owner's illegal command. This option is unavailable when the illegal order to kill is issued by the ruler himself. For this reason, the slave cannot appeal to coercion as an excuse to avoid the legal penalty associated with obeying the slave owner's command.[125]

4. CONCLUSION: DOMAIN-SPECIFIC CONSTRAINTS IN THE PROBLEM OF COERCED MURDER—COMPARISON WITH ANGLO-AMERICAN PHILOSOPHY AND LAW

At the heart of coerced speech jurisprudence lay the diametric opposition between the Ḥanafite and Shāfiʿite positions on coercion's effect on unilateral speech acts. No such clear-cut opposition between the traditions existed in coerced harm jurisprudence. Much of Islamic jurisprudence in this area was devoted to drawing out and articulating the reasoning behind the discordant opinions preserved in each of the traditions. The argumentation used to explain and justify the various opinions displays broad cross-tradition similarities. Both traditions affirmed the proposition that all people have an equal right to security from harm, even if they disagreed on what commitment to this principle required in distributing legal liability for an act of coerced harm. Both similarly held that even if the coerced agent may avoid legal liability for the act of harming another person, he still sins by committing the act. The sin persists even if the liability for legal punishment does not. The various positions on the issues of rape and homicide within the two traditions wrestle with the same conflicting moral and legal values. Ḥanafite and Shāfiʿite scholars strove to reconcile the intuition that causing harm to someone else was wrong with the instinct to give voice to the fact that the physical agent of the harm was coerced in judging the latter's responsibility. The different positions express varying commitments to these values

[125] Ibid., 6:264.4–6.

that pull in different directions. An examination of the writings of modern Anglo-American philosophers and of the reasoning found in the judgments of American and English judges reveals the same broad concerns.

Moral philosophers and jurists, whether committed to deontological or utilitarian approaches to morality, agree on the same premise that united Ḥanafites and Shāfiʿites—namely, that the right to protection from harm applies equally to everyone—even if they disagree on the law that the premise requires in the case of coerced homicide. On implicit deontological grounds, the influential English jurist William Blackstone (d. 1194/1780) held that coercion cannot serve as a defense for homicide. Blackstone insisted that faced with a coercive demand to kill, one ought to die rather than comply.[126] The political philosopher Thomas Hobbes (d. 1090/1679) offered a utilitarian reason for allowing coercion as a defense for homicide:[127] given that the function of punishment is to deter, punishing a coerced killer is pointless, and therefore such a killer ought not to be punished.[128] The utilitarian philosopher Jeremy Bentham (d. 1249/1832) provided a substantially similar justification for the same position.[129] But the legal philosopher H.L.A. Hart (d. 1413/1992) argued that a utilitarian justification can just as well be given for the opposite position—that coercion ought not to serve as an excuse for criminal acts. While the threat of punishment did not deter the coerced murderer, it would plausibly be more effective in deterring others from committing the same crime.[130]

The answer to the question of whether duress has been a successful defense in murder cases is negative. Most American courts have followed Blackstone in specifically excluding duress as an excuse in cases of homicide. Alan Wertheimer, author of an expansive monograph on coercion, claims that these courts may have feared that acknowledging duress might somehow justify homicide. In two British cases from the mid-1970s, the judges explicitly considered the validity of excluding duress as a defense for homicide.[131] In *Abbott v. Regina*, the defendant claimed duress in his role in the grisly stabbing and live burial of a young woman. The Lords seemed

[126] Wertheimer, *Coercion*, 147. [127] Ibid., 148. [128] Ibid.
[129] Ibid., 148–49. [130] Ibid., 149.
[131] See Lord Wilberforce's statement in his judgment in *Lynch v. Director of Public Prosecutions*, quoted by Wertheimer in ibid., 156.

genuinely conflicted on whether to vindicate Abbott's coercion defense. Lord Wilberforce argued against the idea that coercion is specifically excluded as a defense for homicide by noting that "no one can doubt that our law would today allow duress to be pleaded to a charge . . . of wounding with intent" in a case of attempted murder. Why, then, should a defendant be denied the same defense in a murder charge?[132] Other Lords took the opposite view. They reasoned that if the coerced is not punished, the law would effectively disincentivize resistance to coercion to kill. One judge, considering the case, wrote, rather dramatically, "if the law takes away the deep blue sea, a man will go wherever the devil drives."[133] The court agonized over Abbott's claims but ultimately convicted him of the crime.

Actual cases of coerced homicide are few and far between, which poses a difficulty for attempts to uncover the ways in which judges have reasoned about the issue. Much as medieval Ḥanafites and Shāfiʿites drew on the case of people casting others overboard from a sinking ship to think through the problem of coerced homicide, a famous sinking ship case provides a particularly rich source for how judges dealt with necessity defenses and how the legal system reconciled the legal and moral imperative to not kill with the exigent and tragic circumstances faced by those who find themselves stranded at sea. In 1884, when a yacht by the name of *Mignonette* sunk, Tom Dudley, the captain, found himself with three others in a dinghy with little food or water, 1,600 miles from the closest shore. After nineteen days, Dudley suggested that the group kill the sickest and youngest unmarried companion in the dinghy for food. Dudley personally followed through with the act, which sustained him and the others for a while. Eventually the three remaining men were rescued by a passing ship. Dudley recounted the incident to his rescuers. When they reached shore in England, Dudley and the crew were arrested. Dudley took complete responsibility for the incident. A group of five judges convicted him.[134] Lord Coleridge, the chief judge, wrote that the exigent circumstances in which Dudley and the others found themselves did not excuse the homicide for two reasons. While there may be a prima facie

[132] Ibid.

[133] Leo Katz, *Bad Acts and Guilty Minds: Conundrums of the Criminal Law* (Chicago: University of Chicago Press, 1987), 69.

[134] For discussion of the facts of this case, see ibid., 22–24.

duty to sustain one's own life, this duty is not absolute. Circumstances such as war may in fact require sacrificing it. Lord Coleridge also expressed the epistemic difficulties that ensue should necessity permit killing:

> Who is to be the judge of this sort of necessity? By what measure is the comparative value of lives to be measured? Is it to be strength, or intellect, or what?[135]

The guilty verdict and Lord Coleridge's moral difficulties notwithstanding, Dudley was immediately pardoned after the rendition of the judges' verdict. In fact, the home secretary had arranged the pardon ahead of time, and apparently, "when it came to pronouncing the death sentence, the judges did not even wear the black hoods customary on such occasions."[136] The judges' verdict and Lord Coleridge's moral absolutism did not, in the end, translate into a legal punishment for Dudley. If we take both Lord Coleridge's justifications and the way in which the legal institutions acted in the aftermath of the guilty verdict as a representation of the variety of conflicting ethical and legal intuitions in the case of coerced homicide, we come close to the moral and legal analysis of the Abū Ḥanīfa/Shaybānī position within Ḥanafism and the lenient position in Shāfiʿism.

[135] Cited in ibid., 25. [136] Ibid.

Conclusion

1. TECHNICALITY AND PLURALITY OF TRADITIONS

Classical Islamic thought, as found in the disciplines of theology and law, was sustained by a rich culture that prized a vigorous and dynamic exchange of reasons. This culture of argumentation is manifest in the technical textbooks that were produced by scholars belonging to different traditions. By the classical period, Muslim theologians and jurists had developed a sophisticated technical vocabulary to articulate the problems that occupied their disciplines and a robust set of norms for acceptable sources for and methods of reasoning. These inquiries were sustained by traditions that spanned several centuries. For the most part, medieval Muslim societies tolerated the existence of a plurality of such traditions, which set the stage for intense competition among them. The challenge today for scholars of classical Islamic thought lies in interpreting the content and development of the ideas within these parameters.

Two broad approaches characterize scholarship in intellectual history. One approach sees the scholar's job as attempting to identify the function of a text or idea in its larger social context. Typically, this approach tries to read texts as responses to the social, political, or economic situations that their authors were confronting. But when it comes to interpreting classical Islamic theological and legal texts, the intellectual historian committed to this approach is faced with a large challenge. The problems discussed in these texts are often fairly technical and not easily relatable to any immediate feature of a given author's context. Attempting to read a work of Islamic positive law or theology as responding to a particular social and political context is not entirely unlike attempting to read a textbook on logic the same way. Just as we would be rightly skeptical about the correctness of interpreting a logic textbook as somehow a response to a particular political event, we should be similarly skeptical about reading classical legal and theological works in the same way.

A second, idealist approach views classical Islamic texts as expressions of certain essential philosophical values that define individual traditions. The task of the idealist intellectual historian is to discover the singular, perhaps unarticulated, values of a given tradition that in turn explain the argumentation on the variety of subsidiary and tertiary intellectual positions that the tradition avows as in some sense derived from and consonant with its essential values. While aspects of this method are appropriate for seeking to understand the rationality of an Islamic theological tradition, it is unhelpful in interpreting Islamic legal traditions. The legal traditions covered far too many domains of human activity to be reducible to just a few overarching values. Moreover, for both legal and theological traditions, this approach is overly optimistic in regarding how strictly a few ideas or values can determine the content and development of the ideas derived from them. It often mistakes deduction for what is actually ex post facto justification and rationalization. This approach also betrays excessive confidence in trying to explain the persistence of a given legal or theological position over time as reflecting the persuasiveness of the justifications given for it by scholars. Such a view on the relationship between avowed positions and their justifications implies that if a particular argument for a law or theological position is discarded, so must the position that it supported. Yet this is historically simply not the case. A tradition's laws or theological positions are much more stable than the reasons given in support of them. More often than not, when a justification is abandoned, it is simply replaced by one that is regarded as better.[1]

In order to account for the tradition-based rationality and plurality that characterize theological and legal production in classical Islam, I have proposed the constraint and contingency model for understanding the content, logic, and historical development of classical Islamic thought.

[1] On this point, see Sadeghi, *The Logic of Law Making in Islam*, 141–62.

2. A REPRISAL OF THE CONSTRAINT AND CONTINGENCY MODEL OF TRADITION-BASED RATIONALITY

The most important features in the study of tradition-based rationality as found in Islamic discussions about coercion and responsibility are (1) the discursive constraints within which a tradition's rationality unfolds and (2) the contingent features that characterize its context.

By constraints, I mean those features of a tradition-based rationality that relate to the logical force of endorsing a given position, especially the social attitudes that other individuals, whether within one's tradition or outside of it, have toward the act of avowing an intellectual position. Endorsing a position raises questions about whether one is epistemically entitled to endorse it, and what other commitments are logically and substantively entailed by this endorsement. For example, avowing commitment to a position, as required by membership in a tradition, often requires the avower to demonstrate why he is entitled to hold the position. Classical Islamic scholars often did this through interpretation of scripture, empirical observation, citation of a more general principle of which the avowed position was a species, or casuistry. Avowing a position also signals to others that the avower is committed to other positions that are logically entailed by the endorsed one while disavowing positions that are logically incompatible with it, such that if she were to claim simultaneous commitment to a particular position and to something it contradicted, she could rightly be called out for incoherence. This calling out could be done by her fellow tradition members or by scholars outside of her tradition. Given the plurality of traditions that flourished in the classical age, the lively competition among them, and the vigorous internal development of ideas by scholars committed to the same tradition, scholars often pointed contradictions out, and took steps to avoid them.

There are three types of constraints that to a large extent explain the character of a tradition's rationality. Internal constraints are generated by membership in a tradition. They arise from explicit or implicit commitment to a set of positions, principles, values, and methods of reasoning that define a particular tradition and consequently constrain an individual scholar's intellectual output. Internal constraints have two effects on intellectual production. Because avowing a position requires demonstration of entitlement to it, such constraints direct a scholar's energies toward attempting to substantiate and work out the conceptual implications of the position in question. For example, the Muʿtazilites generated the most sophisticated empirical account of the psychology of free choice and compulsion in classical Islam. This account was, no doubt, motivated by their core commitment to a conception of a just God that required He hold human beings responsible only for those acts that they undertake freely. Similarly, the Ḥanafite position that compelling coercion transfers the legal consequences of a bodily act from the coerced to the coercer motivated Dabūsī's formulation of the psychological effects of compelling coercion on the deliberative capacities of the coerced and his resultant choices, along with the articulation of the instrument test for justifying transference.

A second effect of internal constraints is that they commit a scholar to a certain minimal set of positions and require him to demonstrate the coherence among them when needed. Examples of such necessary core commitments are plentiful: No Muʿtazilite could claim that reason cannot recognize at least some acts as morally good or bad, or that God's justice does not require that He act in certain ways. No Ashʿarite could hold that human beings create their own acts or that reason can discern the moral quality of acts. A Shāfiʿite could not easily contradict Shāfiʿī's opinion that coercion cancels the legal consequences of speech acts. A Ḥanafite could not easily hold the view that coercion invalidates a divorce. The commitment to a tradition's positions exerted a certain gravitational pull on any given scholar's writing at a singular moment, and on the argumentation unfolding within a tradition over the course of its history. For example, while Ḥanafite empirical descriptions of the effect of compelling coercion on the psychology of the coerced explained why previously prohibited foods could become permitted or why the coercer could be held legally responsible for homicide, they could not simply overturn the Ḥanafite law on coerced unilateral speech acts. Indeed, Ḥanafite scholars could not easily overturn any of the laws that constituted and constrained Ḥanafite coercion jurisprudence. In fact, despite the perceived inconsistency between the Ḥanafite laws on unilateral speech acts and those on coerced acknowledgments and commercial contracts, the Ḥanafites at no point discarded any of these laws. Nor did Shāfiʿite scriptural arguments and invocation of legal principles persuade Ḥanafites to jettison their law on coerced unilateral speech acts. Rather, constrained by their commitment to all of these laws, the Ḥanafites' coercion jurisprudence consisted of demonstrating the coherence among the laws as well as the consistency between the laws and empirical descriptions, interpretations of scripture, and moral and legal principles.

External constraints—the second type of constraint that shapes a tradition's rationality—are motivated not by the desire to substantiate and demonstrate the internal coherence among the positions held by a tradition, but rather by a quest to establish a particular position's consistency with a position, principle, or authoritative text that is shared among traditions or current in society at large. Since the Ḥanafites adopted what ended up being a marginal, minority position on the issue of coercion's effects on unilateral speech acts, they were at pains to show its reasonableness. One of the founding fathers of the tradition, Shaybānī, cited a number of ḥadīths and precedents to support the Ḥanafite position on this issue, something he did not do for other aspects of his coercion jurisprudence. Subsequent Ḥanafite scholars went out of their way to demonstrate that their position was consistent with scriptural sources and other legal and moral principles. Compared to other aspects of their coercion jurisprudence, the Ḥanafites' coerced speech jurisprudence largely revolved around interpretation of scriptural sources. This, too, was a logical result of the marginality of the Ḥanafites on the issue: they had to appeal to the sources that were most widely shared and regarded as most authoritative to substantiate the legitimacy of their position. The Ḥanafites' approach to coerced speech, shaped by these unique constraints, contrasts with the nature of reasoning that characterized both Shāfiʿite and Ḥanafite jurisprudence on coerced harm. On this issue, both traditions recorded and sustained internal dissent, and neither tradition found itself in the stark minority. Hence, neither Shāfiʿite nor Ḥanafite reasoning on questions of coerced harm made much recourse to scripture to vindicate one position over another. Rather, the arguments put forward within each tradition were broadly similar, consisting of casuistry, application of accepted legal and moral principles, and empirical observation.

In many cases, the solutions that individual tradition-bound jurists and theologians adopted are explainable as the result not just of solely internal or solely external constraints but of both. ʿAbd al-Jabbār's interpretation of the Qurʾānic verse 16:106 on coerced apostasy and Juwaynī's (and Ghazālī's) rejection of the impossible obligations argument are both good examples of this phenomenon. ʿAbd al-Jabbār was externally constrained by the fact that the vast majority of Muslim scholars regarded 16:106 as allowing coercion to make something permissible that was typically prohibited, whether it be lying or apostasy. But he was internally constrained from interpreting 16:106 as providing permission either to lie or to apostatize even under coercion because of the Muʿtazilite commitment to moral objectivism, which required holding the act of lying and professing disbelief as intrinsically evil at all times. His ingenious solution, which deferred to both constraints, was to interpret the verse as allowing one to merely intimate disbelief in the presence of coercion. A similar analysis can be offered for Juwaynī's rejection of the premise that God may impose obligations that humans cannot fulfill in the argument for the position that the absence of coercion is not a condition for moral agency. On the one hand, Juwaynī is externally constrained from endorsing an argument that undermines the idea of individual responsibility, which is a potential logical consequence of admitting that God can impose impossible obligations on human beings and still hold them accountable for their performance. But on the other, he is internally constrained from rejecting the idea that God could impose impossible obligations as something that would be unjust for God to do, since avowing this position would mean endorsing Muʿtazilite moral objectivism. Juwaynī's escape from this dilemma consisted of rejecting the possibility of impossible obligations not because it is unjust, but because it is unintelligible. Since, for Juwaynī, the capacity for linguistic comprehension (*fahm*) is the most important basis for moral agency (a position that also coheres nicely with Ashʿarite Divine Command moral epistemology), an unintelligible command cannot impose an obligation.

The third and final type of constraint on tradition-bound rationality is domain-specific constraints. These are constraints that go beyond any particular historical moment or social situation and transcend the boundaries between traditions. Domain-specific constraints structure inquiry into ethical questions. The problem of coerced homicide best illustrates the nature of domain-specific constraints. Regardless of tradition, culture, and time, any jurist or judge who considered the problem of coerced homicide faced the fundamental conflict between the notion that all people have an equal right to security from harm and the idea that being forced to do something, whether by necessity or coercion, ought to change an agent's accountability for an act.

Beyond the various types of constraints that influence legal and theological argumentation, the character of a tradition's rationality is also shaped by fortuitous historical factors that characterize the discursive context of a tradition. An example of such a factor, which plays an important role in explaining the types of arguments adopted by Ḥanafites and Shāfiᶜites in a given locale, is the particular methods of reasoning that had become widespread in that area. We see this most conspicuously in the relative similarity of the arguments used by Iraqi Ḥanafites and Iraqi Shāfiᶜites, and in the likewise overlapping argumentation of Khurasani/Central Asian Ḥanafites and the Shāfiᶜites of the same region. The Iraqis, both Ḥanafites such as Jaṣṣāṣ and Qudūrī and Shāfiᶜites such as Māwardī, make considerable efforts to reconcile and substantiate their coercion laws with ḥadīth (only the Iraqi Ḥanafite Jaṣṣāṣ makes any reference to a ḥadīth's chain of transmission as relevant to the substantiation of a law). The coercion jurisprudence of Khurasani/Central Asian Ḥanafites and Shāfiᶜites, on the other hand, drew much more on legal and moral principles, casuistry, and empirical observations.

3. TRADITIONS IN MOTION

While much scholarly attention has been devoted to the extent and processes of change in Islamic laws in premodern Muslim societies, little scholarship has focused on changes in the justifications underpinning a given tradition's laws or for that matter on change and development in Islamic theology. It is clear, however, as Sadeghi observed, that the justifications are more variable than the laws and theological positions themselves.[2] This book provides ample examples of change within traditions over time through adjustment, organic growth and development, and internal contestation.

[2] See ibid., 30–32, and 74. Sadeghi made this observation about the Ḥanafite tradition and predicted that it would apply to other legal traditions as well. My study confirmed his prediction and extended it to cover the theological traditions.

Both the Muᶜtazilites and the Ashᶜarites adjusted their subsidiary positions or the arguments they made for particular positions if they thought that either endangered a more important core position of the tradition. For the Muᶜtazilites, the two most important positions were the idea that God's justice requires that He act in certain predictable ways and the claim that good and evil were knowable by human reason. Accordingly, ᶜAbd al-Jabbār rejected the contention of an earlier Muᶜtazilite, Abū al-Hudhayl, that coercion permitted lying about one's theological beliefs, because in ᶜAbd al-Jabbār's view this position undermined the core tenet of moral objectivism. He similarly rejected the claim made by the founders of Basran Muᶜtazilism (Abū ᶜAlī and Abū Hāshim) that acts of injustice committed when asleep or unaware of one's actions cannot be considered evil and therefore do not deserve blame, because he felt that this position, too, would weaken moral objectivism.

The Ashᶜarites modified not their position on coercion and moral agency but the justification given for their position by an earlier scholar (Bāqillānī) in deference to their core doctrinal commitments. Recall that the Ashᶜarites held that the absence of coercion was not a condition for moral agency. No Ashᶜarite ever disavowed this position, but the later Ashᶜarites, Juwaynī and Ghazālī, rejected one of the arguments that Bāqillānī had made in its favor—namely, the claim that God can impose impossible obligations on human beings. By adopting the capacity for linguistic comprehension as the basis of human moral agency, Juwaynī and Ghazālī were able to deny the idea of impossible obligations and thus to reject Bāqillānī's argument without being forced to endorse the opposing Muᶜtazilite position.

The tradition that exhibited the greatest tendency to expand its coercion jurisprudence organically and slowly was Ḥanafism, though elements of this tendency are also found in Shāfiᶜism. Ḥanafite coercion jurisprudence, encompassing, inter alia, the legal formulation of coercion, its effect on speech acts, and harm caused to others, grew in justificatory argumentation over time. Successive scholars within the tradition added new arguments to the unfolding historical conversation, refined inherited ones, and corrected potential inconsistencies. The starting point for Ḥanafite jurisprudence was the laws recorded by Shaybānī as the opinions of the early founders, Shaybānī's own views, and the bare framework of justification for those laws.

Perhaps the best example of the subsequent organic growth is offered by the increasingly coherent Ḥanafite definition of coercion. Shaybānī began by rooting coercion's ability to transform something prohibited into something permitted by interpreting it as a type of necessity that the Qur'ānic verse explicitly mentions as capable of lifting the prohibition from certain types of foods (e.g. carrion, pork). After Shaybānī, Jaṣṣāṣ applied his increasingly technical and sophisticated legal hermeneutic to elucidate how, exactly, the necessity verses in the Qur'ān provide the foundation for the claim that compelling coercion can transform a prohibition. Dabūsī used the same argument, but he located it in a different legal hermeneutic and added an empirical argument and the metaphor of an instrument to explain why compelling coercion is capable of not just transforming an act's legal value but also transferring the legal responsibility for it from the coerced to the coercer. These solutions created their own problems, for one of which Dabūsī himself had an answer. If compelling coercion can transfer responsibility for an act as serious as homicide, why can it not do the same for an act such as divorce? Dabūsī limited the applicability of the instrument metaphor to cases in which it is conceivable that the coercer uses the body of the coerced as a physical instrument to commit the coerced act, thereby excluding speech acts such as divorce from the metaphor's purview. He thus saved himself and Ḥanafite coercion jurisprudence from accusations of gross incoherence. But Dabūsī's empirical argument that compelling coercion so debilitates the coerced agent's deliberative processes that it renders him unable to make a choice was seen as something of an overstatement by later Ḥanafites. Sarakhsī and Bazdawī nonetheless retained aspects of this empirical argument. Bazdawī especially refined it by relating the effects of different types of coercion to different aspects of the psychology of the coerced (contentment and choice) and thus correlating them perfectly with how Ḥanafite laws conceive of legal responsibility for various types of coerced acts.

A similar organic growth of argumentation and increasingly sophisticated conceptualization of conflicting moral and legal intuitions among the Ḥanafites can be seen in the case of coerced homicide. By the time of Sarakhsī and Bazdawī, the Ḥanafites had developed a set of coherent justifications that not only explained the dissenting opinions of the tradition's founding fathers but also accounted for the opinion on which the tradition had come to settle—namely, that while compelling coercion transfers the legal responsibility for a coerced homicide from the coerced to the coercer, the coerced nonetheless still sins by committing the murder. While the instrument test successfully transfers the legal consequences of the act, it cannot transfer the moral consequence of sin, because the coerced has in fact transgressed against two distinct objects in the act of coerced homicide. The transgression against the first object, the harmed victim, admits transference, but that against the second object, the coerced's own religious integrity (*dīn*), is, given its nature, unsusceptible to transference. The two-object analysis of coerced homicide supplied an elegant explanation for the conflicting intuitions informing the case, but it emerged only slowly over several generations of Ḥanafite scholars. The explanation received its most precise and concise formulation in the hands of Bazdawī, the last Ḥanafite addressed in this book.

The phenomenon of organic growth can also be witnessed in Shāfiʿite jurisprudence on coerced homicide. The fifth/eleventh-century Iraqi Shāfiʿite Māwardī adopted Shāfiʿī's framework for analyzing the case of coerced murder, but he expanded on it considerably and also focused in a much more explicit fashion on the effect of the political legitimacy of the commander on the consequences of coercion to commit an illegal homicide.

In contrast to the organic growth that characterized Ḥanafite coercion jurisprudence in the classical period, Shāfiʿism exhibited a tendency toward greater internal contestation and starker breaks in the interpretive frameworks used to frame inherited Shāfiʿite law. The dispute between the Iraqi and some Khurasani Shāfiʿites regarding the legal formulation of coercion is an example of internal debate, while Ghazālī's replacement of the legitimacy of political authority with causal efficacy as an organizing principle in the question of coerced homicide is an instance of an interpretive rupture. Why were the classical Shāfiʿites more willing than the Ḥanafites to dispute forcefully with each other and to break with the tradition's past? I can think of two possible and mutually compatible explanations, one relating to Shāfiʿism and the other to Ḥanafism. Shāfiʿism, especially in its formative stages, emerged as a tradition with an explicit, self-conscious identity that prided itself on following the implications of scripture even if this meant contravening the legal opinions of the founder, Shāfiʿī—an attitude he reportedly encouraged among his immediate followers.[3] If succeeding generations of Shāfiʿites continued to reproduce and emphasize this attitude, their tendency to disagree freely with one another and to reject past interpretive frameworks may reflect the inculcation of this value in the tradition. The second explanation is more speculative and concerns Ḥanafism's tendency toward unity and slow, organic growth. The Ḥanafite tradition has had the good fortune for much of its history to be the recipient of a disproportionately high share of governmental backing in terms of judicial appointments. In the classical period, the two most notable examples are the Abbasid preference for Ḥanafism in the generation after Abū Ḥanīfa, especially with the appointment of his student Abū Yūsuf as chief justice, and the passionate endorsement of Ḥanafism by Turkic tribes from Central Asia who, under the leadership of the Seljuks, established control over most of the Near East in the eleventh century. The fact that the Ḥanafites, for much of the classical period, were applying the law in the courts may have forced Ḥanafite legal scholars to show less tolerance for dissent and to insist on the predictability of the law.

4. THE YIELDS OF COMPARISON

The relationship between the disciplines of law and theology has not been explored much in Islamic studies scholarship, and the studies that exist tend to affirm the way in which premodern Muslim scholars themselves conceived of the relationship: theology proved the premises that law assumed. The most important of these premises were the existence and nature of God and the possibility of prophecy. Aron Zysow has argued that even this conception of theology is far too limited in view of the discipline's actual influence on law. He claims not only that theology produced the foundational assumptions for law, but also that legal scholars, and more specifically legal theorists, argued for certain positions on seemingly technical points of legal theory because of the potential implications that these positions would have on prized theological tenets.[4] In Zysow's conception, then, theology is not

[3] El Shamsy, "The First Shāfiʿī".

[4] Zysow, *The Economy of Certainty: an Introduction to the Typology of Islamic Legal Theory*, 80–85.

just foundational to law but influences the adoption of positions in legal theory because of their theological, as opposed to merely legal, implications.

This study certainly confirms aspects of this view. The explicit question discussed in works of theology was whether or not the absence of coercion is a condition for moral agency. This question is much broader and more foundational than the question of coercion's specific effects on commercial contracts, for instance. ʿAbd al-Jabbār's argument that coercion does not permit outright lying about one's theological beliefs but merely intimating disbelief was motivated by his desire to maintain consistency with the Muʿtazilite position that lies are unconditionally evil, and it thus illustrates how a theological position can affect the adoption of not only a position in legal theory, but also a position in positive law.

However, with that said, a closer examination of the types of arguments that theologians used to support their positions reveals that they were not unwilling to draw on legal arguments to substantiate theological claims. Indeed, both the Ashʿarites and the Ḥanafites did just that. They argued from the fact that all religious scholars agreed that a coerced killer nonetheless sins (a legal position) to the claim that the absence of coercion is not per se a condition for moral agency: God still holds the coerced agent responsible. Theologians not only relied on legal arguments; they also adopted a legalistic explanatory framework for components of their theology. The Muʿtazilites conceived of the possibility that obedience to God's command could result in unjustified harm to victims. They consider the case in which a judge's formal application of the Islamic law of testimony (legitimated by God's command), leads to a substantively unjust outcome (because the testimony is false). In this case the Muʿtazilites hold that God owes other-worldly compensation to victims who suffer harm as a result of the compulsion exerted by God's command. In effect they adopted a compensatory framework that echoes the law of tort. These examples indicate a dynamic traffic in reasons among practitioners of the two disciplines, going both ways.

4.1 Coercion in Islamic Political Thought

The value of liberty is a fundamental component of Western political thought and practice. Many political theorists and philosophers, especially liberal and libertarian ones, have attempted to theorize this value by approaching it from the perspective of its absence—that is, through coercion. Liberal political theorists presume that the state owes prima facie deference to individual liberty and must provide special justification to curtail it through coercion. Libertarian political theorists seek ways to maximize freedom; the examination of coercion as a form of "unfreedom" thus allows them to think about ways in which such a lack of liberty may be minimized. For both groups, especially for scholars working within the Anglo-American tradition of analytical philosophy, the central task of the coercion theorist is simply to describe the necessary and sufficient conditions that characterize its presence.

How does the classical Muslim discourse on coercion compare to these concerns? One of the yields of comparative inquiry, whether in ethics or in political theory, is the light it can shed on the extent to which a given problem, value, or discursive vocabulary captures a transcultural and transhistorical concern. Is the concern with liberty, and by extension with coercion, such a concern, or is it something that emerged contingently in the modern West?

One historian of Islamic thought, Michael Cook, argues that on the whole, the value of liberty is absent from the history of Islamic political thought.[5] My investigation of the history of debates about coercion and responsibility in classical Islamic thought likewise indicates that the value of liberty and the absence of coercion were not essential elements in Muslim religious scholars' conceptions of the normative political order. In fact, Muslim scholars developed a sophisticated analysis of coercion and responsibility in ways that were structurally similar to their modern Western counterparts without making recourse to liberty as a political value—a fact that has implications for how one ought to go about engaging in comparative ethics scholarship. But the absence of the invocation of liberty in Muslim discourses does not mean that coercion played no role in Muslim thinking on political authority. In fact, it is clear that coercion jurisprudence was politicized from the very beginning and that theological and legal thinking about coercion

[5] Michael Cook, "Is Freedom an Islamic Value?," in *Freedom and the Construction of Europe: Volume II*, ed. Quentin Skinner (Cambridge: Cambridge University Press, 2013).

and responsibility seem naturally to have invited consideration of the limits of obedience to those in power, especially when the holders of power enjoyed legitimate authority to exercise it, and the extent to which such power holders are culpable for any illegal and immoral acts they command.

That both the rulers and the religious scholars were keenly aware of the political ramifications of the latter's coercion jurisprudence can be readily seen in the early debate among jurists of the preformative era about whether coercion undermines the validity of divorce. Some second/eighth-century jurists explicitly connected their position on coercion's effects on divorce to its effects on divorce-contingent oaths (e.g., "If I fail to do X, I thereby divorce my wife"). The latter were regularly used throughout premodern Islamic history in oaths of political loyalty. To rule that coercion undermines the validity of divorce-contingent oaths is also to rule, by extension, that it may undermine an instrument that authorities used to ensure compliance. In view of this connection, it is no wonder that Mālik b. Anas, the founder of Mālikism, was reportedly arrested and tortured for circulating a report that implied that coercion undermined the pronouncement of a divorce. Nor is it surprising that one of the co-founders of Ḥanafism, Shaybānī, is said to have been questioned by the political authorities simply because he had written a work on coercion.

Classical Muslim jurists thus used aspects of coercion jurisprudence to indirectly limit the power of the political authorities to ensure obedience. They also directly asserted the supremacy of the Sharīʿa by limiting the scope of a subordinate's duty to obey a ruler to only those commands that the subordinate either knows or presumes to be legal, and by holding rulers legally and morally responsible for any illegal or immoral acts that they coerce their subordinates to commit. These themes are most explicit and prominent in coerced harm jurisprudence, and they are present from the very beginning in both Ḥanafism and Shāfiʿism. Both Shaybānī and Shāfiʿī asserted the primacy of the Sharīʿa over the orders of political rulers by citing a precedent in which the revered caliph Abū Bakr held a government agent responsible for the illegal harm that he had compelled someone to inflict on another person. The majority position on coerced homicide within both traditions was to firmly hold rulers legally and morally responsible for the act. Some early Ḥanafites claimed not only that rulers are morally and legally responsible for coercing acts that harm others, but also that in some cases (those of coerced rape) such coercion disqualifies a ruler from office.

The jurists also considered whether coercion exercised by a ruler is in some sense different from that exercised by other power holders to the point of affecting the distribution of responsibility for the harm caused. Specifically, both Ḥanafites and Shāfiʿites considered the question of whether the mere command of a ruler, unaccompanied by an explicit threat, to commit an illegal homicide counts as coercive. The Ḥanafite Sarakhsī emphatically affirmed that such a command is coercive and consequently relieves the coerced physical killer of legal responsibility, transferring it to the ruler instead. Giving us an insight into how jurists may have imagined the nature of political rule in their time, Sarakhsī noted bluntly that "it is the regular habit of oppressors to refrain from making explicit threats against lives. Rather, they command, and punish only those who oppose their command." On the other hand, the Shāfiʿite Ghazālī endorsed the coerciveness of a ruler's command not on empirical grounds but because he saw the prima facie duty to obey a legitimate ruler's command as itself based on the prudential need for political stability. The fact that such commands have a prima facie claim to legitimacy diminishes the subordinate's ability to discern whether a particular command is in fact legal.

4.2 Domain-Specific Constraints and Comparative Ethics

Given the fact that liberty and the absence of coercion did not play a large role in classical Muslim political thought in the way that they did for Western coercion theorists, can we safely say that the two traditions are incommensurable on the issue of coercion and responsibility? This is manifestly not the case, given the rather similar ways in which modern Western judges and jurists and classical Muslim scholars grappled with the moral problem of coerced homicide. In fact, the similarity suggests, in my view, more fruitful approaches to comparative ethics.

When considering the issue of coerced homicide, both Western coercion theorists and their Muslim counterparts have struggled to reconcile the principle that every individual has an equal right to security from harm with the idea that being coerced ought, in some way, to lessen one's responsibility for an action. The similarity of the ways in which theorists of different times and cultures articulate the reasons for their positions and even their overall conclusions on the issue suggests that both the positions and their rationality are constrained by norms that characterize this particular domain or problem. From one perspective the similarity is surprising: presumably, Muslim religious scholars were committed to overarching values, methods of reasoning, sources of authority, and background cultural assumptions that contrast quite starkly with the commitments of contemporary Western theorists. Muslims operated within a monotheistic religious tradition that gave pride of place to revelation in the articulation of moral and legal norms. Western coercion theorists operate within an explicitly secular framework that does not rely at all on the authority of texts supposedly authored by God. Muslim religious scholars emphasized the superiority of the Sharīʿa, whereas their Western counterparts by and large endorse the primacy of liberty as a political value. Yet commitment to such broadly opposed overarching values had little to no effect on the two groups' handling of the moral problem of coercion and responsibility. The coexistence of dissimilarity in the higher-order normative values that scholars of the two civilizations think characterize their morality, on the one hand, and the striking similarity in the respective premises used by the two groups to tackle this particular ethical problem, on the other hand, makes one skeptical of the idea that the higher-order values (which tend to have a lot of rhetorical force but very little definite content) in fact determine concrete legal and moral positions. Instead, it seems that many different higher-order normative concepts (such as liberty, justice, and Sharīʿa) can equally justify the same positions. This surprising result suggests that a fruitful starting point for comparative ethical inquiry, especially inquiry aimed at the discovery of common ground for ethical action, may be found *not* in an analysis of the overarching values that supposedly characterize specific traditions but rather in an examination of how ethicists from different traditions considered concrete problems.

Bibliography

Abd-Allah Wymann-Landgraf, Umar F. *Mālik and Medina: Islamic Legal Reasoning in the Formative Period*. Leiden: Brill, 2013.

ʿAbd al-Jabbār. *al-Mughnī fī Abwāb al-Tawḥīd wa al-ʿAdl* [in Arabic]. Edited by Ṭāhā Ḥusayn and Ibrāhīm Madkūr. 14 vols. Cairo: Wizārat al-Thaqāfa wa-ʾl-Irshād al-Qawmī, al-Idāra al-ʿĀmma li-ʾl-Thaqāfa, 1960–1969.

Abrahamov, Binyamin. *Islamic Theology: Traditionalism and Rationalism*. Edinburgh: Edinburgh University Press, 1998.

Abrahamov, Binyamin. "A Re-examination of al-Ashʿarī's Theory of *Kasb* according to Kitāb al-Lumaʿ." *Journal of the Royal Asiatic Society* 2, no. 2 (1989): 210–21.

al-Ashʿarī, Abū al-Ḥasan ʿAlī b. Ismāʿīl. *al-Ibāna ʿan Uṣūl al-Diyāna*. 1st ed. Beirut: Dār Ibn Zaydūn, n.d.

al-Ashʿarī, Abū al-Ḥasan ʿAlī b. Ismāʿīl. "Risāla al-Ashʿarī." *Darülfünun İlâhiyat Fakültesi Mecmuası* 3 (1928): 80–108.

al-Ashʿarī, Abū al-Ḥasan ʿAlī b. Ismāʿīl. *The Theology of al-Ashʿarī: the Arabic Texts of al-Ashʿarī's Kitāb al-Lumaʿ and Risālat Istiḥsān al-Khawḍ fī ʿIlm al-Kalām: with Briefly Annotated Translations, and Appendices Containing Material Pertinent to the Study of al-Ashʿarī*. Translated by Richard Joseph McCarthy. Beirut: Imprimerie Catholique, 1953.

al-Bāqillānī, Abū Bakr Muḥammad b. al-Ṭayyib. *al-Taqrīb wa al-Irshād "al-Ṣaghīr"*. Edited by ʿAbd al-Ḥamīd b. ʿAlī Abū Zunayd. 1st ed. 3 vols. Beirut: Muʾassasa al-Risāla, 1993–1998.

al-Bazdawī, ʿAlī b. Muḥammad, and al-Ḥusayn b. ʿAlī al-Saghnāqī. *al-Kāfī: Sharḥ al-Bazdawī*. Edited by Fakhr al-Dīn Sayyid Muḥammad Qānit. 1st ed. 5 vols. Riyadh: Maktabat al-Rushd, 2001.

al-Dabūsī, Abū Zayd ʿAbd Allāh b. ʿUmar. *al-Asrār fī al-Usūl wa al-Furūʿ*. Edited by Salim Özer Keyseri. Turkey: Erciyes University, Turkey, 1997. PhD Dissertation.

al-Dabūsī, Abū Zayd ʿAbd Allāh b. ʿUmar. *Taqwīm Uṣūl al-Fiqh wa Taḥdīd Adillat al-Sharʿ*. Edited by ʿAbd al-Jalīl ʿAṭā. 1st ed. 2 vols. Damascus, Syria; Tripoli, Lebanon: Dār al-Nuʿmān li-ʾl-ʿUlūm; Dār al-Imām Abī Ḥanīfah, 2005.

al-Ghazālī, Abū Ḥāmid Muḥammad b. Muḥammad. *al-Mankhūl min Taʿlīqāt al-Uṣūl*. Edited by Muḥammad Ḥasan Hītū. 2nd ed. Damascus: Dār al-Fikr, 1970.

al-Ghazālī, Abū Ḥāmid Muḥammad b. Muḥammad. *al-Mustaṣfā min ʿIlm al-Uṣūl*. Edited by Muḥammad Sulaymān Ashqar. 1st ed. 2 vols. Beirut: Muʾassasat al-Risāla, 1997.

al-Ghazālī, Abū Ḥāmid Muḥammad b. Muḥammad. *al-Wasīṭ fī al-Madhhab*. Edited by Muḥammad Muḥammad Tāmir. 1st ed. 6 vols. Cairo: Dār al-Salām li-ʾl-Ṭībāʿa wa al-Nashr wa al-Tawzīʿ, 1997.

al-Ghazālī, Abū Ḥāmid Muḥammad b. Muḥammad. *al-Wasīṭ fī al-Madhhab*. Edited by Abū ʿAmr al-Ḥusaynī b. ʿUmar b. ʿAbd al-Raḥīm. 1st ed. 4 vols. Beirut: Manshūrāt Muḥammad ʿAlī Bayḍūn; Dār al-Kutub al-ʿIlmiyya, 2001.

al-Ḥākim al-Jishumī. *Taḥkīm al-ʿUqūl fī Taṣḥīḥ al-Uṣūl*. Edited by ʿAbd al-Salām b. ʿAbbās al-Wajīh. 1st ed. Sanaa: Muʾassasa al-Imām Zayd b. ʿAlī al-Thaqāfiyya, 2008.

al-Jāḥiẓ, Abū ʿUthmān ʿAmr b. Baḥr. *al-Ḥayawān*. 2nd ed. 8 vols. Cairo: Muṣṭafā al-Bābī al-Ḥalabī, 1966.

al-Jaṣṣāṣ, Abū Bakr Aḥmad b. ʿAlī. *Aḥkām al-Qurʾān*. Edited by ʿAbd al-Salām Muḥammad ʿAlī Shāhīn. 3 vols. Beirut: Dār al-Kutub al-ʿIlmiyya, n.d.

al-Jaṣṣāṣ, Abū Bakr Aḥmad b. ʿAlī. *Sharḥ Mukhtaṣar al-Ṭaḥāwī fī al-Fiqh al-Ḥanafī*. Edited by ʿIṣmat Allāh ʿInāyat Allāh Muḥammad and Saʿīd Bakdāsh. 1st ed. 8 vols. Beirut: Dār al-Bashāʾir al-Islāmiyya lil-Ṭibāʿa wa al-Nashr wa al-Tawzīʿ, 2010.

al-Jaṣṣāṣ, Abū Bakr Aḥmad b. ʿAlī. *Uṣūl al-Jaṣṣāṣ al-Musammā al-Fuṣūl fī al-Uṣūl*. Edited by Muḥammad Muḥammad Tāmir. 1st ed. 2 vols. Beirut: Manshūrāt Muḥammad ʿAlī Bayḍūn, Dār al-Kutub al-ʿIlmiyya, 2000.

al-Juwaynī, Abū al-Maʿālī ʿAbd al-Malik b. ʿAbdillāh. *al-Burhān fī Uṣūl al-Fiqh: Makhṭūṭ Yunsharu li-Awwal Marra*. Edited by ʿAbd al-ʿAẓīm al-Dīb. 1st ed. Qatar: Jāmiʿa Qatar, 1399[/1979].

al-Juwaynī, Abū al-Maʿālī ʿAbd al-Malik b. ʿAbdillāh. *al-ʿAqīda al-Niẓāmiyya fī al-Arkān al-Islāmiyya*. Edited by Muḥammad Zāhid b. al-Ḥasan Kawtharī. Cairo: al-Maktaba al-Azhariyya li-ʾl-Turāth, 1992.

al-Juwaynī, Abū al-Maʿālī ʿAbd al-Malik b. ʿAbdillāh. *Irshād ilā Qawāṭiʿ al-Adilla fī Uṣūl al-Iʿtiqād*. Edited by Muḥammad Yūsuf Mūsā and ʿAlī ʿAbd al-Munʿim ʿAbd al-Hamīd. Cairo: Maktabat al-Khānjī, 1950.

al-Juwaynī, Abū al-Maʿālī ʿAbd al-Malik b. ʿAbdillāh. *Nihāyat al-Maṭlab fī Dirāyat al-Madhhab*. Edited by ʿAbd al-ʿAẓīm Maḥmūd al-Dīb. 1st ed. 21 vols. Jeddah: Dār al-Minhāj li-ʾl-Nashr wa-al-Tawzīʿ, 2007.

al-Kawtharī, Muḥammad Zāhid. *al-Ḥāwī fī Sīrat al-Imām Abī Jaʿfar al-Ṭaḥāwī*. Cairo: Maṭbaʿat al-Anwār, 1368 [/1949].

al-Māwardī, ʿAlī b. Muḥammad. *al-Ḥāwī al-Kabīr*. Edited by Maḥmūd Maṭarjī. 1st ed. 24 vols. Beirut: Dār al-Fikr, 1994.

al-Māwardī, ʿAlī b. Muḥammad. *al-Ḥāwī al-Kabīr fī Fiqh Madhhab al-Imām al-Shāfiʿī Raḍiya Allāh ʿanh: wa Huwa Sharḥ Mukhtaṣar al-Muzanī*. Edited by ʿAlī Muḥammad Muʿawwaḍ and ʿĀdil Aḥmad ʿAbd al-Mawjūd. 1st ed. 19 vols. Beirut: Dār al-Kutub al-ʿIlmiyya, 1994.

al-Muzanī, Ismāʿīl b. Yaḥyā. *Mukhtaṣar al-Muzanī fī Furūʿ al-Shāfiʿīyya*. Edited by Muḥammad ʿAbd al-Qādir Shāhīn. 2nd ed. Beirut: Dār al-Kutub al-ʿIlmīyya, 1998.

al-Qudūrī, Aḥmad b. Muḥammad. *al-Mawsūʿa al-Fiqhīyya al-Muqārana: al-Tajrīd*. Edited by Muḥammad Aḥmad Sirāj and ʿAlī Jumʿa Muḥammad. 1st ed. 12 vols. Cairo: Dār al-Salām li-ʾl-Ṭibāʿa wa al-Nashr wa al-Tawzīʿ wa al-Tarjama, 2004.

al-Qudūrī, Aḥmad b. Muḥammad. *Mukhtaṣar al-Qudūrī fī al-Fiqh al-Ḥanafī*. Edited by Kāmil Muḥammad Muḥammad ʿUwayḍa. 1st ed. Beirut: Dār al-Kutub al-ʿIlmiyya, 1997.

al-Qurashī, ʿAbd al-Qādir b. Muḥammad. *al-Jawāhir al-Muḍiyya fī Ṭabaqāt al-Ḥanafiyya*. Edited by ʿAbd al-Fattāḥ Muḥammad al-Ḥulw. 2nd ed. 5 vols. n.p.: Hajar li-ʾl-Ṭibāʿa wa al-Nashr wa al-Tawzīʿ, 1993.

al-Sarakhsī, Abū Bakr Muḥammad b. Aḥmad. *Kitāb al-Mabṣūṭ*. Edited by Abū ʿAbd Allāh Muḥammad Ḥasan Muḥammad Ḥasan Ismāʿīl al-Shāfiʿī. 1st ed. 30 vols. Beirut: Dār al-Kutub al-ʿIlmiyya, 2001.

al-Shāfiʿī, Muḥammad b. Idrīs. *Kitāb al-Umm*. Edited by Rifʿat Fawzī ʿAbd al-Muṭṭalib. 1st ed. 11 vols. al-Manṣūra: Dār al-Wafāʾ li-ʾl-Ṭibāʿa wa al-Nashr wa al-Tawzīʿ, 2001.

al-Shīrāzī, Abū Isḥāq Ibrāhīm b. ʿAlī. *al-Muhadhdhab fī Fiqh al-Imām al-Shāfiʿī*. Edited by Zakarīyā ʿUmayrāt. 3 vols. Beirut: Dār al-Kutub al-ʿIlmiyya, 1995.

al-Shīrāzī, Abū Isḥāq Ibrāhīm b. ʿAlī. *al-Tanbīh fī al-Fiqh ʿalā Madhhab al-Imām al-Shāfiʿī*. 2nd ed. Cairo: Muṣṭafā al-Bābī al-Ḥalabī, 1951.

al-Ṭahāwī, Aḥmad b. Muḥammad. *Mukhtaṣar al-Ṭaḥāwī*. Edited by Abū al-Wafā al-Afghānī. Hyderabad: Lajnat Iḥyāʾ al-Kutub al-Nuʿmānīyya, 1370[/1950].

al-Ṭahāwī, Aḥmad b. Muḥammad. *Sharḥ Maʿānī al-Āthār*. Edited by Muḥammad Zuhrī al-Najjār and Muḥammad Sayyid Jād al-Ḥaqq. 1st ed. 5 vols. Beirut: ʿĀlam al-Kutub, 1994.

al-Zamakhsharī, Maḥmūd b. ʿUmar. *A Muʿtazilite Creed of Az-Zamaḫšarî (d. 538/1144): (al-Minhâǧ fî uṣûl ad-dîn)*. Translated by Sabine Schmidtke. Edited by Sabine Schmidtke. Stuttgart: Deutsche Morgenländische Gesellschaft, 1997.

Alexander, Lawrence A. "Zimmerman on Coercive Wage Offers." *Philosophy & Public Affairs* 12, no. 2 (1983): 160–64.

Ali, Kecia. *Marriage and Slavery in Early Islam*. Cambridge, MA: Harvard University Press, 2010.

Anderson, Scott. "Coercion." In *The Stanford Encyclopedia of Philosophy (Summer 2015 Edition)*. Edited by Edward N. Zalta, 2015. http://plato.stanford.edu/archives/sum2015/entries/coercion/.

Anderson, Scott. "The Enforcement Approach to Coercion." *Journal of Ethics and Social Philosophy* 5, no. 1 (2010): 1–31.

Asad, Talal. *The Idea of an Anthropology of Islam*. Washington, DC: Center for Contemporary Arab Studies, Georgetown University, 1986.

Azam, Hina. *Sexual Violation in Islamic law: Substance, Evidence, and Procedure*. Cambridge: Cambridge University Press, 2015.

Bedir, Murteza. "The Early Development of Ḥanafī *Uṣūl al-Fiqh*." PhD, University of Manchester, 1999.

Bedir, Murteza. "Is there a Ḥanafī Uṣūl al-Fiqh?". *Sakarya Üniversitesi Ilahiyat Fakültesi Dergisi (Journal of Sakarya University Faculty of Theology)* 4, no. 2 (2001): 163–72.

Bedir, Murteza. "Reason and Revelation: Abū Zayd al-Dabbūsī on Rational Proofs." *Islamic Studies* 43 no. 2 (2004): 227–45.

Berman, Mitchell. "The Normative Functions of Coercion Claims." *Legal Theory* 8 (2002): 45–89.

Bosworth, C.E. "Ašʿarī." In *Encyclopaedia Iranica*, edited by Ehsan Yar-Shater. London; Boston, Winona Lake, IN: Routledge & Kegan Paul, 1982.

Boynukalın, Mehmet. *al-Aṣl: al-Muqaddima*. Beirut: Dār Ibn Ḥazm li-ʾl-Ṭibāʿah wa-al-Nashr wa-al-Tawzīʿ, 2012.

Brockelmann, Carl, and Louis Gardet. "al-Djuwaynī, Abu ʾl-Maʿālī ʿAbd al-Malik." In *Encyclopedia of Islam, Second Edition*, edited by P. Bearman, Th. Bianquis, C.E. Bosworth, E. van Donzel and W.P. Heinrichs. Consulted online on 11 August 2016. http://dx.doi.org/10.1163/1573-3912_islam_SIM_2130. First published online: 2012.

Brockopp, Jonathan E. "The Minor Compendium of Ibn ʿAbd al-Ḥakam (d. 214/829) and Its Reception in the Early Mālikī School." *Islamic Law and Society* 12, no. 2 (2005): 141–81.

Bulliet, Richard W. *The Patricians of Nishapur: a Study in Medieval Islamic Social History*. Cambridge, MA: Harvard University Press, 1972.

Burra, Arudra Venkata. "Coercion, Deception, Consent: Essays in Moral Explanation." PhD, Princeton University, 2011.

Calder, Norman. "al-Sarak͟hsī, Muḥammad b. Aḥmad b. Abī Sahl Abū Bakr, S͟hams al-Aʾimma." In *Encyclopedia of Islam, Second Edition*, edited by P. Bearman, Th. Bianquis, C.E. Bosworth, E. van Donzel and W.P. Heinrichs. Consulted online on 11 August 2016. http://dx.doi.org/10.1163/1573-3912_islam_SIM_6620. First published online: 2012.

Calder, Norman. "al-Ṭaḥāwī, Aḥmad b. Muḥammad b. Salāma b. ʿAbd al-Malik al-Azdī al-Ḥad͟jrī Abū D͟jafar." In *Encyclopedia of Islam, Second Edition*, edited by P. Bearman, Th. Bianquis, C.E. Bosworth, E. van Donzel and W.P. Heinrichs. Consulted online on 11 August 2016. http://dx.doi.org/10.1163/1573-3912_islam_COM_1150. First published online: 2012.

Calder, Norman. *Islamic Jurisprudence in the Classical Era*. Edited by Colin Imber. New York: Cambridge University Press, 2010.

Calder, Norman. *Studies in Early Muslim Jurisprudence*. Oxford: Clarendon Press, 1993.

Chaumont, Éric. "al-S͟hāfiʿiyya." In *Encyclopedia of Islam, Second Edition*, edited by P. Bearman, Th. Bianquis, C.E. Bosworth, E. van Donzel and W.P. Heinrichs. Leiden: Brill, 1980–2004.

Chaumont, Éric. "al-S͟hāfiʿī." In *Encyclopedia of Islam, Second Edition*, edited by P. Bearman, Th. Bianquis, C.E. Bosworth, E. van Donzel and W.P. Heinrichs. Consulted online on 11 August 2016. http://dx.doi.org/10.1163/1573-3912_islam_COM_1021. First published online: 2012.

Chaumont, Éric. "al-Shaybānī." In *Encyclopedia of Islam, Second Edition*, edited by P. Bearman, Th. Bianquis, C.E. Bosworth, E. van Donzel and W.P. Heinrichs. Consulted online on 11 August 2016. http://dx.doi.org/10.1163/1573-3912_islam_COM_1051. First published online: 2012.

Chaumont, Éric. "Bâqillânî, Théologien Ash'arite et Usûliste Mâlikite, contre les Légistes à Propos de 'l'Ijtihâd' et de l'Accord Unanime de la Communauté." *Studia Islamica*, no. 79 (1994): 79–102.

Ben Cheneb, Mohammed. "al-Ḳudūrī, Abu 'l-Ḥusayn/al-Ḥasan Aḥmad." In *Encyclopedia of Islam, Second Edition*, edited by P. Bearman, Th. Bianquis, C.E. Bosworth, E. van Donzel and W.P. Heinrichs. Consulted online on 11 August 2016. http://dx.doi.org/10.1163/1573-3912_islam_SIM_4481. First published online: 2012.

Cook, Michael. *Commanding Right and Forbidding Wrong in Islamic Thought*. Cambridge: Cambridge University Press, 2000.

Cook, Michael. "Is Freedom an Islamic Value?". In *Freedom and the Construction of Europe: Volume II*, edited by Quentin Skinner, 283–310. Cambridge: Cambridge University Press, 2013.

Dhanani, Alnoor. *The Physical Theory of Kalām: Atoms, Space, and Void in Basrian Muʿtazilī Cosmology*. Leiden: Brill, 1994.

El Shamsy, Ahmed. *The Canonization of Islamic Law: a Social and Intellectual History*. Cambridge: Cambridge University Press, 2013.

El Shamsy, Ahmed. "The First Shāfiʿī: the Traditionalist Legal Thought of Abū Yaʿqūb al-Buwayṭī (d. 231/846)." *Islamic Law and Society* 14, no. 3 (2007): 301–41.
Ess, Josef van. "Abu ʾl-Hoḏahyl al-ʿAllāf." In *Encyclopædia Iranica*, Vol 1, Fasc. 3, edited by Ehsan Yar-Shater, 318–22. London: Routledge & Kegan Paul, 1982.
Ess, Josef van. *Theologie und Gesellschaft im 2. und 3. Jahrhundert Hidschra: eine Geschichte des Religiösen Denkens im Frühen Islam*. 6 vols. Berlin: Walter de Gruyter, 1992.
Fadel, Mohammad. "The Social Logic of Taqlīd and the Rise of the Mukhtaṣar." *Islamic Law and Society* 3, no. 2 (1996): 193–233.
Frank, Richard M. "al-Ashʿarī." In *Encyclopedia of Religion, Second Edition*, edited by Lindsay Jones, 530–33. Detroit: Macmillan Reference USA, 2005.
Frank, Richard M. *Al-Ghazālī and the Ashʿarite School*. Durham, NC: Duke University Press, 1994.
Frank, Richard M. "Ashʿarīyah." In *Encyclopedia of Religion, Second Edition*, edited by Lindsay Jones, 533–39. Detroit: Macmillan Reference USA, 2005.
Frank, Richard M. "The Autonomy of the Human Agent in the Teaching of ʿAbd al-Ǧabbar." *Le Muséon* 95 (1982): 323–55.
Frank, Richard M. "Elements in the Development of the Teaching of al-Ashʿarī." In *Early Islamic Theology: the Muʿtazilites and al-Ashʿarī, Texts and Studies on the Development and History of Kalām*, edited by Dimitri Gutas, 141–90. Aldershot: Ashgate, 2007.
Frank, Richard M. *The Metaphysics of Created Being According to Abū l-Hudhayl al-ʿAllāf: a Philosophical Study of the Earliest Kalām*. Istanbul: Nederlands Historisch-Archaeologisch Instituut in het Nabije Oosten, 1966.
Friedmann, Yohanan. *Tolerance and Coercion in Islam: Interfaith Relations in the Muslim Tradition*. Cambridge: Cambridge University Press, 2003.
Gesink, Indira Falk. "Chaos on Earth: Subjective Truths versus Communal Unity in Islamic Law and the Rise of Militant Islam." *The American Historical Review* 108, no. 3 (2003): 710–33.
Ghoraba, Hammouda. "Al-Ashʿarī's Theory of Acquisition (*al-Kasb*)." *Islamic Quarterly* 2 (1955): 3–8.
Gimaret, Daniel. "La Notion d' 'impulsion irrésistible' (ilǧâʾ) dans l'éthique Muʿtazilite." *Journal Asiatique* 259 (1971): 25–62.
Gimaret, Daniel. "Matériaux pour une bibliographie des Ǧubbāʾī." *Journal Asiatique* 264, no. 3 (1976): 277–332.
Gimaret, Daniel. *Théories de l'Acte Humain en Théologie Musulmane*. Paris: J. Vrin, 1980.
The Glorious Qurʾan: Text and Explanatory Translation. Translated by Marmaduke William Pickthall. New York: Alavi Foundation, 2001.
Goldziher, Ignaz. *Introduction to Islamic Theology and Law*. Translated by Andras Hamori and Ruth Hamori. Princeton: Princeton University Press, 1981.
Haksar, Vinit. "Coercive Proposals [Rawls and Gandhi]." *Political Theory* 4, no. 1 (1976): 65–79.
Hallaq, Wael. *Authority, Continuity, and Change in Islamic Law*. Cambridge: Cambridge University Press, 2001.
Hallaq, Wael. "From Regional Schools to Personal Schools of Law? A Reevaluation." *Islamic Law and Society* 8, no. 1 (2001): 1–26.

Hallaq, Wael. *A History of Islamic Legal Theories: an Introduction to Sunnī Uṣūl al-Fiqh*. Cambridge; New York: Cambridge University Press, 1997.

Hallaq, Wael. *An Introduction to Islamic Law*. Cambridge: Cambridge University Press, 2009.

Hallaq, Wael. "Was the Gate of Ijtihad Closed?". *International Journal of Middle East Studies* 16, no. 1 (1984): 3–41.

Hāshimī, Sayyid Riḍā. "Bazdawī." In *Dānishnāmah-ʾi jahān-i Islām*, edited by Aḥmad Ṭāhirī ʿIrāqī, Muṣṭafā Mīr Salīm, and Naṣr Allāh Pūrjavādī. Tehran: Bunyād-i Dāʾirat al-Maʿārif-i Islāmī, 1996–. http://rch.ac.ir/article/Details/6656.

Heemskerk, Margaretha T. *Suffering in Muʿtazilite Theology: ʿAbd al-Jabbār's Teaching on Pain and Divine Justice*. Leiden; Boston: Brill, 2000.

Helsinki Group. http://www.cetaceanrights.org/.

Hill, John Lawrence. "Moralized Theories of Coercion: A Critical Analysis." *Denver University Law Review* 74, no. 4 (1997): 907–29.

Hourani, George F. *Islamic Rationalism: the Ethics of ʿAbd al-Jabbār*. Oxford: Clarendon Press, 1971.

Hourani, George F. "A Revised Chronology of Ghazālī's Writings." *Journal of the American Oriental Society* 104 (1984): 289–302.

Hūshangī, Ḥusayn. "Juwaynī." In *Dānishnāmah-ʾi Jahān-i Islām*, edited by Aḥmad Ṭāhirī ʿIrāqī, Muṣṭafā Mīr Salīm, and Naṣr Allāh Pūrjavādī. Tehran: Bunyād-i Dāʾirat al-Maʿārif-i Islāmī, 1996–. http://rch.ac.ir/article/Details/7704#.

Hussain, Mohammed Yusoff. "Al-Ashʿarī's Doctrine of Human Actions." *Islamic Quarterly* 36, no. 2 (1992): 75–83.

Ibn Abī Zayd al-Qayrawānī. *al-Nawādir wa al-Ziyādāt ʿalā mā fī al-Mudawwanah min Ghayri-hā min al-Ummahāt*. Edited by ʿAbd al-Fattāḥ Muḥammad al-Ḥulw. 1st ed. 15 vols. Beirut: Dār al-Gharb al-Islāmī, 1999.

Ibn al-Maḥāmilī, Aḥmad b. Muḥammad. *al-Lubāb fī al-Fiqh al-Shāfiʿī*. Edited by ʿAbd al-Karīm b. Ṣunaytān Amrī. 1st ed. Medina: Dār al-Bukhārī, 1416[/1995].

Ibn al-Malāḥimī, Maḥmūd b. Muḥammad. *Kitāb al-Fāʾiq fī Uṣūl al-Dīn*. Edited by Wilferd Madelung and Martin J. McDermott. 1st ed. Tehran: Muʾassasa-ʾi Pizhūhishī-i Ḥikmat va Falsafa-ʾi Īrān, 2007.

Ibn Farḥūn, Ibrāhīm b. ʿAlī. *al-Dībāj al-Mudhahhab fī Maʿrifat ʿUlamāʾ al-Madhhab*. Edited by Maʾmūn b. Muḥyī al-Dīn al-Jannān. 1st ed. Beirut: Dār al-Kutub al-ʿIlmyya, 1996.

Ibn Fūrak, Abū Bakr Muḥammad b. al-Ḥasan. *Maqālāt al-Shaykh Abī al-Ḥasan al-Ashʿarī, Imām Ahl al-Sunna*. Edited by Aḥmad ʿAbd al-Raḥīm Sāyiḥ. Cairo: Maktabat al-Thaqāfa al-Dīniyya, 2005.

Ibn Ḥazm, Abū Muḥammad ʿAlī b. Aḥmad. *Marātib al-Ijmāʿ fī al-ʿIbādāt wa al-Muʿāmalāt wa al-Muʿtaqadāt*. 1st ed. Beirut: Dār al-Āfāq al-Jadīda, 1978.

Ibn Mattawayh, al-Ḥasan b. Aḥmad. *Kitāb al-Majmūʿ fī al-Muḥīṭ bi-al-Taklīf*. Edited by J. J. Houben, Daniel Gimaret, and Jan Peters. 3 vols. Beirut: Dār al-Mashriq, 1965.

Ibn Nujaym, Zayn al-Dīn b. Ibrāhīm. *al-Baḥr al-Rāʾiq*. Edited by Zakariyya ʿUmayrāt. 1st ed. 6 vols. Beirut: Dār al-Kutub al-ʿIlmiyya, 1418[/1997].

Ibn Nujaym, Zayn al-Dīn b. Ibrāhīm, and Dāwūd b. Yūsuf al-Khaṭīb. *al-Fatāwā al-Ghiyāthīyya*. 1st ed. Cairo: al-Maṭbaʿa al-Āmīrīyya, 1321[/1903].

Ibn ʿAbd al-Barr, Yūsuf b. ʿAbd Allāh. *al-Intiqāʾ fī Faḍāʾil al-Umma al-Thalātha al-Fuqahāʾ: Mālik b. Anas al-Aṣbaḥī al-Madanī, Muḥammad b. Idrīs al-Shāfiʿī al-Muṭṭalibī, wa Abī Ḥanīfa al-Nuʿmān b. Thābit al-Kūfī*. Edited by ʿAbd al-Fattāḥ Abū Ghudda. Aleppo, Syria: Maktab al-Maṭbūʿāt al-Islāmiyya, 1997.

Jackson, Sherman A. *Islamic Law and the State: the Constitutional Jurisprudence of Shihāb al-Dīn al-Qarāfī*. Leiden: Brill, 1996.

Jackson, Sherman A. *On the Boundaries of Theological Tolerance in Islam: Abū Ḥāmid al-Ghazālī's Fayṣal al-Tafriqa bayna al-Islam wa al-Zandaqa*. Karachi: Oxford University Press, 2002.

Jaworska, Agnieszka, and Julie Tannenbaum. "The Grounds of Moral Status." *The Stanford Encyclopedia of Philosophy* (Summer 2013 Edition). http://plato.stanford.edu/archives/sum2013/entries/grounds-moral-status/.

Johansen, Baber. "The Valorization of the Human Body in Muslim Sunni Law." *Interdisciplinary Journal of Middle Eastern Studies* 4 (1996): 71–112.

Kamali, Mohammad Hashim. *Principles of Islamic Jurisprudence*. Revised ed. Cambridge, England: Islamic Texts Society, 1989.

Katz, Leo. *Bad Acts and Guilty Minds: Conundrums of the Criminal Law*. Chicago: University of Chicago Press, 1987.

Kaya, Eyyüp Said. "Continuity and Change in Islamic Law: the Concept of Madhhab and the Dimensions of Legal Disagreement in Hanafi Scholarship of the Tenth Century," In *The Islamic School of Law: Evolution, Devolution, and Progress*, edited by P.J. Bearman, Rudolph Peters, and Frank E. Vogel, 26–50. Cambridge, MA: Islamic Legal Studies Program Distributed by Harvard University Press, 2005.

Kuhn, Thomas S. *The Structure of Scientific Revolutions*. Chicago: University of Chicago Press, 2012.

Lange, Christian. *Justice, Punishment and the Medieval Muslim Imagination*. Cambridge: Cambridge University Press, 2008.

Macdonald, Duncan Black. "Development of Muslim Theology, Jurisprudence, and Constitutional Theory." New York: Charles Scribner's Sons, 1903.

MacIntyre, Alasdair C. *After Virtue: a Study in Moral Theory*. Notre Dame, IN: University of Notre Dame Press, 1984.

MacIntyre, Alasdair C. *Whose Justice? Which Rationality?* London: Duckworth, 1988.

Madelung, Wilferd. "The Late Muʿtazila and Determinism: the Philosophers' Trap." In *Yād-Nāma: in memoria di Alessandro Bausani*, edited by Biancamaria Scarcia Amoretti and Lucia Rostagno. Studi orientali, 245–57. Rome: Bardi editore, 1991.

Madelung, Wilferd. *Religious Trends in Early Islamic Iran*. Bibliotheca Persica. Albany, NY: Persian Heritage Foundation, 1988.

Makdisi, George. "Ashʿarī and the Ashʿarites in Islamic Religious History I." *Studia Islamica* 17 (1962): 37–80.

Makdisi, George. "Ashʿarī and the Ashʿarites in Islamic Religious History II." *Studia Islamica* 18 (1963): 19–39.

Makdisi, George. "The Juridical Theology of Shâfiʿî: Origins and Significance of Uṣûl al-Fiqh." *Studia Islamica* 59 (1984): 5–47.

Mānkdīm, Shashdīw. *Sharḥ al-Uṣūl al-Khamsa*. Edited by Samīr Muṣṭafā Rabāb. 1st ed. Beirut: Dār Iḥyāʾ al-Turāth al-ʿArabī, 2001.

Marshall, David L. "The Implications of Robert Brandom's Inferentialism for Intellectual History." *History and Theory* 52, no. 1 (2013): 1–31.

Martin, Richard C., Mark R. Woodward, and Dwi Surya Atmaja. *Defenders of Reason in Islam: Muʿtazilism from Medieval School to Modern Symbol.* Oxford: Oneworld Publications, 1997.

McDermott, Martin. "Ebn Mattawayh, Abū Moḥammad Ḥasan." In *Encyclopædia Iranica*, Vol VIII, Fasc. 1, edited by Ehsan Yarshater, 39. London; Boston; Winona Lake, IN: Routledge & Kegan Paul, 1982.

Melchert, Christopher. *The Formation of the Sunni Schools of Law, 9th–10th Centuries C.E.* Leiden: Brill, 1997.

The Message of the Qurʾān. Translated by Muhammad Asad. Lahore, Pakistan: Maktaba Jawahar ul Uloom, 1979.

Messick, Brinkley. "Indexing the Self: Intent and Expression in Islamic Legal Acts." *Islamic Law and Society* 8, no. 2 (2001): 151–78.

Murray, Michael J., and David F. Dudrick. "Are Coerced Acts Free?". *American Philosophical Quarterly* 32, no. 2 (1995): 109–23.

Naqīb, Aḥmad b. Muḥammad Naṣīr al-Dīn. *al-Madhhab al-Ḥanafī: Marāḥilu-hu wa Ṭabaqātu-hu, Ḍawābiṭu-hu wa Muṣṭalaḥātu-hu, Khaṣāʾiṣu-hu wa Muʾallafātu-hu.* 1st ed. 2 vols. Riyadh: Maktabat al-Rushd, 2001.

Naysābūrī, Abū Rashīd Saʿīd b. Muḥammad. *al-Masāʾil fī al-Khilāf bayna al-Baṣrīyyīn wa al-Baghdādīyyīn.* Edited by Maʿn Ziyāda and Riḍwān al-Sayyid. Tripoli, Lebanon: Maʿhad al-Anmāʾ al-ʿArabī, 1989.

Nozick, Robert. "Coercion." In *Philosophy, Science, and Method: Essays in Honor of Ernest Nagel*, edited by Sidney Morgenbesser, Patrick Suppes, and Morton White, 440–72. New York: St. Martin's Press, 1969.

Nyberg, Henrick Samuel. "Abuʾl-Hodayl Al-ʿAllāf." In *Encyclopedia of Islam, Second Edition*, edited by P. Bearman, Th. Bianquis, C.E. Bosworth, E. van Donzel and W.P. Heinrichs. Consulted online on 11 August 2016. http://dx.doi.org/10.1163/1573-3912_islam_SIM_0203. First published online: 2012.

Peters, J.R.T.M. *God's Created Speech: a Study in the Speculative Theology of the Muʿtazilī Qâḍī l-Quḍât Abū l-Ḥasan ʿAbd al-Jabbâr Bn Aḥmad al-Hamaḏânī.* Leiden: Brill, 1976.

Peters, Rudolph. *Crime and Punishment in Islamic Law: Theory and Practice from the Sixteenth to the Twenty-first Century.* Cambridge, UK: Cambridge University Press, 2005.

Peters, Rudolph. "What Does it Mean to be an Official Madhhab? Hanafism and the Ottoman Empire." In *The Islamic School of Law: Evolution, Devolution, and Progress*, edited by P. J. Bearman, Rudolph Peters, and Frank E. Vogel, 147–58. Cambridge, MA: Islamic Legal Studies Program Distributed by Harvard University Press, 2005.

Powers, Paul R. *Intent in Islamic law.* Leiden: Brill, 2006.

The Qurʾan: a New Translation. Translated by Thomas Cleary. United States: Starlatch, 2004.

Rabb, Intisar. *Doubt in Islamic Law: a History of Legal Maxims, Interpretation, and Islamic Criminal Law.* Cambridge, MA: Cambridge University Press, 2015.

Renard, John. *Islamic Theological Themes: a Primary Source Reader*. Oakland: University of California Press, 2014.
Ryan, Cheyney C. "The Normative Concept of Coercion." *Mind* 89, no. 356 (1980): 481–98.
Sadeghi, Behnam. "The Authenticity of Two 2nd/8th Century Ḥanafī Legal Texts: the Kitāb al-Āthār and al-Muwaṭṭaʾ of Muḥammad b. al-Ḥasan al-Shaybānī." *Islamic Law and Society* 17 (2010): 291–319.
Sadeghi, Behnam. *The Logic of Law Making in Islam: Women and Prayer in the Legal Tradition*. Cambridge: Cambridge University Press, 2015.
Schacht, Joseph. *An Introduction to Islamic Law*. Oxford: Clarendon Press, 1964.
Schacht, Joseph. *The Origins of Muhammedan Jurisprudence*. Oxford: Clarendon Press, 1950.
Schwarz, M. "'Acquisition' (*kasb*) in Early Kalām." In *Islamic Philosophy and the Classical Tradition. Essays Presented by his Friends and Pupils to Richard Walzer on his Seventieth Birthday*, edited by S.M. Stern, Albert Hourani, and Vivian Brown, 355–87. Columbia, SC: University of South Carolina Press, 1973.
Schwarz, M. "Some Notes on the Notion of Iljāʾ (constraint) in Muʿtazilite Kalām." *Israel Oriental Studies* 2 (1972): 413–27.
Shaybānī, Muḥammad b. al-Ḥasan. *al-Aṣl*. Edited by Mehmet Boynukalın. 13 vols. Beirut: Dār Ibn Ḥazm lil-Ṭibāʿah wa-al-Nashr wa-al-Tawzīʿ, 2012.
Shihadeh, Ayman. "The Argument from Ignorance and its Critics in Medieval Arabic Thought." *Arabic Sciences and Philosophy* 23, no. 2 (2013): 171–220.
Shihadeh, Ayman. "From al-Ghazālī to al-Rāzī: 6th/12th Century Developments in Muslim Philosophical Theology." *Arabic Sciences and Philosophy* 15 (2005): 141–79.
Shihadeh, Ayman. *The Teleological Ethics of Fakhr al-Dīn al-Rāzī*. Leiden: Brill, 2006.
Spies, O. "al-Dj̲aṣṣāṣ, Aḥmad b. ʿAlī Abū Bakr al-Rāzī." In *Encyclopedia of Islam, Second Edition*, edited by P. Bearman, Th. Bianquis, C.E. Bosworth, E. van Donzel and W.P. Heinrichs. Consulted online on 11 August 2016. http://dx.doi.org/10.1163/1573-3912_islam_SIM_2017. First published online: 2012.
Syed, Mairaj U. "Coercion in Classical Islamic Law and Theology." Dissertation, Princeton University, 2011.
Syed, Mairaj U. "Review of Mālik and Medina." *Islamic Law and Society* 22 (2015): 301–7.
The American Society for the Prevention of Cruelty to Robots. www.aspcr.com/.
Tsafrir, Nurit. *The History of an Islamic School of Law: the Early Spread of Hanafism*. Cambridge, MA: Islamic Legal Studies Program Distributed by Harvard Law School, 2004.
Vasalou, Sophia. "Equal before the Law: the Evilness of Human and Divine Lies ʿAbd al-Ğabbār's Rational Ethics." *Arabic Sciences and Philosophy* 13, no. 2 (2003): 243–69.
Vasalou, Sophia. *Moral Agents and their Deserts: the Character of Muʿtazilite Ethics*. Princeton, NJ: Princeton University Press, 2008.
Watt, W. Montgomery. "Ibn Fūrak, Abū Bakr Muḥammad b. al-Ḥasan." In *Encyclopedia of Islam, Second Edition*, edited by P. Bearman, Th. Bianquis, C.E. Bosworth, E. van Donzel and W.P. Heinrichs. Consulted online on 11 August 2016. http://dx.doi.org/10.1163/1573-3912_islam_COM_0321. First published online: 2012.
Watt, W. Montgomery. "The Origin of the Islamic Doctrine of Acquisition." *Journal of the Royal Asiatic Society of Great Britain and Ireland*, no. 2 (1943): 234–47.

Weiss, Bernard G. *The Search for God's Law: Islamic Jurisprudence in the Writings of Sayf al-Dīn al-Āmidī*. Salt Lake City: University of Utah Press, 1992.

Weiss, Bernard G. *The Spirit of Islamic Law*. Athens, GA: University of Georgia Press, 2006.

Wertheimer, Alan. *Coercion*. Princeton, NJ: Princeton University Press, 1987.

Wertheimer, Alan. "Remarks on Coercion and Exploitation." *Denver University Law Review* 74 (1997): 889–906.

Wheeler, Brannon M. *Applying the Canon in Islam: the Authorization and Maintenance of Interpretive Reasoning in Ḥanafī Scholarship*. Albany: State University of New York Press, 1996.

Wizāra al-Awqāf wa al-Shuʾūn al-Islāmiyya. "Nafīyy." In *al-Mawsūʿa al-Fiqhiyya*, 41:118–32. Kuwait: Wizāra al-Awqāf wa al-Shuʾūn al-Islāmiyya, 1987–2006.

Wizāra al-Awqāf wa al-Shuʾūn al-Islāmiyya. "Riḍāʿ." In *al-Mawsūʿa al-Fiqhiyya*, 238–56. Kuwait: Wizāra al-Awqāf wa al-Shuʾūn al-Islāmiyya, 1987–2006.

Wolfson, Harry Austryn. *The Philosophy of the Kalam*. Cambridge, MA: Harvard University Press, 1976.

Zaman, Muhammad Qasim. *Ashraf ʿAli Thanawi: Islam in Modern South Asia*. Makers of the Muslim World. Oxford: Oneworld, 2008.

Zimmerman, David. "Coercive Wage Offers." *Philosophy and Public Affairs* 10, no. 2 (1981): 121–45.

Ziryāb, ʿAbbās. "Bāqillānī." In *Dānishnāmah-ʾi Jahān-i Islām*, edited by Aḥmad Ṭāhirī ʿIrāqī, Muṣṭafā Mīr Salīm and Naṣr Allāh Pūrjavād ī. Tehran: Bunyād-i Dāʾirat al-Maʿārif-i Islāmī, 1996–.

Zysow, Aron. *The Economy of Certainty: an Introduction to the Typology of Islamic Legal Theory*. Atlanta, GA: Lockwood Press, 2013.

Index

Printed and bound by CPI Group (UK) Ltd, Croydon, CR0 4YY